C000030233

ISBN 0-9553725-0-X

ISBN 978-0-9553725-0-6

Published by **Melvyn Mckeown** Freelance Graphic Designer

First published in Great Britain in 2006

I

Contents

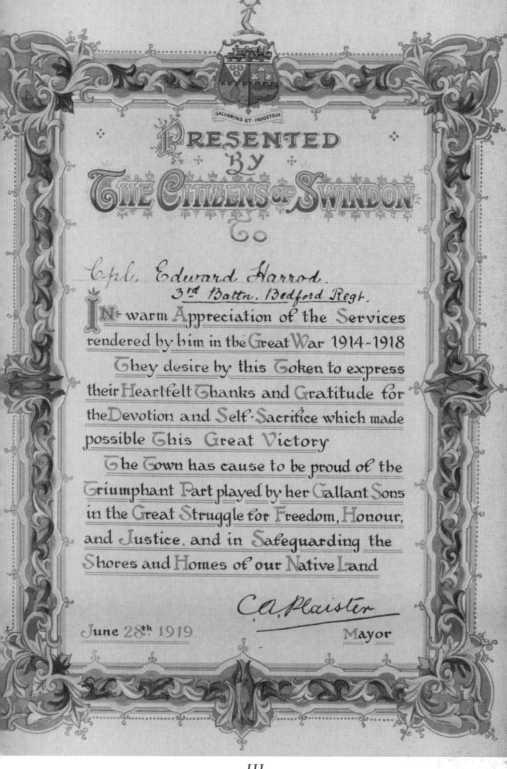

PRESENTED
BY
THE CITIZENS OF SWINDON
To

Cpl. Edward Harrod.
3rd Battn. Bedford Regt.

IN warm Appreciation of the Services
rendered by him in the Great War 1914-1918

They desire by this Token to express
their Heartfelt Thanks and Gratitude for
the Devotion and Self-Sacrifice which made
possible This Great Victory

The Town has cause to be proud of the
Triumphant Part played by her Gallant Sons
in the Great Struggle for Freedom, Honour,
and Justice. and in Safeguarding the
Shores and Homes of our Native Land

C.A.Plaister

June 28th 1919

Mayor

Tell Them of Us
Remembering Swindon's Sons of the Great War 1914 - 1918

In November 2003, my Father, a Deacon of Holy Rood Church in Swindon, was asked to lead a service of remembrance in the old technical college in Victoria Road. The service was held in front of a stained glass window in the entrance hall, that commemorates 44 men who were students of the college, and were killed in the Great War. A number of relatives attended the service. I was intrigued by this window, and, after viewing it had to find out more about these men. With the friendly and very helpful advice from the staff of the reference library in Swindon, a new door to my lifelong interest opened.

The First World war has interested me for as long as I can remember. I would read books on the subject, collect memorabilia from the period and watch intently anything that appeared on the television in the way of films or documentaries. This has not changed. My wife and family can vouch for that!
I had, and still have, a great interest in the 'Pals' regiments that were formed in Britain. I have read many stories of the comradeship of this citizen army, that held the men together and bought them through this terrible experience. I had never thought about, though, the men of my home town, Swindon, until, that is, I saw for the first time the memorial in the Town hall. Commemorating 920 men who died, the memorial rests out of public sight, behind curtains in the Swindon dance studio. I felt guilty for not realizing the impact that war had on my town.

Using as a basis, the information of W Bavin's, 'Swindons War Record' of 1922, I have put together a record that tells a story of its own. His book gives us a complete record of the events that took place in the five years from 1914 to 1919. All I have done is used his official list together with the records of those who died and the original documents of the 'Committee of Comforts for the Troops' and gathered together many photographs, kindly loaned to me by the relatives of the men. In W Bavins book, under the Roll of Swindon men who served, he wrote the following about the roll -
'It will be a thousand pities if these sheets remain unused, and it would be a public service on the part of anyone with sufficient leisure and patience who would transcribe them, properly arranged and checked, into a well bound volume to be placed amongst the town records or in the museum.'

Swindon has changed so much since Bavin's time and I'm sure he would frown on what Swindon has become! We have lost what the town was built on, the railways, and there is not much of that history left in the town. Swindon's Rail museum 'Steam' is excellent but, without its hard worked staff and the many volunteers who help keep the records together and its exhibits looking so bright, I really think we would have lost that along with many of our towns original and many beautiful buildings that have been demolished in the name of progress. That though, is down to politics and I would be best to stay very well clear of something these soldiers thought very little of.

I hope though, that Mr Bavin would approve of my effort. This work is not a history of the Towns involvement as Bavins was. My book, like me, is simple! It contains the 'Roll of Honour' Those that died, using information from the Commonwealth War Graves Commission, the records of Soldiers Died, and also relatives records themselves. It also contains the roll of those who survived. You will see that there is a mixture of information on the men listed, some have a page or half a page of information on them, others I have nothing but their name. But I wanted each one mentioned so all will be remembered.

The real story of this time, could only have been told by those men who had taken part in those fearful years. But they have all now passed on.

I had the honour, and the privilege to have known and spoken to some of these men, whom I regarded, and still regard as my heroes'. As I have grown older, I wish now, I had asked these, very humble but great men, many more things than I did back then. But alas, that is the way of things. My old neighbour, 'AJ' Alfred Gray, a veteran whose name is included in this book, was typical of these men. He spoke very little about his experiences, but spoke fondly of his chums. I don't have a photo of 'AJ' nor do I remember the Regiment he served with, though I recall the Somerset Light Infantry mentioned, Somerset being his birth place, but I proudly remember him and in my home I treasure the steel helmet he gave me that he had worn through his service.

This work, though, would not have been possible without the help of the Swindon Advertiser. Through their support by the appeals for information in their pages, many relatives would not have contacted me. Without the relatives of these men, I would never had been able to put this all together. (See acknowledgements) What I am pleased with, though, is that when anyone has asked me about this project, nobody has asked why have I wanted to do this? I still don't think I need to answer that!

Over 5,000 men from Swindon served. These men, through their suffering, showed spirit, determination and great courage, in the face of despair and impossible odds. We can learn much from their stories. They believed in what they were doing, and that it was the right thing to do. They had a job to do and they would play the game out to the last. They were true to their word. They succeeded. But when it was over, things were different. Their own country let them down. Politicians, as they have and always will do, came out on top. Large amounts of money were generously awarded to members of the war cabinet and other political leaders.

The soldiers who survived, came back to very little. To a world who could not understand their state of mind. Besides physical scars, men had to hide mental scars. Many were hidden away in Roundway hospital in Devizes and remained there until they passed away years later. Many survivors suffered for years afterwards, some for the rest of their lives from the effects of that awful weapon of WW1, gas.

If you have the opportunity to make a pilgrimage to the hallowed grounds of France and Flanders or of any of the Great War cemeteries, visit the graves of the Swindon men that lay in that now very peaceful place. Or, closer to home, honour those also that are buried in the cemeteries of Radnor Street, Christchurch, St Marys and Whitworth Road.

The war dead will be remembered, as is fitting. They gave the ultimate sacrifice. War cemeteries and memorials all over Britain, France, Belgium, Dardanelles, the Middle East and many other places, will continue to remind us of these dead heroes'. But what of the men who survived to return home. What memorials are there, to these who went through the same, and had to live on with the legacy of that terrible war.

This is for all our Lads from Swindon

Memorial Window in Victoria Road Technical College

ACKNOWLEDGEMENTS

I have been so privileged to share in the memories of these men I regard as my heroes' by talking to many of their relatives. None of this would have been possible without the help of the following to whom I would like to express my deepest gratitude.

The Swindon Advertiser, who allowed me through their pages, to appeal for information for the book. They remain where they were during the Great War, at the heart of Swindon's community. Roger Trayhurn and the Staff of the Swindon Reference Library. The staff of Bath Road Museum. The staff of the library of 'Steam' Swindon's Railway Museum. Mr and Mrs J Holt and Mr Holt senior, for proof reading, editing and support. Their advice has been so invaluable. The Swindon Society in which I am proud to be a member myself. The information and support I have received from this welcoming club has never ceased. Bert Evans, for all your work in tracing the towns memorials. Les and Ruby Thompson, their recollection of Swindon families proved so accurate. I wish Les could have seen the book finished. We will miss you Les. To my parents for your support in everything I do, thanks Mum and Dad. My wife Theresa, for your love and patience. My children - Nicholas, for your time at the reference library and teaching me the mysteries of the computer. Jessica, for your hours researching the roll of honour. Francesca, for just being you. At the end of a hard day your smiles always lift me. I'm so proud of my children who are part of the next generation who will take up the torch for these Swindon men. Alan Nix for the many times you've loaned me the projector. Last but by no means least, my pal Tony Fox. This is as much your book as it is mine. You've seen it from the start, listened to my many ramblings, helped with so much research and supported me throughout, also thanks for doing all the driving whenever we go to France.

The following have all contributed to the book. Without them, much of this could not have been possible. They have kindly loaned me very precious photographs and given me valuable details of their relatives. I hope I have not omitted any names, but if I have then please accept my most sincere apologies.

Lesley Aldridge, Jean Allen, The Late Brian Archer, Margaret Archer, Margaret Baker, Perry Barrett, Mr Bint, Mr and Mrs E Bizley, Kevin Bizley, Ann Blackett, Mrs Bone, George Bray, Clive Bright, Lou Butler, Tony and Michael Carter, Peter Chappell, David Clark, Robert J Collett, Merle Cooper, Mr and Mrs Crewe, Ron Culling, Jenny Morse (Culling), Pearl Curathers, Mr and Mrs Davies, Lorna Dawes, Mr G H Day, Paul Dixon, Chris Done, Ian Dunbar, Michael Ellis, Diane Everett, Marjorie Farrell, Neil Farrell, Fred Ferris, Les Ferris, Ms D Francis (Swindon College), Charles Gee, Mr and Mrs Gibbs, Mr R Gilbert, Mr Gray, Robert 'Dan' Gurney, Mrs Haines, Mrs J Hawketts, Mr and Mrs Hazell, Peter Hedges, Beryl Henderson, Rose Hodges, Kevin Hood, Donald Howse, Mrs Hunt, Mr and Mrs J Iles, Eileen Jenkins, Barry Jobson, David Lacey, Eric Langaster, Mr Lavington, Mr R Linnegar, Neil Lover, Dick Mattick, Joyce Murgatroyd, Mr and Mrs Myall, Robert Myers, John Oliver, Anthony Osbourne, Jim Osman, Mrs Painter, Mr and Mrs Parry, Ann and Clive Partridge, Jan Peters, Mr and Mrs Rawling, Marion Reeves, Colin Rowland, Robert Sheppard (The Highworth Branch of the British Legion), Mr Shilton, Ron Slade, Mr and Mrs R Smith, Mr and Mrs Starr, Ken and Mary Sturgess, Mrs P Summerhayes, Terry Swaine, Brenda Taylor, Mike Taylor, Brian and Jean Timbrell, James Turner, Ron Viveash, Mr Walter, Joyce Walters, Philip Webb, Mr Westall, Millie White (Bevan), Stuart Witts, Mrs M Woodman, Mrs Wynn, Bill Yeo, All Members of The Lounge, (Ex-rail workers) The Western Front Association.

Together we Remember

The Roll of Honour
The men of Swindon who made the supreme sacrifice

**For the Mothers, Fathers, Wives and Children
who lost Sons, Husbands and Fathers**

Only those who have loved and lost can understand

ABBOTT, A.E.
Albert Edward
Corporal 14219 8th Battalion Kings Own Yorkshire Light Infantry
Killed in Action 2nd October 1915
23 years old
Son of Edward and Alice Abbott of Wolverton, Buckinghamshire
D. I. X Farm Cemetery La Chappelle D'Armentieres
Born in Swindon

ACOTT, H.G.
Herbert George
Private 12160 6th Battalion Wiltshire Regiment
Killed in Action 26th September 1915
Panel 102 Loos Memorial
Lived in Swindon

ALDER, A.E.
Albert Ernest
Private 10484 1st Battalion Wiltshire Regiment
Killed in Action 29th June 1915 at Hooge
23 years in old
Son of Frederick Alder of 28 St. Margarets Road, Swindon
Panel 53 Menin Gate Memorial
Born in Swindon
Labourer in No 23 Shop GWR Works, Swindon
Remembered on Plaque in Christchurch, Old Town

ALDER, W.G.
Walter Gee
Private 78870 5th Battalion Tank Corps (Formerly 270063 ASC)
Killed in Action 22nd March 1918
Panel 90-94 Pozieres Memorial
Lived in Swindon
Remembered on Plaque in Christchurch, Old Town

ALLARD, W.F.
Walter Frank
Private 9212 2nd Battalion Wiltshire Regiment
Died of Wounds 25th October 1914
26 years old
Son of Henry Joseph and Annie Allard of 11 Hythe Road, Swindon
A. 1. 9. Ypres Town Cemetery
Lived in Swindon

ALLAWAY, A.H.J.
Alfred Henry James
Private 8682 1st Battalion Wiltshire Regiment
Died of Wounds 7th June 1917
111.C.327 Bailleul Communal Cemetery Extension
Born in Stratton St. Margaret

ALLEN, J.
Jesse
Private 8980 1st Battalion Wiltshire Regiment
Died of Wounds 28th October 1914
19 Years Old
Son of Mr and Mrs Henry Allen of 2 Farm Cottages, Rodbourne Road.
Bethune Town Cemetery 111.A.9.
Born in Swindon

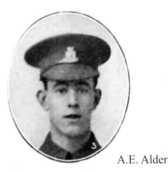

A.E. Alder

AMOR, G.
George
Private 13565 7th Battalion Wiltshire Regiment
Died 16th September 1916 in Salonika
33 years old
Son of John and Annie Amor of Swindon
Husband of Florence Ann Amor of 88 Redcliffe Street, Swindon
416 Salonika (Lembet Road) Military Cemetery
Born in Swindon

AMOS, E.R.
Edwin Reginald
Private 202945 2/4th Royal Berkshire Regiment
Killed in Action 22nd August 1917
25 years old
Son of Mr Edwin and Mrs F H Amos of 69 Goodhind, Stapleton Road, Bristol
Panel 105-106 + 162 Tyne Cott
Born in Swindon

ANDERSON, H.F.
Horace Frank
Sergeant 62650 124th Field Company
Royal Engineers
Died 11th July 1916
Pier and Face 8A + 8D Thiepval Memorial
Attended Swindon Technical College
Victoria Road in 1906. Remembered on
its stained glass window.

ANNAND, S.
Stewart
Trumpeter 14958 6th Reserve Regiment
of Dragoons (Formerly 2616 Royal
Berkshire Yeomanry)
Died 1st June 1917. 17 years old
Son of George and Ellen Annand of
Coombe Park, Whitchurch, Oxon
D.I. Tidworth Military Cemetery
Born in Swindon

ANSTY, F.C.
Frederick Cecil
Private 10293 2nd Battalion Wiltshire
Regiment
Died of Wounds 15th June 1915
Panel 33-34 Le Touret Memorial
Born in Swindon

ARCHER, A.E.
Arthur Edwin
Private 328080 1/8th Battalion
Lancashire
Fusiliers (Formerly 1976 Gloucestershire
Regiment)
Killed in Action 28th June 1918
21 years old
Son of A E and Esther Archer of Bristol
Plot 2, Row D, Grave 18 Bertrancourt
Military Cemetery
Born in Swindon

ARCHER, C.G.E.
Clarence George Edward
Private 16605 M. G. C. Infantry 19th
Battalion (Formerly 106604 Royal Welsh
Fusiliers)
Killed in Action 26th October 1916
X I. R. 2 Guards Cemetery Lesboeufs
Born in Swindon

ARCHER, F.J.
Francis John
Private 33486 2nd Battalion Wiltshire
Regiment
Killed in Action 21st March 1918
Panel 64 Pozieres Memorial
Born in Haydon Wick

ASH, F.
Francis
Private 22938 2/7th Battalion West
Riding Regiment Formerly 9231 Wiltshire
Regiment
Died 14th November 1918. 22 years old
Son of Mary Ash of Hinton Parva,
Swindon In South West Part, Hinton
Parva New Burial Ground
Lived in Swindon

ATTWOOD, A.
Arthur
Driver 94701 'C' Battery 52nd Brigade
RFA
Died of Wounds 4th August 1917
X V.11 .G. 16 Lijssenthoek Military
Cemetery
Born in Swindon

A Attwood

AUSTIN, A.G.
Arthur George
Boy 2nd Class J/93548 Royal Navy HMS Powerful'
Died 18th January 1919. 17 years old
Son of Henry Melinda Austin of 4 The Green,
Rodbourne Cheney
8.16 St. Mary's, Rodbourne Cheney

AUSTIN, F.C.
Francis Charles
Private M2/166861 ASC. 1st Ammunition Sub.Park
Died 29th November 1916
Son of Charles and Mary Austin of Trossocks Lodge,
Warminster Road, Bath
11.B. 15 A Boisguillaume Communal Cemetery
Born in Swindon

AVERIES, H.
Harold.
Private 32300 1st Battalion Wiltshire regiment
Killed in Action 22nd March 1918
Bay 7 Arras memorial France.
Born in Wroughton Lived in Swindon

AXFORD, A.W.J.
Arthur William James
Corporal 1709 Wilts Battery 3rd Wessex Brigade
Royal Field Artillery
Died of Malaria, 7th July 1915
24 years old
Youngest son of Mr Thomas and Mrs Axford of 8
Folkstone Road, Swindon
Delhi 1914 – 1918 Memorial

BADEN,F.
Frank
Private 9413 5th Battalion Wiltshire Regiment

F. Baden

Killed in Action 19th July 1915
19 years old
Youngest Son of Mr. Frank Baden of 60 Kingshill Road.
Sp. Memorial 121 Pink Farm Cemetery, Helles Dardanelles
Born in Swindon and remembered on plaque in Christchurch, Old Town
Formerly worked in Number 14 shop in the G. W. R.
He and three others were in a dug - out when a land slide occurred. All four were buried, two were rescued but Private Baden and another suffocated.

BAILEY, C.N.
Clifford
Private 7718 1st battalion Wiltshire regiment.
Killed in Action 30th October 1914
11 A 22 Ypres town cemetery extension. Belgium
Buried with A Booth Staffordshire Regiment.

BAILEY, F.
Fred
Private MS/1085 Royal Army Service Corps
Died of Wounds 7th June 1918
1 K. Diss. 1600 Manchester Southern Cemetery
Born in Swindon lived in Manchester

BAILEY, F.
Frederick
Private 10824 2nd Battalion Wiltshire Regiment
Died of Wounds 23rd August 1915
18 years old
Son of Frederick and Rose Bailey of Hodson, Chiseldon
1.D. 71 Chocques Military Cemetery
Lived in Swindon

BAILEY, F.T.
Frederick Thomas
Corporal 305770 10th Tank Corps
Died 25th July 1918. 30 years old
Son of Mrs A Bailey of Brinkworth
Husband of Voilet Bailey of 47 Cambria Place, Swindon
X11. A. 29 Geeviller British Cemetery
Formerly a Clerk in the G. W. R. Locomotive Department

F.T. Bailey

BAILEY, H.
Died No Details.

BAILEY, T.W.
Sapper 520019 1st Wilts Fortress
Battalion Royal Engineers
Died 13th March 1917. 42 years old
Husband of Emma P.J. Bailey of 151
Rodbourne Road, Swindon
IV C. 16 Grove Town Cemetery Meaulte
Served in South African Campaign

BAGGS, A.
Arthur
Private 46251 1st Battalion Wiltshire
Regiment
Died of Wounds 27th October 1918
XIII. A. 11 Rocquigny – Equancourt Road,
British Cemetery Manancourt
Born in Swindon

BAKER, E.F.
Edgar Frank
Private 14146 5th Battalion Wiltshire
Regiment
Killed in Action 10th August 1915
Panel 156-158 Helles Memorial
Born in Swindon
Formerly worked in GWR in Loco Dept.
Offices
Joined the Wiltshire Regiment in
September 1914

E.F. Baker

BAKER, E.J.
Ephram John
Gunner 189167 'A' Battery 38th Brigade
Royal Field Artillery
Died 7th August 1917. 33 years old
Son of William and Sarah Baker of
Swindon
VII.A. 2 Railway Dugouts Burial Ground
Transport Farm

BAKER, F.
Frederick
Lance-Sergeant 9039 2nd Battalion
Bedfordshire Regiment
Died of Wounds 6th July 1915
28 years old
Husband of C.H. Baker of 8 Ponting
Street, Swindon
B. 3315 Radnor Street Cemetery

T.W. Bailey

BALCH, F.A.
Frederick Arthur
Private 399088 17th Battalion Tank Corps
Killed in Action 2nd September 1918
20 years old
Son of Arthur and Eva Mary Balch of 8
Bath Road, Swindon
Panel II VIS-EN Artios Memorial
Born in Swindon – Educated at Swindon
High School Remembered on plaque in
Christchurch.

BALDRY, A.E.
Bombardier 24501 4th Siege Battery
Royal Garrison Artillery
Killed in Action 27th December 1915
V.B. 9. Duhallow A. D. S. Cemetery

BALL, F.A.
Fred Avery
Private 6986 1st Battalion Wiltshire
Regiment
Killed in Action 19th October 1914
Panel 33 and 34 Le Touret Memorial
Born in Swindon

BALL, F
Frederick.
Gunner. 3754 Royal Field Artillery. 'D'
Battery 2nd Brigade.
Killed in Action 13th October 1915
23 years old.
Son of Mrs Eliza Ball of 68 Telford Road
Rodbourne Cheney
Fosse 7 Military Cemetery. Mazingarbe,
France.

F. Ball

BALL. G.
George.
Lance-Corporal 5065 2nd Battalion
Wiltshire Regiment
Killed in Action 24th October 1914
36 years old
Son of William and Emily Ball of Badbury
Wick, Chiseldon
Husband of Agnes Ellen Ball of 15
Bradford Road
Panel 53 Menin Gate Memorial
Also served in South African Campaign

BALL. G.G.
Private 33800 7th Battalion Norfolk
Regiment
Killed in Action 7th March 1918
30 years old
Son of Mr and Mrs George Ball of 2
Station Road
I F 7 Tournai Communal Cemetery Allied
Extension.
He had been rejected twice for Military
Service, before succeeding with the
Norfolk Regiment.

BALLARD, J.H.
Private 942 2nd Division Cyclist Company
Army Cyclist Corps
Killed in Action 26th July 1915
27 years old
Son of Joseph and Mary Ann Ballard
Husband of Harriett Ballard of 2
Lansdowne Gardens, South Lambeth
London

41 Beuvry Communal Cemetery France.
Formerly worked in Number 16 shop in
the GWR

J.H. Ballard

BALLINGER, B.W.
Bertie William
Private 18554 9th Battalion Worcester
shire Regiment
Killed in Action 20th April 1916
36 years old.
Son of Thomas and Sarah Ann Ballinger,
of Shrivenham, Berks.
Panel 18 and 63 Basra war memorial. Iraq
Lived in Swindon

BARBER, H.H.
Horace Henry
Private G/23252 1st Battalion Queens
Own Royal West Kent Regiment
Killed in Action 26th October 1917
28 years old
Husband of Helen Barber of 19 Kingshill
Road, Swindon
V.I. A. D. 10. Hooge Crater Cemetery.
Belgium

BARKER, A.J.
Arthur James
Private 63031 1st Garrison Battalion
Worcestershire Regiment
Died 7th July 1918. 39 years old
Son of Joshua and Hanna Barker, of
Swindon
Husband of Sarah A. Barker of 7 Osborne
Road, Willesden Green, London
B. 22. 13. Cobh Old Church Cemetery,
County Cork, Republic of Ireland

BARLING, H.
Harry
Private 11174 19th Queen Alexandra's
Own, Royal Hussars
Killed in Action 8th October 1918
19 years old
Son of Harry Barling and Kate Louisa

Barling, of 20 Hamlet Road, Norwood, London
V1 C. 27 Busigny Communal Cemetery Extension France
Lived in Swindon

BARNES, A.A.S.
Arthur Alison Stuart
Ordinary Signalman J/32146 Royal Navy
HMS 'Queen Mary'
Died 31st May 1916. 18 years old
Son of Harry and Charlotte Barnes, of 18 Medgebury Road Swindon
13 Plymouth Naval Memorial

BARNES, W.H.F.
William
Private 12494 'B' Company 2nd Battalion Wiltshire Regiment
Died 12th April 1917. 18 years old
Son of Harry and Charlotte Barnes, of 18 Medgebury Road, Swindon
V111 C. 6 Warlincourt Halte British Cemetery
France
Brother of Arthur Barnes

BARNETT, R.T.F.
MBE. Cavalier of the Order of the Crown of Italy.
Captain Royal Army Medical Corps
Died 12th February 1920
B366 Penmaenmawr Owygyfycch Cemetery. Wales.
Attended North Wilts Technical college Victoria Road in 1901 Remembered on its stained glass window

BARRETT, J.
Private 22505 3rd Battalion Wiltshire Regiment
Transferred to 312447 439th Agricultural Company Labour Corps
Died 5th March 1918. 21 years old
Son of Maurice and Amelia Barrett, of Dadgrove Cottages, Fairford, Gloucestershire
D1958 Radnor Street Cemetery
Born in Broad Hinton Lived in Swindon

BARRETT, J.F.
James Frederick
Private 33804 10th Battalion Loyal North Lancashire Regiment
Died 11th April 1917. 21 years old
Son of Walter Frank and Harriet Kate Barrett, of 66 Manchester Road

Brother of Walter Frank (Below)
I.C. 23 Windmill British Cemetery Monchy
– Le – Preux
Enlisted into the Army Cyclist Corps in Bristol

BARRETT, W.F.
Walter Frank
Company-Quarter-Master-Sergeant
T4/061133 2nd Company 41st Division Train Army Service Corps
Died 29th May 1918. 26 years old
Son of Walter Frank and Harriett Kate Barrett of 66 Manchester Road
Brother of James Barrett (Above)
XIV G 4 Dozinghem Military Cemetery

W.H.F. Barnes

BARRETT, M.
Maurice
Private 3134 6th Battalion Royal Munster Fusiliers
Formerly 12610 Wiltshire Regiment
Died 11th December 1915 in Egypt
B. 43 Alexandria (Chatby) Military and War Memorial Cemetery
Lived in Swindon

BARRETT, P.S.
Percival Sydney
Private 6460 1st Battalion Wiltshire Regiment
Killed in Action 31st October 1914
29 years old
Son in Law of Mrs. M. A. Winters, of 1 Frome Cottages, The Green, Colwall, Malvern
Panel 33 – 34 Le Touret Memorial
Born in Swindon

BARTLETT, F.
Frank
Sergeant 21788 13th Battalion Gloucestershire Regiment
Killed in Action 22nd March 1918
23 years old

Son of Harvey Bartlett and Husband of Elizabeth, of 33 Catherine Street, Swindon
III.H. 31 Peronne Communal Cemetery Extension

BARTLETT, T.E.
Thomas Edward
Private 71191 'A' Staff (GABBAN) Royal Army Medical Corps
Died 24th October 1918. 53 years old
Son of Mrs. Mary Ann Bartlett, of 7 North Street, Swindon
IV.A. 9. Taranto Town Cemetery
Served in South African Campaign
Remembered on plaque in Christchurch, Old Town

BARTON, E.
Ernest
Private 7362 2nd Battalion Oxfordshire and Buckinghamshire Light Infantry
Killed in Action 16th May 1915
29 years old
Son of the late David and Ann Barton and Husband of Ada Beatrice Barton of Flackwell Heath, High Wycombe, Buckinghamshire
Panel 26 Le Touret Memorial
Army Reservist Formerly a telegraph linesman in the signal department GWR

E. Barton

BATHE, G.
George
Private 10221 1st Battalion Wiltshire Regiment
Killed in Action 20th January 1915
25 years old
Son of George and Charlotte Francis Bathe, of 69 Kingshill Road
H. 20 Kemmel Chateau Military Cemetery
Born in Shrivenham Lived in Swindon
Former Swindon Town football player

BEALES, E.N.
Edwin Ninian
Private 90673 140th Field Ambulance Royal Army Medical Corps
Died 23rd March 1918. 26 years old
Son of James and Helen Beales, of 32 Commercial Road
Bay 10 Arras Memorial
Attended North Wilts Technical College Victoria Road, in 1905 Remembered on its Stained Glass Window

BEAMES, C.T.
Charles Thomas
Pte 1644 15th Battalion, Royal Warwickshire Regiment
Killed in Action 12th June 1916
23 years old
Son of Mrs Ellen Johnson 16 Premier Street, Nechells Birmingham.
I D 42 Faubeurg D'Amiens cemetery Arras. France

BEARD, F.
(Died)No Details

BEASANT, F.A.
Frederick Ashley
Private 7/15224 'C' Company 7th Battalion Royal Dublin Fusiliers
Died 29th March 1918. 23 years old
Son of George and Emma Beasant, of 63 Brunswick Street
F 47. Jerusalem War Cemetery

Grave of George Bathe

8

F.T. Bailey

BAILEY, H.
Died No Details.

BAILEY, T.W.
Sapper 520019 1st Wilts Fortress
Battalion Royal Engineers
Died 13th March 1917. 42 years old
Husband of Emma P.J. Bailey of 151
Rodbourne Road, Swindon
IV C. 16 Grove Town Cemetery Meaulte
Served in South African Campaign

BAGGS, A.
Arthur
Private 46251 1st Battalion Wiltshire
Regiment
Died of Wounds 27th October 1918
XIII. A. 11 Rocquigny – Equancourt Road,
British Cemetery Manancourt
Born in Swindon

BAKER, E.F.
Edgar Frank
Private 14146 5th Battalion Wiltshire
Regiment
Killed in Action 10th August 1915
Panel 156-158 Helles Memorial
Born in Swindon
Formerly worked in GWR in Loco Dept.
Offices
Joined the Wiltshire Regiment in
September 1914

E.F. Baker

BAKER, E.J.
Ephram John
Gunner 189167 'A' Battery 38th Brigade
Royal Field Artillery
Died 7th August 1917. 33 years old
Son of William and Sarah Baker of
Swindon
VII.A. 2 Railway Dugouts Burial Ground
Transport Farm

BAKER, F.
Frederick
Lance-Sergeant 9039 2nd Battalion
Bedfordshire Regiment
Died of Wounds 6th July 1915
28 years old
Husband of C.H. Baker of 8 Ponting
Street, Swindon
B. 3315 Radnor Street Cemetery

T.W. Bailey

BALCH, F.A.
Frederick Arthur
Private 399088 17th Battalion Tank Corps
Killed in Action 2nd September 1918
20 years old
Son of Arthur and Eva Mary Balch of 8
Bath Road, Swindon
Panel II VIS-EN Artios Memorial
Born in Swindon – Educated at Swindon
High School Remembered on plaque in
Christchurch.

BALDRY, A.E.
Bombardier 24501 4th Siege Battery
Royal Garrison Artillery
Killed in Action 27th December 1915
V.B. 9. Duhallow A. D. S. Cemetery

BALL, F.A.
Fred Avery
Private 6986 1st Battalion Wiltshire
Regiment
Killed in Action 19th October 1914
Panel 33 and 34 Le Touret Memorial
Born in Swindon

BALL, F
Frederick.
Gunner. 3754 Royal Field Artillery. 'D' Battery 2nd Brigade.
Killed in Action 13th October 1915
23 years old.
Son of Mrs Eliza Ball of 68 Telford Road Rodbourne Cheney
Fosse 7 Military Cemetery. Mazingarbe, France.

F. Ball

BALL. G.
George.
Lance-Corporal 5065 2nd Battalion Wiltshire Regiment
Killed in Action 24th October 1914
36 years old
Son of William and Emily Ball of Badbury Wick, Chiseldon
Husband of Agnes Ellen Ball of 15 Bradford Road
Panel 53 Menin Gate Memorial
Also served in South African Campaign

BALL. G.G.
Private 33800 7th Battalion Norfolk Regiment
Killed in Action 7th March 1918
30 years old
Son of Mr and Mrs George Ball of 2 Station Road
I F 7 Tournai Communal Cemetery Allied Extension.
He had been rejected twice for Military Service, before succeeding with the Norfolk Regiment.

BALLARD, J.H.
Private 942 2nd Division Cyclist Company Army Cyclist Corps
Killed in Action 26th July 1915
27 years old
Son of Joseph and Mary Ann Ballard
Husband of Harriett Ballard of 2 Lansdowne Gardens, South Lambeth London

41 Beuvry Communal Cemetery France.
Formerly worked in Number 16 shop in the GWR

J.H. Ballard

BALLINGER, B.W.
Bertie William
Private 18554 9th Battalion Worcestershire Regiment
Killed in Action 20th April 1916
36 years old.
Son of Thomas and Sarah Ann Ballinger, of Shrivenham, Berks.
Panel 18 and 63 Basra war memorial. Iraq
Lived in Swindon

BARBER, H.H.
Horace Henry
Private G/23252 1st Battalion Queens Own Royal West Kent Regiment
Killed in Action 26th October 1917
28 years old
Husband of Helen Barber of 19 Kingshill Road, Swindon
V.I. A. D. 10. Hooge Crater Cemetery. Belgium

BARKER, A.J.
Arthur James
Private 63031 1st Garrison Battalion Worcestershire Regiment
Died 7th July 1918. 39 years old
Son of Joshua and Hanna Barker, of Swindon
Husband of Sarah A. Barker of 7 Osborne Road, Willesden Green, London
B. 22. 13. Cobh Old Church Cemetery, County Cork, Republic of Ireland

BARLING, H.
Harry
Private 11174 19th Queen Alexandra's Own, Royal Hussars
Killed in Action 8th October 1918
19 years old
Son of Harry Barling and Kate Louisa

BEASANT, M.G.
Driver 966462 Royal Field Artillery
Died 4th November 1918
9.34. St. Mary's, Rodbourne Cheney

BECKETT, H.
Hubert
Lance-Corporal 39584 11th Battalion Somerset Light Infantry (Formerly 5618
Wiltshire Regiment)
Killed in Action 5th November 1918. 34 years old
Son of John and Sarah Beckett, of Swindon
Husband of Annie Beckett (nee Chapman), of 161 Manchester Road
On the South Boundary – Obigies Communal Cemetery
Born in Swindon Seen previous service in South Africa.He was working as a labourer
in the GWR works before volunteering for service again. He joined the Wilts on 5th
November 1914 and sent out to France. He was later transferred to the Dorset Regt
then on to the Somerset LI.
In a letter to Huberts wife Annie Rev Campling wrote the following.
11th Somersetshire Light Infantry
BEF France November 12th

Dear Mrs Beckett, I am afraid I have some very sad news for you – that your husband
has been killed. It occurred on the morning of November 5th. We were ordered to
make an advance as news had come that the Germans had evacuated the village on
the opposite bank of the river, over against our positions. In the morning the advance
began, but some machine guns opened fire and several of our men were killed and
wounded – and amongst them your husband. It will be very sad news indeed for you
especially now as the end of the war has come and we are all looking forward to
being with our friends and relations again. I am sure you have my sympathy.

I have heard some of the officers who
knew your husband speak most highly of
him. They respected him as a soldier and
they liked him. He was a good soldier
and I am sure must have been a good
husband. I feel for you very much in your
loss. He has been buried in the village
churchyard at Obigies on the east bank
of the Scheldt near to where he fell.
I am sure this war brings home to us the
certainty of a life to come. It ends so
suddenly and it makes us look forward to
that future life when we shall be with our
loved ones in His presence. It will be a
wonderful life. And the disappointments
and bereavements here are to make us
look forward to the life to come and to
draw nearer to our Lord Himself. I pray
that he will comfort you at this time.

Yours sincerely

(The Rev) W C Campling C.E Chaplin to
the 11th Somerset Light Infantry

BEDWELL, R.
Robert
Private 21069 5th Battalion Wiltshire Regiment
Killed in Action 9th April 1916
18 years old
Son of Robert Lily Elija Bedwell, of 31 Union Street
Panel 30 and 64 Basra Memorial
Lived in Swindon Remembered on plaque in Christchurch

BELBIN, E.J.G.
Acting Lance-Corporal 504536 503rd Field Company Royal Artillery
Died of Wounds 27th June 1918
11 D. 17 Pernois British Cemetery Halloy – Les – Pernois
Born in Swindon

BELCHER, C.
Charles
Private 15248 7th Battalion Royal Dublin Fusiliers
Killed in Action 17th November 1915
Son of Laurence and June Belcher, of Goosey, Faringdon, Berkshire
Doiran Memorial

BELCHER, W.H.
William
Private 240367 1/5th Battalion Gloucestershire Regiment
Died 18th November 1916. 21 years old
Son of William and Eliza Belcher, of Duntisbourne, near Cirencester, Glos.
111 E. 31. Warlencourt British Cemetery France

BENBOW, J.L.
John Lewis
Private STK/2305 26th Battalion Royal Fusiliers City of London Regiment
Died of Wounds 18th September 1916
lll.G. 6. Guards Cemetery Lesboeufs
Lived in Swindon

BERRY, W.W.
Walter Ward
Private TR/830566 51st Training Reserve Battalion Hampshire Regiment
Died 12th November 1918. 18 years old
473 Christchurch Cemetery, Swindon
Remembered on plaque in Christchurch, Old Town

BERWICK, R.T.
Robert
Able-seaman Z/2069 Royal Navy Reserve
Collingwood' Royal Navy Division
Died 4th June 1915
Panel 8 – 15 Helles Memorial

BEVAN, E.W.R.
Edward William Reginald
Engine Room Artificer 3rd Class M/1189
H. M. S. Submarine 'E 16'
Died at Sea 22nd August 1916
Husband of Mable Hurst of Southbrook Street.
14 Plymouth Naval Memorial
Born in Stratford on Avon – Lived in Swindon (Wellington Street)
The E.16 was last sighted 35 miles East of Yarmouth by the E38. She later observed a group of warships moving North in the vicinity of Terschelling. Splashes were seen near to one of the warships which may have been depth charges exploding. Reports of enemy vessels attacking a periscope on 22nd August may have been against the E16.

E. Bevan

BEVAN, F.H.
Francis Herbert
Lance-Corporal T/240411 1/5th Battalion East Kent Regiment
Died 26th June 1918
IV. C. 6. Baghdad (North Gate) War Cemetery
Born in Swindon Lived in Ashford Kent

BEVAN, G.
George
Private 20624 2nd Battalion Wiltshire Regiment
Died of Wounds 26th December 1916
30 years old
Husband of Lillie Bevan, of 104 Goddard Avenue, Swindon
BIO. I. 407 Birmingham (Lodge Hill) Cemetery

BEZZANT, A.F.
Albert Fred
Private 10527 2nd Battalion Wiltshire Regiment
Died of Wounds 23rd June 1915
I. A. 166 Longuenesse (St. Omar) Souvenir Cemetery
Formerly a Labourer in Number 1 shop in the GWR

A.F. Bezzant

BICK, C.A.
Charles Albert
Private 12307 7th Battalion Wiltshire Regiment
Killed in Action 24th April 1917 in Salonika
Son of Albert and Margaret Bick, of 47 County Road, Swindon
Doiran Memorial

BIGNALL, S.
Died No Details.

BIGGS, E.L.
Private Royal Engineers
Remembered on plaque in Christchurch, Old Town
No Other details.

BIGGS, L.
Pioneer. WR./279572 Royal Engineers attached to the Direction of General Transportation

Died 27th October 1918
Plot 8. Row D. Grave 8. Montecchio Precalcino Communal Cemetery Extension Italy.

BILLETT, H.
Harold
Private 8492 1st Regiment South African Infantry
Killed in Action 18th October 1916
Pier and face 4C Thiepval Memorial
Born in Swindon, lived at Bright Street prior to emigrating to South Africa.
Attended North Wilts Technical College Victoria Road 1902 Remembered on its Stained Glass Window
Became Astronomer Royal in South Africa

H Billett South African Infantry

BINT, W.H.
William Henry
Lance-Corporal 8782 2nd Battalion Wiltshire Regiment
Died 2nd January 1915. 27 years old
Son of Charles Thomas and Charlotte Bint
Sp. Memorial 27 Kortrijk (St. Jan) Communal Cemetery
Born in Inkpen, Berkshire Lived in Swindon

BIRCH, F.W.
Frederick
Lance-Corporal 12010 2nd Battalion Hampshire Regiment (Formerly 13558 Duke of Cornwalls Light Infantry)
Killed in Action 7th October 1915
32 years old
Son of William and Sarah Agnes Birch of 17 Milton Road
IV. D. 1. Pink Farm Cemetery Helles

Dardanelles
Born in Swindon Remembered on plaque in Christchurch
Worked in his Fathers grocery in Commercial Road later He left Swindon to work in a grocery establishment in London.

BIRKS, A.O.
Alfred Owen
2nd Lieutenant 1st Battalion Dorsetshire Regiment
Died of Wounds 13th March 1918
Son of Mr and Mrs John Birks, of 97 County Road
Grave I. D. 2. Haringhe (Badaghem) Military Cemetery
Educated at Sanford St school, and attended North Wilts Technical College Victoria Road in 1904.
Formerly employed in the clerical department of the GWR, he volunteered for service in 1914. He joined as a private and left England for France as a Sergeant – Major in the Army Service Corps. He was gazetted to the Dorset regiment in July 1917. He had only just returned to the front, after a spell of leave, when on the 13th March, he was shot through the chest and died that same evening. He was married and had two children.

W H Bint (standing) with his brother Gerry Bint of the Hampshire Regiment

BIRKS, G.A.
George Allen
Air-mechanic 1st Class 7432 RAF
Died 14th July 1918. 22 years old
Son of John Birks
D. 1226 Radnor Street Cemetery

BISHOP, J.H.
James Henry
Private 42769 1st Battalion Royal Iniskillin Fusiliers (Formerly 122613 Army Service Corps)
Died of Wounds 24th April 1918
Son of Joseph W. and Annie Bishop, of 4 Francis Road, Upper Parkstone
B. Q. Q. 11. C. Poole (Branksome) Cemetery
Born in Swindon

BISHOP, L.W. (ALIAS GYLBY)
Leonard William
Lance-Corporal 9532 B Company 2nd Battalion Royal Berkshire Regiment
Killed in Action 25th September 1915
22 years old
Son of Ernest and Annie Gylby, of 60 North Street
Panel 7 and 8 Ploegsteert Memorial
Served as Bishop, real name was Gylby

BISHOP, T.A.
Thomas Albert
Private 2883 2nd Battalion Gloucester shire Regiment
Killed in Action 9th May 1915
Panel 22 and 34 Menin Gate Memorial
Born in Swindon

BIZLEY, A.
Arthur
Driver T. F. 846019 3rd Section 61st Division Ammunition Corps Royal Field Artillery
Killed in Action 5th December 1917
24 years old
Son of Mr and Mrs A Bizley of 9 Medgebury Road
II. E. 13. Finnis New B Cemetery, Sirel Le Grand
Lived in Swindon and was employed as a barman in the Whale Inn.

BIZLEY, R.C.
Private 024304 125th Company Army Ordnance Corps.
Died 26th November 1918
Son of Margaret Bizley

of 126 Cricklade Road
504 Kirechkoi – Hortakoi Military
Cemetery

R.C. Bizley

BLACKFORD, J.B.
John Bertie
21913 8th Battalion Gloucestershire
Regiment
Died 28th July 1917. 41 years old
Son of Joseph and Roshanna Blackford,
of 41 Rolleston Street.
Panel 22 and 34 Menin Gate Memorial

BLAKE, F.B.
Died No Details

BLAKE, R.A.
Reginald Albert
Gunner 61630 'X' 12th Medium Trench
Mortar Battery Royal Garrison Artillery
Died 28th June 1916. 18 years old
Son of James and Sarah Ann Blake, of
Stanton Fitzwarren, Highworth
Pier and Face 8A Thiepval Memorial

BLOXSOM, F.
Francis
Gunner 199136 'C' Battery 86th Brigade
Royal Field Artillery
Died of Wounds 3rd September 1918
20 years old
Son of Mr. and Mrs. Smith, of 116
Kingsdown Road, Stratton
IV.B. 7 Ligny – St Flochel British
Cemetery
Averdoingt France
Lived in Swindon

BLOXSON, H.
Harry
Private 11287 6th Battalion Wiltshire
Regiment
Killed in Action 26th September 1915
Panel 102 Loos Memorial

BLUNSDON, F.A .
Frederick Albert.
Private 3/583 1st Battalion Wiltshire
Regiment
Killed in Action 25th September 1915
36 years old
Son of Mr Charles Blunsdon of 62
Edinburgh Street Gorse Hill
Wife and daughter of 56 Argyll Street
Panel 53 Menin Gate Memorial.
Worked in GWR as a striker in No 14
Shop.
Served previously with the Wiltshire
Regiment in south Africa.

F. Blunsdon

BOND, C.J.
Charles John
Private 53049 8th Battalion Essex
Regiment
Died 31st August 1921. 21 years old
Son of William and Sarah E. Bond, of 401
Ferndale Road
C. 3555 Radnor Street Cemetery
Buried in same plot with his father

F.H. Bloxsom

13

BOND, W.
William
Rifleman 204553 22nd Battalion Rifle Brigade
Transferred to 388505 816th Company Labour Corps
Died 11th December 1918. 54 years old
Husband of Sarah E. Wild (Bond), of 401 Ferndale Road
Father of Charles John Bond, private in the Essex Regiment
C. 3555 Radnor Street Cemetery

BOULTON, E.R.
Ernest Rice
Sapper 3706 2/2nd Field Company Royal Engineers
Died of Wounds 28th July 1916
Son of Alfred William and Ellen Boulton of 46 Birch Street
Husband of E M Boulton (Died some months previously to Ernest)
Brother of Reginald (Below)
IV.A. 19. Longuenesse (St. Omer) Souvenir Cemetery
Formerly a painter in the Locomotive Works in the GWR
Remembered on Family plot together with Reginald in Radnor Street Cemetery

BOULTON, R.C.
Reginald Cyril
Private 19423 5th Battalion Wiltshire Regiment
Died 11th December 1915. 19 years old
Son of Alfred William and Ellen Boulton, of 46 Birch Street
B. 49. Alexander (Chatby) Military and War Memorial Cemetery
Born in Swindon

BOWEN, E.
Edward
Signalman 230362 RFR/PO/B/2774 H. M. S. 'Good Hope'
Died 1st November 1914. 31 years old
Husband of Ellen Bowen, of 76 St. Chads Avenue, North Ends, Portsmouth
3.Portsmouth Naval Memorial
Born in Swindon

BOWEN, W.
Walter
Private 241632 2/6th Territorial Force Battery South Staffordshire Regiment
Killed in Action 30th November 1917
26 years old

Son of Edward and Lucretia Bowen, of 'Hill View', Milton Road, Repton, Derby
Panel 7. Cambrai Memorial Loverval
Lived in Swindon

BOWERING, J.E.
John Edwin
Lance-Corporal 35898 20th Army Troops Company Royal Engineers
Died 27th April 1918
II F5 Gwalia Cemetery Belgium
Attended North Wilts Technical College Victoria Road 1907 Remembered on its Stained Glass Window. Was employed by Redman Civil Engineers. Recommended for a commission.

E R Boulton

BOWERS, T.
Thomas
2nd Leutenant Army Cyclist Corps
Died 31st July 1919. 28 years old
Son of George and Eliza Bowers of Upwell Norfolk
Husband of Phylis Constance Bowers of 88 Manchester Road
Upwell St Peters Churchyard Norfolk
Remembered on memorial in Radnor St Cemetery

BOWLES, W.H.
William Henry
Sergeant 3/811 1st Battalion Wiltshire Regiment
Killed in Action 2nd September 1917
Panel 119 – 120 Tyne Cott
Born in Stratton

BOWLEY, E.
Edward
Private 22709 6th Battalion Wiltshire Regiment
Killed in Action 2nd July 1916
Pier and Face 13A Thiepval Memorial
Born in Swindon Remembered on plaque in Christchurch

BOWRNE, S.B.
Died No Details

BOWRON, F.
Frank
Private 30003 8th Battalion Gloucester shire Regiment
Died 9th July 1917. 31 years old
Son of William Bowron and Husband of Constana Jessie Bowron, of 28 Turner Street
Panel 22 + 34 Menin Gate Memorial

BOWRON, P.
Percy
Lance-Corporal 42269 9th Battalion Yorkshire Regiment
Formerly 183429 Royal Field Artillery
Killed in Action 4th November 1918
II B. 14 Le Cateau Military Cemetery
Born in Swindon

BOYLES, T.H.
Thomas Henry
Private 22096 Wiltshire Regiment
Transferred to 90670 152nd Company Labour Corps
Son of Henry and Ann Boyles, of Ogborne St. George, Marlborough, Wiltshire
II.B. 5. Solferino Farm Cemetery

BRADFIELD, T.H.
Thomas Henry
Private 11201 2nd Battalion Welsh Regiment
Killed in Action 9th May 1915
Panel 23 and 24 Le Touret Memorial France
Born in Swindon Lived in Wales

BRADLEY, H.W.
Horace.W
2nd Lieutenant 5th Battalion Royal Welsh Fusiliers
Killed in Action 10th February 1917
Son of Thomas W. and and Emma Ellen Bradley, of 225 Ferndale Road
1V C. 2. St. Vaast Post Military Cemetery Richebourg, L'auoue
Attended North Wilts Technical College Victoria Road 1908 Remembered on its Stained Glass Window

BRAIN, W.T.
William Thomas
Private 10402 1st Battalion Wiltshire Regiment

Killed in Action 16th June 1915
Panel 53 Menin Gate Memorial
Born in Swindon

BRAMBLE, W.
William
Sapper 193713 Royal Engineers
Died 3rd January 1917. 27 years old
Son of Mr. G. and Mrs. F. Bramble, of 27 Newport Street
Husband of Mrs. R. Bramble, of Toronto, Canada
C. 3401 Radnor Street Cemetery

BREWER, S.G.
Sidney George
Private 32983 2nd Battalion Wiltshire Regiment (Formerly 2091 Royal Wiltshire Yeomanry)
Died of Wounds 12th March 1917
21 years old
Son of Henry James and Caroline Jane Brewer, of 21 Stafford Street
C. 16 Auesnes – Le – Comte Communal Cemetery Extension
Born in Seend, Wiltshire – Lived in Swindon

BREWER, W.A.
William Arthur
Private 10398 'D' Company 1st Battalion Wiltshire Regiment
Killed in Action 13th November 1914
21 years old
Son of George and Sarah Brewer of 81 Wood Lane Chippenham
Panel 53 Menin Gate memorial
Served as a Territorial for 3 years Played for Swindon Town Football Club.

BRIDGEMAN, A.
Arthur
Private 22600 2nd Battalion Wiltshire Regiment
Killed in Action 18th October 1916
V1 D. 38. Warlencourt British Cemetery
Lived in Swindon

A. Bridgeman

BRIDGEMAN, C.O.
Charles Oliver
C. H./20209 RMLI H. M. S. 'Vanguard'
Died 9th July 1917. 18 years old
Son of George and Emily Bridgeman, of
44 Princess Street, Swindon
25 Chatham Naval Memorial

BRIDGEMAN, H.
Henry
Private 10407 1st Battalion Wiltshire
Regiment
Died of Wounds 25th January 1915
28 years old
11 F. 17. Locre Churchyard Belgium.
Born in Swindon.
Formerly a Labourer in the Signal
Department in the G. W. R.

BRIGHT, A.J.
Alfred John
Private T/205332 1st Battalion Queens
Royal West Surrey Regiment
Killed in Action 12th April 1918
21 years old
Son of H. J. Bright, of 146 Oxford Road,
Windsor, Berkshire
Panel 1 and 2 Ploegsteert Memorial
Belgium
Born in Swindon

BRIGHT, J.C.G.
Joseph Charles George
Corporal 5695 21st Battalion (First Surrey
Rifles) London Regiment
Killed in Action 15th September 1916
20 years old
Son of Joseph and Emma Bright, of
Millfield Rectory Road, Hadleigh, Essex
Pier and Face 13C Thiepval Memorial

BRISTON, C.
Clayton
Corporal R/4502 13th Battalion KRRC
Killed in Action 11th April 1917
D. 5 Houdain Lane Cemetery
Born in Swindon Lived in West Ham
London

BRITTAIN, H.V.
Harry Varney
Driver T2/13452 RASC attached to XVI
Corps Ammunition Company
Died 3rd October 1918. 24 years old
Son of H. J. and Annie Sarah Brittain, of
Wiltshire
D. 696 Sarigol Military Cemetery

Kriston Balkans
Born in Swindon

BROADHURST, B.
Benjamin
Sergeant 11243 16th Battalion
Lancashire Fusiliers
Killed in Action 1st July 1916
Pier and Face 3C and 3D Thiepval
Memorial

H. Bridgeman

BROCKWAY, T.H.
Thomas Henry George
Private 6484 1st Battalion Wiltshire
Regiment
Killed in Action 20th September 1914
Sp. Memorial 31 Valley British Cemetery
(Sur-Aisne)
Born in Swindon

BROOKES, R.
Richard
Private 32817 A Company 6th (Service)
Battalion York and Lancaster Regiment
Killed in Action 13th June 1917
23 years old
Son of William and Eliza Brookes, of 28
Barking Street, Carbrook, Sheffield
A. 18. Cabin Hill Cemetery
Born in Swindon

BROOKHAM, F.
Died No Details

BROOMFIELD, R.M.
Richard Mc Allistor
Private 10105 8th Battalion Northamber
land Fusiliers
Died of Wounds 4th November 1915
Son of Elizabeth and Murray Broomfield.
Husband of Elizabeth Broomfield, of 52
Worcester Street, Gateshead.
III.E. I. Hill 10 Cemetery
Born in Swindon

BROTHERIDGE, W.J.
William
Private 310871 Warwickshire Yeomanry
Died at Sea 27th May 1918
Son of Mr and Mrs William Brotheridge of 90 Montague Street.
Chatby Memorial
Lived in Swindon He was on board the transport ship 'Learowe Castle' when it was sunk by a torpedo. He had spent 2 ½ years on active service with the Egyptian Expeditionary Force and was on his way for home leave and looking forward to celebrating his 21st Birthday at home.

BROWN, C.G.
Charles George
Private 25870 6th Battalion Wiltshire Regiment
Killed in Action 10th April 1918
Panel 119 to 120 Tyne Cott Memorial
Lived in Swindon

BROWN, H.
Henry
Private 11078 4th Battalion Worcester shire Regiment
Killed in Action 6th August 1915.
30 years old
Brother of William Brown, of 27 Jackson Road, Alum Rock, Saltey, Birmingham
Panel 104 – 113 Helles Memorial
Born in Swindon

J Brown

BROWN, J.E.
John Edwin
Private 22647 3rd Battalion Coldstream Guards (Formerly 2545 Household Btn)
Killed in Action 13th April 1918.
37 years old
Son of Edwin Ernest and Mary Jane Brown, of 39 Hatfield Road, Gloucester-shire
Husband of Georgena May Brown, of 67 Albany Street, Gloucestershire

Panel 1 Ploegsteert Memorial
Born in Swindon

BROWN, N.F.T.
Norman Frederick Theodore
Private 20714 'D' company 5th Battalion Wiltshire regiment.
Killed in Action 29 March 1917
21 years old.
Son of Mrs Uriania Maria Johnson. 3 Lulworth Terrace, Rodbourne Cheney.
Panel 30 and 64 Basra war memorial Iraq.
Born in Stratton

N.F.T Brown

BROWN, P.O.
Percy Osman
Pte 90674 140th Field Ambulance Royal Army Medical Corps
Died 23rd March 1918
Bay 10 Arras Memorial France.

BROWN, W.A.J.
William Alfred John.
Ordinary seaman. J/39301 Royal Navy HMS 'Defence'
Killed in Action 31st May 1916.
18 years old.
Son of William and Eliza Brown 1A Murray St New, North Road, London.
16 Chatham Naval memorial.
Lived in Swindon.
HMS Defence, 1st Cruiser squadron of the Grand Fleet, was blown up by German Gunfire, during the Battle of Jutland.
Of the 4 ships of this Squadron,-Defence, Warrior, Duke of Edinburgh and Black Prince, Only Duke of Edinburgh survived.

BRUNSDON, W.T.
Walter Thomas
Private 7851 1st Battalion Wiltshire Regiment
Died of Wounds 30th October 1914

23 years old
Son of Mr. And Mrs. Walter Brunsdon, of
Cirencester
I.A. 5A. Wintruex Communal Cemetery
Born in Swindon

BRYANT, A.E.
Allan Edgar
Sergeant 504565 503rd Field Company
Royal Engineers
Killed in Action 20th September 1917
27 years old
Son of Albert and Mary Ann Bryant of
Swindon
E. 21 Buffs Road Cemetery

BRYANT, A.R.
Arthur Reginald
Private 26561 103rd Company Machine
Gun Corps (Formerly 17664 Somerset
Light Infantry)
Killed in Action 1st July 1916
19 years old
Son of James Thomas and Sarah Ann
Bryant The Cottage, High St, Portishead,
Bristol
Pier and Face 5c and 12c Thiepval
Memorial France
Born in Swindon

BRYANT, G.E.
Gilbert Edward
Private 10796 5th Battalion Wiltshire
Regiment
Died of Wounds 10th August 1915
Son of Albert and Mary Ann Bryant,
Bletchley Surrey.
Brother of Reginald (Below)
Panel 156 to 158 Helles Memorial
Dardanelles
Born Bletchingley, Surrey – Lived in
Swindon

G.E Bryant

BRYANT, R.W.
Reginald Walter
11271 Air Mechanic 1st Class 28th
Squadron Royal Air Force
Died 10th November 1918. 26 years old.
Son of Albert and Mary Ann Bryant,
Bletchley Surrey.
Brother of Gilbert (Above)
DIV 62 11 05 STE Marie Cemetery Le
Harvre France
Born in Bletchingley, Lived in Swindon.

BUCKLAND, R.H.
Reginald
Private 33200 1st Battalion Wiltshire
Regiment
Died of Wounds 8th November 1918
30 years old
Brother of Winifred Buckland, of 7
Ipswich Street, Swindon
V.II. N. 3A Mont Huon Military Cemetery
Le – Treport
Lived in Swindon

BULL, A.
Arthur
Private 3163 1st Battalion Wiltshire
Regiment
Killed in Action 19th June 1917
28 years old
Son of Thomas and Emily Bull, of
Monkton, Wiltshire
G. 11 Poperinghe New Military Cemetery
Lived in Swindon

BULL, D.G.
Daniel George
Lance-Corporal 7525 5th Battalion
Wiltshire Regiment
Died 31st August 1916. 27 years old
Son of Thomas and Fanny Bull,
Husband of Eleanor Betty Bull, of Upper
Square, Purton
V.E. 11 Basra War Cemetery
Lived in Swindon

BULL, J.
James
Private 18662 2nd Battalion Wiltshire
Regiment
Killed in Action 15th June 1915
28 years old
Son Thomas and Emily Bull, of 188
Winterbourne Monkton
Panel 33 – 34 Le – Touret Memorial
Lived in Swindon

BUNCE, F. J.
Frederick John
Gunner 62524 'A' Battery 86th Brigade
Royal Field Artillery
Killed in Action 21st November 1917
XIV.D. 11. The Huts Cemetery
Born in Swindon

BURCHELL, W.E.
William Eli
Private 10835 2nd Battalion Wiltshire
Regiment
Killed in Action 15th June 1916
35 years old
Son of the late William Eli Burchell, of
Hunt Mill Road, Wootton Bassett
Pier and Face 13A Thiepval Memorial
Born in Wootton Bassett Lived in
Swindon

BURBRIDGE, J.H.
John
Private 5895 1st Garrison Battalion Royal
Irish Regiment (Formerly G/27331 Royal
Irish Fusiliers and 11122 Royal Worcester-
shire Regiment)
Died 30th May 1918
Pier and Face 5C and 12C Thiepval
memorial France
Born in Swindon

BURNESS, W.J.
William John
Private 33501 2nd Battalion Wiltshire
Regiment
Killed in Action 31st July 1917
37 years old
Son of J. Burness of Reading
Husband of Mrs. K. C. Burness, of 46
Goddard Avenue, Swindon
Panel 53 Menin Gate Memorial
Born in Canning Town

BURGESS, F.J.
Francis John
Private 22941 1st Battalion Wiltshire
Regiment
Died of Wounds 28th November 1916
Born in Purton Lived in Swindon

BURNS, C.S.
Charles Stewart
Lance-Corporal 45822 89th Field
Company Royal Engineers
Killed in Action 10th December 1915
VI.A. 6. Duhallow A. D. S. Cemetery
Lived in Swindon

BURT, C. S.
Christopher Stigant
Corporal 200497 1/4th Battalion
Hampshire Regiment
Killed in Action 21st January 1916
22 years old
Son of Christopher and Clara Burt, of
'Darien' Whitworth Road
Panel 21 and 63 Basra Memorial

BURTON, O.E.
Owen Edgar
Engine room Artificer 1st class. Royal
Navy. HMS 'Indefatigable'
Killed in action 31st May 1916. 38 yrs old.
Son of Matthew and Mahila Burton
75 Radnor Street.
Husband of Elsie Amelia Burton 12
George street Davenport.
14 Plymouth Naval Memorial.
Born in Swindon. Had been in Navy for
15 years.

BUTCHER, A.E.
Albert Edward
Private 22470 6th Battalion Wiltshire
Regiment
Killed in Action 2nd July 1916
18 years old
Son of Joseph and Annie Butcher, of 9
Ipswich Street
Pier and Face 13A Thiepval Memorial
Born in Fulham, London Lived in
Swindon

BUTCHER, A.S.
Arthur Stewart
Private 11032 'B' Company 2nd Battalion
Wiltshire Regiment
Died of Wounds 29th October 1917
21 years old
Son of John and Annie Butcher, of 10
Dixon Street
III.E. 86. Bailleul Communal Cemetery
Extension (Nord)
Born in Stratton

BUTCHER, G.E.
George Edward
Private 12334 2nd Battalion Wiltshire
Regiment
Killed in Action 26th April 1918
28 years old
Son of Mrs. Sarah Butcher, of Buttlewell,
Purton
Panel 119 – 120 Tyne Cott
Lived in Swindon

BUTLER, E.J.
Edward John
Private 11492 7th (Service) Battalion
Gloucestershire Regiment
Killed in Action 8th August 1915
Panel 101 – 104 Helles Memorial
Dardanelles
Born in Swindon

BUTLER, F.C.
Frederick Charles
Company-Sergeant-Major 3/478 6th
Battalion Wiltshire Regiment
Killed in Action 23rd February 1916
I.F. 7. Rue du Bacquerot Number 1
Military
Cemetery, Laventie
Lived in Swindon

BUTLER. F.T.
Frederick Thomas
Private 46974 2nd Battalion Wiltshire
Regiment
Killed in Action 19th October 1918
Son of Mr A T Butler of Broad Hinton
IV B 19 St Aubert Britiash Cemetery
Lived in Swindon

BUTLER, J.
John
Sapper 125 1/1st Wilts Fortress

Company Royal Engineers
Died of Wounds 23rd March 1915
21 years old
Son of George B. and Mary Butler, of 35
Gooch Street
B. 3290 Radnor Street Cemetery
He was involved in a gun incident, and
was hospitalised in Liverpool Military
Hospital, where he died. His body was
brought back to Swindon. His funeral
Service was conducted at St. Pauls where
he was a member of St. Pauls F.C.
His pall Bearers were other members of
the football team: R. C. Mortimer, C. Fry,
A. W. Summers, E. J. Tyler.
He had worked at the G. W. R. as a
carpenter in the Carriage Department.

BUTLER, R.H.
Robert Herbert
Private M/282793 Reserve Mechanical
Transport General Head Quarters Army
Service Corps
Died 26th October 1918. 30 years old
Son of Alfred Robert and Sarah Annie
Butler
Husband of Lily Louisa Butler, of Swindon
Plot 3 Row D. Grave 7. Giavara British
Cemetery Arcade

The Menin Gate. Ypres
Inside on each wall is the inscription 'Here are recorded the names of officers and men who fell in the Ypres salient but to whom the fortune of war denied the known and honoured burial given to their comrades in death' On these panels are engraved the names of about 55,000 men of the British Empire, who were killed in the Salient from August 1917 whose remains were never found.A further 34,000 missing men who died between August 1917 till the end of the war, have their names carved on panels at Tyne Cott. Many Swindon men are commemorated at both places.

BUTT, W.H.F.
William Frederick Handley
Private 14228 8th Royal Berkshire
Regiment
Died 3rd September 1916. 26 years old
Son of Frederick Handley Butt, of Great
Malvern Worcestershire
Husband of Florence Mary Handley Butt
of 56 Medgebury Road
Pier and Face 11D Thiepval Memorial

CANN, R.G.F.
Richard George Fred
Private 10512 1st Battalion Wiltshire
Regiment
Died of Wounds 30th June 1915
19 years old
Eldest son of Richard and Liliean Cann, of
10 Avening Street, Gorse Hill
VIII. B. 54. Boulogne Eastern Cemetery
Lived in Swindon

CANNINGS, E.
Ernest
Rifleman S/3496 12th Battalion Rifle
Brigade
Died 28th February 1916. 20 years old
Son of Ernest and Alice Cannings, of 17
Holbrook Street
VI. D. 28. Etaples Military Cemetery
Born in Swindon

CANNINGS, S.
Sidney
Sergeant 5828 1st Battalion Wiltshire
Regiment
Died of Wounds 8th August 1917
IV.13. 12 Mendinghem Military Cemetery
Born Ashbury (Berkshire) Lived in
Swindon

S. Cannons

CANNONS, S.
Sidney
Sergeant 5828 1st Battalion Wiltshire
Regiment

Killed in Action 8th August 1917
IV.B. 12. Menclinghen Military Cemetery
Formerly worked as a Labourer in the
Loco and Carriage Department at the
GWR

T. Canter

CANTER, T.
Tom
Private 14509 8th Battalion Royal
Berkshire Regiment
Killed in Action 25th September 1915.
30 years old
Son of Thomas and Dinakz Canter, of
Silver Street, Minety Wiltshire.
Husband of Ella Alice Cantor, of 11 Unity
Street, Chippenham
Panel 93 – 95 Loos Memorial. France.

J. Carey

CAREY, J.
John
Private 18104 1st Battalion Wiltshire
Regiment
Died of Wounds 27th June 1915
XIII.B. 2. Harlebeke New British Cemetery
Born and Lived in Swindon
Worked as a frame builders assistant in
21A shop in the GWR

CARPENTER, W.H.E.
William Edwin
Private 25535 1/4th Wiltshire's
(Territorial Force)

Formerly 23855 Somerset Light Infantry
Killed in Action 23rd November 1917.
20 years old
Son of Thomas William and Sarah Ann
Carpenter, of 65 Hythe Road
C. 48. Jerusalem War Cemetery
An old pupil of Lethbridge School and
a member of the Baptist Tabernacle
Secondary
School. He served an apprenticeship to
Grocer W Haynes of Westcott Place. He
joined up under the Derby scheme and
was called up in March 1916. As a result
of being a member of the Volunteer
Training Corps, he was sent out to France
quickly. He later qualified as a sniper
then went on to train as a bomber. He
was wounded in Easter 1917. When he
had recovered, he was transferred to the
Wilts and sent out to Egypt.

CARTER, B.
Bertram
2nd Lieutenant 1st Battalion Cam
bridgeshire Regiment
Killed in Action 18th September 1918.
26 years old
Son of George Henry and Kate Carter, of
Broughton, Ketteriy,
Husband of Elsie Carter
LD. 23. Epehy Wood Farm Cemetery
Epehy

CARTER, H.
Henry
Private 18106 8th Hussars (Kings Royal
Irish)
Killed in Action 9th August 1918
Panel 2 Vis – en – Artois Memorial.

CARTER, P.C.
Percy Charles
Gunner 68328 Royal Field Artillery
Killed in Action 23rd August 1914.
19 years old
Son of Mr. C. and Mrs. E. Carter, of 34
Martins Avenue, Seven Sisters, Neath
Glam
La Ferte – Sous Jouarre Memorial
Labourer in the Loco and Carriage
Department at the GWR

CARTER, W.
William
Private 21224 1st Battalion Wiltshire
Regiment
Killed in Action 24th March 1918.

24 years old
Son of John and Honour Carter, of Ham
Cottages, Kempsford, Fairford, Glouces-
tershire
Bay 7 Arras Memorial. France
Born in Stenton, Wiltshire Lived in
Swindon

CARVEY, E.
Edward
Private 10391 2nd Battalion Wiltshire
Regiment
Killed in Action 26th September 1915
Panel 102 Loos Memorial. France
Born in Swindon

CASTLE, E.G.
Ernest George
Private 6875 1st Battalion Wiltshire
Regiment
Died of Wounds 29th October 1914.
32 years old
Lived 177 Beatrice Street
Panel 33 and 34 Tyne Cott Belgium.
Born in Swindon Worked as a Wagon
Examiner in the GWR

E.G. Castle

CASWELL, E.E.
Ernest Edward
Private 20638 5th Battalion Wiltshire
Regiment
Died 4th December 1915
I.E. 18. Hill 10 Cemetery Dardanelles
Born in Swindon
Worked as a porter in the Traffic
Department in the GWR

CAVILL, W.
William
Sapper 23383 33rd Base Park Company
Royal Engineers
Died 31st October 1918 in Salonika.
24 years old
Son of Edwin and Rose S. Cavill,

Husband of Mrs. A. V. Cavill, of 11 Rycroft Street, Gloucestershire
405 Kirechkoi – Hortakoi Military Cemetery
Born in Swindon

CHAMBERS, G.A.
George Austin
Tpr 831779 'C' Battery 306th Brigade Royal Field Artillery
Died of Wounds 15th August 1917.
19 years old
Son of John William and Alice Chambers
A. 21. New Irish Farm Cemetery
Born in Swindon

CHAMBERS, S.W.
Sydney William
Private 286567 Labour Corps 641st Employment Company
Formerly 10207 Army Cyclist Corps
Died 14th October 1918. 23 years old
Son of Robert and Kate Chambers, of 71 Ashford Road
K. 1052 Radnor Street Cemetery
Born in Swindon

CHANDLER, C.E.
Charles, E
Private 14231 1st Battalion Royal Berkshire Regiment
Died of Wounds 5th April 1918.
22 years old
II.A. A. 2. Le Quesnoy Communal Cemetery
Born in Swindon

C.E. Chandler

CHANDLER, S.T.
Samuel Thomas
Private 3/9676 2nd Battalion Wiltshire Regiment
Killed in Action 24th October 1914.
21 years old
Son of Mr. and Mrs. Chandler, of 9 Telford Road
Panel 53 Menin Gate Memorial

CHANNON, J.
James
Sergeant 13130 7th Battalion South Lancashire Regiment
Killed in Action 22nd July 1916.
25 years old
Son of James and Mary Channon, of 6 Tyny Rheoc Terrace, Brynoch, Neath Glam
Pier and Face 7A and 7B Thiepval Memorial
Born in Swindon

CHANTER, S.H.
Sidney Harold
Lance-Corporal 13693 2nd Battalion Wiltshire Regiment
Killed in Action 11th March 1915.
25 years old
Son of Richard and Harriette Chanter, of 'Ranelagh' 48 Burlleigh Road, West Southbourne, Bournemouth
Panel 33 and 34 Le Touret Memorial
Born in Swindon

C.L Chaplin

CHAPLIN, C.L.
Cyril L.
Sapper 520166(319) 142nd Army Troops Company Royal Engineers
Killed in Action 2nd December 1917.
20 years old
Son of Mr. and Mrs. R. Chaplin, of 25 Belgrave Street
I.A. 9. Hermies Hill British Cemetery
Formerly an apprentice in Locomotive and Carriage Department at the GWR works.

A letter was sent to Mr. and Mrs. Chaplin, December 1917.

Dear Mr and Mrs Chaplain

It is with very deep regret that I have to announce to you, the death of your son. About 4 o'clock yesterday afternoon, he was engaged with the rest of the company on a piece of work when the enemy started shelling and he was hit on the head and seems to have died instantaneously. He was buried in the military cemetery near by.

Your son had not been very long with the unit, but in the short time he was with us, he had made himself a favourite with everybody and both officers and men desire me to send to you their heartfelt sympathy in the great sacrifice you have been called on to make.

Capt. J Renwich

CHAPMAN, J.G.
James George
Sergeant 12990 8th Battalion Royal Fusiliers
Died of Wounds 3rd September 1916. 26 years old
Husband of Lily E. Chapman, of 42 Swindon Road
B. 6A Etaples Military Cemetery
Former axle box pad maker in the GWR
Remembered on Plaque in Christchurch

J.G Chapman

CHAPMAN, W.J.
Private 98457 'D' Battery 147 Brigade Royal Field Artillery
Killed in Action 24th June 1916.
23 years old
Son of Frederick and Mary Ann Chapman, of 1 Turl Street
II.B. 13 Doullens Communal Cemetery

Extension number 1
Served in the Dardanelles, Egypt and France

CHEQUER, H.J.
Herbert Jeffrey.
Gunner 78142 Royal Garrison Artillery
Died 31st December 1917. 28 years old
Son of Henry Lewis and Annie Chequer
Husband of Elsie Chequer of 10 Handle Street Gorse Hill
A144 Alexandria (Hadra) War Memorial Cemetery. Egypt.

H.J Chequer

CHESTERMAN, P.T.
Percy Thomas
Driver T4/045363 Royal Army Service Corps (Formerly 14467 Royal Berkshire Regiment)
Died 6th June 1918
Son of Thomas and Martha Chesterman, of 'Poplar House' Broad Town
III.A. 21. Lahana Military Cemetery Balkans
Lived in Swindon

CHEW, A.
Alfred
Private 46453 2nd Battalion Welsh Regiment
Killed in Action 7th November 1917. 38 years old
Husband of Mrs. A. L. Chew, of 3 Duffin Back Terrace Church Village, Pontypridd, Gloucestershire
Panel 93 to 94 Tyne Cott
Born in Swindon

CHILD, A.R.
Alfred Robert
Private 10635 2nd Battalion Wiltshire
Regiment
Killed in Action 18th October 1916.
21 years old
Son of Mr and Mrs Charles E. Child, of
Regents Close
IV. B. 14 Warlencourt British Cemetery

CHIRQWIN, H.
Herbert
Private 204201 2/5th Battalion
Lancashire Fusiliers
Killed in Action 31st July 1917
Panel 33 Menin Gate Memorial
Born in Swindon

CLACK, G.E.
Gerald Elphinstone
Private 203592 6th Battalion Wiltshire
Regiment
Killed in Action 10th April 1918
Panel 119 to 120 Tyne Cott
Born in Swindon

CLAPHAM, F.
Frederick
Private 45868 8th Battalion Royal
Berkshire Regiment
Died 5th September 1918. 18 years old
Son of Frederick and Jane Clapham, of 27
Farnsby Street
VIII. B. 20. Dernancourt Communal
Cemetery Extension
Born in Swindon

CLARK, C.
Cecil
Corporal 94082 'V' 12th Trench Mortar
Battery Royal Field Artillery
Died of Wounds 5th July 1917.
27 years old
Son of Mrs Sarah Peart, of 12 Lansdown
Road
IV.J. 21. Fanbourg D' Amient Cemetery,
Arras
Born in Swindon

CLARK, F.
Frank
Private 9206 5th Battalion Wiltshire
Regiment
Died of Wounds 13th April 1916.
18 years old
Son of William Clark, of Wickfield Lane

Wootton Bassett
VI. H. 12. Amara War Cemetery
Born in Bath Lived in Swindon

CLARKE, H.
Henry
Lance-Corporal 15465 2nd Battalion
South Wales Borderers
Killed in Action 19th June 1915
44 years old
Husband of Mary Ann Clarke, of 6 Hillside
Terrace Hashilleth, Newport, Mon
XI.F. 1. Twelve Tree Copse Cemetery
Dardanelles
Born in Swindon

W. Clarke

CLARKE, H.
Henry
Private 6079 7th Service Battalion
Gloucestershire Regiment
Killed in Action 8th August 1915
Panel 101 – 104 Helles Memorial
Dardanelles
Born in Swindon

CLARKE, J.
James
Sergeant 3/7699 1st Garrison Battalion
Dorsetshire Regiment
Died 29th January 1917. 37 years old
Husband of Rose S. Clarke, of 97 St.
Marks Terrace Albion Street
168 Durrington Cemetery Amesbury
connected with Larkhill Camp

CLARKE, J.
John
Driver 24205 Royal Field Artillery 6th
Brigade Ammunition Company
Killed in Action 29th April 1915
III B. 10. Ypres Town Cemetery Extension

CLARKE, W.H.
William Henry
Private 22165 8th Battalion Wiltshire

Regiment
Died 11th November 1915
St. Mary's Rodbourne Cheney
Lived in Swindon

CLIFFORD, A
Albert.
Private 203551 6th Battalion Wiltshire
regiment (Wilts Yeomanry)
Killed in Action 23rd March 1918.
Bay 7 Arras memorial. France
Lived in Swindon.

CLIFFORD, A.G.
Albert Godfrey
Gunner 74681 128th Battery Royal Field
Artillery
Killed in Action 18th April 1917.
21 years old
Son ofAlbert and Agnes J. Clifford, of 64
Rosebery Street
D. 8. Athies Communal Cemetery
Extension

CLIFFORD, W.G.
William George
Private 7200 1st Wiltshire Regiment
Died of Wounds 19th January 1915.
30 years old
Son of Mr G. Clifford, of 85 Kingshill Road
C. 6. 1660. Netley Military Cemetery
Born Clevancy, Wiltshire Lived in
Swindon
He had left for Canada in 1913, but
returned to join the 1st Wiltshires.
He was wounded in the thigh by a bullet
and a piece of shrapnel, then admitted to
Netley Hospital on Christmas day, 1914.
He also had two brothers, Francis Henry
Clifford who served in India, and Alfred
Clifford.

COLE, J.
James
Private 3/824 1st Battalion Wiltshire
Regiment
Killed in Action 16th June 1915
Husband of Daisy Sarah Cole, of 101
Bright Street, Gorse Hill.
Father of 6 children, eldest was 15 and
youngest was 3.
Panel 53 Menin Gate Memorial
Born in Tewkesbury Lived in Swindon
Forgemans assistant in Number 18 shop
in the GWR

J. Cole

COLEMAN, F.C.
Frederick Charles
2nd Lieutenant 6th Battalion Wiltshire
Regiment
Killed in Action 25th September 1915
24 years old
Son of Henry and Grace Coleman, of 58
Eastcott Road
Panel 102 Loos Memorial
BSc Bristol University. Attended North
Wilts Technical College Victoria Road in
1905 Remembered on its Stained Glass
Window

COLES, C.
Charles
Corporal 71124 'B' Battery 161st Brigade
Royal Field Artillery
Died of Wounds 14th July 1918
Son of Mr and Mrs Coles, of Swindon
Husband of H. L.Coles, of 17 Hawkins
Street
III.D. 2. Bagneux British Cemetery
Gezaincourt
Born in Swindon Labourer in the Loco
and Carriage Department in the GWR

C. Coles

26

COLLETT, E.G.
Ernest George
Private 7646 1st Battalion Wiltshire Regiment
Killed in Action 12th March 1915
Son of Mr and Mrs W. Collett, of 13 Page Street,
Husband of E. Townsend, of 3 Gordon Gardens
Panel 53 Menin Gate Memorial
Born in Stratton Formerly a machinist in 21A Shop in the GWR
1 of 6 brothers who served. Brother of John (Below)

Ernest Collett

COLLETT, J.
John
Sergeant 8108 2nd Battalion Wiltshire Regiment 'D' Company
Killed in Action 9th April 1917
26 years old
Son of William John and Ellen Collett, of 13 Page Street
B. 13 Neuville Vitasse Road Cemetery
Joined the Wilts Regiment 8th March 1908
Served in South Africa and Gibraltar
Born in Stratton Brother of Ernest

J. Collett

COLLINS, G.
Gilbert
Lance-Corporal 14230 8th Battalion Royal Berkshire Regiment
Died of Wounds 18th October 1915
21 years old
Son of Mr and Mrs E. Collins of 261 Cricklade Road, Gorse Hill
A. 13. 7 St. Sever Cemetery Rouen
Born in Swindon Commemorated on plaque in St. Barnabas Church, Gorse Hill

COLLYER, H.
Harry
Private 28721 1st Battalion Royal Berskshire Regiment
Died 19th November 1916. 39 years old
Husband of Mercy Collyer, of 44 Omdurman Street
XXX. A. 4A. Etaples Military Cemetery
Born in Ipswich Lived in Swindon

COMLEY, J.
John
Private 3/232 5th Battalion Wiltshire Regiment
Killed in Action 10th August 1915
37 years old
Son of Jacob and Sarah Comley, of Wootton Bassett
Panel 156 – 158 Helles Memorial
Lived in Swindon

P.H Comley

COMLEY, P.H.
Percy Harold
Sapper 218815 No. 2 LT Railway OP Company Royal Engineers
Died of Wounds 1st October 1917.
28 years old
Son of Albert and Mary Ann Comley, Husband of Mary E. Comley of the Schoolhouse Sedgebarrow, Evesham
XXV.J. 6. Ljissenthoek Military Cemetery. Belgium.

Born in Swindon Formerly worked in the G. W. R.

COOK, A.
Albert
Sapper 140182 80th Field Company Royal Engineers
Died of Wounds 4th June 1917.
29 years old
Son of John and Sarah Ann Cook (Stepmother), of 15 Taunton Street
III.D. 184. Bailleul Communal Cemetery Extension (North)
Born in Swindon

COOK, A.E.
Albert Edward
Private 19170 6th Battalion Wiltshire Regiment
Killed in Action 24th July 1916.
27 years old
Son of W. H. Cook and Mary Cook, of 14 Marlbrough Road
7.H. 9. London Cemetery and Extension Longueval
Born in Swindon

COOK, E.F.
Edwin Frank
Private 40542 1/8th Battalion Durham Light Infantry
Killed in Action 6th November 1917
25 years old
Son of Henry and Mary Elizabeth Cook of 7 Moredon Road, Rodbourne Cheney
Panel 128 – 131 and 162 + 162A Tyne Cott
Born in Swindon

COOK, H.
Private 4844 3rd Battalion Wiltshire Regiment
Died 6th May 1919. 40 years old
C. 3566 Radnor Street Cemetery, Swindon

COOK, H.J.
Hubert James
Corporal 94712 88th Battery 14th Brigade Royal Field Artillery
Died 3rd December 1917. 25 years old
Son of James and Elizabeth Cook, of Swindon,
Husband of Mildred Cook, of 19 Tennyson Street
XV.A. 3. The Huts Cemetery

"He Died that we may live,We loved him well,But Jesus loved him best."

COOK, R.J.
Ralph Joseph
Driver 806778 2nd Battery Territorial Force Royal Field Artillery
Killed in Action 19th December 1917
II.G. 35. Metz – En – Couture Communal Cemetery British Extension
Born in Swindon

COOK, S.
Stuart
Private 19888 2nd Battalion South Wales Borderers
Killed in Action 25th October 1916
22 years old
Son of Edward Jasper Cook and Mary Louisa Cook
Pier + Face 4A Thiepval Memorial

COOK, W.C.
William Charles
Private 305849 7th Battalion Tank Corps
Died of Wounds 8th October 1918 34 years old
Son of Eleanor Cook of Wroughton
Husband of Elsie May Cook of 18 Wells Street.
I V F 37 Terlincthun British cemetery Wimille
Worked as a clerk in accounts office Loco Dept. He enlisted into the Royal Engineers in October 1915. He was wounded in France on September 28th 1918 and died of his wounds 10 days later.

COOK, W.H.
William
Private 3/865 1st Battalion Wiltshire Regiment
Killed in Action 8th January 1915
Husband of A. E. Cook, of 6 Winifred Street
I.A. 21. La Laiterie Military Cemetery
Lived in Swindon

COOK, W.J.
Walter James
Private 8966 1st Battalion Wiltshire Regiment
Killed in Action 16th June 1915
21 years old
Son of William and Emily Blanch Cook, of

8 John Street
Panel 53 Menin Gate Memorial
Born in Swindon
Letter from Corporal F. Timming, Royal Army Medical Corps, with the 1st Battalion Wiltshire Regiment:
"Dear Madam,
I am forwarding the photograph enclosed with this letter at the request of your Son, who I am extremely sorry to say was killed in action on 16th June. He was struck by a bullet from a machine gun and died almost immediately. He did not suffer much and passed away peacefully.
He was buried at night by us. We send to you our greatest sympathy in your sad bereavement. I sincerely hope that your dark hours may be strengthened by the knowledge that your Son did his duty and died a hero."

A Cooper

COOK, W.J.
William John
Private 7669 1st Battalion Wiltshire Regiment
Died of Wounds 19th September 1914
La Forte – Sous – Jouarre Memorial

COOKE, F.
Frank
Gunner 14212 Royal Field Artillery
Died of Wounds 27th September 1916
Pier and Face 1A – 8A Thiepval Memorial
Born in Swindon

COOKSEY, C.F.
Charles Frederick
Private 3/12 1st Battalion Wiltshire Regiment
Killed in Action 13th March 1915
23 years old
Son of Benjamin and Emily Cooksey
Panel 53 Menin Gate Memorial
Born in Wandsworth, London Lived in Swindon

COOPER, A.
Arthur
Private 13910 5th Battalion Wiltshire Regiment
Died of Wounds 31st January 1917
22 years old
Son of Isaac and Bertha Cooper, of 79 Dean Street
XIV.6. 33. Amara War Cemetery
Born in Basingstoke Lived in Swindon

COOPER, E
Ernest
Private 10633 1st Btn Wiltshire Regiment.
Killed in Action 22nd November 1914
Panel 53 Menin Gate Ypres Belgium.

COOPER, H.
Hubert
Sergeant 11246 Coldstream Guards
Killed in Action 28th September 1915
Panel 7 and 8 Loos Memorial
Born in Withrell Ford, Lancashire Lived in Swindon

CORBETT, A.
Arthur
Private 3/9668 2nd Battalion Wiltshire Regiment
Killed in Action 23rd February 1915
I.H. 48. Rue – Duvil Military Cemetery, Fleurbaix

E Corbett

CORBETT, E.
Edward
Corporal 2798 6th Battalion Royal Munster Fusiliers
Died of Wounds 16th August 1915
K. 114 Alexandria (Chatby) Military Cemetery + War Memorial
Born in Swindon
Worked as a riveter in Number 13 Shop in the GWR

CORNISH, A.
Arthur
Private 203254 6th Battalion Wiltshire
Regiment
Killed in Action 23rd March 1918
Bay 7 Arras Memorial France
Born in Swindon

CORSER, H.
Horace
Sapper 44058 79th Field Company Royal
Engineers
Died 11th January 1918. 25 years old
Son of William and the late Elizabeth Ann
Corser, of 1 Broad Street
II.B. 57. Bleuet Farm Cemetery,
Elverdinghe Belgium
Brother of Reginald (Below)

CORSER, R.
Reginald
Engine Room Artificer 4th Class Royal
Navy H. M. S. 'Defence' M/11896
Died 31st May 1916. 25 years old
Son of William and Elizabeth Ann Corser,
of 1 Broad Street.
Husband of Lily B. Corser, of 94 Deacon
Street
14 Plymouth Naval Memorial
Brother of Horace Corser (Above)

COTTON, C.
Cyril
Private 80914 1/8th Durham Light
Infantry
Died 9th April 1918
Panel 8 and 9 Ploegsteert Wood
Cemetery. Belgium.
Attended North Wilts Technical College
Victoria Road 1908 Remembered on its
Stained Glass Window

COTTON, R.
Ralph
Private 10419 1st Wiltshire Regiment
Died of Wounds 18th March 1915.
19 years old
Son of Rev. James William and Ruth
Cotton, of 'The Maise' 3 Stratford Square,
Wakefield
III.D. 39. Boulogne Eastern Cemetery.
France
Born in Chinnor Oxon Lived in Swindon
Formerly served an apprenticeship with
Gilberts house furniture.
Joined in September 1915 He was sent
out to France in January 1915, His father

was supt. Minister of the Primitive
Methodist connection associated with
the Prospect Church, Swindon

COULDREY, H.A.
Horace Arthur
Private33258 6th Battalion Wiltshire
Regiment (Wiltshire Yeomanry)
Formerly 1140 Royal Field Artillery
Killed in Action 7th April 1917.
22 years old
Youngest Son of Thomas James and
Margaret Couldrey, of 141 Goddard
Avenue.
V.I. C. 2. Elzenwalle Brasserie Cemetery
Born in Bombay, India
Attended North Wilts Technical College
in 1908 Remembered on its Stained Glass
Window . Also remembered on plaque in
Christchurch

H.A.Couldrey

COVE, E.
Ernest
Private 13723 2nd Battalion Wiltshire
Regiment
Killed in Action 15th June 1915
Panel 33 and 34 Le Touret Memorial
Lived in Swindon
Worked in L2 Shop in the Loco and
Carriage Department GWR
Remembered memorial plaque in the
Outlet Village, Swindon

COVE, H.
Henry
Private 18422 2nd Battalion Wiltshire
Regiment
Died of Wounds 15th September 1918.
29 years old
Husband of Mrs A. Westall (Cove), of 17
Davis Street
I.A. 10. Lapuqney Military Cemetery

COWLEY, F.W.
Frederick Williams
Private 6357 Coldstream Guards
Killed in Action 15th September 1916
VI.H. 4. AIF Burial Ground
Born in Swindon

COWLEY, J.
James
Corporal 204633 1st Battalion Wiltshire Regiment
Killed in Action 26th April 1918
Panel 119 to 120 Tyne Cott. Belguim.
Born in Cricklade Lived in Swindon

COWLEY, J.F.
James Frederick
Sergeant 200106 1/4 Battalion Wiltshire Regiment
Died of Wounds 13th November 1917
Son of Mr and Mrs Cowley of 30 Read Street.
XV.II. A. 10. Gaza War Cemetery
Born in Swindon
Formerly worked as a boilermaker in the Loco and Carriage Department in the GWR. He was a keen footballer who played for the 'Brotherhood' and Swindon Imperials.

J.F Cowley

COX, A.H.
Albert Harry
Private 11615 5th Battalion Wiltshire Regiment
Died 8th March 1917 (as a Prisoner of War) 25 years old
Son of Mr and Mrs Frederick Cox, of 37 Iffley Road
XXI.Y. 23. Baghdad (North Gate) War Cemetery. Iraq.

COX, I.
Isaac
Private 18049 1st Battalion Wiltshire Regiment

Killed in Action 11th August 1917.
31 years old
Son of John Cox, of Highworth.
Husband of Edith Emily Cox, of 11 Kings Hill
Panel 53 Menin Gate Memorial Belgium.
Born in Swindon
Worked in B B Shop GWR. He served 4 months in the Dardanelles, where he was wounded. After returning to service in 1916, he was wounded again on the Somme battlefields in November 1916. After recuperation, he returned again to active service. He was killed later in 1917, while carrying a wounded man to the dressing station.

I. Cox

COX, W.P.
William Percival.
Corporal. 57180 106th field Company Royal Engineers.
Died 18th November 1915. 19 Years Old
Son of Albert Edward and Elizabeth Cox.
Kings Farm Longcott, Berkshire.
11 A 37 London Rifle Brigade Cemetery Belgium

COX, T.
Thomas
Corporal 11359 Coldstream Guards
Died of Wounds 29th December 1914
I.C. 12. Wimereux Communal Cemetery
Machinist in Number 13 Shop in the GWR

T. Cox

CRADDOCK, C.W.
Charles William
Private 8th Battalion Surrey Regiment
Died of Wounds 16th October 1918.
32 years old
Son of George and Louisa Craddock, of
Crookham Fleet, Hants.
Husband of Alice Maud Craddock, of 129
Rodbourne Road
C. 3545 Radnor Street Cemetery,
Swindon

CREBER, S.W.V.
Stafford William Vernon
Airman 1st Class 6180 Royal Flying Corps.
Salonika Aircraft Park
Died 7th October 1917. 21 years old.
Son of Albert and Annie Creber of 128
Clifton Street
129 Mikra British Cemetery Kalamaria.
Salonika

CREIGHTON, S.
Sidney
Private 103324 15th Battalion Notting
hamshire and Derbyshire Regiment
Died of Wounds 30th January 1919.
19 years old
Son of Fred and Elizabeth Creighton, of
Broad Chalk, Salisbury
XIII.B. 21 Terkincthun British Cemetery
Wimille
Born in Swindon

CREWE, P.
Philip
Private 1613 1st/6th Battalion
Manchester Regiment
Died 15th June 1915. 25 years old
Son of Rowland and Eliza Crewe, of 894
Stockport Road, Longsight, Manchester
Panel 158 – 170 Helles Memorial.
Dardannelles
Attended North Wilts Technical College
in 1905 Remembered on its Stained Glass
window

CRISP, T.
Thomas
Private 57276 M. C. G. Infantry 52nd
Company
Formerly 29861 Gloucestershire
Regiment
Killed in Action 9th November 1917
Panel 154 to 159 and 163A Tyne Cott
Belguim.
Born in Cheltenham   Lived in Swindon.

CROCKER, G.A.
George Augustus
Private 90679 Royal Army Medical Corps
Died of Wounds 15th March 1918.
29 years old
Son of George Augustus and Kate
Crocker, of 63 Exmouth Street
PV. R. 2B. St. Sever Cemetery Extension
Rouen. France
Born in Swindon

R.H. Crocket

CROCKET, R.H.
Ralph Henry
Private 11524 5th Battalion Wiltshire
Regiment 'B' Company
Died 29th June 1916. 21 years old
Son of Mr and Mrs J. Crocket, of 2
Theobold Street
Panel 30 + 64 Basra War Cemetery
Formerly a Machinist in the Locomotive
and Carriage Department GWR

CROOK, A.
Arthur
Private 7059 1st Battalion Wiltshire
Regiment
Killed in Action 5th December 1914.
26 years old
Son of Thomas and Eliza Ann Cowles, of
School House, Hinton Parva
33 + 34 Le Touret Memorial
Born in Bishopstone Lived in Swindon

A. Crook

CROOK, H.
Henry
Private 10387 2nd Battalion Wiltshire
Regiment
Died of Wounds 13th July 1916
35 years old
Son of Mr and Mrs L Crook of the
Quarries Old Town
V. G. 3. Abbeville Communal Cemetery
Born in Hullavington Lived in Swindon

CROOK, J.J.W.
John James William
Gunner 109739 Royal Field Artillery 'A'
Battery 150th Army Brigade
Killed in Action 4th September 1917
19 years old
Son of William John and Clara Crook
IX. H. 21. Vlamertinghe New Military
Cemetery. Belgium.
Remembered on plaque in Christchurch

CULLINGFORD, F.E.
Able Seaman R/5413 RNVR Hood
Battalion Royal Navy Division
Killed in Action 15th March 1918.
37 years old
Son of F. T. M. Cullingford, (Dentist) of 95
Victoria Road
Husband of M. M. A. Cullingford, of 79
Victoria Road, Swindon
II.E. 1. Ribecourt British Cemetery
He had volunteered only 8 months
previously. A letter was received from
the battalion. -

Dear Mrs Cullingford,
It is with deep regret that I have to
inform you that your husband was killed
on March 14th by a shell. It may be some
slight consolation for you to know, that
death was instantaneous and therefore,
he suffered no pain. Your husband had
been so short a time with us, that I did
not get the opportunity to get to know
him well, but his work was always
excellently carried out, and am sure, had
he been spared would have made a
name for himself. He was one of those
we can ill afford to loose. Please accept
my deepest sympathy in your
bereavement. Believe me to be yours
very truly,
H. Grant-Dalton Lt RNVR Hood Btn.

CULLIP, G.W.
Private 65840 26th Battalion Royal

Fusiliers (secondary unit) Royal Engineers
attached to 184th Tunnelling Company
Died 23rd August 1918
XXIV.A. 26A. Lijssenthoek Military
Cemetery

CUMNER, V.G.
Victor George
Sapper 520333 478th Field Company
Royal Engineers
Died 4th June 1917. 22 years old
Son of Mr G. H. and Mrs E. Cumner, of 14
Radnor Street
I.G. 2. Tilloy British Cemetery Tilloy – les
– Moftlaimes

V.G. Cumner

CURTIS, S.H.
Sydney Herbert
Private 201591 1/4th Battalion Wiltshire
Regiment
Died 11th December 1918. 23 years old
Son of Mr H S and Mrs M. E. Curtis, of 4 St.
Pauls Street
A. 52 Ramleh War Cemetery
Born in Swindon

S.H. Curtis

CURTIS, W.G.
William George
Pte 7209 1st Battalion Wiltshire
Regiment
Killed in Action 31st October 1914
Panels 3 and 34 Le Touret Memorial
France

CUSS, C.
Cyril
Private 10509 Honourable Artillery
Company (infantry)
Died 25th March 1917
M.(C) 624 Cricklade Cemetery
Lived in Swindon

C.H. Cuss

DADGE, G.G.
Gilbert George
Private 10196 2nd Battalion Wiltshire
Regiment
Died of Wounds 15th June 1915
21 years old
Son of Mr George and Mrs M. J. Dadge, of
15 Oxford Street
Panel 33 + 34 Le Touret Memorial
France

DARLING, A.L.
Arthur Lancelot
Private 19472 7th Battalion Wiltshire
Regiment
Killed in Action 24th April 1917
22 years old
Son of Richard and Louisa Darling, of 5
Horsell Street
Doiran Memorial, Salonika
Born in Swindon

DASH, J.
John
Private 18459 2nd Battalion Wiltshire
Regiment
Died of Wounds 13th March 1915
Panel 33 + 34 Le Touret Memorial France
Lived in Swindon

C.H. Cuss

Memorial Plaque in Christchurch

34

DASH, P.
Percy Edward
Private 20888 5th Battalion Wiltshire
Regiment
Died 9th April 1916. 18 years old
Son of Francis James and Ellen Dash,
of 36 Clifton Street
XVI.L. 1 Amara War Cemetery

DAVENPORT, H.
Harold
2nd Lieutenant 122nd Siege Battery
Royal Garrison Artillery
Killed in Action 21st March 1918
Panel 10 Pozieres Memorial France

DAVENPORT, Z.B.
Zakariah Bartley
Private 13022 6th Battalion Royal
Berkshire Regiment
Killed in Action 29th June 1916
23 years old.
Son of George Henry and Alice Amelia
Davenport of Swindon
Husband of Annie Eliza Davenport 82
Whiteman Street
Q 13 Carnoy Military Cemetery. France

DAVID, H.W.
Henry William
Driver T4/249301 925th Horse transport
company Army Service Corps
Killed in Action 24th October 1918
25 years old
3B 48 Ramleh War Cemetery Israel
Born in Swindon

DAVIES, P.E.
Phillip Edgar
Corporal TR/10/20189 10th Battalion East
Surrey Regiment
Died 24th January 1917. 28 years old
Son of Mr and Mrs M Davies of 'St Osyth'
4 Buckingham Road Newbury
1537 Newton Road Cemetery Newbury
Born in Swindon

DAVIS, E.A.
Ernest Alfred
Bombadier 62958 45th Trench Mortar
Battery Royal Field Artillery
Killed in Action 30th June 1916
I F 9 Sucrerie Military Cemetery
Colincamps
France
Born in Swindon

DAVIS, H.V.
Henry Victor
Private 22205 5th Battalion Wiltshire
Regiment 'B' Company
Killed in Action 29th March 1917
19 years old
Son of Frank and Maria Phillipa Davis,
of 7 Newport Street
Panel 30 and 64 Basra Memorial Iraq
Born and resided in Swindon

DAVIS, L.D.
Lewis Dennis
Sapper 495174 479th Field company
Royal Engineers
Died 1st June 1918. 26 years old
Son of Reuben and Julia Davis 44 Bright
Street Gorse Hill
111 B 13 Aire Communal cemetery.
France
Born in Stroud Glos.

DAVIS, S.J.
Acting Company Quarter-Master-
Sergeant 8357 Coldstream Guards
Died of Wounds

DAVIS, W.J.
William John
Private 19177 1st Wiltshire Regiment
Died of Wounds 9th May 1916
23 years old
Son of Mrs S. A. Davis, of 133 Westcott
Place
I.B. 33. Aubigny Communal Cemetery
Extension
Born in Swindon

W. Davis

DAY, A.H.
Arthur Herbert
RFM 2939 7th Battalion West Yorkshire
Regiment POWO
Died 29th July 1915. 30 years old
Son of George and Emily Day, of 32
Newport Street

Plot 1 Row 1 Grave 8 Ferme – Oliver Cemetery, France
'If death be the price of Victory, He paid in full.'
In Memorium:
In loving memory of a dear Son who laid down his life for king and country.
He bravely answered duty's call, his life he gave for one and all, but the unknown grave is the bitterest blow.
None but an aching heart can know.
From his sorrowing Mother and May Wheatsheaf, in Newport Street, Swindon.

In loving memory of our dear Brother, Could we have been there at the hour of death, to catch the last sigh of his parting breath? His last feint whisper we might have heard and breathed in his ear just one parting word.
From his Sister and Brother – law.
Farliegh House, 54 Hythe Road, Swindon.

DAY, B.R.
Bertie Roland
Private 33828 8th Battalion Devonshire Regiment
Killed in Action 26th October 1917
Panel 38 to 40 Tyne Cot Memorial
Born in Swindon

DAY, E.J.
Edwin James
Private 319470 2nd Battalion Welsh Regiment
Killed in Action 25th July 1916
Pier and Face 7a and 10a Thiepval Memorial
Born in Swindon

DAY, M.
Maurice
2nd Lieutenant 2nd Battalion Royal Berkshire Regiment
Killed in Action 9th May 1915
23 years old
Son of Rev. Benjamin Day, Rector of St. Peters, Sandwich, Kent, and Mary Sophie Day
Panel 7 and 8 Ploegsteert Memorial Belgium

DEACON, C.G.M.
Charles Godfrey Montague
Private 127423 15th Battalion Lancashire Fusiliers
Died of Wounds 27th September 1918

(Gas) 33 years old
Son of Rose Deacon and the late William Deacon, of 39 Rolleston Street
B. 2819. Radnor Street Cemetery, Swindon

DEACON, W.J.
William James
Able Seaman 191882 Royal Navy. HMS Good Hope'
Died 1st November 1914
2 Portsmouth Naval Memorial

W. Deacon

DEAN, G.F.
George Frederick
2nd Lieutenant 162nd Brigade Royal Field Artillery
Killed in Action 16th October 1917
Son of Mr and Mrs R. Dean, of 11 Gloucestershire Terrace
Panel 4 – 6 + 162 Tyne Cott
Attended North Wilts Technical College in 1901and remembered on its Stained Glass Window.
Educated at Sanford Street School His Father was well known in the town as district secretary of the Order of Foresters.
His brother Sergeant J. L. Dean (RAMC) transferred to Hants Regiment, and survived the war.

2Lt. G. Dean

DEAVE, A.G.
Arthur George
Private 240445 43rd Battalion Royal Fusiliers
Died 17th November 1918. 29 years old
Eldest Son of George and Kezia Deave, of 70 Oxford Buildings, Rodbourne
VI. G. 11A. Les Boraques Military Cemetery Sangatte France
Born in Swindon

DENNIS, H.V.
Driver 826246 'C' Battery 155th Battery Royal Field Artillery
Killed in Action 8th March 1917
I.H. 14 Euston Road Cemetery Colincamps

DENT, B.R.
Bertram Robert
Private 326027 1st Battalion Cam bridgeshire Regiment
Killed in Action 31st July 1917
23 years old
Husband of Ethel B. Sanders, of 12 Gloucestershire Terrace
Panel 50 + 52 Menin Gate Memorial

DENTON, W.W.
Walter William
Private 19417 1/4th Battalion Wiltshire Regiment
Killed in Action 10th May 1918
23 years old
Son of Walter and Amelia Denton, of 23 Oriel Street
N. 24. Ramleh War Cemetery Egypt
Lived in Swindon

W. Denton

DEWE, E.E.
Eli Edward
Sergeant 21540 21st Company MGC Infantry
Killed in Action 15th August 1916

24 years old
Adopted Son of Mrs K. Cooper, of 75 Elmina Road
II. D. 4. Gorre British and Indian Cemetery

DEWE, F.H.J.
Frederick Henry James
Private 8249 1st Battalion Wiltshire Regiment
Killed in Action 23rd October 1914
Panel 33 and 34 Le Touret Memorial
Born in Swindon

DICKSON, J.C.
James Cambell
Trooper 734 Household Battalion
Killed in Action 18th February 1917
Pier and Face 1a Thiepval Memorial
Born in Swindon

DIFFORD, W.M.
William Membry
Lieutenant 8th battalion Manitoba Regiment Canadian Infantry.
Attached 8th Squadron Royal Air Force.
Killed in Action 3rd October 1918
25 years old
Son of S G and Annie Difford of 42 Lansdown Road
11 B 11 Canada cemetery Tilloy – Les – Cambrai. France

DIXON, E.A.
Edgar Arnold
Private 34390 2/4th Battalion Oxfordshire and Buckinghamshire Light Infantry
Killed in Action 12th September 1918
19 years old
Son of Mr W. T. and Mrs A. A. Dixon, of 14 Park Lane
Brother of Norman Dixon (Below)
Panel 7 Ploegsteert Memorial
Born in Swindon

N. Dixon

DIXON, N.R.W.
Norman Reginald Walter
Sapper 520289 565th Wiltshire Field
Company Royal Engineers
Killed in Action 19th September 1918
22 years old
Son of Walter Tate Dixon and Ada Ann
Dixon, of 14 Park Lane, Swindon
E. 22. Beaumetz Cross Road Cemetery,
Beaumetz – Les – Cambrai

DIXON, W.
Wilfred
Private 9418 1st Battalion Warwickshire
Regiment
Killed in Action 26th May 1915
III A 14 Whitehouse Cemetery   Belgium
Born in Swindon

DIXON, W.J.
William James
Private 20629 2nd Battalion Wiltshire
Regiment
Killed in Action 17th October 1916
19 years old
Son of Mrs Ellen Dixon, of 20 Summers
Street, Swindon
Pier + Face 13A Thiepval Memorial
France
Born in Wooton Bassett – Lived in
Swindon

DOBSON, A.J.
Arthur James
Private 22995 1st Battalion Wiltshire
Regiment
Killed in Action 6th July 1916
Pier and Face 13A Thiepval memorial.
France

DOBSON, F.
Francis
Gunner 9874 'C' Battery 71st Brigade
Royal Field Artillery
Killed in Action 9th April 1917
28 years old
Son of Mr A J Dobson of 'St Ives' Kingston
Lewes Sussex
A26 Beaurains Road Cemetery Beaurains
France
Born in Swindon

DOWERS, F.J.
Francis John
Sapper 520020 565th Army Troops
Company (Wilts) Royal Engineers
Died 18th November 1918. 26 years old

Influenza
Son of Mr and Mrs F Dowers of 20
Beatrice Street
Husband of Elizabeth Dowers of 12 Bath
Place Stroud Glos.
C. 8. Douai British cemetery Cuincy.
France

F. Dowers

DREW, C.T.
Christopher Tom
Private 242152 1st Battalion Royal West
Kent Regiment
Killed in Action 3rd October 1917
VIA C 9 Poelcapelle British Cemetery
Lived in Swindon

DREWETT, S.G.
Stanley George
Private 65001 1/2nd London Regiment
Royal Fusiliers
Killed in Action 27th August 1918
20 years old
Son of William Frank and Mary Ann
Drewett, of 72 Medgbury Road
I.B. 4. Summit Trench Cemetery, Croisilles
Born in Swindon

DRIVER, W.G.
William George
Lance – Corporal 15367 1st Battalion
Royal Dublin Fusiliers (Formerly 12988
Wiltshire Regiment)
Killed in Action 1st July 1916
19 years old
Son of George and Annie Driver 84 Albert
Road North, Buckhurst Hill Essex
Pier and Face 16C Thiepval Memorial

DRURY, H.P.
Henry Philip
Private 6444 1st Battalion Wiltshire
Regiment
Killed in Action 22nd September
La Ferte Sous – Douarre Memorial
Lived in Swindon

DRURY, P.C.
Philip Charles
Gunner 3259 86th Army Brigade Royal Field Artillery
Killed in Action 30th September 1917
22 years old
VIII.D. 14. The Huts Cemetery Belgium
Son of Mrs Drury, of 66 Westcott Place
Formerly worked in the Loco and Carriage Department as a Labourer in the GWR

F.E. Duck

Philip Druary

DRURY, W.
Corporal 18450 Clerk 25th Battery 7th Field Artillery Brigade Australian Imperial Force
Died 6th October 1917
IV.B. 12. Nine Elms British Cemetery
Attended North Wilts Technical College Victoria Rd and remembered on its stained glass window.

DUCK, F.E.
Frederick Ernest
Private 13587 2/4th Battalion Royal Berkshire Regiment
Killed in Action 22nd August 1917
23 years old
Son of Frederick John and Mary Ann Duck, of 25 Shelly Street
Panel 105 – 106 and 162 Tyne Cott
Born in Swindon Formerly worked in L2 shop Loco Department in the GWR
Remembered on plaque in Outlet Village, Swindon

DULIN, W.W.M.
William Walter Motta
Lieutenant Central Despatch Pool Royal Air Force
Killed in Action 29th July 1918
Terlinchun Wimille British Cemetery, Boulogne France
Attended North Wilts Technical College in 1912 and was an apprentice in the Loco Dept GWR.

Lt. Dulin

DUNN, H.W.
Horace W
Private 13893 9th Battalion Worcester shire Regiment
Died 5th April 1916
Panel 18 and 63 Basra Memorial
Worked in paint shop Carriage and Wagon dept GWR

Horace Dunn

DUNSDON, P.
Percy
Corporal 26533 10th Battalion Duke
of Cornwalls Light Infantry
Killed in Action 7th June 1917
31 years old
Son of William and Alice Jane Dunsdon
Husband of Beatrice Annie Dunsdon, of
13 Hythe Road
I. B. 5. Orchard Dump Cemetery,
Arleux – en – Gohelle
Born in Swindon

DYER, F.E.
Frank Edward
Private 21940 2nd Battalion Wiltshire
Regiment
Killed in Action 4th December 1917
Son of Mrs S A Dyer of 90 Beatrice Street
Panel 119 – 120 Tyne Cott
Lived in Swindon

DYER, P.W.
Private 7918 1st Battalion Wiltshire
Regiment
Died 22nd September 1918
B. 2756 Radnor Street Cemetery,
Swindon

DYKE, F.
Fred
Private 3/9865 1st Wiltshire Regiment
Killed in Action 17th November 1914
20 years old
Son of Alfred and Fanny Dyke, of 5
Swindon Road
Panel 53 Menin Gate Memorial
Born in Swindon

EDGE, C.
Charles
Private 12317 7th Battalion Wiltshire
Regiment
Killed in Action 18th October 1918
III F 9 Highland cemetery Le Cateau.
France
Born in Swindon Formerly worked in L2
shop in the Locomotive Department at
the G. W. R.
Remembered on plaque in the Outlet
Village, Swindon

EOIS, C.F.
Cyril Frances
Private 29237 1st Battalion Somerset
Light Infantry (Formerly T2/12487 Royal

Army Medical Corps)
Killed in Action 29th March 1918
Bay 4 Arras Memorial France
Lived in Swindon

EDWARDS, A.
Arthur
Sergeant 3/178 5th Battalion Wiltshire
Regiment
Killed in Action 10th August 1915
Panel 156 – 158 Helles Memorial
Dardanelles
Born in Swindon

EDWARDS, J.
John
Private 5867 1st Battalion Hampshire
Regiment
Killed in Action 7th November 1914
Panel 6 Ploegsteert memorial
Born in Swindon Formerly worked in L2
shop in the Loco Department GWR
Remembered on plaque in the Outlet
Village, Swindon

J. Edwards

EGGLETON, T.E.
Thomas Edward
Private 6361 1st Battalion Wiltshire
Regiment
Died of Wounds 10th October 1914
Born in Swindon

EGGLETON, H.J.P.   MM
Henry James Pitt
Guardsman 26636 2nd company 1st
Battalion Grenadier Guards
Died 5th November 1918. 20 years old
Son of Benjamin and Julia Eggleton of
Glitchbury, Brinkworth.
77 Brinkworth Cemetery.
Born in Swindon

ELLIS, A.C.
Arthur Cecil
Sapper 349569 'C' Company 6th Reserve
Battalion Royal Engineers
Died 24th September 1918. 19 years old
Son of A. M. Ellis, of 38 Farnsby Street
E. 8623 Radnor Street Cemetery,
Swindon

A. Ellis

EMBLING, F.G.
Francis George
Lance-Corporal 70266 Berkshire
Yeomanry

Died 15th November 1917. 23 years old
Son of Mrs E. Embling, of 20 North Street
X.42. Jerusalem War Cemetery

EMBURY, T.H.
Thomas Henry
Private 13936 2nd Battalion Wiltshire
Regiment
Killed in Action 18th October 1916
24 years old
Son of Charles and Ellen Elizabeth
Embury, of Church Path, Purton
V.I. E. 28. Warlencourt British Cemetery
Lived in Swindon

EMERY, P.C.
Percy Charles
Lance-Corporal 1566 Berkshire Yeomanry
Died 26th October 1915. 22 years old
Son of Mrs Thirga Emery, of 75
Dennington Road, Reading
D. 163. Cairo War Memorial Cemetery
Born in Swindon

ENGLISH, F.J.
Francis James
Signal Man J/7209 HMS 'Tipperary' Royal
Navy
Died 1st June 1916 22 years old.
Son of James and Ruth English 6
Savernake Street
14 Portsmouth Naval Memorial

EVANS, T.D.
Thomas David
Private 46863 2nd Battalion Wiltshire
Regiment
Killed in Action 5th November 1918
19 years old
Son of William John and Theodosia
Euans, of 41 County Road
II.B. 6. Cross Roads Cemetery, Fontaine
– Au – Bois
Lived in Swindon

T. Evans

41

EVELEIGH, W.C.
William Charles
Private 25773 6th Battalion Wiltshire Regiment
Died 24th October 1918
Panel 119 – 120 Tyne Cott
Born in Hallsbrow, Somerset Lived in Swindon

EVERETT, F.A.
Francis Aubrey
Private 7605 1st Battalion Wiltshire Regiment
Killed in Action 13th October 1914
24 years old
Son of Mrs E. Everett, of 22 Cyril Road, Rauboil Hill, Worcestershire
Panel 33 + 34 Le Touret Memorial
Born in Wantage, Berkshire Lived in Swindon

EYELS, E.
Edward
Private 203292 1/4th Battalion Oxfordshire and Buckingham Light Infantry.
Died 12th February 1917. 34 Years old
Son of Joseph and Esther Annie Eyels of Swindon
Husband of Dora nee Higgins 7 Kings Rd Rusden Northants
I C 7 Hem Farm Cemetery Hem – Monacu France

FAITHFULL, W.
William
Private 2803 5th Battalion Royal Irish Regiment (Formerly 12858 Royal Inniskilling Fusiliers and 13071 Duke of Cornwalls Light Infantry)
Died 23rd February 1916. 24 years old
Son of Mrs Phoebe Faithfull, of 12 York Terrace, Cato Street, Sultley, Birmingham
84.Salonika (Lembet Road) Military Cemetery
Born in Swindon

FARMER, F.H.
Francis Henry
Private 31367 9th (Service) Battalion Devonshire Regiment
Died of Wounds 1st November 1917
19 years old
Son of Joseph Richard and Sarah Jane Farmer, of 18 Regent Place
VI.F. 15. Wimereux Communal Cemetery
Lived in Swindon

FARMER, W.
Walter
Corporal A.3443 7th Battalion K Royal Air Corps
Killed in Action 15th May 1917
21 years old
Son of Issabelle Farmer, of 19 College Street
V.F. 26. Warlencourt British Cemetery
Lived in Swindon

FARNDELL, C.
Charles
Lance-Corporal 15044 12th Battalion (Bristols Own) Gloucestershire Regiment
Killed in Action 30th July 1916
Pier and Face 5A and 5B Thiepval Memorial

Corporal Charles Farndell Glostershire Regiment worked previously in No.6 Shop GWR

FELL, C.G.
Colin Garret
Corporal 31634 4th Battalion Worcestershire Regiment
Died of Wounds 24th April 1917
32 years old
Son of Stephen and Emma Fell, of Calne
Husband of L. C. Elvina Fell, of 76 The Mall
II.K. 2. Duisans British Cemetery

FELL, T.C.
Thomas Curtis
Private 46474 17th Battalion Lancashire Fusiliers (Formerly 196828 Royal Army Service Corps)
Killed in Action 28th September 1918
20 years old
Son of Emily Fell, of 5 King John Street

Men of the GWR 'Somewhere in France'

XXI. L.19. Hooge Crater Cemetery
Belgium
Born in Swindon He was a member of St Pauls Young Mens Club and an apprentice in the Wagon Dept GWR. A letter was sent to his Mother from his Lieutenant which read as follows - 'It is to express our sincere sympathy with you and your family that I write these few lines in the sad loss you have sustained by the death of your son, T C Fell. Although I had only just taken over the platoon, of which your son was gunner, I noticed he carried out his duties in a soldier like manner and always did his best. He was a favorite with the members of section and I am Born in Swindon

T.C. Fell

FEW, R.J.D.
Robert James Donald
Lieutenant 1st Battalion Dorset Regiment
Died of Wounds 27th October 1918
23 years old
Son of Charles Robert and Helena Few, of 49 Victoria Road
II.139. Oxford Botley Cemetery

FENNER, C.
Charles
Private 1955 5th Battalion Wiltshire Regiment
Died 1st May 1917
IV.K. 18. Basra War Cemetery Iraq
Lived in Swindon

FERRIS, F.J.
Sapper 155570 74th Field Company Royal Engineers
Killed in Action 19th November 1916
22 years old
Husband of A E Ferris 2 Siemens Terrace Telford Road Rodbourne Cheney
IV C 22 Dernancourt Communal cemetery Extension France

FIELD, C.
Charles
Private 240430 2/5th Battalion Gloucestershire Regiment
Killed in Action 29th October 1918
B. 5. Bermerain Communal Cemetery
Born in Swindon

FISHER, E.
Ernest
Private 205663 10th Battery West Kent Regiment
Died 31st July 1917
Panel 45 + 47 Menin Gate Memorial
Attended North Wilts Technical College Victoria Rd in 1910 and remembered on its stained glass window.

FISHER, H.E.
Harold Ernest
Private 19502 7th Battalion Wiltshire Regiment
Killed in Action 18th October 1918
18 years old
Son of Mrs J. Gibbs, of 22 Chester Street
III.F. 1. Highland Cemetery, Le Cateau
Born in Swindon

FISHER, J.C.H.
James Charles Hugh
Private 541 6th Battalion Wiltshire Regiment (Transferred to 29199 6th Battalion Royal Dublin Fusiliers)
Killed in Action 17th October 1918
Son of James Thomas and Emma Fisher 65 Ferndale Road.
A 9 Forest Communal Cemetery France

FISHLOCK, A.V.
Albert Victor
Lance-Corporal 225939 1st Battalion Monmouthshire Regiment
Killed in Action 8th October 1918
A. 20. Sequehart British Cemetery Number 1
Born in Swindon

FLETCHER T.
Sergeant 69298 26th Battalion New Brunswick Regiment Canadian Infantry.
Killed in Action 28th August 1918
33 years old
Son of George and Martha Fletcher of 85 Redcliffe Street.
D 13 Sur-Quary Cemetery Cherisy France
He had served an apprenticship in the Loco and carriage Dept GWR, before

leaving for Canada in 1912. He worked then for the Canadian Pacific Railway Company workshops at Montreal. He joined the army in November 1914.

FLOREY, H.
Henry
Private 19416 5th Battalion Wiltshire Regiment
Killed in Action 17th January 1917
XV111 D. 11. Amara War Cemetery
Lived in Swindon

H. Florey

FLOWER, E.B.
Edwin Brian
Sapper 189875 No. 9 Light Railway Operation Company Royal Engineers
Died of Wounds 4th October 1917
I.D. 28. Rocquigny Equancourt Road, British Cemetery Manancourt
Born in Swindon

E. Flower

FORD, D.
Dan
Sergeant 18058 M. G. C. Attached to 1st Battalion Wiltshire Regiment
Died of Wounds 9th May 1917
II.K. 5. Wimereux Communal Cemetery
Born in Swindon

FORD, V.R.
Victor Reginald
Private 48949 16th Battalion Lancashire Fusiliers
Killed in Action 5th April 1918
21 years old
Son of Mrs Clara Godwin Ford, of 166 Adelaide Road Swiss Cottage, London
A. 6. Quesnoy Farm Military Cemetery
Born in Swindon

FORD, W.F.
William Frank
Private 59954 9th battalion Devonshire Regiment
Killed in Action 26th October 1917
26 years old.
Son of William Thomas and Matilda Ford.
96 Westcott Place
Panel 38 – 40 Tyne Cot Memorial
Belgium

FOREST, J.H.J.
James Herbert John
Private 13105 5th Battalion Royal Berkshire Regiment
Died of Wounds 4th October 1916
Born in Swindon

FOREST, W.
Walter
Corporal 20149 70th Battery Royal Field Artillery
Died 23rd August 1914
La Ferte-Sous-Jouarre Memorial France

FORTEATH, W.V.
Private 40861 22nd Battalion (Tyneside Scottish) Northumberland Fusiliers
Killed in Action 9th April 1917
Son of W Forteath, Roclincourt, Culver Road Shanklin Isle of Wight
III F 7 Roclincourt Valley cemetery France

FORTUNE, J.
John
Captain (TP) Royal Army Medical Corps
Attached to 27th CCS
Died 27th December 1918
Panel 5 Column 1 Tehran Memorial

FOSTER, E.
Ernest
Private Territorial Force 292429
21st Battalion Middlesex Regiment
Killed in Action 9th April 1918

28 years old
Husband of M. Foster (nee Martin), of 10 Clarendon Place Landsport, Portsmouth
Panel 8 Ploegsteert Memorial
Born in Swindon

FOSTER, S.F.
Private 100034 20th Squadron MGC
Died 4th November 1918
Nephew of Ernest Foster 'Haysley', of 28 Leaphill Road, Pokesdown, Hants
A. 175 Alexandria Hadra Memorial Cemetery. Egypt
Attended North Wilts Technical College in 1910 remembered on its stained glass window.

FOWLER, H.J.
Herbert James
Private 11088 2nd Battalion Wiltshire Regiment
Died of Wounds 8th July 1916
24 years old
Son of Charles Henry and Martha Fowler, of 18 Kembrey Street
Pier and Face 13A Thiepval Memorial

H. Fowler

FOWLER, T.
Thomas
Private 26933 (26923) 6th Battalion Somerset Light Infantry
Formerly 22200 Wiltshire Regiment
Died of Wounds 16th September 1916
Husband of Mrs A. Fowler, of 39 East Lulworth Wareham, Dorset
II. A. 70. Dartmoor Cemetery Becordel Becourt France
Born in Swindon

FOX, J.W.
Joseph William
Sergeant 71868 5th Battalion Royal Fusiliers
Died 8th January 1918
B2 799 Radnor Street Cemetery
Born in Swindon

FOX, W.H.
William Henry
Private 14473 10th Battalion Notting hamshire and Derbyshire Regiment (Sherwood Foresters)
Killed in Action 14th February 1915
19 years old
Son of Edward and Mary Ann Fox, of 76 Haig Street, Creation, Derby
Panel 39 + 41 Menin Gate Memorial
Born in Swindon

FRANKLIN, C.S.
Charles Stanley
Private 22646 1st Battalion Wiltshire Regiment
Died of Wounds 3rd September 1916
20 years old
Son of George Robert and Sophia Franklin, of 38 Priors Hill, Wroughton
Pier and Face 13A Thiepval Memorial
Born in Swindon

FRANKLIN, G.
George
Private 10570 2nd Battalion 'C' Company Wiltshire Regiment
Killed in Action 13th March 1915
22 years old
Son of Mr and Mrs George Franklin, of Steeple Ashton, Trowbridge
Panel 33 – 34 Le Touret Memorial
Born in Swindon

FRANKLIN, H.C.
Hollister Clare
Private 10888 2nd Battalion Hon Artillery Company
Died 22nd January 1918 34 years old
Plot 4. Row B. Grave 7. Giavera Arcade British Cemetery Italy
Attended North Wilts Technical College Victoria Rd in 1896 and remembered on its stained glass window.

FRANKLIN, H.T.
Henry Thomas
Bombardier 57627 C Battery 93rd Brigade Royal Field Artillery
Killed in Action 10th September 1918
30 years old
Son of James Franklin, of 32 Swindon Road
I.E. 1. Favreuil British Cemetery. France
Born in Swindon

FRANKLIN, L.
Leonard
Private 58281 13th Battalion Welsh
Regiment
Formerly 58774 South Wales Borderers
Killed in Action 18th September 1918
Panel 7 – Vis En – Artois Memorial
Born in Wootton Bassett – Lived in
Swindon

FRANKLIN, S.W.
Stafford William
Private 14291 9th Service Battalion South
Staffordshire Regiment
Killed in Action 10th July 1917
30 years old
Son of Henry Franklin, of 'Trenance'
Milton Avenue, Weston – Super – Mare
II.B. 12. Dickebusch New Military
Cemetery Extension Belgium
Born in Swindon

FREARSON, B.H.
Pioneer 237853 'A' Signal Department
Bedford Royal Engineers
Died 4th February 1918 19 years old
Son of Mr H. J. Frearson, of Adstone
Farm, Ashbury, Shrivenham
A/C Screen Wall Reading Cemetery
Attended North Wilts Technical College
Victoria Rd in 1911 and remembered on
its stained glass window

FREEBURY, E.
Edward
Private 7159 1st Battalion Wiltshire
Regiment
Killed in Action 27th December 1914
27 years old
Son of John and Louisa Freebury, of 14
Union Street
Panel 53 Menin Gate Memorial
Born in Wroughton

FRICKER, A.C.
Albert Charles
2nd Lieutenant 10th Battalion East
Yorkshire Regiment
Killed in Action 27th February 1917
23 years old
Son of Albert Edwin and Mary Ann
Fricker, of Close Cottage, Rodbourne
Cheney
III.L. 2. Euston Road Cemetery,
Colincamps. France
Bsc London University

Attended North Wilts Technical College
Victoria Road 1906 and remembered on
its Stained glass window

FROST, F.H.
Frederick Harold
Private 8225 D Company 2nd Battalion
Wiltshire Regiment
Died 20th December 1918. 28 years old
Son of Frank Frost
1V H 4 Nivelles Communal Cemetery
Belgium
He had been held as a prisoner of war in
Limburg, Germany but died in hospital
soon after his release.

FRY, W.
William
Driver 9408 Royal Field Artillery
Died of Wounds 4th November 1917
Son of William and Annie Meria Fry, of 46
Exmouth Street
VI.G. 5A Wimereux Communal Cemetery
Formerly worked in L2 shop in the
Locomotive Department in the G. W. R.
Remembered on plaque in the Outlet
Village, Swindon

FULKER, J.N.
Private 42333 10th Battalion Yorkshire
Regiment
Killed in Action 11th April 1917
Cojeul British Cemetery, St Martin-Sur-
Cojeul France

FULLAWAY, W.J.T.
William John Thomas
Private 2918 6th Battalion Royal Munster
Fusiliers (Formerly 12696 Wiltshire
Regiment)
Killed in Action 1st September 1915
Panel 185 – 190 Helles Memorial
Dardanelles
Born in Swindon

FULLER, E.F.
Edward Fleetwood
Private 1028 POWO Royal Wiltshire
Hussars
Died 8th October 1914
Lived in Swindon

GADD, W.
William
Private 5275 1st Battalion Wiltshire
Regiment.

Killed in Action 26th August 1914.
31 years old
Son of Harry and Matilda Gadd of 52
Cricklade Rd.
La ferte – Sous – Jouavre memorial.

GALE, H.W.
Herbert William
Private 11028 2nd Battalion Wiltshire
Regiment
Killed in Action 8th July 1916.
26 years old.
Son of George and Harriet Gale
Pier and face 13A Thiepval.

GAPP, E.J.
Edmund John
Trooper. 422 Royal Horse Guards
Killed in Action 3rd May 1917
Bay 1 Arras Memorial.
Born in Swindon

GARDINER, A.D.
Gunner 135427 D Bty 50th Brigade Royal
Field Artillery
Died 14th June 1917. 26 years old
Husband of Mrs R E Gardiner 29 Elmina
Road
I E II Point-du-Jour Military cemetery
Athies France

GARDINER, C.W.
Charles William
Gunner 148405 Royal Field Artillery
Killed in action 3rd May 1917
Son of Mr C J Gardiner 30 Omdurman
Street
B 8 Bunyans cemetary Tilloy – Les –
Mofflares.

GARLAND, E.C.
Ernest Charles
Lance -corporal 33321 1st Battalion Royal
Berkshire Regiment
Died of wounds 30th November 1917.
39 years old
Son of Thomas and Angela Garland of
Swindon.
Husband of Rose Garland of 6 Atlas road
Victoria Park Bristol.
1.Q. 20 Achiet – Le Grand communal
cemetery extension
Born in Swindon

GEE, A.G.
Albert.
Private. 52879. 2nd Battalion West

Yorkshire Regiment.
Killed in Action. 29th May 1918.
24 years old.
Son of John and Jane Gee, 31 Bengess
Broham, Chippenham Wiltshire.
Soissons Memorial. France.

GEE, W.H.
William Henry.
Private. 6868 1st Battalion Wiltshire
Regiment.
Killed in Action. 26th October 1914.
32 years old.
Son of William Gee.
Husband of Annie Gertrude Gee of 59
Omdurman Street. Gorse Hill,
Panel 33 and 34 Le Touret Memorial
France

G.W. Gee

GEE, G.W.
George Wilfred.
Lance – Corporal. 13960. 2nd Battalion
Wiltshire Regiment.
Killed in Action 15th June 1915
Panel 33 and 34 Le Touret memorial.
France.

GEORGE, H.G.
Herbert Gladstone.
Battery Sergeant- Major 860804 6th
Brigade Royal Field Artillery.
Killed in Action. 7th May 1917.
28 years old.
Son of Ruben and Clara G George.
Husband of Lilian George of Swindon.
Karachi war cemetery. India.

GEORGE, W.E.
William Ernest
Sergeant. 8223 2nd Battalion Wiltshire
Regiment.
Died of Wounds. 26th October 1916.
26 years old.
Woolea road, West Torring, Worthing,

Sussex.
V111. D.3A Etaples Military cemetery.
France.
Born in Swindon.

GENT, G.A.
George Alfred.
Private 9856. 1st Battalion Gloucester-
shire regiment.
Died of Wounds. 27th December 1914.
20 years old.
Son of Arthur and Mary Gent 150 The
Butts, Frome, Somerset.
111 B 18 Lillers communal cemetery.
France
Born in Swindon.

GIBBS, H.
Harry.
Private 53961. 15th Battalion Welsh
Regiment.
Killed in Action. 4th August 1917.
Panel 37 Menin Gate memorial. Belgium.
Born and lived in Swindon.

GIBBS, J.
Joseph
Private 22243 7th Battalion Wiltshire
Regiment
Died 7th October 1918
Panel 9 Vis – en – Artois Memorial
Born in Swindon

J. Gibbs

GILL, G.
Giles.
Private. 10531. 1st Battalion Wiltshire
Regiment.
Killed in Action. 23rd January 1915.
Memorial 4 Wytscheete military
cemetery. Belgium.

Born in Rodbourne.
Worked in L2 shop. Loco dept GWR.
Named on plaque in Outlet village
centre.

GILLARD, S.T.
Samuel Tyler.
Private. 27762. 8th Battalion Somerset
Light Infantry.
Died of Wounds. 31st June 1917
Panel 21 Menin gate memorial. Belgium.
Born in Swindon.

S Gillard

GILLESPIE, A.H.
Alfred Howard.
Private. 1533892. Machine gun corps.
Died of Wounds. 18th September 1918.
Formerly 22063 Wiltshire regiment.
No details of burial.
Born in Swindon.

GLASS, A.
Albert
Private. 5732. 5th Battalion Wiltshire
Regiment.
Died of Wounds. 27th February 1917.
43 years old.
Husband of Adelaide Daisy Glass of 1
Church road, Swindon.
X111 B 19 Amara war cemetery. Iraq.

GLASS, A.
Arthur.
Sergeant 6886. 1st Battalion Wiltshire
Regiment.
Killed in Action. 18th October 1914.
Panel 33 and 34 Le Touret memorial.
France.
Born in Swindon.

GLASS, H.S.
Hebert Stanley.
Private. 38371. 11th battalion Worcestershire regiment.

Killed in Action. 24th April 1917.
27 years old.
Brother of Mrs Emily Maud Dark 52
Gooch Street.
Doiran memorial. Salonika.
Born in Swindon.

GLEED, F.J.
Francis James
Pte 456089 231st Field Ambulance Royal
Army Medical Corps
Died 25th November 1918. 25 years old
Son of Thomas and Elizabeth Gleed of
Swindon
XI E 23 Terlincthun British cemetery
Wimille France

GODDARD, B.
Bertram.
Private. 7598. 3rd battalion Wiltshire
Regt.
Died 17th October 1915.
A.351 Radnor street cemetery. Swindon.

GODDARD, F.
Frank.
Private.2922 3rd battalion Royal Munster
Fusiliers (Formerly 13226 Wiltshire
Regiment)
Died 30th March 1916.
B 21 7 Cobh old Church cemetery.
Born in Swindon.

GODDARD, W.J.
Walter John.
Private 5436. 1st battalion Wiltshire
Regiment.
Killed in Action. 27th October 1914.
32 years old.
Son of Thomas Goddard of 64 Prospect
Lane.
Husband of Louisa Goddard 76 Stafford
street.
Panel 33 and 34 Le Touret memorial.
France.

GODWIN, H.J.
Harold John.
Sergeant 203174. 6th Battalion Wiltshire
regiment.
Died 10th August 1918.
1.D.10 Hamburg cemetery. Germany.
Died as a result of TB while a prisoner of
war.
Lived in Swindon.

GOLBY, H.L.
Horace Lett.
AM.11 123583 Royal Air Force.
Died 30th March 1918.
1590 Radnor Street cemetery, Swindon.

GOLBY, J.H.
John Henry.
Private 22661 6th Battalion Duke of
Cornwalls light infantry.
Died of Wounds 23rd April 1917
37 years old.
Son of James and Mary Golby of Gorse
hill.
Husband of Blanche L. Golby of 61
Whiteman street Gorse hill.
11.F.5 Abbeville communal cemetery
extension. France

H. Golby

GOODENOUGH, A.J.
Albert Jesse
Private 10462 2nd Battalion South Wales
Borderers
Died 25th April 1915. 23 years old
Son of Mr and Mrs T H Goodenough of 58
Argyle Street Gorse Hill
Panel 80 – 84 and 219 – 220 Helles
Memorial
Brother of Sidney (Below)

GOODENOUGH, S.T.
Sidney Thomas
Private 9980 2nd Battalion Oxfordshire
and Buckinghamshire Light Infantry
Killed in Action 16th May 1915
19 years old
Son of Mr and Mrs T H Goodenough of 58
Argyle Street Gorse Hill
Panel 26 Le Touret Memorial
Brother of Albert (Above)

GOODMAN, H.H.
Harold.
Private 10507 1st Battalion Wiltshire Regiment.
Died of wounds 28th June 1915.
18 years old.
Son of Ernest Walter and Annie Goodman of 5 Shelly Street.
V111 B 52 Boulogne Eastern Cemetery. France.
Worked in L2 shop loco department GWR and named on plaque in Outlet Village.

GOODWIN, J.W.
John Wilfred
Lance Sergeant 470 Welsh Horse Yeomanry
Died 5th January 1918. 35 years old
1931 Radnor Street Cemetery

GORTON, F.W.
Frederick Woolford.
Lance Corporal 14540 Coldstream Guards.
Killed in Action 15th September 1916.
29 years old.
Son of the late Mrs Ellen Gorton.
Pier and face 7 D and 8 D Thiepval Memorial France.
Born In Swindon

GOSLING, H.A.
Harold Austin.
Private 35046 12th Battalion East Surrey Regiment.
Died of Wombs 3rd October 1918.
20 years old.
Son of Jacob and Alice Gosling of Swindon.
111.B.65 Haringhe (Bandaghem) Military Cemetery, Belgium.
Born in Swindon.

GOSLING, W.H.
William Henry.
Private 1st Battalion Hampshire Regiment.
Killed in action 22nd of April 1918.
19 years old.
Son of Mr F and Mrs E.L Gosling of 48 Whitemans Street Gorse hill.
111.D.21 Saint Venant Robecq Road British cemetery, Robecq. France
Was a Trimmers apprentice in the loco and carriage department GWR.

W.H. Gosling

GOSS, P.F.
Percy Frank.
Corporal 19124 2nd Battalion Wiltshire Regiment.
Killed in Action 17th October 1916.
19 years old.
Son of Mr F and Mrs E.B Goss of 90 Albion Street Swindon.
11.E.15 Bulls Road Cemetery Flers, France.
Born in Jersey.

GOUGH, F.
Frank.
Private 9409 5th Battalion Wiltshire Regiment.
Killed in Action 19th June 1915.
19 years old.
Son of George and Mrs M.A Gough of 52 Clifton Street
Special Memorial 148 Pink Farm Cemetery Helles. Dardanelles.

F. Gough

GOUGH, F.G.
Frederick George.
Private 6796 2nd Battalion Wiltshire Regiment.
Killed in Action. 24th October 1914.

51

27 years old.
Son of the late John and Elizabeth Gough.
Panel 53 Menin gate Memorial. Belgium.
Born in Wroughton. Lived in Swindon.

GOVIER, A.J.
Alfred J
Private 6289 ASC Transferred to 5/10670 852nd Area Employment Company Labour Corps.
Died 22nd March 1918
Bay 10 Arras Memorial

GOVIER. W.J.
Walter John.
Private. 44435 13th Battalion Devonshire Regiment
Died. 13th March 1917. 23 years old
Son of Francis Albert and Mary Ann Govier of 17 Edmund Street.
C.1751. Radnor Street cemetery. Swindon

GRACE, W.J.
William James
Private CH/308S 1st Royal Marine Battalion Royal Naval Division Royal Marine Light Infantry.
Killed in Action 13th November 1916
29 years old
Son of T and L Grace of Quainton Allysbury Buckinghamshire
Husband of M Odine Grace of 2 Dixon Street
Pier and Face 1A Thiepval Memorial

Lt. W. T. Grainger

GRAINGER, W.T.
William Thomas.
Lieutenant. 3/4th Battalion Wiltshire Regiment.
Died of Wounds 21st September 1917.
24 years old.
Son of Mr and Mrs Thomas Granger 40 Park Lane Chippenham.
6.1.6 Bus House cemetery. Belgium

Worked in Loco and carriage dept as a clerk, GWR. He joined up in September 1914.

GRANT, J.
John
Lance – Corporal. 20756 6th Battalion Wiltshire regiment.
Died of Wounds. 28th March 1918.
25 years old.
Son of Mr A Grant of 21 Princes Street.
V111 B 5 H A C cemetery Ecoust – St – Mein. France

GRANT, W.
William
Private 36518 10th battalion Notting hamshire and Derbyshire Regiment.
Killed in Action. 31st October 1916.
Pier and face 10c, 10d and 11a Thiepval memorial. France.
Born in Swindon.

GRAY, F.J.
Frederick James.
Private 35812. 2nd Battalion Wiltshire regiment.
Died 23rd September 1918.
R.2 Neuve Chapelle farm cemetery. France
Lived in Swindon.

GRAY, T.C.
Thomas Charles
Lance – Corporal. 10220. 2nd Battalion Wiltshire regiment.
Killed in Action. 13th March 1915.
Panel 33 and 34 Le Touret memorial. France.
Lived in Swindon.

T. Gray

GREEN, A.R.
Archibald Rowland.
Private 18551 6th Battalion Wiltshire regiment.
Died of Wounds 11th October 1915.
11.A.56 Longuenesse St Omer Souvenir
cemetery. Belgium.
Lived in Swindon.

GREEN, A.L.
Arthur Leonard.
Private G/23722 10th Battalion Queens own West Kent Regiment.
Died of Wounds 4th August 1917.
XX11 O 22A Etaples military cemetery. France.
Formerly 20979 Somerset Light Infantry.
Born in Blunsdon, Lived in Swindon.

GREEN, E.R.B.
Edward Reginald.
Private 62376. 130th company, Machine Gun Corps.(Formerly 1563 Wiltshire Regt)
Died 11th October 1918. 24 years old.
Son of Edward Joseph and Emma Selina Green, 9 Crombey Street
8.B.16 Dehli war cemetery. India.

GREEN, H.A.
Henry Arthur.
Private 207945 22nd Battalion Middlesex regiment.(TF Depot)
Died 5th November 1918. 23 years old.
Son of Henry William and Mary Jane Green of 56 Gooch Street.
D 700 Radnor street cemetery. Swindon.

GREEN, J.
John.
Private 202777 6th Battalion Northamptonshire regiment. (Formerly 632 Middlesex Regt)
Killed in Action. 19th September 1918.
1 G 2 Unicorn cemetery Vend'huile. France.
Born in Swindon.

GREENING, L.H.
Leonard Harvey
Sergeant 14836 7th Battalion Shropshire light Infantry
Died of Wounds 22nd April 1917
Foster – Son of Mrs C Boss of 46 Jewel street, Barry dock, Glamorgan.
1V A 2 Duisans British cemetery

extension. France.
Born in Swindon

GREENMAN, W.M.
Wilfred Manley
Private 33245 2nd Battalion Wiltshire Regiment
Killed in Action 31st June 1917.
22 years old
Son of Mr and Mrs T Greenman of 128 Victoria Road
Panel 53 Menin gate memorial. Belgium.
He had worked with his Father on the Management of 'Nightingale Farm' He had signed up with the Wiltshire Yeomanry in April 1916 later being transferred to the Wiltshire Regiment. A letter was sent to his parents –

'It is with the very deepest pain, that I have to write to you to confirm the death in action of your son W Greenman on August 1st. He was the Gunner of my Lewis Gun team and I always thought a great deal of him as he was such a good upright boy. I believe he had been in the Royal Wilts Yeomanry, which is my own regiment. He followed me closely in the attack of the day before . He and I were first in the enemy's trench. It is characteristic of him, that although a first class soldier, he was very kind – hearted and I shall never forget the way he stopped me killing the German he and I captured. All through the battle he behaved with great gallantry. He was severely wounded by a shell in the evening of 1st of August and died before we could get him to the dressing station. He is buried in the German position which he helped to capture.
Yours faithfully   *S Collier 2nd Lt.*

F. Gregory

53

GREGORY, F.J.
Frederick John
Sergeant 1636 C Battery 227th Brigade
Royal Field Artillery
Died 18th August 1916. 32 years old
Son of John and Mary Gregory
Husband of E A Gregory of 50 Rosebery
Street
Face 3 Madras 1914 – 1918 War Memorial
Chennai.
Buried in Bangalore (Hosur Road)
Cemetery India
Served in the South African War

GRIBBLE, F.
Stoker 1st Class K/2533 Royal Navy HM
Submarine E41
Died 15th August 1916. 29 years old
Son of William Gribble 31 Cricklade Road
RN Plot 107 Shotley (St Mary)
Churchyard, Suffolk

GRIFFIN, M.G.
Mervyn Granville
Private 44014 2/4th Battalion Royal
Berkshire regiment (Formerly 46134
Hampshire Regiment)
Died of Wounds 9th June 1918.
18 years old.
Son of W.M and Bertha Griffin of 27
Broad street.
111 B 26 Aire communal cemetery.
France
Born in Swindon

GRIFFIN, P.C.
Percy Charles
Private 70451 A company, 2nd Battalion
Devonshire regiment.
Killed in Action. 24th April 1918.
19 years old.
Son of Charles and Eliza Griffin 12
Alexandra road, Swindon.
11 O 28 Adelaide cemetery Villers
Bretonneux. France.
Attended North Wilts Technical college
Victoria Road in 1910 Remembered on
its Stained Glass window.

GROVES, E.W.
Ernest William
Lance Corporal 61151 152nd Field
Company Royal Engineers.
Died 2nd October 1917. 35 years old
Son of William and Harriett Groves
Husband of Mary Ellen Groves of 4
Marlborough Road

XXV E 7 Lijssenthoek Military Cemetery
Belgium

GROVES, W.A.
Private 20509 13th Battalion Royal
Fusiliers
Killed in Action 19th December 1917
II C 10 Spoilbank Cemetery Belgium

GUBBINS, J. MM
Jesse
Company Quarter Master Sergeant 9699
D Company 7th Battalion Oxfordshire
and Buckinghamshire Light Infantry
Died 29th October 1918. 40 years old
Son of Henry and Harriet Gubbins of
Wootton, Woodstock, Oxon
Husband 0f E Gubbins of 26 Pembroke
Street Swindon
701 Mikra British Cemetery Kalamaria

J. Gubbins

GULEY, E.G.
Edward George
Private 11523 5th battalion Wiltshire
regiment.
Killed in Action. 29th March 1917.
Panel 30 and 64 Basra memorial. Iraq.
Born in Swindon.

E. Guley

54

GULLIS, W.
William
Sergeant 18226 A company, 2nd
battalion, Wiltshire regiment.
Killed in Action. 9th April 1917.
25 years old
Son of John and Sarah Jane Gullis of 10
Badbury.
Bay 7 Arras memorial. France.
Lived in Swindon

GUTHRIE, R.C.
Lance-Corporal 93960 217th Army
Troops
Company Royal Engineers Transferred to
Royal Flying Corps as AM 2nd Class.
Killed in Action 13th April 1918
Son of Mr and Mrs T G Guthrie of 164
Clifton Street
V E 3 Villers Brettoneux Military Cemetery
France
Apprentice in Loco and carriage dept
GWR

R.C. Guthrie

HACKER, A.
Arthur
Trooper 13/487 Auckland Mounted Rifles
New Zealand Forces
Killed in Action 19th May 1915
Brother of Elizabeth Hacker of 6
Corporation Street
I B 6 Walkers Ridge Cemetery Anzac
Dardanelles
Born in Swindon

HACKER, G.T.
Sapper 216 Wilts Fortress Company
Royal Engineers.
Died 29th April 1915
E 7724 Radnor street cemetery. Swindon.

HACKER, L.T.
Driver 2730 3/3 Battalion Wessex
brigade, ammunition column. Royal Field
Artillery.
Died 24th December 1915
B 1815 Radnor street cemetery. Swindon

HACKMAN, C.
Clifford
2nd Lieutenant. Royal Air Force.
Killed in a flying accident. 7th April 1918.
20 years old.
Son of Mr and Mrs E F Hackman of 73A
Hythe Road
Winchcome cemetery near Cheltenham.
He was killed while landing in a Sussex
aerodrome. His wing was hit by another
plane while landing, he jumped clear but
broke his neck in the fall.
Born at Winchcome. Educated at
Swindon High School and was a clerk in
the GWR.

HAGGARD, C.E.
Charles
Private 8380 3rd Battalion Wiltshire
regiment.
Died 7th February 1919. 37 years old
Son of Samuel G Haggard 60 Stafford
street.
E 7227 Radnor street cemetery. Swindon
Died suddenly in Swindon 3 weeks after
his return from internment in Germany
as a prisoner of war, as a result of
starvation and exposure.

HAINES, J.
James
Private 7175 1st Battalion Wiltshire
Regiment
Killed in Action 24th October 1914
28 years old
Son of William and Elizabeth Haines 9
Baker Road Wroughton
Panel 33 and 34 Le Touret Memorial
Lived in Swindon

HALL, A.W.
Albert William
Private 88345 Royal Army Medical Corps
Died 13th July 1920. 23 years old.
Son of William John and Esther Tucker
Hall 86 Ponting street.
D 1088 Radnor street cemetery. Swindon

HALL, E.G.
Private 106873 20th Battalion Machine
gun corps.

Died 13th November 1918
C 3525 Radnor street cemetery Swindon

HALL, J.W.
James William
Private 8010 1st Battalion Coldstream Guards
Killed in Action 14th September 1914
6 B 29 Chauty Communal Cemetery British Extension
Born in Swindon

HALL, S.
Sidney
Private 13643 1st Battalion South Wales Borderers
Killed in Action 10th November 1917
Panel 65 to 66 Tyne Cot Memorial
Born in Swindon

HALL, W.J. DSM
William Jasper
Engine room artificer 3rd class M/19438
Royal Navy HMS 'Victory'
Died 14th September 1918. 32 years old.
Son of Mr T H Harding 30 Argyle street
E 7464 Radnor street cemetery Swindon.

HALE, A.
Private. 3655 Wiltshire regiment.
Died 7th November 1919. 49 years old.
Husband of Mary Jane Hale 163 Beatrice street.
C3653. Radnor street cemetery. Swindon.
Served previously in the South African campaign. His son Alfred also died

A. Hale

HALE, A.
Alfred
Private 200214 C Company 1/4th Battalion Wiltshire Regiment
Died 21st February 1919. 24 years old
Son of A and Mary Hale of 163 Beatrice Street

EE 70 Ramleh War Cemetery
Remembered on his fathers headstone in Radnor Street Cemetery.

HALLETT, H.
Harry.Lance-corporal. 4968. 2nd Battalion Wiltshire regiment.
Killed in Action 29th May 1915.
Panel 102 Loos memorial.
Born Swallowcliffe Wiltshire, lived in Swindon.

HAMBIDGE, W.A.
William Arthur.
Private, 9492. 1st Battalion Wiltshire regiment.
Died of wounds 15th March 1915.
Son of William John and Caroline Hambidge of Stratton St Margaret.
J 29 Bailleul communal cemetery. France
Lived in Swindon

HAMBIDGE, E.F.
Ernest Frederick.
Private 11120 5th Battalion Wiltshire regiment.
Killed in Action. 9th April 1916.
Panel 30 and 64 Basra memorial. Iraq.
Born in Stratton Brother of William Arthur

HAMILTON, R.E.
Robert Ernest
Private TF 203051 13th Battalion Middlesex Regiment
Killed in Action 10th October 1918
29 years old
Son of Robert Ernest Hamilton
Husband of Frances Matilda Hamilton of 162 Shipbourne Road Tonbridge Kent
III B 5 St Aubert British Cemetery
Born in Swindon

HANCOCK, E.W.
Ernest William
Lance- corporal. G/34635 2nd Battalion Royal Fusiliers.
Killed in Action. 28th November 1916.
28 years old.
Son of William Joseph James Hancock and Truphena Hancock 11 Eastcott Hill.
1X P 4 Guards cemetery, Lesboeufs. France.

HARDING, T.N.
Thomas Neate
Lance – corporal W/R 554096, Inland

Waterways and Docks Royal Engineers Died 12th February 1920, 32 years old. Son of Mr TH Harding of 30 Argyle street. B1271 Radnor street cemetery. Swindon. Related to WJ Hall DSM RN mentioned earlier. Also buried in Radnor street. Commemorated on plaque in St Barnabas Church Gorse Hill.

HARDYMAN, H.E.
Henry Edgar.
Corporal. 24057 Royal garrison artillery. Died 31st August 1914. Special memorial, Templebreedy cemetery. Republic of Ireland. Co. Cork Lived in Swindon.

HARMAN, C.
Charles
Private 7008. 1st Battalion Royal Berkshire regiment. Killed in Action 11th November 1914 Husband of Mrs C Harman 61 Kingshill road. Swindon Father of 3 children. Panel 45 Menin gate memorial. Belgium. Lived in Swindon. Worked as a driller in boiler shop GWR.

HARRIS, F.
Frederick
Private 18372 11th Battalion Notts and Derbyshire Regiment (The Sherwood Foresters) Killed in Action 14th July 1918 38 years old Son of Henry and Susan Jane Harris of Arkwright Town Chesterfield Husband of Sarah Ann Harris Plot 4 Row A Grave 6 Montecchio Precalcino Communal Cemetery Extension Born in Swindon

HARRIS, J.H.
James Henry
Corporal 331354 1st/8th Battalion Hampshire Regiment (Formerly 11573 Wiltshire Regt) Died 19th April 1917. 21 years old Son of William and Isabella Harris of 38 Pinehurst Road. Panels 28 and 29 Jerusalem Memorial Born in Southampton

HARRIS, R.
Rawley.
Private 8567 2nd Battalion Wiltshire regiment.

Killed in Action, 23rd October 1914 21 years old. Son of Mr and Mrs C Harris, of 53 Kingsdown road, Upper Stratton. Panel 53 Menin gate memorial Belgium. Lived in Swindon.

HARRISON. A.
Arthur
Private 28267 2nd Battalion Wiltshire regiment. (Formerly Wiltshire Hussars) Killed in Action 4th September 1918. 18 years old. Son of Walter and Charlotte Harrison, of the Queens Royal Hotel, Tap yard, Wellington street Swindon. E 19 Le Vertannoy British cemetery Hinges. France Lived in Swindon.

HART, R.P.
Reginald Percy.
Private 23659 5th Battalion Royal Berkshire Regiment Killed in Action 9th August 1916. 21 years old. Only son of Mr E J and Mrs E Hart of 9 Carisbrook, Chiseldon. Pier and face 11D Thiepval memorial. France.

HARTLEY, H.E.
Harold Ernest
Lance-corporal 33201 2nd Battalion Wiltshire Regiment Killed in Action. 9th April 1917 Bay 7 Arras memorial. France. Born in Swindon

HARTWELL, W.W.
Private 20792 5th Battalion Wiltshire regiment. Died 24th August 1916. 20 years old Son of Walter and Annie Hartwell of 6 Percy street Swindon V G 9 Basra war cemetery. Iraq.

W.W. Hartwell

HATCHER, G.L.
George Leonard
Sapper 520092 565th Army Troops company Royal Engineers.
Killed in Action, 18th September 1918.
22 years old.
Son of Albert Thomas and Mary Annie Hatcher, 41 Lansdown road Swindon.
M 6 Ruyaulcourt military cemetery.
France

G.L. Hatcher

HATHERELL, A.P.
Albert Prior.
Gunner 119294. 'B' Battery, 160th Brigade. Royal field artillery.
Died 19th May 1917. 20 years old.
Son of William Jesse and Leah Jane Hatherell of 32 St Margaret's road.
1 V L 54 Duisans British cemetery Etrun. France

HAWARD, F.
Private 545009 60th Sanitary Section, Royal Army Medical Corps.
Died 19th October 1918. 24 years old.
Son of John Haward of Paddington London.
Husband of Ethel Beatrice Haward of 71 Ponting Street Swindon.
Z 8 Ramleh war cemetery. Egypt

HAWKINS, A.E.
Albert Edward.
Private 57909 2/8th Battalion Worcester shire regiment
Died of Wounds 9th September 1918.
(Gas) 18 years old.
Son of Mr and Mrs Hawkins of 48 Clifton Street
111 C 40 Terlinctum British cemetery. Wimille. Belgium.
Lived in Swindon.

HAWKINS, C.A.D.
Conrad Alexander Douglas
Lance Corporal 18374 6th Battalion Wiltshire Regiment
Killed in Action 23rd March 1918
27 years old
Son of Joseph and Isabella Hawkins of Townsend Farm Bridport Dorset
Bay 7 Arras Memorial
Lived in Swindon

HAWKINS, C.T.
Charles Titcombe
Private 35150 6th Battalion Wiltshire Regiment
Killed in Action 10th April 1918
Panel 119 to 120 Tyne Cot memorial
Born in Swindon Lived in Wroughton

HAWKINS, W.H.
Walter Henry
Acting Bombardier. 605. 194th Heavy Battery Royal Garrison Artillery.
Died 11th December 1916. 29 years old
Son of Mrs M Hawkins of 451 Ferndale road.
AF 2033 Aldershot military cemetery. UK

HAYDON, C.
Charles
Private 29858 11th Hussars
Died 10th October 1918
No Burial Details
Born in Swindon Lived in Stanford in the Vale

HAYDON, J.
James
Corporal G/1362 2nd Battalion Royal Sussex Regiment
Died 18th September 1918. 29 years old
Husband of Mrs Haydon (nee Robinson) of 66 Conway St Hove Brighton
II J 5 Roisel Communal Cemetery Extension
Born in Swindon

F.C. Haylock

HAYLOCK, F.C.
Lance-corporal. 13941 5th Battalion
Wiltshire regiment.
Killed in Action 1st February 1917.
XXV Amara War cemetery. Iraq

HAYNES, O.M.
Oliver Mark
Private 7365 1st Battalion Royal
Berkshire Regiment
Killed in Action 16th May 1915.
Panel 30 Le Touret memorial. France.

HAYNES, W.E.
William Ewart
Gunner 123127 'X' 5th Trench Motor
Battery Royal Field Artillery
Killed in Action 28th June 1918
20 years old
Son of Mr and Mrs Haynes of 72
Sandholme Road Brislington Bristol
Plot 3 Row D Grave 6 Tannay British
Cemetery Italy
Born in Swindon

HAYWARD, A.
Albert
Private 5943 13th Battalion Manchester
Regiment
Died 23rd February 1916
Husband of E Hayward of 17 Mansland
Street Chorlton on Medlock Manchester
87 Salonika (Lembet Road) Cemetery
Born Swindon

HAYWARD, W.A.
William Alfred
Private 46452 2nd Battalion Wiltshire
regiment
Killed in Action 4th November 1918.
19 years old.
Son of Mr A and Mrs L S Hayward of 69
Chapel street. Swindon.
11 B 19 Cross roads cemetery Fontaine
au – bois. France.
Born in Stratton

HAZELL, E.J.
Edward James
Private 7703 1st Battalion Royal
Berkshire Regiment
Killed in Action 15th November 1914.
27 years old
Son of Edwin and Ann Hazell,
Brightwalton, Wantage, Berks.
Husband of Edith Ellen Hazell,
Northbrook Place Newbury, Berkshire
Panel 45 Menin Gate Memorial. Belgium

E.J. Hazell

HEAD, W.H.
William Head.
Private 52651 21st Battalion Manchester
regiment. (Formerly 110376 Army
Service Corps)
Killed in Action 27th October 1917.
34 years old.
Son of William and Sarah Ann Head, of 68
Newport street.
Panel 120 to 124 and 162 to 162a and
163a Tyne Cot memorial. Belgium.

HEAP, R.W.
Richard William
Corporal 43710. 154 field company Royal
Engineers
Killed in Action 16th November 1916.
Pier and Face 8a and 8d Thiepval
memorial France.
Born in Swindon.

R.W. Heap

HEATH, G.
George
Private 38563 2nd Battalion Welsh
Fusiliers.
Killed in Action 5th November 1916.
25 years old.
Son of William and Martha Heath, 157
Clifton street.
Pier and Face 4a Thiepval memorial.
France.
Formerly 38644 Welsh Regiment.

Son of Frank Hedges 20 Cricklade road.
V1 N 22 Bucquoy road cemetery, Ficheux.
France

G. Heath

S.H. Heavens

HEATH, H.T.
Harry Thomas
Corporal 19475 5th Battalion Wiltshire
regiment.
Died 29th December 1916. 20 years old.
Son of Mrs L Heath of 16 Eastcott road.
X111 A 14 Amara war cemetery. Iraq.

HEMMINS, R.A.
Roy Allnutt.
Private 11335 2nd Battalion Wiltshire
regiment.
Killed in Action 8th July 1916.
21 years old.
Son of Tom Allnutt Hemmins.189
Ferndale Road Swindon.
Pier and Face 13a Thiepval memorial.
France.
Lived in Swindon.

H.T. Heath

R.A. Hemmins

HEATH, J.W.
Joseph William
Private 7937 1st Battalion Wiltshire
regiment.
Killed in Action 24th August 1914.
D 9 Ors British cemetery. France
Born in Gorse hill and commemorated on
a plaque in St Barnabas Church.

HEMMINGS,W.J.
William James
Chief Engine Room Artificer 2nd Class
HMS 'Defence' Royal Navy
Died 31st May 1916
14 Plymouth Naval Memorial

HEAVENS, S.H.
Sidney H
Able Seaman SS/2056 HMS 'Pegasus'
Died 1st October 1918
E D 2566 Dumfermline Cemetery

HEMSLEY, M.S.
Maurice Swinnerton
Private 205671 7th Battalion Royal West
Kent Regiment
Killed in Action 21st March 1918
27 years old
Son of Henry and Catherine Hemsley of
Whistable Kent
Panel 58 and 59 Pozieres Memorial
Born in Swindon

HEDGES, W.E.
William Edward.
Private 20795 2nd Battalion Wiltshire
regiment.
Killed in Action 9th April 1917.
21 years old.

HENDON, E.E.
Ernest Edward
Lance-corporal 10523 2nd Battalion
Wiltshire regiment.
Killed in Action 9th April 1917
Son of Mrs W B Hendon 14 Hinton Street,
Gorse hill.
V1 E 20 Wancourt British cemetery.
France.

HENSTRIDGE, R.R.
Reginald Robert
Rifleman A/201845 18th Battalion Kings
Royal Rifle Corps.
Killed in Action 31st July 1917
Panel 51 and 53 Menin Gate memorial.
Belgium.
Lived in Swindon.

HERMAN, J.
Jesse
Private 13900 Coldstream Guards
Killed in Action 15th September 1916.
Pier and Face 7D and 8D Thiepval
memorial. France.
Lived in Swindon.

J. Herman

HEWLETT, J.H.
Joseph Harbird
Private TF/2010 4th Battalion East Kent
Regiment (Buffs)
Killed in Action 4th April 1915
22 years old
Son of Henry and Louisa Hewlett of St
Margarets at Cliffe Dover
R C 839 Netley Military Cemetery
Born in Swindon

HIBBARD, A.E.
Albert Edward
Private 22121 6th Battalion Wiltshire
Regiment
Killed in Action 2nd July 1916
18 years old
Son of Mr F J Hibbard of 20 Gloucester

Road Boscombe Hants.
Pier and Face 13A Thiepval Memorial
Born in Swindon

HIBBERD, A.E.
Alfred Edward
Corporal 1514 1st/1st Battalion London
Regiment Royal Fusiliers
Killed in Action 9th May 1915
21 years old
Son of Clara L Hibberd 31 Mantau Street
Battersea
10 Ploegsteert memorial
Lived in Swindon

HIBBERD, E.G.
Ernest George
Private 18314 5th Battalion Berkshire
regiment.
Died of Wounds 10th May 1917.
25 years old.
Son of William Joseph and Sarah Hibberd
12 Florence Street.
XV111 2 12 Etaples military cemetery.
France.

HICKS, F.H.
Francis Harold.
Gunner 636355 'D' Battery 256th Battery
Royal Field Artillery. T/F
Killed in Action 17th July 1917.
22 years old.
Son of Thomas and Ellen Hicks of 13
Union Street
11 D 30 Poperinghe New Military
cemetery. Belgium.
Born in Swindon.
Family plot in Christchurch cemetery,
remembers him- " In memory of our son
Francis Harold Hicks Killed in France 17th
July 1917" His Father served in the Army
Veterinary Corps

HIETT, G.F.
George Frederick.
Lance – Corporal. 6486 2nd Battalion
Wiltshire regiment
Died 19th November 1915. 30 years old.
Son of Henry and Kate Hiett of Port Farm
Hannington Highworth.
Panel 102 Loos memorial. France.
Lived in Swindon.

HIGGS, W.G.
William George
Gunner 956489 Royal Field Artillery. T/F
Killed in Action 18th March 1918
24 years old

Son of William and Mary A Higgs 10
Telford Road Swindon
1V A 15 Reninghelst New Military
cemetery. Belgium.

HILL, J.
James
Private 7745 1st Battalion Wiltshire
regiment
Killed in Action 16th September 1914
La ferte – Sous – Jouarre memorial.
France.
Born in Swindon

HILLARD, H.C.
Herbert Charles
Driver 34706 Royal Field Artillery.
Killed in Action 19th July 1916
1 F 23 Peronne Road cemetery
Maricourt. France
Lived in Swindon.

H.C. Hillard

HILLIER, C.S.
Died No Details

HILLIER, C.T.
Christopher Thorpe
Private 10591
Killed in Action 31st December 1914
21 years old.
Son of William Hillier of 71 Chapel Street
Gorse hill.
Panel 8 Ploegsteert memorial Belgium
Commemorated on plaque in St
Barnabas Church.

C. Hillier

HILLIER, R.R.
Lance Corporal 46090 9th Battalion
Machine Gun Corps.
Died 6th January 1919. 21 years old
Son of Henry and Emily Hillier,
of 9 Kent Road
LXX11 A 17 Etaples Military Cemetery

R.R. Hillier

HIND, F.W.
Gunner 196643 255th Siege Battery
Royal Garrison Artillery
Died 18th October 1918
SII J 14 St Sever Cemetery Extension
Rouen

HINDER, C.G.
Christopher George
Private 290939 9th Battalion Devonshire
regiment.
Killed in Action 26th October 1917
Panel 38 to 40 Tyne Cot memorial
Belgium
Born in Wroughton lived in Swindon.

P. Hinder

HINDER, P.
Percy
Private 37880 12th (Bristols Own)
Battalion Gloucestershire Regiment
Killed in Action 7th August 1917
32 years old.
Son of William and Jessie Hinder of
Swindon
Husband of Clara May Hinder of 118
Chapel Street Gorse hill.

P11 F A St Sever cemetery extension
Rouen. France

HINDER, R.J.
Richard John
Private Po/16033 Royal Marine Light
Infantry HMS ' Viknor '
Died 13th January 1915. 22 years old
Son of Mr and Mrs G Hinder 36 Dover
Street
9 Portsmouth Naval Memorial

HINTON, C.
Christopher
Private 37451 1/5th Battalion Duke of
Cornwalls Light Infantry
Killed in Action 17th April 1918
Son of George and Mercy Hinton of
Grittenham, Dauntsey
Panel 68 Loos Memorial
Born in Swindon

HINTON, E.J.
Edgar John
Private 203294 D Coy 6th Battalion
Wiltshire Regiment
Killed in Action 21st March 1918
24 years old
Son of Frederick and Clara Coleman
Hinton of the Croft Wanbrough
Bay 7 Arras Memorial
Born in Swindon

HINTON, G.E.
George Emanuel
Private 21125 5th Battalion Wiltshire
Regiment
Died of Wounds 14th April 1916
Panel 30 and 64 Basra Memorial
Born in Swindon

HINTON, H.
Harry
Private 37248 12th Battalion (Bristols
Own) Gloucestershire Regiment
Killed in Action 8th May 1917
31 years old
Son of Mrs Ellen Hinton of 49 Kensington
Terrace Albion Street
Bay 6 Arras Memorial

HISCOCK, A.
Albert
Guardsman 14364 1st Battalion
Grenadier Guards
Died 29th October 1915
Panel 9 and 11 Ypres Menin Gate
Memorial. Born in Swindon

HISCOCK, F.
Fred
Private 21231 6th Battalion Wiltshire
regiment.
Killed in Action 13th January 1917
11 H 12 Sailly – Au – Bois military
cemetery France
Born in Swindon.

HITCHCOCK, M.
Maurice
Private 25135 1st Battalion Gloucester
Regiment
Died of Wounds 25th August 1916
B 26 35 St Sever Cemetery Rouen

HOBBS, G.C.H.A.
George Charles Henry Andrew
Bombardier 128333 'A' Battery 178th
Brigade Royal Field Artillery
Killed in Action 25th March 1918
23 years old
Son of Georg and Florence Amelia
Hobbs of 64 Argyle Street Gorse Hill
Bay 1 Arras Memorial

HODDINOTT, E.
Ernest
Corporal B/203075 9th Battalion Rifle
Brigade
Died 30th June 1918. 35 years old
Son of Edward and Emily Hoddinott of 43
The Street Stratton St Margaret
B 4 Selestat (Schlestadt) Communal
Cemetery
Born in Swindon

HODGES, S.P.
Sidney Philip
Private 306819 2/8th Battalion Royal
Warwickshire Regiment
Killed in Action 27th August 1916
22 – 25 Loos Memorial

HODGES, W.R.
William Ralph
Driver 7963 1st Battalion Gloucester
Regiment
Killed in Action 29th October 1914
27 years old
Son of John and Annie Hodges of 15
Victory Road Gloucester.
I H 44 Maroc British Cemetery Grenay.
Born in Swindon

HOLLAWAY, W.A.
William Alexander
Private 18864 5th Battalion Oxfordshire

and Buckinghamshire Light Infantry
Died 30th July 1916, No Burial Details
Born in Swindon

HOLE, C.H.
Charles Henry
Private 103921 2nd battalion Notting
hamshire and Derbyshire regiment
Killed in Action 10th October 1918
20 years old
Son of Herbert and Priscilla Hole of 20
Curtis Street.
111 C 10 Busiqny communal cemetery
extension. France

HOLLEY, F.T.J.
Francis Thomas John
Sapper 1338 1st (South Midland) Field
Company Royal Engineers
Killed in Action 23rd May 1915
22 years old
Son of Thomas John Holley 106 Somerset
Road, Knowle Bristol.
Lived in Beatrice Street
11 0 37 Trois Arbres Cemetery
Steenweck France

F.T. Holley

HOLLEY, S.P.
Stanley Percy
Private 42329 2nd Battalion Hampshire
regiment
Killed in Action 13th April 1918
18 years old.
Son of Walter Ayshford Holley 2 Gordon
Road Swindon
Panel 6 Ploegsteert memorial Belgium

HOLLICK, E.W.
Edward William
Private 10479 1st battalion Coldstream
Guards.
Killed in Action 29th September 1915
19 years old
Son of Jacob and Clara Annie Hollick
12 Drew Street Rodbourne
Panel 7 and 8 Loos memorial. France

E.W. Hollick

HOLLISTER, C.
Charles
Private 11415 16th Lancers
Killed in Action 17th January 1917
32 years old
Son of William and Margaret Hollister.
Husband of Jean Hollister 46 Crown
Avenue. Clydebank Glasgow.
V C 33 Lillers communal cemetery. France
Born in Swindon

HOLMES, A.
Albert
Private 22276 2nd Battalion Wiltshire
regiment
Killed in Action 2nd January 1917
24 years old
Son of Elizabeth Ann Holmes of 16
Avening Street Gorse hill
111 J 4 Warlincourt Halte British
cemetery. France
Lived in Swindon

HOLMES, H.
Henry
Lance Corporal 266074 C Company 2nd
Battalion Monmouthshire Regiment
Killed in Action 12th April 1918
38 years old
Son of Daniel and Elizabeth Holmes of 47
Bright Street Gorse Hill
Husband of Florence Holmes of 10 Dean
Street Larkbeare Exeter
Panel 10 Ploegsteert Memorial
Born in Swindon

HOLT, H.H.
Harold
Private S/43659 5th Battalion Seaforth
Highlanders (Formerly 22620 Veterinary
Corps)
Killed in Action 13th October 1918
A 28 Avesnes -Le Sec communal
cemetery extension. France
Born in Swindon.

HOLTHAM, W.C.
Wilfred Charles
Private 34128 2/4th Battalion (City of Bristol) Gloucester Regiment
Died 3rd December 1917
Panel 6 Cambrai Memorial

HOOD, N.
Norman
Private 29659 15th Battalion Hampshire Regiment
Killed in Action 7th October 1916
Pier and Face 7c and 7b Thiepval Memorial
Lived in Swindon

HOOK, S.P.
Sidney Pevensey
Private 5013 1/8th Battalion Warwickshire Regiment
Died of Wounds 29th December 1916
Brother of Edward James Hook of 62 Manchester Road
O IV C 7 St Sever Cemetery Rouen
Lived in Swindon

HOPKINS, C.J.
Charles John
Sapper 29959 6th AT Company Royal Engineers
Died 8th December 1915. 37 years old
Son of Charles and Nelly Hopkins of 'Fairfield' Goddard Ave.
Husband of Emily Hopkins of 77 Chickerell Road Weymouth
B C 2288 Weymouth Cemetery
Born in Swindon

HORLER, E.
Edwin
2nd Lieutenant 122 company Machine gun corps
Killed in Action 31st July 1917
29 years old
Son of John and Emma Horler Stoney Littleton Shoscombe Bath
1 E 21 Voormezeele Enclosure No 1 and 2 Belgium
Attended North Wilts Technical college in 1903 Remembered on its window
'He died in a foreign land, far from home and friend'

HORNBLOW, E.A.F.W.
Edward Albert Frederick William
Sergeant 44410 'B' Battery 84th Brigade Royal Field Artillery
Killed in Action 17th August 1917
28 years old
Son of Edward and Fanny Hornblow of 6 Church Street Caversham Reading
I A 24 Artillery Wood Cemetery
Born in Swindon

HORTON, V.J.
Victor John
2nd Lieutenant 'D' Battery 161st Brigade Royal Field Artillery
Died 2nd December 1917. 20 years old
Son of Noah Horton
II D 16 Duhallow ADS Cemetery. Belgium
Educated at Swindon High School and Dauntsey College, he volunteered in August 1914 when he was 17, and entered as a private in the Royal Field Artillery. He was promoted to corporal in August 1915. Sent to Gallipoli where he was wounded in October. He returned to service in France in February 1916. He served on the Somme with a French Mortar battalion attached to the RFA. He was promoted to Sergeant and was also mentioned in depatches and after offered a commission. He returned to England for Officer training and was sent back to France as a 2nd Lt in November 1916. On 2nd December 1917 he was in an advanced observation post with another Officer and7 OR's, when a shell scored a direct hit killing them all.

HOWARD, C.R.
Charles Robert
Private 3/230 5th Battalion Wiltshire Regiment
Killed in Action 10th August 1915
36 years old
Son of Joshua Frederick and Annie Howard of Swindon
Panel 156 to 158 Helles Memorial Dardanelles
Lived in Swindon

G. Howell

65

HOWELL, G.
George
Private 46451 2nd Battalion Wiltshire regiment
Killed in Action 5th November 1918
20 years old
Son of Mr F G Howell and Mrs L J Howell
75 Swindon road Wroughton
1 E 19 Cross road cemetery Fontaine – Au – Bois. France.
Born in Wroughton lived in Swindon Worked in L2 shop Loco dept GWR and remembered on memorial in Outlet Village Rodbourne.

HOWES, C.
Charles
Private 11014 1st Battalion South Wales Borderers
Killed in Action 31st October 1914
19 years old
Son of Henry and Margaret Howes of 61 Church Street Aberbargoed, Mon.
Panel 22 Ypres Menin Gate Memorial
Born in Swindon

HOWSE, R.
Richard
Rifleman Z/717 2nd Battalion Rifle Brigade
Killed in Action 28th October 1915
24 years old
Son of Richard and Harriett of Swindon
L16 Y Farm Military Cemetery Bois Grenier. France.

W.G. Howse

HOWSE, W.G.
William
Private 11347 116th company Machine Gun Corps.
Killed in Action 4th November 1916
19 years old.
Son of William and Florence Howse of Rodbourne Cheney.
111 E 26 Contay British cemetery Contay France

Was an apprentice boiler smith Loco and carriage dept GWR
Remembered on plaque in St Mary's Church Cheney Manor.

HUGHES, A.S.
Arthur Stanley
Private G/24501 10th Battalion East Kent regiment
Killed in action 21st September 1918
19 years old
Son of Henry and Louisa Hughes 518 Christiancy Street, Lansing Michigan USA
Panel 3 Vis – en – Artois memorial France.
Lived in Swindon

HUGHES, C.N.
Charles Normandale
Driver 860793 Royal Field Artillery
Died 3rd December 1918. 19 years old
Son of Albert Henry and Minnie Hughes
38 Morris Street Brother of Walter (below)
D192 Radnor street cemetery Swindon

HUGHES W.G.D.
Walter George David
Sapper 47266 97th Field company Royal Engineers
Killed in Action 26th June 1916
23 years old
Son of Albert Henry and Minnie Hughes
38 Morris Street
B2 Ville Sur Ancre communal cemetery France
Brother of Charles (previous)

HUGHES, G.J.
George James
Lance Corporal G/24845 11th Battalion Royal Sussex Regiment
Killed in Action 3rd April 1918
Panel 46 and 47 Pozieres Memorial

HUGHES, H.J.
Henry James
Gunner 119299 12th battery 35th brigade Royal Field Artillery
Killed in Action 9th October 1917
22 years old
Son of James and Alice Hughes 123 Morrison street
111 D 6 Birr Cross roads cemetery Belgium

HUGHES, S.J.A.
Stephen John Arthur
Private 21244 H company 2nd battalion
Wiltshire regiment
Died of wounds 23rd June 1917
20 years old
Son of Mr A and Mrs Rose Hughes of
30 Eastcott Road
X1V D 2A Ljissenthoek military cemetery.
Belgium

HUGHES, W.
William
Private 10468 1st battalion Wiltshire
regiment
Killed in Action 12th January 1917
11 C 41 London Rifle Brigade cemetery
Belgium
Born in Swindon

HUMPHRIES, E.C.
Ernest Charles
Private 18212 2nd battalion Wiltshire
Regiment
Died of Wounds 8th June 1915
30 years old
Son of Mr and Mrs C Humphries
Husband of L C Humphries 20 Ripley road
454 Christ Church cemetery

HUMPHRIES, F.
Frank
Private 9835 2nd Battalion Wiltshire
Regiment
Killed in Action 12th March 1915
Panel 33 and 34 Le Touret Memorial
Lived in Swindon

HUMPHRIES, L.J.
Levi John
Driver 504542 503rd field company
Royal Engineers
Killed in Action 6th September 1918
21 years old
Son of John and Agnes Humpheries 98
Commercial road
11 F 61 Bronfray Farm Military cemetery
Bray – Sur – Somme France.

HUNT, A.G.
Albert George
Private 20657 6th Battalion Wiltshire
Regiment
Killed in Action 20th March 1916
II U 3 St Vaast Post Military Cemetery
Richebourg L'Avour France
Lived in Swindon

HUNT, A.V.
Albert Victor
Private 8308 2nd Battalion Wiltshire
regiment
Killed in Action 5th July 1916
25 years old
Son of Thomas Stephen and Elizabeth
Hunt 19 Oxford street.
Pier and Face 13A Thiepval memorial
France.

HUNTER, W.S.
Wallace Samuel
2nd Lieutenant 9th Battalion Royal west
Kent regiment
Died 1st February 1916. 21 years old
Son of William Wallace Hunter and Mary
Hunter of 'Bonnie Doon' Beach road
Weston Super Mare.
C2015 Radnor Street cemetery Swindon
Lived in Swindon.

HUNTLEY, J.H. MM
John Henry
Gunner 87361 'C' Battery 62nd Brigade
Royal Field Artillery
Killed in Action 25th October 1916
26 years old
Son of Mrs Ellen Huntley of 9 Andover
Street Swindon
11 E 6 Guards Cemetery Lesboeufs
France

J.H. Huntley

HURFORD, S.J.
Stanley James
Private 1/3583 1st/5th Battalion East
Kent Regiment
Died 24th June 1916
VI S 8 Basra War Cemetery
Born in Swindon

HURSEY, T.H.
Private 18479 1st Battalion Wiltshire
Regiment
Killed in Action 4th May 1916
1 J 6 Ecoivres Military Cemetery, Mont
– St Eloi. France

HURST, W.J.
Private 22265 7th Battalion Gloucestershire Regiment
Died 15th December 1916
Panel 17 Basra Memorial, Iraq

W.J. Hurst

HUTCHINSON, J.F.
John Frederick
Private 240707 1st/5th battalion Gloucestershire regiment
Killed in Action 16th August 1917
Son of Robert and Eleanor Hutchinson 7 Strouds Hill Chiseldon
Panel 72 to 75 Tyne Cot memorial Belgium
Born in Swindon.

HYLAND, H.
Herbert
Sergeant S/7378 12th Battalion Argyle and Sutherland Highlanders
Died 8th May 1917. 22 years old
Son of William and Agnes Hyland of 37 Weston Street
Doiran Memorial Salonika
Born in Swindon

ILES, B.
Bert
Private 18247 2nd Battalion Wiltshire regiment
Killed in Action 8th July 1916
26 years old

Son of John and Elizabeth Iles,
20 Kingsdown Road, Stratton
Pier and Face 13a Thiepval memorial France.

IRELAND, R.P.
Reginald Pearse
Private 277774 10th Battalion Princess Louises Argyle and Sutherland Highlanders
Died 2nd October 1918. 21 years old
Son of Frederick and Mary Ireland 51 Inglefield Street Glasgow.
V1 1 8 Bellincourt British cemetery France.
Born in Swindon

ISAACS, F.H.
Frederick Hollaway
Private 203069 2nd Battalion Wiltshire Regiment
Died of wounds 3rd August 1917.
111 E 16 Mendingham Military cemetery Belgium
Formerly 4892 Somerset Light Infantry.
Lived in Swindon.

JACKSON, R.J.
Reginald John
Acting Corporal S/2439 Rifle Brigade
Died of wounds 13th February 1916
22 years old
Son of Mrs T Jackson 14 Ripley Road.
11 D 44 Ljissenthoek Military Cemetery Belgium

JACOBS, H.
Harry
Private 554 1st Battalion Welsh Guards
Killed in Action 27th September 1915
21 years old
Son of Mr and Mrs W Jacobs 0f 11 Cambria Cottages Canal Side
Panel 10 Loos Memorial

JAGO, R.
Reginald
Brigade Quarter Master Sergeant 218th
Brigade Royal Field Artillery
Died 16th May 1918. 45 years old
Husband of Mable Jago 35 Prospect
Place
Dehli War Memorial

He was the bandmaster for the Wessex Brigade in Swindon and a well known figure in the town. He was serving in India when he wrote the following letter to Mr A T Ward of the Victoria Hotel in June 1915.

'You have undoubtedly been expecting to hear from me before this, but I have been particularly busy up to now and after I finish my work in the office, I can assure you I don't feel like writing letters, especially with a temperature of 108' in the shade which we registered yesterday. I am glad to feeling very fit and well, taking all things into consideration and my shadow doesn't seem to grow much less. We are doing plenty of hard work and good training and pleased to say we are shaping up more like soldiers every day.

Our day starts of 5am. The first thing I see when I open my eyes is the 'Nappy' the Barber – a nigger, standing over me with a razor inhis hand shaving me! He has on more than one occasion, shaved me without me knowing it! (I must have been tired the night before). Well, we parade at 5.30am, harness up and hook in the guns and off on drill order. Parade at 6am. We have some very wild country to maneuver over and we usually get back at 8.30 or 9.00am. This occurs twice a week. Tuesday morning is spent in sports a very ingenious invention of the authorities to give the men a rest. This consists of driving, jumping, harness, fitting and other numerous competitions. I am pleased to say that the Wilts Battery have been very successful, winning four or five of the six events each week up to now.

We do nothing in the afternoon up to 5.00pm, then we have riding, gun laying, fuze setting etc p to about 6.30pm. We have a half days holiday on Tuesdays and Thursdays. I can assure you the men could do with it and the heat takes a great deal out of one. One of the things most wanted here is a good old English feed. We live very well considering the country, but when you see a sheep here, averages a weight of 16 lbs, you know there is a lot of meat. A leg of mutton would make a decent feed for one man, provided there are plenty of vegetables and bread. Again, fowls are plentiful here, very massive brutes they are too! We can buy them for 6p each but I think the price would work out at 3s a pound. I should say a fowl would weigh roughly half a pound if well stuffed – of course the heavier the stuffing the heavy the fowl. From an eating point of view, unless the stuffing is composed of minced meat, the amount of meat found would be the same as a sausage.

Our half day holidays, after 5pm are spent largely in sports, football and hockey, chiefly and we turn out some very decent football teams in different Batteries. The great drawback to football, is that they play on a gravel pitch, no grass pitches being available and it often occurs that half a dozen or more of the 22 players retire prematurely with gravel rash through being roughly grassed. Well, I get the Swindon Advertiser and the North Wilts Herald sent out every week, so keep in touch with the old country a little. I was greatly amused this week with the annual squabble about concerts in the Town Gardens. I have always, up to now, been interested in these and can look on this years and I expect future years, with an unbiased eye. This annual council meeting has always given the different musical representations of the bands in the concert, an opportunity of giving their knowledge. I notice with satisfaction, that one member, a bandsman of some years standing, has discovered the fact, that the better the band, the more attendances at the gardens and the larger the letting of chairs. Good! We are improving! I am also surprised to find a great change in another member of the council. I was always preferred to think of him as the member of the 'Tired mothers division of Swindon' He always advocated concerts in the recreation grounds. He has quite changed now, getting quite mercenary in fact! Well, do hope they will have a very successful season. It has become an old joke here on Wednesday or Sunday for someone to say 'whose up at the Town Gardens today Mr Jago?' It often sets me thinking though. I picture the band of well, let us say, the --- ----- playing martial airs to the crowded audience composed mostly of men who are sitting back in the chairs looking for bombs preferred. I say 'Composed largely of me'. Advisedly as we understand here that 'Sister Susies sewing shirts for soldiers'. Well I suppose most of the men or shall of say, some of them, have reasons and good ones for not joining the colours?

We Terriers, here in India, look as if we were out of it as far as actual warfare is concerned, but we have a certain amount of satisfaction knowing that we have relieved better soldiers to do the scrapping and are daily working hard to get efficient to take the field when we are relieved by, let us say, some of those who are at home listening to concerts in the Town Gardens. I must be getting rather serious so I will try and become normal again!.....

I have been enjoying splendid health in fact, all our boys are. I have had a touch of prickly heat, youwill know what that is having been in this country, but as everyone here says, it is a sign of good health. I havn't grumbled although I have felt inclined to doubt it. We are anxiously waiting for the monsoon season to start , due yesterday. We had a small shower of rain but we want a lot to cool off a bit! ......

JAMES, A.H.H.
2nd Lieutenant Royal Field Artillery
Died 20th December 1918. 24 years old
B3226 Radnor Street cemetery Swindon

2Lt. A.H. James

JAMES, F.A.
Frederick
Private 27806 2nd Battalion Hampshire Regiment
Killed in Action 27th May 1917.
11 D 3 Feuchy British cemetery
Born in Swindon

JAMES, H.
Herbert
Corporal 35796 'B' Bty 117 Brigade Royal Field Artillery
Died 14th October 1918. 29 years old
Husband of Mrs E V James, 9 Forest View, Manor Road, London
S11 X 15 St Sever Cemetery Extension Rouen, France
Born in Swindon

JAMES, S.
Samuel
Private 18039 2nd Battalion Wiltshire Regiment
Died of wounds 18th June 1915
Son of Mrs Winchurst, 13 Havelock Street, Swindon
11.C.43 Lillers Communal Cemetery

JANAWAY, R.L.P.
Reginald Lethbridge Pleydell
Corporal 9231 1st Bn Royal Berkshire Regiment
Killed in Action 1st November 1914
24 years old
Son of Catherine Elizabeth Dobson Baydon
Husband of May Olivier Ivy, House Farm Thicket, Wantage
Panel 45 Menin Gate Memorial, Belgium
Born in Swindon

JEFFCUTT, S.
Samuel
Private 10575 1st Battalion Wiltshire Regiment
Killed in Action 12th March 1915
Panel 53 Menin Gate Memorial, Belgium
Born in Swindon

JEFFERIES, A.H.
Albert Henry
Private M2/167494 562nd Motor Transport Company. Army Service Corps
Died 16th March 1919. 27 years old
Husband of Lilly Elizabeth Harman of The Square, High Street
570 Chiseldon Cemetery

JEFFERIES, W.
William
Private 9408 5th Battalion Wiltshire
Regiment
Died of Exposure 29th November 1915
23 years old.
Son of Joseph Jefferies 81 Gothic
Cottage, Kingshill Road.
11 E 14 Greenhill Cemetery   Dardanelles
Born in Swindon. Was a Labourer in Loco
and Carriage Dept GWR.

W. Jefferies

JEFFERIES, W.H.
William Henry
Private 33531 1st Battalion Wiltshire
Regiment.
Killed in Action 12th August 1917
Panel 53 Menin Gate Memorial. Belgium
Born in Swindon

JEFFERY, W.
William
Lance Corporal 552 22nd Battalion The
Rifle Brigade
Died 5th May 1919. 44 years old
Son of James and Elizabeth Jeffery
Husband of Emma Jane Jeffery of Church
Cross Buckfastleigh Devon
C G 795 Radnor Street Cemetery
"Your memory is as dear today as in the
hour you passed away"

JEFFORD, L.A.
Leslie Arthur
Acting Bombardier 302398 40th Battery,
10th Brigade, Canadian Field Artillery
Died of Wounds 27th May 1917
27 years old
Son of Mr and Mrs John Frederick Jefford
of Bath Road, Swindon
Husband of Hannah Headley Jefford of
20 Fisher Street, Toronto, Canada
1V B 13 Lapugnoy Millitary Cemetery,
France
Memorial in Christchurch, Old Town "In

Memory of Leslie Arthur Jefford, 3rd son
of John Frederick Jefford"

JENNER, A.J.
Arthur John
Pioneer 148096 5th Army HQ Signal
Company Royal Engineers
Killed in Action 27th October 1917
V B 7 Bard Cottage Cemetery, Belgium
Born in Swindon, lived in Wroughton

JEW, A.E.
Albert Edward
Chief Engine Room Artificer 2nd class
269506 Royal Navy HMS Invincible
Killed in Action 31st May 1916
39 years old
Son of Joseph and Elizabeth Jew of
Swindon
Husband of Issabelle Iddison, Three
Wood Close, Bessboro Road, Harrow,
Middlesex
15 Portsmouth Naval Memorial

JOBBINS, P.
Percy
Lance Corporal 19881 2nd Battalion
South Wales Borderers
Killed in Action 14th April 1917
33 years old
Son of Ezra and Eliza Jobbins of Ashley,
Tetbury, Gloucestershire
1 B 23 Feuchy Chapel British Cemetery
Wancourt, France
Born in Swindon

JOHNSEY, L.
Leonard
Sergeant 8541 2nd Battalion Wiltshire
Regiment
Killed in Action 9th April 1917
23 years old
Son of Isaac Johnsey and Flora K Harris of
7 Radnor Street
D 7 Neuville – Vitasse Road Cemetery,
France
Born in Swindon

JOHNSON, A.
Albert
Sapper 520211 565th A T Company Royal
Engineers
Killed in Action 18th September 1918
M 6 Ruyaulcourt Military cemetery.
France
Worked in L 2 Shop, Loco Department,
GWR and remembered on a Memorial in
The Outlet Village

JOHNSON, E.L.B.
Edmund Leake Burns
Corporal 29381 8th Battalion East Surrey
Regiment.
Killed in Action 18th September 1918
24 years old
Son of Mrs E Johnson of Ivy Nook, Shillets
Road, Upper Parkstone Dorset
I D 9 Unicorn Cemetery Vend'huile. Aisne
France

JOHNSON, H.E.
Henry Edward
Driver 109862 'A' Battery 104th Brigade
Royal Field Artillery
Killed in Action 25th November 1917
X1V D 13 The Huts Cemetery, Belgium

H.E. Johnson

JOHNSON, J.
John
Private 3/210 5th Battalion Wiltshire
Regiment
Killed in Action 27th September 1915
B XV11 5 Picta Military Cemetery
Gallipoli
Lived in Swindon

JOHNSON, R.
Reginald
Private 2386 2nd/3rd North Midland
Field Ambulance Royal Army Medical
Corps
Died 29th March 1916. 21 years old
Son of George and Alice Johnson 41
Midland Road Gloucestershire
3959 Gloucester Old Cemetery
Born in Swindon

JOHNSTON, C.W.T.
Cecil William
Sapper W520116 565th A T Company
Royal Engineers
Died 17th April 1917. 21 years old
Son of W and Julie Johnston of 11
Portsmouth Street Swindon
1 J 81 Varennes Military cemetery France

C.W.T. Johnson

JOLLIFFE, A.
Augustine
Private SD/2419 11th Battalion Royal
Sussex Regiment
Killed in Action 26th March 1918
Panel 46 and 47 Pozieres Memorial
Born in Swindon

JONES, A.W.E.
Private 28409 1st Battalion Hampshire
Regiment
Killed in Action 11th July 1918
19 years old
Son of Harry and Lily Kate Jones of 18
Poulton Street Gorse Hill
I K 2 Mont Bennanchon British Cemetery
Gonnehem France

JONES, C.E.
Charles Edwyn
Ordinary Seaman 2/6162 RNVR Royal
Navy London Depot (Crystal Palace)
Died 17th March 1918. 38 years old
Son of Edwyn Jones
Husband of Ethel Elizabeth Jones of
Church
Street Warmington nr Peterborough.
D 15 75 Radnor Street cemetery
Born in Swindon

JONES, T. DCM
Thomas
Sergeant 15377 12th Battalion Northumberland Fusiliers
Died of Wounds 17th December 1916
V F 28 Vermelles British Cemetery France
Born in Swindon, Lived in Stackton Durham

JONES, F.
Fred
Lance Corporal 34816 2nd Battalion Wiltshire Regiment
Killed in Action 30th May 1918
19 years old
Son of Fred and Emily Jones of 5 Marlborough Road
Soissons Memorial France
Born in Swindon

JONES, F.G.
Frederick George
Private 29342 6th Battalion Duke of Cornwalls Light Infantry
Killed in Action 16th October 1917
18 years old
Son of Mr G and Mrs E J Jones of 41 Cheltenham Street
XV G 15 Hooge Crater Cemetery
Formerly 19212 Royal Berkshire Regiment

JONES, F.W.
Francis Walter
Private 59237 25th Battalion Northumberland Fusiliers (Formerly 09640 Army Ordnance Corps)
Killed in Action 24th March 1918
19 years old
Son of Samuel N and Kate C Jones of 39 Elmina Road
Bay 2 – 3 Arras Memorial
Commemorated on plaque in St Barnabas Church Gorse Hill

JONES, G.E.
George Thomas
Private G/157 3rd Battalion Royal West Surrey Regiment
Died 2nd December 1915. 31 years old
Son of Richard and Sarah Louisa Jones of Swindon
1348 Fort Pitt Military Cemetery (Chatham Kent)
Born in Swindon

JONES, H.H.
Harry Harold
Private 70419 Berkshire Yeomanry
Killed in Action 24th August 1917
Panel 4 Jerusalem Memorial
Lived in Swindon

JONES, S.W.J.
Driver 935 3rd Wessex Brigade Ammunition Column Royal Field Artillery
Died 24th January 1915. 27 years old
Son of Mr J Jones of 52 Clifton Street
C 24 Radnor Street Cemetery Swindon

JONES, W.
William
Sergeant 13688 9th Battalion Worcestershire Regiment
Killed in Action 19th April 1916
20 years old
Son of Alfred and Elizabeth Jones
26 Enville Road Wall Heath Dudley Worcestershire
Panel 18 and 63 Basra War Memorial Iraq
Born in Swindon

W.A. Jones

JONES, W.A.
Wilfred Arthur
Private 10984 3rd Battalion Wiltshire Regiment
Died 11th March 1916. 25 years old
Son of Edwin and Elizabeth Annie Jones
38 Western Street Swindon
565 Portland Royal Naval Cemetery
Born in Swindon

JONES, W.H.
William Henry
Private 61587 135th company Machine gun corps (Formerly 20825 Wilts)
Killed in Action 21st April 1917
Panel 41 Basra Memorial Iraq
Born in Swindon

A.V. Jordan

JORDON, A.V.
Albert Victor
Driver 3715 Royal Field Artillery
Died 15th August 1915
Buried in Middle East (No Further Details)
Commemorated on Plaque in St
Barnabas Church Gorse Hill.

JOYCE, W.H.
William Henry
Lance Corporal 10216 2nd Battalion
Wiltshire Regiment
Killed in Action 27th September 1915
21 years old
Son of Annie Elizabeth Smith 2 High
Street Lambourne Wiltshire
Panel 107 Loos Memorial

The memorial at Paddington Station London, which commemorates 25,479 men of the GWR who served in the Great War. 2524 were lost in the conflict. Today the memorial also commemrates those of the Second World War.

KEEL, H.A.
Private 10983 1st Battalion Wiltshire Regiment
Killed in Action 12th March 1915
21 years old
Son of Albert and Margaret Keel
Qualicum Beach, Vancover Island
British Columbia
1 B 9 La Laiterie Military Cemetery
Born in Swindon

H.A. Keel

KEEN, J.
James
Private 5441 1st Battalion Berkshire Regiment
Killed in Action 15th May 1915
Panel 30 Le Touret Memorial
Born in Swindon

KEEN, P.G.
Percy George
Leading Stoker K/3608 H M Tug 'Desire'
Royal Navy
Died 24th January 1918. 28 years old
Son of Alfred and Susan Keen Eddington
Herne Bay Kent
Husband of Jessie Keen 80 Maygrove Road Brondesbury London
29 Chatham Naval Memorial
Born in Swindon

KEEN, W.H.
Wilfred Henry
Corporal 7967 6th Battalion Wiltshire Regiment
Killed in Action 3rd May 1917
25 years old
Son of Edith Barnes of 4 Avening Street
VI J 3 Vlamertinghe Military Cemetery

KEENE, A.
Arthur Daniel
Private 9528 1st Battalion Dorset Regiment
Killed in Action 22nd October 1914
21 years old

Son of Arthur and Elizabeth Keene of 37 Bathampton Street Swindon
Panel 22 and 23 Le Touret Memorial. France

KEEVIL, J.
John.
Private TF 207943 21st Battalion Middlesex Regiment
Killed in Action 25th march 1918
Bay 7 Arras memorial. France
Lived in Swindon

KENT, A.J.
Arthur James
Private 55221 1/5th Battalion Somerset Light Infantry (Formerly 4218 Wiltshire Regiment)
Died 24th October 1918
B 190 El Belah War Cemetery. Israel
Born in Swindon

KENT, C.
Fitter 5880 31st Brigade HQ Royal Field Artillery
Died 27th November 1918. 36 years old
Son of James and A Kent of 108 Chapel Street
507 Kirechkoi – Hortakoi Military cemetery

KENT, F.J.
Private 7569 2nd Battalion Wiltshire Regiment
Died 15th March 1920. 31 years old
Son of Thomas and Ann Kent of Groundwell Blunsdon
A 25 39 Radnor Street cemetery
Swindon

KENT, G.
George
Private 22412 5th Battalion Wiltshire Regiment
Killed in Action 15th January 1917
XVIII C 14 Amara War Cemetery Iraq
Born in Swindon

KENT, W.G.
William George
Private 13789 2nd Battalion Wiltshire Regiment
Killed in Action 15th June 1915
Panel 33 and 34 Le Touret Memorial France
Born in Swindon

KETHERO, C.E.
Charles Edwin
Private 22372 2nd Battalion Wiltshire Regiment
Killed in Action 2nd July 1916
21 years old
Son of William Allen and Annie Kethero of 33 Eastcott Hill
Pier and Face 13A Thiepval Memorial France
Lived in Swindon

KIBBLEWHITE, E.H.
Ernest Herbert
Sergeant 7252 5th Battalion Wiltshire Regiment
Killed in Action 10th August 1915
27 years old
Son of Mr and Mrs W Kibblewhite of Station Road Purton
Husband of Racheal Mary Kibblewhite (nee Rees) of 20 Bryn Road Neath Glam
Panels 156 and 158 Helles Memorial Dardanelles
Born in Swindon

Monmouthshire Regiment
Killed in Action 26th May 1915
Panel 50 Ypres Menin Gate Memorial
Born in Swindon

KING, E.T.
Edward Thomas
Private 8358 2nd Battalion Royal Berkshire Regiment
Died of Wounds 19th March 1915
CE 591 Grange Gorman Military Hospital Dublin Ireland (From George V hospital grounds)
Born in Swindon

KING, F.R.
Frederick Richard
Private 12407 7th Battalion Border Regiment
Killed in Action 9th July 1916
22 years old
Son of Mr and Mrs King of 14 Merton Street. Swindon
Plot 1 Row C Grave 53 Corbie Communal extension Cemetery

C. Kibblewhite

F. King

KIBBLEWHITE, G.F.
Private 163123 32nd Battalion Machine Gun Corps
Died 15th August 1919
X11 C 8 Cologne Southern Cemetery

KILBY, J.
John.
2nd Lieutenant 10th Battalion Gloucestershire Regiment (Attached 7th Trench Mortar Battery)
Died of Wounds 21st August 1916
27 years old
Son of Annie and Harry Kilby of Swindon
Forceville Communal Cemetery   France

KILMINSTER, H.W.
Herbert William
Sergeant 1124 2nd Battalion

KIRBY, C.P.
Charles Parker
2nd Lieutenant 33rd Battalion Australian Imperial Forces.
Died of Wounds 18th February 1917
27 years old
Son of John Peter (Clerk to the Swindon and Highworth board of Guardians) and Annie Susanna Kirby of Swindon
V11 B 13 Boulogne Eastern Cemetery
Charles had received his commission into the AIF. He had managed to visit his parents in Swindon while on leave from the front in the Autumn of 1916. He was later mortally wounded in France.
A letter was received by his father, from Lt-Col L J Morshead, 11th Feb 1917
' My dear Mr Kirby,
It is with feelings of deep regret that

76

I write to you of your sons wound received on the 8th. On that afternoon we bombarded the enemy trenches, and later the Boches retaliated with pineapple bombs. During the bombardment one of Lt Kirby's men was badly wounded and he at once hurried to his assistance and rendered First Aid under heavy shell fire. Hearing a bomb coming towards him, he leant over the wounded man to save him from further injury and took the whole of the explosion himself. His leg had to be amputated above the knee. Throughout your Son displayed great courage and coolness. I know that you will be very proud of him. You have reason to be so!' John (below) had been educated at Sanford Street school and had been a Lieutenant in the Hertfordshire Volunteers. He and Charles had emigrated to Australia to set up a farm together in New South Wales which they named 'Swindon' Farm. When war broke out he applied for a commission but was refused. He decieded then to join the ranks of the AIF. By January 1915 he had been promoted to Colour Sergeant. He left for Gallipoli, witnessing the destruction of the German ship the Emden, on route. He wrote to his father describing the action. He was later killed in action in Gallipoli.

KIRBY, J.H.
John Hopkins
Company Sergeant Major 904 1st Battalion Australian Imperial Forces
Killed in Action 2nd May 1915
35 years old
Son of John Peter and Annie Susanna Kirby of Swindon
12 Lone Pine Memorial. Gallipoli
The brothers are commemorated at Christchurch and on a family plot alongside their Parents.

KIRBY, G.F.
George Felix
Private 14/1263 'B' Company 14th Battalion Warwickshire Regiment
Killed in Action 23rd July 1916
20 years old
Son of Felix John and Marianne Kirby of Middle Barton Oxford
Pier and Face 9a 9b and 10b Thiepval memorial
Born in Swindon

KIRBY, M.
Manfred.
Private 881 1st Battalion Wiltshire Regiment
Killed in Action 31st October 1914
23 years old
Son of William and Sarah Kirby 103 Eastcott Hill
Panel 33 and 34 Le Touret Memorial France

KNAPP, C.E.
Charles Edward
Corporal 218907 20th Broad Gauge Railway Operating Coy Royal Engineers
Killed in Action 16th April 1918
39 years old
Son of Edward Thomas and Caroline Elizabeth Knapp
Husband of Lilian Knapp of 79 Ashford Road
XXV1 FF 8A Lijssenthoek Military Cemetery Belgium

C.E. Knapp

KNEE, A.E.
Archibald Edward.
Lance Corporal 21233 'D' Company 1st Battalion Wiltshire Regiment
Killed in Ac tion 29th May 1916
25 years old
Son of Mr and Mrs F Knee 31 Catherine Street Swindon
V D 13 Etaples Military Cemetery

KNEE, D.A.
Dennis Arthur
Gunner RMA/13723 Royal Marine Artillery HMS 'Vanguard'
Died 9th July 1917 22 years old
Son of Arthur and Eliza Knee
78 Medgbury Road Swindon
27 Portsmouth Naval Memorial

KNIGHT, F.
Frank
Private 12367 7th Battalion Wiltshire

Regiment
Killed in Action 24th April 1917
35 years old
Son of Thomas Knight of Durrington
Salisbury
Husband of Lilian Eva Knight of 28
Redcliffe Street
Doiran Memorial Salonika

F. Knight

KNIGHT, G.E.
George Edward.
Private 12238 7th Battalion Wiltshire
Regiment
Killed in Action 24th April 1917
24 years old
Son of Mrs Sarah Ann Shergold 12 Hinton
Street Gorse Hill
Doiran Memorial Salonika

G.E. Knight

LACEY, H.
Harry
Acting Sergeant 9755 'C' Company 1st
Battalion Royal Berkshire Regiment
Killed in Action 16th May 1915
21 years old
Son of Clifford Charles and Mary Lacey of
63 Sherman Road Reading
Panel 30 Le Touret Memorial
Born in Swindon

LAFFORD, G.V.
George Vernon
Rifleman Z/102 7th Battalion Rifle
Brigade
Died of Wounds 13th October 1917

22 years old
Son of John William and Mary Lafford of
317 Ashley Road Parkstone Dorset
I P 46 Godewaersvelde British Cemetery.
France
Born in Swindon

LAMBDIN, R.G.
Reginald George
Pte 46993 C Company 2nd Battalion
Wiltshire Regiment
Died 4th November 1918. 19 years old
son of John and Elizabeth Lambdin 10
Rayfield Grove
Near North West Corner Eth Communal
cemetery
Born Stratton St Margaret.

R.G. Lambdin

LAMBERT, E.A.
Ernest
Pte 22058 6th Battalion Wiltshire
Regiment
Died 14th April 1916
II E 24 Le Touret Military Cemetery
Richebourge L'Avoue
Born in London Lived in Swindon

LAMBERT, F.C.
Frederick Charles
Private 10519 46th Field Ambulance
Royal Army Medical Corps
Died of Wounds 24th April 1917
24 years old
Son of Robert and Mary Ann Lambert of
Chelsea London
III D I Duisans British Cemetery Etrun
Born in Swindon

LAMBOURNE, A.H.
Albert Henry
Private 18561 5th Battalion Wiltshire
Regiment
Died of Wounds 8th August 1915
17 years old
Son of Charles and Martha Louisa
Lambourne of 6 Cheltenham Street
Panel 156 -158 Helles Memorial
Dardanelles

LAMBOURNE, E.
Driver 1800 1st S W Mntd Brigade Field
Ambulance Royal Army Medical Corps.
Accidentally Killed 3rd June 1915
23 years old
Son of Mr C Lambourne of Deacon Street
B3316 Radnor Street Cemetery

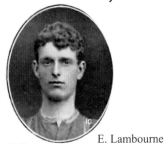
E. Lambourne

LANDER, C.C.
Private 50523 1/6th Battalion North Staf-
fordshire Regiment
Died 18th May 1918. 33 years old
Son of John and Meg Lander
Husband of Susan Lander 12 Queens
Street Father of 5 young children
C 3514 Radnor Street Cemetery

A reservist. He died in The City of London
Hospital.

LANDFEAR, W.J.
William John
Private 13705 1st Battalion Wiltshire
Regiment
Killed in Action 12th March 1915
Panel 53 Menin gate memorial Ypres
Born in Stratton

Sqt A.E. Lanfear

LANE, W.A.G.
William Alexander Gunning
Bombardier 114614 351st Siege Battery
Royal Garrison Artillery
Killed 13th June 1917. 40 years old
Son of James and Ellen Lane
II M 7A Wimereux Communal Cemetery

LANFEAR, A.E.
Alfred Edward
Sergeant 3/698 2nd Battalion Wiltshire
Regiment
Killed in Action 17th May 1915
V A 6 Pont-Du-Hem Military cemetery La
Gorgue
Born in Broad Hinton Lived in Swindon

C. Lang

LANG, C.
Cecil
Private 10573 1st Battalion Wiltshire
Regiment
Killed in Action 16th June 1915

26 years old
Son of Mrs Mercy Lang 46 Havelock Street
Panel 53 Menin Gate memorial Ypres
Born in London Lived in Swindon

LAPPINGTON, W.F.
William Frederick
Private 20225 1st Battalion Dorsetshire Regiment
Killed in Action 8th March 1918
XLVIII D 5 Poelcapelle British Cemetery
Born in Swindon Lived in Lechlade.

LAPWORTH, J.
Joseph
Private 240468 5th Battalion Gloucestershire Regiment
Died 8th March 1919. 21 years old
Son of William and Sabina Lapworth of 55 Cheltenham Street
D1084 Radnor Street cemetery

LAUNCHBURY, C.E.
Charles Edwin
Private 9984 6th Battalion Oxfordshire and Buckinghamshire Light Infantry
Died 27th February 1917
Pier and Face 10a and 10d Thiepval memorial

LAW, H.G.
Harold George
Private 21036 5th Battalion Wiltshire Regiment
Died 25th January 1917
XVII A 13 Amara war cemetery
Born and lived in Swindon

H.G Law

LAW, J.W.A.
John William Arthur
Lance-Corporal 10433 1st Battalion Wiltshire Regiment
Killed in Action 12th March 1915
20 years old

Son of Maurice and Agnes Mary Law of 122 Morrison Street
Panel 53 Menin Gate Memorial Ypres
Born in Malmsbury Lived in Swindon

LAWES, A.G.
Private 41685 8th Battalion Royal Inniskilling Fusiliers
Died of Wounds 4th September 1917
19 years old
Son of Albert and Elizabeth Lawes of 5 Ponting Street
XXV O 7A Etaples Military cemetery.
He had been Injured in one leg which resulted in amputation and he died shortly after. He had been educated in Sanford Street School and had worked for C H Carpenter Grocers of Manchester Road.

LAWRENCE, F.C.
Frederick Cyril
Lance Corporal 285148 'C' Coy 2/1st Battalion Oxfordshire and Buckinghamshire Light Infantry
Killed in Action 2nd September 1917
21 years old
Son of Harry and Minnie Lawrence of 13 Lethbridge Road
Panel 96 – 98 Tyne Cott
He had been working for Halfords Cycle Company in Regent Street. He was transferred to the Bath branch then promoted to management in the Southampton depot. In November 1915, he enlisted and joined the Cycle Corps of the Hampshire Regiment. He was later moved to the Royal Ordnance College, Woolwich in June 1916, where he passed out at the top of the list of 120 competitors. He was promoted to Lance Corporal and made an artificer. He qualified in May 1917, as a Bombing Instructor. Just after, he was sent to France. A letter he wrote home to his parents on August 22nd 1917, was as follows.
'During the past few weeks, I have been up the line and over the top. I am safe but nerves a little shakey. Don't worry. I will tell you a few of my experiences. We went into the front line on Monday night, walked up there in the open. The trench was just a lot of shell holes connecting up, affording little cover. On Tuesday morning, Fritz got his wind up and thought we were going to attack.

He dropped a barrage fire on our trench. It lasted about an hour. I got partially buried. On wednesday morning we attacked. Our barrage was something terrific. I never thought it would be anything like it really was. I went right through to the objective. Our fellows fell like rain. I jumped down into a shell hole and an explosive bullet from a German Machine Gun, hit the sole of my right boot and embedded itself there. I thought it had gone into my foot, but was much surprised to find it had not touched me. It only stunned my foot for about 3 hours. Owing to the flanks not coming up, our fellows had to withdraw. I could not walk, so I lay in that shell hole from 5.15am until dark at 9.15pm, about 16 hours. I had 4 wounded fellows with me. We dared not move because there was a German machine gun each side of us with heaps of snipers about. The Germans tried to counter attack in the afternoon and our people dropped a barrage on the ground where we were. A shell burst about a yard from me and a large piece of earth hit me in the face, breaking the skin in several places. That night we went back to the English line, about 800 yards behind and arrived about 2am. I fell in the enemy's wire in the dark and cut my right wrist a little. All day Thursday, we kept low in the new line that had pushed forward. Only one German shell dropped in it causing 3 casualties. On Thursday night we went about 200 yards into no mans land and dug another trench behind 2 enemy strongpoints which were causing a lot of trouble. We stopped out there until we were relieved by another battalion. At 11.30pm, we made our way back very quickley and a train carried us to our billetts. When we arrived we were made a great fuss of and fed well. I never want to have another time like that I had in no mans land. I am lucky to be alive. Many of my pals are wounded or killed. It would be easy to write a book about it all.
PS. We are still smiling. Going to see a concert party tonight.
Just a few days later, his parents received another letter, written by CQMS W F Taylor of the Oxs and Bucks Ll.
'Dear Madame , I am sorry to inform you that your Son, Lance Corporal 285148 F C Lawrence was killed early this morning. He was one of the carrying party when a shell exploded among them, killing your son instantly. Please accept the deepest sympathy from officers NCOs and men of C coy and may God comfort you in your great loss'

LAWRENCE, G.W.
George Wellman
Private 8330 2nd Battalion Wiltshire Regiment
Killed in Action 19th January 1915
I H 49 Rue-Davis Military Cemetery Fleurbaux
Born in Swindon

LAWRENCE, H.
Harry
Private 8545 2nd Battalion Royal Berkshire Regiment
Killed in Action 10th March 1915
No Burial details
Born in Swindon lived in Durham

LAWRENCE, H.H.A.
Herbert Henry Allan
Pioneer 147264 5th Battalion Special Brigade, Royal Engineers
Died 26th April 1916. 19 years old
Son of Frederick John Harris and Maria Lawrence of The Square Baydon.
Plot C Row 3 Grave 13 Calais Southern Cemetery
Lived in Swindon

LAWRENCE, H.C.
Henry Charles
Private 7133 1st Battalion Wiltshire Regiment
Died of Wounds 20th October 1914
26 years old
Husband of Ada Lawrence (nee Wood) of 6 The Castle York
Panel 33 and 34 Le Touret Memorial
Born in Swindon

LAWRENCE, J.
Jesse
Private B178 6th Battalion Royal Munster Fusiliers
Died of Wounds 16th August 1915
30 years old
Son of Harry and Annie Lawrence of Cromwell Street
Husband of Martha Lawrence of Hook Piece Wootton Bassett
Panel 185 – 190 Helles Memorial Dardanelles

of 142 Albion Street
VII D 6 Harelbeke New British Cemetery

J. Lawrence

LAWRENCE, W.J.
William John
Private 18227 2nd Battalion Wiltshire Regiment
Killed in Action 9th April 1917
V E 35 Warncourt British Cemetery
Born in Stratton

LEA, T.
Thomas
Private 1074 6th Battalion Leinster Regiment (Previously 13408 Wiltshire Regt)
Killed in Action 11th August 1915
Panel 184 and 185 Helles memorial Dardanelles
Lived in Swindon

LEE, F.G.
Frederick George
Private G/41573 1st Battalion Middlesex Regiment
Died 14th December 1916. 30 years old
Son of FG and EL Lee of 14 Greenford Avenue Hanwell Middlesex
Pier and Face 12D and 13B Thiepval Memorial
Born in Swindon

LEE, G.
George
Acting Bombardier 94703 Royal Field Artillery
Died of Wounds 28th April 1917
21 years old
Son of Henry and Mary Ann Lee of Church Road Liddington
I H 9 St Nicolas British cemetery
Born in Swindon

LEE, S.G.
Sapper 342205 205th Field Company Royal Engineers
Died 20th October 1918. 19 years old
Son of Sidney and Ada Lee

S.G. Lee

LEGG, G.
George
Gunner 91143 118th Battery Royal Field Artillery
Killed in Action 24th September 1914
20 years old
Son of Mr and Mrs Richard Legg of 23 Devizes Road
La Ferte-Sous-Jouarre Memorial

LEGG, S.H.
Septimus Henry
Private 10435 1st Battalion Wiltshire Regiment
Killed in Action 16th June 1915
35 years old
Husband of Lily Legg (nee Edwards) of 29 Drew Street.
Panel 53 Menin Gate.
Born in Middlesborough

LEGGETT, E.G.
Ernest George
Lance-Corporal 10982 1st Battalion Wiltshire Regiment
Killed in Action 3rd September 1915
21 years old
Son of Mr W and Mrs I Leggett of 282 Ferndale Road
Panel 53 Menin Gate Memorial

LEGGETT, W.S.
William Stephen
Lance – Corporal 10981 1st Battalion Wiltshire Regiment
Killed in Action 16th June 1915
22 years old
Son of Mr W and Mrs I Leggett of 282

Ferndale Road
Panel 53 Menin Gate Memorial
Brother of Ernest (Above)
In a letter to his mother, Ernest wrote of Williams death -
" We made the charge all right, and then we had to retire a little, and dear old Bill got hit, just about a dozen yards from the trench we were holding. They carried him into one of the dugouts and I was very soon with him and stayed by his side until he passed away. We did everything for him that we possibly could. He was a brave chap and very happy, right up to the last. I was proud of the way he stuck it out. Tell his pals that he died like a Soldier and a Man."
Lance-Corporal F Parker, 1st Wilts of Ferndale Road, wrote of the incident to his own Mother. -
" Two companies were in the charge. First of all, our artillery bombarded the German trenches. I don't know how many Germans would have lived through it all. Our artillery were at their best and the Germans lost a tremendous lot. The Germans prayed for our chaps not to kill them. I am sorry to say Billy Leggett was killed. One of our chaps told me that Ern was with him as well and he said that Billy died very calm and like a hero. He was shot through the stomach and the bullet came out at the hip."

Ernest Leggett

William Legget

LEIGHFIELD, I.J.
Isaac James
Private 8119 1st Battalion Wiltshire Regiment
Killed in Action 20th February 1915
24 years old
Son of William and Ellen Maria Leighfield of Shaw.
Panel 53 Menin Gate Memorial
Lived in Swindon

LEIGHFIELD, S.F.
Sydney Francis
Driver 3017 31st Brigade, Ammunition Column, Royal Field Artillery
Died 19th September 1918. 22 years old
Son of Mr F and Mrs J Leighfield 56 Edinburgh Street
305 Mikra British Cemetery Kalamaria.

LEONARD, E.J.
Private 8/10220 52nd Battalion Devonshire Regiment
Died 1st March 1918. 18 years old

Son of Mr and Mrs Pewsey of 2 Ladds Mill Swindon
491 Christ Church Cemetery Swindon

LEONARD, F.C.
Frederick Charles
Driver 860887 3rd Wessex Brigade Royal Field Artillery
Died 6th October 1918
Face 2 Kirkee 1914-1918 Memorial India
Born in Swindon

F.C. Leonard

LEONARD, P.H.
Percy Harold
Gunner 183782 A Battery 173rd Brigade
Royal Field Artillery
Killed in Action 18th July 1917
19 years old
Son of George and Elizabeth Louisa
Leonard of 7 Warwick Road
I G 18 Vlamertinghe New Military
Cemetery Belgium
Worked in Loco and Carriage Dept GWR

LESTER, H.N.
Harry Nevill
Private M2/174851 695th Mechanical
Transport Company Army Service Corps.
Died 3rd August 1916. 23 years old
Son of Frederick and Annie Lester
III N 7 Basra War Cemetery
Born in Swindon

LEVEAUX, R.F.H.
Reginald Frederick Herbert
Lance-Corporal 37223 9th Battalion
Norfolk Regiment
Killed in Action 8th October 1918
Panel 4 Vis-en-Artois Memorial France
Born in Swindon

LEWIS, C.
Charles
Corporal 504770 12th Field Company
Canadian Engineers
Died 28th October 1917
11 35 Ypres Reservoir Cemetery

LEWIS, E.
Edward
Gunner 4335 12th Heavy Battery Royal
Garrison Artillery
Died 19th November 1915
Plot 1 Row B Grave 9 Corbie Communal
Cemetery. France
Born in Swindon

LEWIS, F.J.   MM
Frederick James
Sergeant 43518 15th Signal Company
Royal Engineers
Died 17th January 1918. 30 years old
Son of Caroline Lewis of Lambeth
London
III D 4 Anzin St Aubin British Cemetery
France

LEWIS, H.
Harry
Private 8805 2nd Battalion Wiltshire
Regiment
Died of Wounds 23rd October 1914
21 years old
Son of Eliza Lewis of Griffins Barn Cottage
Malmesbuy Charlton London
D. 19 Ypres Town Cemetery
Born in Swindon

LEWIS, H.
Harry
Gunner 111609 172nd Brigade Royal
Field Artillery
Died of Wounds 1st February 1917
20 years old
Son of Francis and Harriett Lewis of
Commonplatt
IC 20 Hazebrouck Communal Cemetery
France
Born in Swindon

LEWIS, H.A.
Harold Augustus
Private 11192 5th Battalion Wiltshire
Regiment
Died of Wounds 2nd February 1917
XXV Amara War Cemetery
Born in Chippenham Lived in Swindon

LEWIS, H.S.
Henry Stephen
Private 26252 1st Battalion Wiltshire
Regiment
Killed in Action 12th April 1918
20 years old
Son of Benjamin James and Sarah
Georgina Lewis of 37 Jennings Street
Rodbourne
X Q 9 Strand Military Cemetery Belgium

F.J. Lewis

LEWIS, J.W.
John William
Sapper 269356 12th Light Railway Operations Company Royal Engineers (Formerly 22001 Wiltshire Regt)
Died of Wounds 22nd July 1917
44 years old
Husband of Mrs Lewis of 47 Winifred Street.
I V 6 Trois Arbres Cemetery Steenwerck
Born in South Marston Lived in Swindon
He was in hospital at a casualty clearing station in France, when a German plane dropped a bomb on the hospital. He had worked in the GWR. When he was 17, he joined the army and enlisted into the Ox and Bucks Light Infantry. He served in the Boer War where he was wounded and discharged with a pension. He returned to work in the GWR works and later worked for Vickers in Barrow in Furness. When war broke out he returned to Swindon and enlisted.

LEWIS, T.A.   Croix de Guerre.
(Belgium) Thomas Arthur
Corporal 387134 6th Seige Company Royal Engineers
Killed in Action 2nd November 1918
24 years old
Son of Mr and Mrs Lewis of Swindon
Husband of Ellen Lewis of 12 Brunel Street
VI F 53 Terlincthun British Cemetery Wimille. France

T.A. Lewis

LIDDINGTON, W.E.
Wilfred Edmund
Private 8314 2nd Battalion Hampshire Regiment
Died 6th August 1915. 29 years old
Son of John and Sarah Liddington
Panel 125-134 225-226 228-229 and 328
Helles Memorial Dardanelles

LIDDEN, W.
Walter
Private 8016 2nd Battalion Wiltshire Regiment
Killed in Action 24th October 1914
Panel 53 Menin Gate Memorial Ypres
Lived in Swindon

LIDDON, J.H.
John Henry
Lance-Sergeant 22499 2nd Battalion Wiltshire Regiment
Killed in Action 27th December 1917
XVI J II Hooge Crater Cemetery
Born in Swindon

LINDSEY, E.A.
Ernest Albert
Private 19454 6th Battalion Wiltshire Regiment.
Killed in Action 2nd July 1916
19 years old
Son of Mr and Mrs Lindsey of 130 Beatrice Street
Pier and Face 13A Thiepval Memorial
Born in Swindon
Worked in L2 Shop Loco Dept and remembered on memorial in the Outlet Village.
'My dear Mother, just a few more lines in answer to your welcome letter which found me in the pink. Well dear Mother, I am very pleased to hear Flo went up and saw Will in Reading and so pleased to hear he is getting on fine. Well dear Mother, you say Will may be home this weekend, well I am sorry to say I shan't be in England then, for I have to tell you, by the time that you get these lines I shall be in France, for I am off tonight. I do hope the Lord will guard you in my absence. I shall go with a good heart and come back again, for I am going to march straight through to Berlin without stopping, for nothing can stop the Wilts.

Dear Mother, I expect to join the 1st Wilts, so I shall be the 1st Wilts instead of the 8th. Well dear Mother, I am sorry I can't see Will before I go, but we must make the best of it. Well dear Mother, as you say, you have heard from Dad and that he is alright and he said he wants to come home, I hope to see him. I am so sorry to hear that poor little Arthur is not out yet, well I do hope he will soon be home. Well dear Mother, I expect Fred told you that I had a good Easter.

As you say, I should have liked to have been home along with those nice girls. Well not half, for it would have been worth a lot to speak to a girl. Well you would not realise how we are situated up here..................
Well, give my love to those girls and tell them I have gone at last to the front. Mother, I do hope you won't put yourself about me, for I shall be alright and I will write as soon as I get a chance. That will be my first thing to do after I get out of the trenches. Well I can tell you, Edie is terribly upset about it, but as I told her, she must make the best of it and wait for me if she wants me. For as the Country needs me and I must go and make the best of it. I am sorry to hear that Fred had been a rascal this holiday. Well the best thing you could do, would be to send him in the Army and make a man of him. Tell him that I broke my watch last week when we were playing football and one took my watch to be a football! Well never mind. I must close now with love. Don't write anymore until you hear from me, as I can't leave you an address yet. Goodbye and God bless you. Till we meet again. Will write more next time.
Your everloving son, Ern xxx.
Ps tell Mrs Heath, 65 Argyle Street.
His father John Lindsey was serving in the Royal Engineers. Two brothers of his, William and Frederick also served and survived. Edie was his Fiancee who lived at 65 Argyle Street. She never married.

LITTLE, A.W.R.
Sergeant 520087 Royal Engineers
Died 7th February 1918. 25 years old
Son of William Charles and Clara Ann Little of 39 Telford Road
I 12 St Mary's Church Rodbourne Cheney

A.W.R. Little

LITTLE, H.G.
Private 44064 9th Battalion Kings Own Yorkshire Light Infantry
Died 25th April 1917
A70 Cojeul British Cemetery St Martin Sur Cojeul

H.G. Little

LODER, R.A.
Reginald Arthur
Private 10274 5th Battalion Wiltshire Regiment
Died of Wounds 28th January 1917
XIII B 7 Amara War Cemetery
Born in Swindon Lived in Sutton, Surrey

R.A Loder

LOCKE, H.S.
Harold Smith
Private 263059 2/8th Battalion Worcestershire Regiment
Killed in Action 19th August 1917
Panel 75 – 77 Tyne Cot Memorial
Born in Swindon

LOCKEY, A.W.
Arthur William
Private 19102 5th Battalion Wiltshire Regiment
Killed in Action 25th January 1917
19 years old
Son of Charles and Caroline Lockey of 4 Winifred Street
XVII A 10 Amara War Cemetery

LOCKEY, T.
Thomas
Private 9777 5th Battalion Wiltshire
Regiment
Killed in Action 10th August 1915
34 years old
Son of Thomas Lockey of Blind Lane
Lambourne
156 – 158 Helles Memorial

LOMAS, G. DCM
George Archibald Colin
2nd Lieutenant 1/20th London Regiment
Killed in Action 22nd May 1916
Son of Rev. Charles and Kate E Lomas 149
Dornley Road Gravesend Kent
III E 6 Caberet Rouge British Cemetery
Souchez Arras
Attended Swindon Technical College
Victoria Road and remembered on its
Stained Glass window.

LONG, C.H.
Charles Henry
Private 6256 1st Battalion North
Lancashire Regiment
Killed in Action 28th September 1914
La Ferle – Sous -Jouarre Memorial France
Born in Swindon Brother of Edward
(below)

LONG, E.
Edward
Lance-Corporal 5924 1st Battalion North
Lancashire Regiment
Died (in captivity) 31st March 1915
XIII D I Berlin South Western Cemetery
Born in Swindon Brother of Charles
Henry (above)

LONG, T.
Thomas
Private 10521 1st Battalion Wiltshire
Regiment
Killed in Action 16th June 1915
Son of Worthy and Minnie Long of South
Cerney
Panel 53 Ypres Menin Gate Memorial

LOOKER, S.
Samuel
Gunner 3085 D Battery 107th Brigade
Royal Field Artillery
Killed in Action 4th April 1918
A 32 Morevil Communal Cemetery Allied
Extension

LORD, R.C.
Robert Charles
Private 50758 1st Battalion Somerset
Light Infantry
Killed in Action 21st October 1918
19 years old
Son of Robert Tanstall and Ada Georgina
Lord of 6A High Cowes
Panel 4 Vis-en-Artois Memorial
Lived in Swindon

R.C. Lord

LOVE, W.R.
Died No Details

LOVEDAY, A.W. DCM + Bar
Arthur William
Company Sergeant Major 6975 B
Company 1st Battalion Wiltshire
Regiment
Killed in Action 18th September 1918
31 years old
Son of Mr P Loveday of 106 Stafford
Street.
Husband of Ellen Hilda Loveday
31 Stafford Street
VIII E 17 Gouzeaucourt New British
Cemetery.
Born in Swindon

In December 1916, Arthur wrote to his
wife, telling her of his exploits when he
won his first DCM.
' I am going to tell you what occurred last
Sunday morning, December 19th, which I
will never forget as long as I live. About 4.30
am a young officer of my company asked
me and another sergeant , if we would go
with him across to the German trenches
and do some damage, and if possible, take
a prisoner. We volunteered and got seven
other men as well. So off we went over

the parapet, and crawled across to the German barbed wire. Armed with bombs, revolvers and heavy sticks weighted with iron. We cut our way through their wire and crawled on through water and mud, until we heard some Germans coughing badly. We went as near to their dug-out as we possibly could then the Officer, myself and the other Sergeant decided to get into their trench and take our chances, the others remaining on the parapet. So in we went and as we got in we were up to our knees in mud and water. The noise at this aroused the Johnnies, and I saw one big German well over 6' in height step outside the dug out and then draw back. He must have seen us. I gave the other two the tip and around the corner we popped.

A.W. Loveday

The Officer held the big German up with his revolver and then came two more from the dug out. One we had to shoot, and the other got away down the trench. I shall never forget what happened after. As our young Officer was asking the big fellow at the point of the revolver to become a prisoner, he knocked our Officer's arms up and grappled him around the waist nearly hugging the life out of him and all the time shouting at the top of his voice and hadn't he some lungs. We hit him on the head and put two shots into him and even then he would not give in. I shall never forget the look of defiance on his face. Well, during this struggle the shouting and firing had roused all the Germans in the trench and down they came in large numbers towards us throwing bombs and firing as they came, shouting also at the tops of their voices. We saw then that it was life or death so my chums put two bullets into the big Germans head. We had to shoot the poor fellow in the head though he did not deserve it. He was a brave soldier and fought to the last. When the rest got to within 15 yards of us I had the presence of mind to pitch two bombs right in amongst them and oh you should have heard the cries and the moaning. That was a bit of luck for us for it stopped them and gave us a chance to get out of their trench and run for it, which we did, reaching our own trench quite safe but exhausted. I shall never forget the sight – bombs and bullets flying all around us, the flashes and spits of flame from their rifles, the bursting of the bombs, the blood and the shouts of agony and pain. We were lucky in not one of us being hit, the only damage done was that I had a large hole torn through the right sleeve of my jacket, cardigan and shirt by a piece of German bomb but it never so much as scratched my arm, a bit of luck for me I can tell you. I offered a prayer when I came back as well as before going out. Our Colonel and my Captain and Medical Officer were waiting and congratulated us when we came sauce and the daring of it to get into the enemies trench, three of us and kill and wound about 15 of them and then get back safe and well. I shall never do it again.'

A further letter to his wife dated 28th December including the following;
'When I rejoined the Regiment yesterday, I was met with congratulations from my Officers down to my chums. I have won the DCM for bravery, my pal has done the same and my young Officer the Military Cross for that affair I told you of.........................'
The raid was carried out by 2nd Lieutenant Cordon, Sergeants Loveday and Ingram, and 7 other ranks. The purpose was to capture a double sentry post. His DCM was presented to him and Sgt Ingram on 12th February 1916 by Corps Commander Sir Charles Ferguson.

Arthur Loveday had gone to France as a Private at the outbreak of war. He had been wounded twice up to the time he wrote the letters and had a lucky escape when a snipers bullet penetrated and became embedded in two cartridges in his bandolier which luckily failed to explode. A postcard commemorating this event was published in Swindon. He later won his second DCM. On 18th September 1918 the battalion was in the line at Equancourt, in France. It went into action behind an artillery barrage.

It proved to be a successful operation. The loss to the battalion was 12 killed including Arthur Loveday, and 75 wounded.

LOVEDAY, F.
Frederick
AM I 11201 No 1 Transport Depot RAF
Died 6th November 1918
Husband of Adeline Loveday
10 Summers Street
C 3524 Radnor Street Cemetery
Died as a result of Influenza.

F. Loveday

LOVEDAY, H.U.
Hedley Uriah
Private 37199 Duke of Cornwalls Light Infantry
Died 6th October 1919. 20 years old
Son of Uriah and Mary Loveday of 40 Dryden Street
D 1519 Radnor Street Cemetery.

LOVEDAY, R.G.
Sergeant 861016 'C' Battery 3rd Wessex Brigade Royal field Artillery
Died 20th October 1918. 28 years old
Son of Arthur Loveday of 96 York Road
Delhi 1914 – 1918 War Memorial.

R.G. Loveday

LOVEDAY, W.G.T.
William George Thomas
Private 43589 4th Battalion South Staffordshire Regiment
Killed in Action 27th May 1918
Soissons Memorial   France
Born in Swindon

LOVEGROVE, B.
Died No Details

LOVEGROVE, W.J.
William
Sergeant 7135 1st Battalion Gloucestershire Regiment
Killed in Action 5th November 1914
28 years old
Son of James Winifred Lovegrove of 45 Whiteman Street
Panel 22 and 34 Menin Gate Memorial

LOVELOCK, C.
Charles
Private 8892 5th Battalion Wiltshire Regiment
Died of Wounds 28th January 1917
XXIII K 13 Amara War Cemetery
Born in Rodbourne Cheney and Lived in Wootton Bassett

LOVELOCK, F.G.
Frederick Graham
Sergeant 200921 1/7th Battalion Middlesex Regiment
Died 28th September 1920. 31 years old
Son of Tom and Elizabeth Lovelock
Husband of Nora Annie Lovelock of 43 William Street.
D 1191 Radnor Street.
Attended North Wilts Technical College Victoria Road and remembered on the college stained glass window.

LOVELOCK, V.R.
Victor Roland
Private 24210 2nd Battalion Wiltshire Regiment
Killed in Action 8th May 1918
20 years old
Son of George and Mary Jane Lovelock
Panel 119 – 120 Tyne Cot Memorial
Born in Broad Hinton

LOVERIDGE, E.
Edward
Lance Corporal 10273 5th battalion Wiltshire Regiment

Died 18th April 1916. 24 years old
Son of John and Louisa Loveridge
Panel of 30 and 64 Basra Memorial
Also served in France

LOVERIDGE, T.
Thomas
Private 3231 Gloucestershire Regiment
Died 25th November 1916
Husband of Adelaide Loveridge of 4 Cow
Lane
A1 947 Cheltenham Cemetery

LOVESEY, H.
Harry
Private 19737 2nd Battalion Berkshire
Regiment
Killed in Action 1st July 1916. 21 years old
Son of Herbert and Mary Lovesey of
Winterbourne Bassett
Pier and Face 11D Thiepval Memorial
Lived in Swindon

LUCAS, T.H.
Lieutenant Royal Air Force
Died 15th May 1918
Son of Mr and Mrs Lucas of 6 Lorne
Terrace Station Road
D 169 Cairo War Memorial
He worked in the GWR and joined up
at the outbreak of war as an Engineer
sapper.
He was drafted to the Wiltshire regiment,
then to the Hampshire Regiment. He was
later transferred to the Royal Flying
Corps. He returned to England to train as
a pilot and was sent to Egypt in 1917.

Lt. T.H. Lucas

LUGG, W.J.
Private 26201   1st Battalion East Surrey
Regiment
Killed in Action 6th November 1917
24 years old
Son of John Thomas and Eveline
Elizabeth Lugg of 2 Merton Street
VIII A 9 Hooge Crater Cemetery Belgium

Was a Machine Man in the GWR and
previously worked for H James, Grocers
of Fleet Street.

W.J. Lugg

LUSTY, G.H.
George Howard
Private 33552 7th Battalion Cameronians
Killed in Action 23rd November 1917
Panel 25 Jerusalem Memorial
Born in Swindon

LYNN, H.T.
Henry Thomas
Private 18232 2nd Battalion Wiltshire
Regiment
Killed in Action 17th May 1915
Panel 33 and 34 Le Touret Memorial
France
Born in Lydiard Tregoze Lived in Swindon

H.T. Lynn

LYNES, N.
Norman
Private 200776 1st/7th Battalion
Middlesex Regiment
Died 16th September 1916
Pier and face 12D and 13B Thiepval
Memorial

MABBERLEY, H.
Henry
Engine Room Artificer 2nd Class Royal Navy H M Submarine 'E 26'
Died 6th July 1916. 30 years old
Husband of Mrs Daisy Mabberley of 5 Merton Street
14 Plymouth Naval Memorial
Worked as an apprentice in the GWR. He was a member of St Marks Football team.

MALIN, C.
Died No Details

MACQILLVRAY, R.K.
Ronald Kirkpatrick
Private 6751 Coldstream Guards
Died 22nd October 1918. 36 years old (Died in Captivity)
Cousin of Charles Franklin of 36 Hythe Road
VIII A II Berlin South Western Cemetery
Born St Johns Middlesex lived in Swindon

MAISEY, W.
Walter
Private 3/9902 2nd Battalion Wiltshire Regiment
Died 2nd October 1917. (Died in captivity)
II C 23 Cologne Southern Cemetery
Born in Haydon Wick lived in Swindon

MANNERS, B.
Bertrand
Private 18107 2nd Battalion Wiltshire Regiment
Killed in Action 17th May 1915.
36 years old
Son of Alfred and Caroline Manners of Watchfield
Husband of Elizabeth Annie Manners of 27 Stafford Street
Panel 33 and 34 Le Touret Memorial.

B. Manners

MANNERS, F.J.
Frederick James
Private 26622 2nd Battalion Wiltshire Regiment (Formerly 18398 Dorset Regiment)
Killed in Action 18th October 1916
Pier and Face 13A Thiepval Memorial
Born in Swindon

MANNERS, W.F.G.
William Frederick George
Sergeant 7252 1st Battalion Wiltshire Regiment Regiment
Killed in Action 18th October 1914
Panel 33 and 34 Le Touret Memorial
Born in Warminster and lived in Swindon

MANNINGS, A.
Alfred
Rifleman P/153 16th Battalion Rifle Brigade
Killed in Action 3rd September 1916
Pier and Face 16B and 16C Thiepval Memorial
Born in Swindon

J.T. Manning

MANNING, J.T.
John Thomas
Private 90695 Royal Army Medical Corps
Died 13th April 1917. 31 years old
Son of William Gauntlet and Emily Manning of Swindon
Husband of Elizabeth Amy Manning of 24 Spring Gardens
G 10 Athies Communal Cemetery Extension
Born in Swindon

MANT, F.
Frank
Lance-Corporal 19418 5th Battalion Wiltshire Regiment
Died of Wounds 8th April 1916
Panel 30 and 64 Basra Memorial
Born in Swindon

MARCHANT, A.
Alfred
Private 5050 2nd Battalion Wiltshire
Regiment
Died 22nd October 1914. 34 years old
Son of Mr and Mrs William Marchant
Husband of Ellen Rose Marchant of
24 Dixon Street
X B 28 Perth Cemetery (China Wall)
Born in Ramsbury and Lived in Swindon

A. Marchant

MARCHANT, A.E.
Arthur Ernest
Private 20635 2nd Battalion Wiltshire
Regiment
Died of Wounds 10th April 1917
20 years old
Son of Albert and Annie Marchant
A 10 Gauy – en – Artois Communal
Cemetery Extension
Born in Swindon.

MARKS, C.
2nd Lieutenant Royal Air Force
Died 6th January 1919
560 Christchurch Cemetery

MARSH, J.L.
Jesse Lewellyn
Lance-Corporal 21622 2nd Battalion
Bedfordshire Regiment (Formerly
M2/266698 RASC)
Killed in Action 23rd October 1918
20 years old
Son of John and Elizabeth Marsh of 29
Union Street
II B 77 Highland Cemetery Le Cateau.
Born in Swindon

MARSH, L.E.
Lemuel Enos
Private 20682 5th Battalion Wiltshire
Regiment
Died 17th January 1917
XIII D 13 Amara War Cemetery
Lived in Swindon

L.E. Marsh

MARSHALL, A.
Arthur
Stoker 1st Class K/7872 HMS Hampshire
Royal Navy
Died 5th June 1916. 25 years old
Son of Joseph Angus and Elizabeth
Marshall
19 Plymouth Memorial
MARSHALL,T W Died No Details

MARSTON, E.
Edgar
Private 235012 1st Battalion Somerset
Light Infantry
Died 3rd May 1917. 22 years old
Son of Stephen James and Alice of 106
County Road
Bay 4 Arras Memorial

MARTIN, T.
Tom
Lance/Sergeant CL/1582 21st Lancers
Died 30th July 1915
Face 1 Dehli Memorial (India Gate)
Buried in Newshera Military Cemetery N15
Born in Purton and lived in Swindon

MARTIN, F.
Frederick
Private 8/3460 53rd Battalion Hampshire
Regiment
Died 31st December 1917
D 5 Tidworth Military Cemetery
Born in Newmarket lived in Swindon

MARTIN, F.C.
Frank Clewley
Rifleman S/33502 Rifle Brigade
Killed in Action 2nd December 1917
32 years old

Son of Thomas and Fanny Martin
Husband of Sarah Anne Dorothy Martin
of 97 Pinehurst Road
Panel 10 and 11 Cambrai Memorial
Louveral
Born Chelsea London. Lived in Swindon

MARTIN, L.F.
Lesley Frank
Private 276931 1st Battalion Somerset
Light Infantry (Formerly 20794 Wiltshire
Regiment)
Died of Wounds 20th May 1918
22 years old
Son of Mr and Mrs A H Martin of Swindon
I F 13 Fernes British Cemetery
Born in Swindon

MARTIN, W.E.
Died No Details

MARTIN, W.J.
Walter John
Private 22876 6th Battalion Wiltshire
Regiment
Killed in Action November 4th 1915
24 years old
Son of Mr and Mrs Martin of 154
Rodbourne Road

Tom Martin (front right)Delhi India 1915

IX M 19 Regina Trench Cemetery
Grandcourt

MASLIN, T.H.
Thomas Henry
Private 29237 1st/6th Battalion TF. Royal
Warwickshire Regiment (Formerly 9029
Wiltshire Regiment)
Killed in Action 3rd December 1917
Panel 3 Cambrai Memorial Louveral
Born in Devizes and Lived in Swindon

MASON, A.
Arthur
Private 18491 1st Battalion Wiltshire
Regiment (Formerly 63970 Durham
Light Infantry)
Died of Wounds 23rd October 1918
I F 4 Brandhoek Military Cemetery
Belgium
Born in Marlbrough and Lived in
Swindon

MASKELL, E.N.
Ernest Nelson
Gunner 150181 Royal Field Artillery
Killed in Action 8th January 1918
20 years old
Son of John and Kate Maskell of East
Farm Broad Town
V C 43 Bard Cottage Cemetery
Born in Swindon

MATTHEWS, H.J.
Harold James
Sapper 23669 5th Field Company Royal
Engineers (Formerly 8711 Wiltshire
Regiment)
Killed in Action 8th November 1917
29 years old
Son of Frederick and Mary Matthews of
Manchester
XIII D 20 Tyne Cot Cemetery
Born and lived in Swindon

MATTHEWS, J.E.
John Edgar
Sergeant 8292 1st Battalion Wiltshire
Regiment
Killed in Action 17th February 1917
26 years old
Son of Mrs A Matthews of Swindon
Husband of Gertrude A Matthews of the
'Nook' Church Road Earley Reading
I 0 18 Berks Cemetery Extension
Born in Swindon

MATTHEWS, J.E.
Jacob Ernest
Bombardier 57311 Attd' 'V' 19th Trench Mortar Battery Royal Garrison Artillery
Died of Wounds 26th March 1918
28 years old
Husband of S A Matthews of 51 Pinehurst Road
IX C 5 St Pierre Cemetery Amiens.

MATTHEWS, S.W.
Stanley Welcome
Private 10465 1st Battalion Wiltshire Regiment
Killed in Action 16th June 1915
Lived in Telford Road Swindon
Panel 53 Menin Gate Memorial
Born in Swindon

S.W. Matthews

MATTHEWS, W.
Walter
Private 10997 2nd Battalion Wiltshire Regiment
Died of Wounds 21st September 1915
22 years old
Son of Mr and Mrs W Matthews of 73 Kingsdown Road Upper Stratton
I D 108 Chocques Military Cemetery
Born in Stratton

MATTOCK, F.E.
Frederick Ernest
Private 11092 2nd Battalion Wiltshire Regiment
Killed in Action 21st March 1918
24 years old
Son of Ebenezer and Kate Mattock
47 Princes Street
Panel 64 Pozieres Memorial
Born in Swindon.

Mc DOUGAL, A.
Died No details

Mc GRATH, W.A.
William Arthur
Private 172600 Labour Corps (Formerly 26395 Devonshire Regiment)
Died of Wounds 24th May 1918
II D 20 Esquelbecq Military Cemetery
Born in Swindon

Mc IIVRIDE, G.
George
Corporal 28207 10th Hussars
Died of Wounds 17th December 1917
III G 10 Tincourt New British Cemetery
Born in Dundee and Lived in Swindon

Mc NALLY, G.
George
Private 320872 Royal Wiltshire Hussars POWO
Killed in Action 23rd March 1917
Pier and Face 1A Thiepval Memorial
Born in Swindon

MEARS, G.N.
Died No details

G. McNally

MELLON, P.
Percival
Rifleman S/36651 1/7th London Regiment Rifle Brigade (Formerly M/319327 RASC)
Killed in Action 6th October 1918
20 years old
Son of Henry and Annie Mellon
38 Trefusis Road Redruth Cornwall.
VI D 40 Ration Farm Military Cemetery La Chapelle D'Armentierers
Born in Bolton Lancs Lived in Swindon
One of 3 Sons Killed

Grave of H.J. Matthews

the whole time, and it was bitter cold. We had not been in the trenches long before the Germans started sending star shells to try and locate our positions, and we experienced a lively 2 hours. I am not exaggerating when I tell you we were working up to our knees in mud, and every time they sent one of these star shells over, we had to lay down flat on our stomachs. If you had seen us you would had thought we had been in the trenches for a month. However, we had very few casualties – 3 killed and 10 wounded was our total. I can assure you it was not a pleasant experience for there were dozens of dead Germans lying about the parapets of the trenches. One of our fellows caught hold of a dead German and thinking at first it was one of our fellows asleep. It gave him a shock. Please send us some cakes and chocolates as we have been living on biscuits and bully beef for a fortnight and a bit of cake is a luxury.'

Another letter he wrote home was dated November 18th 1917 Just 10 days before he was killed. -

'Dear Mother and Dad, Just a few lines to let you know that I am in the best of

Mc KAY, A.
Alexander
Private 11725 1st Battalion Royal Berkshire Regiment
Killed in Action 19th May 1915
Stepson of R W Menham and Son of Bessie McKay of the Castle Hotel
I C 36 Chocques Military Cemetery France

MENHAM, R.W.
Reginald William
Private 13602 Coldstream Guards
Killed in Action 28th November 1917
Son of Councillor R W Menham of the Castle Hotel
I A 5 Orival Wood Cemetery Flesquieres
Born in Wigan Lived in Swindon
A Letter He sent to his parents 1915 -

'Dear Mother and Dad, I hope this will find you all in the best of health. We have already been in action on 3 occasions but we are now having a short rest behind the firing line. We engaged in trench digging on Thursday night. Our work consisted of digging a commu nication trench, and we were shelled

Alexander McKay

health and going on alright. I received your parcel alright and it came in very acceptable. Things are just the same as usual. We have been having very funny weather lately, rain and frost. I wish the next parcel you send you would send a couple of pairs of socks. Hows Archie going on. Did he go to Coventry? Tell him to write me a letter when he has time..... I should have liked to have him home at the same time as George King. Did he say what part of the line he came from. Has Reg Porter been home on leave yet? I have never seen no more of him. I think ours will be a very lonely Xmas this year as I think we shall still be up the line. Well I think this is all for now. Don't forget to write as soon as possible.

With Love from your affec son
Reg

XXX

Menham & McKay

Reginald Menham

Reginald in his sporting days

Reginald Manham standing at the back as Goalkeeper

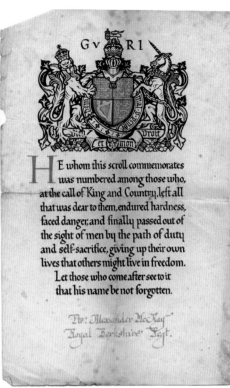

HE whom this scroll commemorates was numbered among those who, at the call of King and Country, left all that was dear to them, endured hardness, faced danger, and finally passed out of the sight of men by the path of duty and self-sacrifice, giving up their own lives that others might live in freedom.

Let those who come after see to it that his name be not forgotten.

Pte: Alexander McKay
Royal Berkshire Regt.

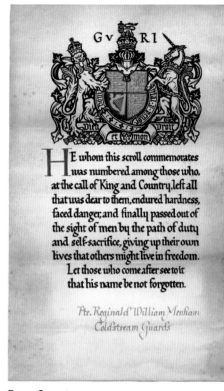

HE whom this scroll commemorates was numbered among those who, at the call of King and Country, left all that was dear to them, endured hardness, faced danger, and finally passed out of the sight of men by the path of duty and self-sacrifice, giving up their own lives that others might live in freedom.

Let those who come after see to it that his name be not forgotten.

Pte. Reginald William Menham
Coldstream Guards

MERCHANT, S. MM
Sidney
Sergeant 70217 Machine Gun Corps (Inf)
(Formerly 12171 Wiltshire Regiment)
Killed in Action 26th March 1918
25 years old
Son of William and Alice Merchant of ' Ye Red Lion' Faringdon Berkshire
Bay 10 Arras Memorial
Born in Stratton

MERRETT, H.J.
Acting Bombardier 35900 B Battery 117th Brigade Royal field Artillery
Died 3rd August 1917
D 165 Alexandria (Hadra) War Memorial Cemetery

MILDENHALL, C.J.
Cecil John
Private 172239 4th Battalion Canadian Infantry (Central Ontario Regiment)
Killed in Action 16th September 1916
27 years old
Husband of Beatrice Mildenhall of 91

Dean Street
I Q 13 Wimereux communal Cemetery

MILES, A.B.
Arthur Bertie
Acting Lance-Corporal 37406 611th Fortress Company Royal Engineers.
Died 31st October 1918. 31 years old
Son of George and Maria Miles of Swindon
Husband of Emily Miles of Henley on Thames
I CE 482 Bootle Cemetery

MILES, C.A.
Charles Albert
Private 314441 2/5th Battalion Gloucestershire Regiment
Died 19th April 1918
II D 24 Aire Communal Cemetery
Born in Swindon

MILES, F.H.
Frederick Henry
Private 16045 1st Battalion Royal

Berkshire Regiment
Killed in Action 23rd May 1916
29 years old
Son of Alfred Henry and Esther Miles of Newbury
Husband of Lucy Alice Miles of 3 Market Street Newbury
II A 20 Zouave valley Cemetery Souchez
Born in Swindon

MILES, R.E.H.
Sapper 43519 77th Field Company Royal Engineers
Died of Wounds 14th February 1916
22 years old
Son of Charles Edward and Julie Miles of 25 Islington Street
II C 5 Enclosure No2 Bedford House Cemetery
Born in Swindon
' Father in Thy Gracious keeping,leave we now Thy servant sleeping'

R.E.H. Miles

MILLER, H.E.B.
Herbert Edward Bowen
Guardsman 26929 1st Battalion Grenadier Guards
Died in Wounds 28th September 1917
24 years old
Son of Thomas and Agnes Miller 170 Cricklade Road
P III I 5A St Sever Cemetery Extension Rouen

MILLER, H.J.G.
Henry John Gardner
Stoker 1st Class PO/K/33007 HMS Leviathan Royal Navy
Died 5th September 1918. 22 years old
Son of Charlotte Miller of 49 Mortimer Road Southampton
Husband of H Miller of 19 Henrietta Street Portsmouth
37 Ocean View Sec. Cemetery New York City Brooklyn 'The Evergreens' USA
Born in Swindon

MILLIN, T.G.
Thomas Geoffrey
Private 28758 15th Battalion Hampshire Regiment
Killed in Action 9th August 1918
19 years old
Son of Mr A G Millin and Mrs J Millin of 9 Marlborough Road
Panel 88 to 90 and 162 Tyne Cot memorial
Born in Christian Melford

MILLIN, W.R.
William Richard
Private 242398 2/6th Battalion Lancashire Fusiliers
Killed in Action 21st March 1918
19 years old
Son of Alfred George and Jane Millin of 9 Marlborough Road
III F 17 Roisel Communal Cemetery Extension
Brother of Thomas Geoffrey (Above)

MILLS, A.W.
Arthur William
Private 20779 6th Battalion Wiltshire Regiment
Died of Wounds 8th July 1916
34 years old
Son of William and Eliza Mills
Husband of Mabel Mills of 79 Dixon Street
VIII C 102 Boulogne Eastern Cemetery
Born in Castle Eaton

MILLS, E.G.
Edward George
Sergeant 87972 K Battery Royal Field Artillery
Died of Wounds 10th October 1918
XII C 2 Highland Cemetery Le Cateau
Born in Swindon

MILLS, H.
Henry
Private 18333 5th Battalion Wiltshire Regiment
Killed in Action 19th April 1916
39 years old
Son of William and Elizabeth Mills
Husband of Emily Hannah Mills of 5 Council Houses Chisbury Little Bedwyn
Panel 30 and 64 Basra Memorial

MILLS, H.G.
Harry George
Private 202815 1st Battalion Wiltshire Regiment
Died 15th July 1918. 22 years old

Son of Robert and Amelia Anne Mills of
Eastrop Cottage Highworth
IA 12 Braine Le Comte Communal
Cemetery
Lived in Swindon

MILLS, S.J.
Sidney John
Private 3/9753 1st Battalion Wiltshire
Regiment
Killed in Action 31st October 1914
Panel 33 and 34 Le Touret Memorial
Born and Lived in Swindon

MILTON, A.
Albert.
Bombardier 151944 B Battery 64th
Brigade Royal Field Artillery
Killed in Action 11th October 1917
31 years old
Son of John and Emily Milton
38 Kimberworth Park Road Rotherham
Husband of Agnes 6 Stansfield Street
Sunderland
Panel 4 – 6 and 162 Tyne Cot
He played as left back for Swindon Town
Football Club and made 27 league and
2 FA cup appearances for the club in the
1914 -15 season. Previously he played for
Sunderland in 1908 – 1913 and South
Kirby, Barnsley in 1907

Albert Milton

MINETT, J
AM III 1485.49 No 10 Acceptance Park
RAF (Formerly Wiltshire Regt)
Died 1st November 1918. 27 years old
Son of C and E Minett of 13 Rosebery
Street
C 942 Radnor Street Cemetery Swindon
Died of Pneumonia

J. Minett

MOBEY, F.R.
Francis Richard
Private 142995 25th Battalion Machine
Gun Corps
Killed in Action 10th April 1918
32 years old
Son of William and Ellen Mobey
Husband of Emily Mobey of 33 Woodrow
Road Melksham
Panel 11 Ploegsteert Memorial
Worked in Stores dept GWR

MOODY, W.J.
William Joseph
Private 19405 5th Battalion Wiltshire
Regiment
Killed in Action 5th April 1916
31 years old
Son of Frederick and Caroline Moody of
70 Stafford Street
Panel 30 and 64 Basra Memorial
Born in Brinkworth. Worked in Stores
Dept GWR

MOORE, F.G.
Francis George
Corporal 17255 1st Battalion Somerset
Light Infantry
Killed in Action 10th April 1917
23 years old
Son of Alfred and Caroline Moore
Brompton Ralph, Somerset
Husband of Hannah Jane Moore 233
Nantgarw Road Caerphilly Cardiff
Bay 4 Arras Memorial
Born in Swindon

MOORE, G.E.
George Ernest
Private 4208 9th Battalion East Surrey
Regiment
Died of Wounds 3rd October 1915
XII B I Caberet Rouge British Cemetery
Souchez
Born in Swindon

MOORE, L.F.
Gunner 152985 230th Siege Battery
Royal Garrison Artillery
Died 28th March 1918. 28 years old
Son of William and Emily Moore of 2
Grove Villas Drove Road
IV B 22 Roccincourt Military Cemetery

MOORE, W.H.W.
William Henry Walker
2nd Lieutenant D Company 6th Battalion
Wiltshire Regiment
Killed in Action 25th September 1915
18 years old
Son of Dr S J Moore of Walton Grange,
Bath Road
I F II Browns Road Military Cemetery
Festubert
Born in Hersham Walton on Thames
Also had an older brother serving as an
Officer in the Wiltshire Regiment
Remembered on plaque in Christchurch
and also by way of a brass plaque

MORAN, T.
Thomas
Sergeant 20461 1st Company Machine
Gun Corps (Formerly 13096 Royal
Berkshire Regiment)
Killed in Action 14th July 1916
28 years old
Son of Mr Thomas Moran of Regents
Place. Ostler of Riflemans Hotel
Pier and Face 5C and 12C Thiepval
Memorial
Born in Didcot lived in Swindon and was
a forman in the GWR
The following is a letter received by his
father from his son's Officer:

'Dear Sir,
It is my painful duty to inform you that
your son, Sgt T Moran, has been killed in
Action. He was my section Sgt these last
few days and he took all the opportuni-
ties which his position offered of proving
himself to be a brave and capable soldier.
At the time of his death I was not with
him, but so far as I can gather the facts,
they are these;
He was in charge of two of my guns in a
recently captured village. He had
relieved me the night before and I had
advanced with my remaining guns. The
place was being heavily shelled when
one unfortunately accurate shot blew
in the dug out where he was, killing him

instantly. The time was about 8.00pm on
the 13th July. It is all the luck of the
game, that dug out had been mine and
had I decided to send him forward, he
would be alive now and I would be dead.
I valued him much as a courageous
solider and I will miss him greatly.
Permit me to assure you of my heartfelt
sympathy.
Yours faithfully, F Lismore, Lt
Brigade MGC BEF France 18th July 1916'

MOREMAN, R.P.E.
Reginald Percy Edgar
Acting Lance Corporal 207475 22nd
Battalion Rifle Brigade (Formerly 2824
25th Battalion Rifle Brigade)
Died 31st October 1918. 28 years old
Eldest son of Mrs Hillier of Swindon
Husband of Beatrice E Moreman of 36
Frampton Road, Gloucestershire
I B 13 Doiran Military Cemetery Balkans
Born in Swindon

MOREMAN, W.H.
Sapper 3128 3/1st Wessex Division
Signal Company Royal Engineers
Died 11th April 1916
C3359 Radnor Street Cemetery
Born in Watermore Gloucestershire lived
in Swindon

MORGAN, A.C.
Alfred Charles
Private 10986 1st Battalion Wiltshire
Regiment
Killed in Action 21st October 1916
III D 2 Regina Trench Cemetery
Grandcourt France
Born in Camberwell lived in Swindon
worked in Stores dept GWR

A. Morgan

MORGAN, F.
Francis
Driver T/35223 18th Corps Transport
Depot Army Service Corps
Died 7th December 1915. 18 years old
Son of William and Kathleen Morgan of 9
Alfred Street Reading
III D 126 East Mudros Military Cemetery
Greece.
Born in Swindon

MORGAN, F.J.W.
Francis James William
Private 9029 2nd Battalion Dorset
Regiment
Died 9th September 1915
Son of Mr F Morgan of 179 Cricklade
Road
V D 13 Amara War Cemetery
Born and lived in Swindon

MORGAN, F.J.
Frederick John
Corporal 571st Field Company Royal
Engineers
Killed in Action 15th February 1915
20 years old
Son of John and Emily Morgan of 55
Oxford Street Totterdown Bristol
C 5 Dickebusch Old Military Cemetery
Belgium
Lived in Swindon and an apprentice in
the Engineers Department of GWR

MORGAN, H.E.
Henry Edward
Private 9083 2nd Battalion Dorset
Regiment
Died 6th December 1914
VI D 18 Basra War Cemetery
Born in Swindon

MORRIS, C.V.
Died No Details

MORRIS, S.
Sidney
Private 90696 18th Field Ambulance
Royal Army Medical Corps
Died 21st March 1918 21 years old
Son of Edwin James and Elizabeth Morris
of 34 Avenue Road
Bay 10 Arras Memorial
Born in Swindon Brother of Walter
(right)

MORRIS, W.G.
Walter Gilbert
Corporal 22527 Grenadier Guards
Killed in Action 12th September 1916
28 years old
Son of Edwin James and Elizabeth Morris
of 34 Avenue Road
XIV E 10 Serre Road Cemetery No 2
Brother of Sidney (previous)

MORRIS, S.R.
Died No Details

MORRIS, W.
Died No Details

MORRIS, W.T.
William Thomas
Private 102737 52nd General Hospital
Royal Army Medical Corps
Died 4th September 1919. 31 years old
Husband of Lillian Alethea Morris
I.G.7 Haidar Pasha Cemetery Turkey

W.T. Morris - with family

MORRIS, S.S.
Septimus Summers
Private 12361 7th Battalion Wiltshire
Regiment
Died 15th August 1916. 23 years old
Son of W E and Bessie Morris of 10
Devizes Road
311 Leribet Road Military Cemetery
Salonika
Born in Christchurch, Dorset lived in
Swindon

MORSE, A.J.
Albert James
Private G/51523 2/10th Battalion
Middlesex Regiment (Formerly
S4/146149 ASC)
Died 29th October 1918
XXV11 F 7 Gaza War Cemetery
Born in Swindon

MORSE, F.
Frank
Private 8497 2nd Battalion Wiltshire
Regiment
Died of Wounds 9th January 1917
30 years old
Son of James and Maria Morse of New
Cottages, Lower Wanborough
III J 8 Warlincourt Halte British Cemetery
Born in Shrivenham   lived in Swindon

MORSE, G.
Private 25404 2nd Battalion Wiltshire
Regiment
Killed in Action 9th April 1917
VI E 16 Wancourt British Cemetery
France

MORSE, H.
Henry
Private 203315 6th Battalion Wiltshire
Regiment (Wilts Yeomanry)
Died of Wounds 15th April 1918
Panel 119 – 120 Tyn Cott Memorial
Born and Lived in Swindon

MORSE, J.
John
Private 3/9632 2nd Battalion Wiltshire
Regiment
Killed in Action 12th March 1915
Panel 33 and 34 Le Touret Memorial
France
Born in Swindon

MORSE, P.L.
Percy Lapper
2nd Lieutenant 1/4th Battalion Glouces-
tershire Regiment
Died of Wounds 20th November 1917
31 years old
Son of Levi and Winifred Morse of
Swindon
Husband of Margery Morse of Barton on
Sea Hants
Buried of St Sever Cemetery Rouen

MORSE, R.H.D.
Richard Hunt Dennis
Lance Corporal 11569 6th Battalion
Wiltshire Regiment
Killed in Action 13th November 1916
24 years old
Son of Peter and Ellen Morse of 110
William Street
IV D 50 Pozieres British Cemetery Ovillers
La Boisselle
Born in Swindon

R.H. Morse

MORSE, T.
Thomas
Lance Corporal 8398 1st Battalion
Wiltshire Regiment
Killed in Action 29th July 1916
II E 21 Hamel Military Cemetery
Beaumont-Hamel
Born in Swindon

MOSS, J.
James
Sergeant 240365 1/5th Welsh Regiment
Killed in Action 25th January 1918
P 117 Jerusalem War Cemetery
Born and lived in Swindon

MUGFORD, H.N.
Sapper 520171 365th Army Troop
Company Royal Engineers
Killed in Action 19th September 1918
23 years old
Son of Mrs L M Mugford of 36 Kenilworth
Avenue, Wimbledon
II D 15 Sunken Road Cemetery Boisleux
St Marc
Attended Technical College Victoria Road
1909 worked in R Shop GWR

MULLARNEY, E.
Ernest
Lance Corporal 1434 2nd Battalion Mon-
mouthshire Regiment
Killed in Action 25th October 1916
24 years old
Son of George and Mary Anne Mullarney
of 91 Kingsdown Road Upper Stratton
XXII C 4 Beucourt British Cemetery
Born in Swindon lived in Newport

MUTTON, E.G.
Ernest Granville
Private 14472 5th Battalion Dorset
Regiment
Killed in Action 26th September 1916

Pier and Face 7 B Thiepval Memorial France
Born in Stroud Glos, lived in Swindon

E. Mullarney

MYALL, E.G.   Order of St George 4th Class (Russia)
Edwin George
Lance Sergeant 10057 9th Battalion East Surrey Regiment
Killed in Action 26th September 1915
21 years old
Son of James and Elizabeth Myall of 19 Church Road Bromley, Kent
Panel 65/67 Loos Memorial France
Born in Swindon

NASH, C.
Charles
Sapper 504580 63rd Field Company Royal Engineers
Died of Wounds 19th October 1918
33 years old
Son of James Robert and Elizabeth Nash of 21 Longground Frome
A 71 Kortrijk (St Jan) Communal Cemetery
Born in Warminster Lived in Swindon and worked in Loco Dept GWR.

NASH, G.W.F.
George William Frederick
Engine Room Artificer 3rd Class M/2325
HMS Monmouth Royal Navy
Died 1st November 1914. 26 years old
Son of James and Harriet Nash of 23 Dixon Street
2 Plymouth Naval Memorial

C. Nash

NEALE, W.G.
William George
Gunner 208285 B Battery 306th Brigade Royal field Artillery
Killed in Action 28th April 1918
27 years old
Son of Charles William and Amelia Neale of 41 Wells Street, Camberwell London
P XI J IB St Sever Cemetery Extension Rouen

NETHERCOT, H.H.
Herbert Harold
Private G/54944 11th Battalion Royal Fusiliers (Formerly 3784 Royal Fusiliers)
Killed in Action 22nd August 1918
20 years old
Son of Walter Herbert and Miriam Evelyn Nethercot of 108 Springfield Road Brighton
II D 9 Albert Communal Cemetery Extension
Born in Swindon

NEVILLE, C.
Charles
Private M2/177685 Royal Army Service Corps
Died 30th April 1918
Husband of Alice Rozina Neville
H 537 Belfast City Cemetery
Born in Swindon

NEW, B.H.C.
Bertram Henry Charles
Private 170915 307th Home Service
Employment Company Labour Corps
(Formerly 10034 Royal Sussex Regt)
Died 26th October 1918. 36 years old
Son of Henry and Ann New of Ivy
Bungalow Berrow Burnham on Sea,
Somerset
AF 2116 Aldershot Military Cemetery
Born in Swindon

NEW, W.C.
William Charles
Bombardier 81701 D Battery 84th
Brigade Royal field Artillery
Died of Wounds 3rd October 1918
V J 25 Tincourt New British Cemetery
Born in Swindon

NEWMAN, B.
Bennett
Private 305811 4th Battalion Tank Corps
(Formerly 617 Wilts Royal Engineers)
Killed in Action 10th August 1918
Panel 11 Vis en Artois Memorial
Born in South Cerney Lived in Swindon

NEWMAN, F.
Frank
Private 5102 1st Battalion Wiltshire
Regiment
Killed in Action 22nd June 1915
33 years old
Son of John and Esther Newman
Panel 53 Menin Gate Memorial
Born in Swindon

NEWMAN, F.W.
Private 137251 6th Battalion Machine
Gun Corps
Died 5th April 1919. 20 years old
Son of Frederick G and Catherine
Newman of 82 Bright Street
C 3572 Radnor Street Cemetery

F.W. Newman

NEWMAN, J.
John
Private 8208 2nd Battalion Wiltshire
Regiment
Died of Wounds 7th December 1914
24 years old
Son of Frederick James and Emily
Newman of Christian Malford
I L 22 Merville Communal Cemetery
Lived in Swindon

NEWMAN, V.R.
Victor Reuben
Private 12577 2nd Battalion Royal
Warwickshire Regiment (Formerly 56092
Royal Garrison Artillery)
Killed in Action 3rd September 1916
19 years old
Son of Ellen Newman
Pier and Face 9A, 9B and 10B Thiepval
Memorial
Born in Swindon and lived in Wootton
Bassett

NEWTON, A.E.
Albert Edward
Corporal 22560 2nd Battalion Wiltshire
Regiment
Killed in Action 31st July 1917
40 years old
Husband of Elizabeth H Newton
82 Cricklade Road Gorse Hill
Panel 53 Menin Gate Memorial

A.E. Newton

NICHOLAS, E.J.
Edgar John
Driver 2689 D Battery, 79th Brigade Royal
Field Artillery
Killed in Action 1st April 1917
20 years old
Son of John and Florence Emily Nicholas
of Swindon

IV C 7 Maroevil British Cemetery
Born in Swindon

NICHOLAS, J.
John
Private 14919 2nd Battalion Welsh
Regiment
Killed in Action 25th May 1915
Panel 23 and 24 Le Touret Memorial
Born in Swindon

E.J. Nicholas

NICHOLS, W.E.
Died. No Details

NIPPRESS, F.
Frank.
Private 1983 3rd Battalion Monmouth
shire Regiment
Killed in Action 2nd May 1915
26 years old
Husband of Elizabeth Jane Nippress
23 Thomas Street Rodbourne
Panel 50 Menin Gate Memorial

NOBLE, E.L.D.
Pte 34344 7th Battalion Somerset Light
Infantry
Died 23rd April 1918. 20 years old
Son of Edwin and F E Noble of 89
Redcliffe Street
II H I Tournai Communal Cemetery Allied
Extension
Born in Chiseldon and Lived in Swindon

NORGROVE, E.J.
Edgar John
Private 41400 3rd Battalion Worcester-
shire Regiment (Formerly 161632 RASC)
Killed in Action 10th April 1918
Special Memorial F 16 Croix Du Bac
British Cemetery Steenwerch
Born in Swindon

NORRIS, J.
Died No Details

NORTH, A.S.
Arthur Sydney
Corporal 453 25th Battalion Australian
Infantry
Died 3rd May 1917. 27 years old
Son of William and Ann of 139 Cricklade
Road
Villers Brettoneux Memorial

NORTON, E.G.
Edgar George
Private 15390 2nd Battalion Coldstream
Guards.
Killed in Action 16th September 1916
31 years old
Son of Henry Thomas and Mary Norton of
Swindon
Husband of Louisa R Norton of Albion
House Cambria Bridge Road
XXXII H 7 Delville Wood Cemetery
Longueval
Born in Swindon

NOTT, V.G.
Vernon George
Private 27863 6th Battalion Duke of
Cornwalls Light Infantry (Formerly 24085
Somerset Light Infantry)
Killed in Action 16th September 1916
Pier and Face 6B Thiepval Memorial
Born in Swindon

E.G. Norton

NURDEN,W.J.
Lance Corporal 1st Company Wilts
National Reserve
Killed by Accident 11th December 1914
He was hit by a train while crossing the
line to relieve a sick railway guard.
(The Swindon company National reserve,
were made up from volunteers to
become railway guards. These men were
mainly elderly or with homes and
dependants).

OAK, J.P.
John Park
Private 285162 2/1st Bucks Battalion
Oxfordshire and Buckinghamshire Light
Infantry (Formerly 2558 Hampshire
Regiment)
Killed in Action 22nd August 1917
41 years old
Son of Charles Oak
Husband of Elizabeth Ann Oak of 80
Ponting Street.
Panel 96 to 98 Tyne Cot Memorial

W.J. Nurden

OAKES, L.
Leonard
Private 23635 5th Battalion Berkshire
Regiment (Formerly 21779 Somerset
Light Infantry)
Killed in Action 9th August 1916
22 years old
Son of George and Louisa Oakes of 24
Lethbridge Road
Pier and Face II D Thiepval Memorial
Born in Swindon

O'BRIEN, D.
Died No Details

O'BRIEN, H.F.
Harold Frederick
Gunner 94084 D Battery 82nd Brigade
Royal Field Artillery
Killed in Action 21st October 1917
19 years old
Son of Frederick and Eliza May O'Brien of
60 Elmina Road
I B I Minty Farm Cemetery
Born in Swindon

O'CONNELL, D.J.
Daniel James
Private 202777 6th Battalion Royal West
Kent Regiment (Formerly 21208
Wiltshire Regiment)
Killed in Action 22nd May 1918
II N 2 Maillywood Cemetery

Born in Swindon and worked as a
boilermaker in the GWR.

H.F. O'brien

ODEY, J.H.
John Henry
Private 54286 13th Battalion Durham
Light Infantry (Formerly 164457 RFA)
Killed in Action 8th June 1917.
34 years old
Son of Mrs James Odey of 7 Southville
Terrace Lyncombe Vale Bath
Husband of Rosie Mary Odey of 3 Stanley
Street
Panel 36 and 38 Menin Gate Memorial
Born in Bath

O'KEEFE, T.
Timothy
Lance-Corporal 11089 1st Battalion
Wiltshire Regiment
Died of Wounds 24th September 1915
22 years old
Son of John and Fanny O'Keefe of
33 Oriel Street
I F 5 Brandhoek Military Cemetery
Born in Swindon Joined the army
September 1914. He left the front in
January 1915. He was formerly employed
as a boiler maker's assistant in the GWR
'He died not in rescuing a few ancient
places as in the days of chivalry, but for
the desecrated shrines of human faith
and love, and the holy temples of justice
and freedom.'

OCKWELL, R.T.
Sapper 62893 151st Field Company Royal
Engineers
Killed 5th September 1917
Son of Mr and Mrs G Ockwell
Husband of Bertha Emily Ockwell of
Alreasford Hants

IV F 19 Bard Cottage Cemetery
Born in Stratton.

T. O'Keefe

ORAM, F.
Gunner L/3813 Royal Field Artillery
Killed in Action 16th August 1917
V C 38 Vlamertinghe New Military
Cemetery
Lived in Swindon

F. Oram

OSBORN, G.H.
George Henry
Private 87558 11th Battalion Kings
Liverpool Regiment (Formerly 1980
RAMC)
Killed in Action 21st March 1918
22 years old
Son of James and Ellen Osborn
Panel 21 to 23 Pozieres Memorial
Born in Swindon

PACKER, E.G.
Edward George
Lance Corporal 35323 14th Battalion
Royal Warwickshire Regiment
Killed in Action 26th September 1918
C36 Neuville-Bourjonval British Cemetery
Born in Swindon

PACKER, J.
Joseph
2nd Lieutenant Royal Airforce
Died 20th August 1918. 21 years old
Son of Joseph Frederick and Anne Packer
of 37 North Street

535 Christchurch Cemetery
Enlisted in RAMC June 1914 Transferred
to RE 1915 Served in France and Flanders
Gazetted April 1918
He was flying in a training exercise over
Oxfordshire when his plane collided with
another. Both pilots were killed.

PACKER, J.
John
Private 8278 2nd Battalion Wiltshire
Regiment
Killed in Action 4th November 1914
Panel 53 Menin Gate Memorial
Born in Swindon

PACKER, W.M.
Died No Details

PADGET, W.G.
William George
Corporal 23417 16th Battalion Welsh
Regiment
Killed in Action 5th April 1916
III P 4 Guards Cemetery Windy Corner
Cuinchy
Born in Swindon

G.H Osborn

PAGE, C.J.
Charles J
Sapper 504573 3rd Field Company
Canadian Engineers
Killed in Action 15th August 1917
31 years old
Son of John and Alice Page of Cricklade
Road
Husband of Carrie Page of 15 Alexander
Street Toronto Canada
II D 16 Mazingarbe Communal Cemetery
Extension France
A stained glass window was installed in

A wedding party in Albion Street in 1917.
Canadian Hooper Gates (left) and Bert Marfleet (right) married sisters Agnes and Elsie Morse

Bert Marfleet Army Service Corps and Elsie Morse
Bert died a few weeks later in France

St Barnabas Church with the inscription -'In Loving memory to Charles J Page by his Devoted wife and parents.'

PAGE, F.J.
Frederick James
Private 72987 15th Battalion Notting hamshire and Derbyshire Regiment
Killed in Action 24th May 1918
No Details of Burial Place
Born in Swindon (Brother of William Page below)

PAGE, W.J.
William John
Private 6081 1st Battalion Wiltshire Regiment
Killed in Action 21st October 1914
32 years old
Brother of Frank Page of 3 Church Road
Panel 33 and 34 Le-Touret Memorial
Born in Swindon (Brother of Frederick Page above)

PAGET, E.J.
Ernest John
Private 3/9323 2nd Battalion Wiltshire Regiment
Killed in Action 24th October 1914
Panel 53 Menin Gate
Lived in Swindon

PAGET, M.R.
Private 56909 447th Agricultural Company Labour Corps (Formerly RAMC)
Died 23rd March 1919
10 12 St Mary's Church Rodbourne Cheney

PAGINTON, G.A.
George Arthur
Private 15230 7th Battalion Royal Dublin Fusiliers
Killed in Action 16th August 1915
28 years old
Son of George and Louisa Paginton of 4 Telford Road Rodbourne
Panel 190 – 196 Helles Memorial

PAINTER, A.
Albert
Sergeant 2nd Division Australian Imperial Forces
Killed in Action 10th June 1917
Son of Mr and Mrs Painter of 65 Winifred Street
No details of burial
Born in Swindon, Emigrated to Australia

in 1913. He volunteered for the army at the outbreak of war and was sent to the Dardanelles, later to France. He had been wounded in July 1916.

G.A. Paginton

PAINTER, G.
Sergeant 437328 Labour Corps (Formerly 7990 Wilts Regt)
Died 15th February 1919. 27 years old
Son of Charles Painter
Husband of Ellen Rosina Painter of 34 Albion Street
5 24 SS John the Baptist and Helen Churchyard Wroughton.

PAINTER, W.E.
William Edward
Lance Corporal 205626 1st Battalion Royal Fusiliers (Formerly 1636 RAMC)
Killed in Action 18th September 1918
22nd years old
Son of Henry and Sarah Painter of 60 Albion Street
III B 17 Flesquieres Hill British Cemetery
Born in Swindon

W.E. Painter

PAINTIN, J.E.
Sapper 520262 565th Army Troops Company Royal Engineers
Died 31st December 1918
B 1578 Radnor Street Cemetery

PALMER, A.G.
Arthur Gilbert
Lance Corporal 17610 1st Battalion
Grenadier Guards
Killed in Action 10th-12th September
1916
Pier and Face 8D Thiepval Memorial
Born in Swindon

PALMER, R.T.
Richard Thomas
Lance Corporal 10622 1st Battalion
Wiltshire Regiment
Killed in Action 12th March 1915
20 years old
Son of Richard James and Elizabeth
Palmer of 41 Whiteman Street, Gorsehill
I B 8 La Laiterie Military Cemetery
Lived in Swindon

PALMER, W.W.
Walter William
Private 18942 3rd Company 4th
Battalion Grenadier Guards
Died 11th June 1916. 38 years old
Son of Stephen and Sylvia Palmer
Husband of Jessie Palmer of 25 Deburgh
Street
A 460 Radnor Street Cemetery

PANNELL, A.J.
Alfred John
Sapper 222960 509th Field Company
Royal Engineers
Killed in Action 21st March 1918
38 years old
Son of Thomas and Martha Pannell
Husband of Maria Pannell of 14 Ganwarf
Road, Portsmouth
Bay 7 Arras Memorial
Born in Swindon

PANTOLL, A.J.
Alfred James
Staff Sergeant Major S4/072094 Royal
Army Service Corps (Formerly 15733
Royal Irish Rifles)
Died of Wounds 22nd May 1916
25 years old
Son of Samuel James and Sarah Jane
Pantoll of Cirencester
Husband of Alice M Pantoll of 57 Edridge
Road, Croydon
V D 21 Bethune Town Cemetery
Lived in Swindon

PARROTT, S.G.
Simon George
Private 22139 2nd Battalion Wiltshire
Regiment
Killed in Action 8th July 1916
Pier and Face 13A Thiepval Memorial
Lived in Swindon

PARSONS, E.C.
Ernest Charles
Private M2/031929 Mechanical Transport
Attached Anti Aircraft Battery Royal
Army Service Corps
Died of Wounds 31st March 1917
27 years old
Son of Charles and Emily Parsons of
Bodenham Salisbury
V I E 26 Dernancourt Communal
Cemetery Extension
Born in Swindon

PARSONS, F.
Frank
Private 318940 1st Battalion Wiltshire
Regiment
Killed in Action 31st October 1914
Panel 33 and 34 Le Touret Memorial
Born in Swindon

PART, F.G.
Frederick George
Trooper 3196 Household Battalion
(formerly 2nd Life Guards)
Killed in Action 22nd January 1917
29 years old
Son of Mr and Mrs John Part
Husband of Amy Part of 4 Corporation
Street
II M 10 Grove Town cemetery Meaulte
France
Born in Swindon

PARTRIDGE, R.A.
Ralph Allen
Private 97132 K Company Royal Army
Medical Corps
Died 19th January 1917
D 874 Radnor Street Cemetery
Born in Swindon

PARTON, T.
Thomas
Private 27597 1st Battalion Royal
Warwickshire Regiment (Formerly 3849
6th Bn South Staffordshire Regt)
Killed in Action 23rd October 1916
Pier and Face 9A 9B and 10B Thiepval
Memorial. Lived in Swindon

PAYNE, F.G.
Frederick George
Private 381139 2nd Battalion Hampshire
Regiment
Killed in Action 11th April 1918
III D 8 Trois Arbres Cemetery Steenwerck
France.
Lived in Swindon

PAYNTOR, A.E.
Albert Edward
Gunner 80024 9th Trench Motor Battery
Royal Field Artillery.
Killed in Action 9th May 1917
I E 7 Point Du Jour Military Cemetery
Athies
Born in Swindon

A.E. Paynter

PEARCE, A.C.
Sapper 261781 Railway Operating
Division Royal Engineers
Died 29th June 1918. 53 years old
Son of William Pearce of 36 William
Street
C 1848 Radnor Street Cemetery

PEARCE, A.J.
Alfred James
Driver T2/14157 53rd Divisional Train
Royal Army Service Corps
Died 17th August 1915
II F 93 East Murdros Military Cemetery
Egypt
Lived in Swindon

PEARCE, F.S.
Died No Details

PEARCE, G.E.
George Ewart
Driver 860861 Royal Field Artillery
Died 21st October 1918
India
Lived in Swindon

PEARSE, W.
Died No Details

PEART, H.G.
Horace George
Private 22404 7th Battalion Wiltshire
Regiment (Formerly 34654 Machine Gun
Corps)
Died of Wounds 16th October 1918
I B21 Roisel Communal Cemetery
Extension
Lived in Swindon

PEART, J.J.
Joseph John
Private 8238 2nd Battalion Wiltshire
Regiment
Died of Wounds 8th July 1916
Pier and Face 13A Thiepval Memorial
Lived in Swindon

PEDDER, A.L.K.
Alfred Leslie King
Private 42454 4th Battalion Worcester-
shire Regiment
Killed in Action 10th April 1918
19 years old
Son of Alfred and Emma Pedder of 28
Brunswick Street
Panel 5 Ploegsteert Memorial
Lived in Swindon

PEGLER, P.J.
Percy John
Private 25909 5th Battalion Wiltshire
Regiment
killed in Action 29th March 1917
29 years old
Son of Mr and Mrs H Pegler of Fountain
Street Nailsworth Stroud Glos.
Husband of Verney Kate Ellen Pegler of
245 Cricklade Road Gorse Hill.
Panel 30 and 64 Basra Memorial

PEOPLE, O.C.
Owen Cyril
Gunner 14453 Royal Marine Artillery
HMS 'Natal'
Died 30th December 1915. 18 years old
Son of Charles and Sarah Annie People of
37 Telford Road
9 Portsmouth Naval Memorial

PERRY, T.H.
Thomas Henry
Private 19010 E Company 2nd Company
Wiltshire Regiment

Killed in Action 21st March 1918
34 years old
Son of John and Mary Ann Perry of
Levershulme Manchester
Husband of Lilly Perry of 101 Osmaston
Park Road Derby.
Roupy Road German Cemetery Menn 29
Savy British Cemetery
Lived in Swindon

PETTIFORD, E.H.W.
Edward Henry William
Private CH/1811 Royal Marine Light
Infantry, Royal Marine RN Division
Died 28th April 1917. 22 years old
Son of Josiah and Mary Augusta Pettiford
of 288 Cricklade Road
Bay 1 Arras Memorial France

PHILLIMORE, C.
Charles
Gunner 861151 108th Royal Field
Artillery
Died of Wounds 18th July 1917
Panel 3 and 60 Basra Memorial
Born in Swindon

PHILLIPS, A.H.
Arthur Henry
Private 22960 A Company 6th Battalion
Wiltshire Regiment
Died of Wounds 5th July 1917
25 years old
Son of George and Ellen Phillips of
Swindon
II N 12 Wimereux Communal Cemetery
Lived in Swindon

PHILLIPS, G.N.V.
George Nigel Victor
Private 5180 1/6th Battalion Gloucester-
shire Regiment
Died of Wounds 12th November 1916
28 years old
Son of Thomas and Mary Jane Phillips of
Silver Street Dursley Glos.
O I P3 St Sever Cemetery Extension
Rouen France
Born in Swindon

PHILLIPS, S.R.
Sidney Richard
Private 306970 Tank Corps
Killed in Action 8th August 1918
Panel II Vis en Artois Memorial

PICKERING, V.G.A.
Sergeant 20640 1st Battalion Wiltshire

Regiment
Died 31st May 1917. 19 years old
Son of Mr W and Mrs B A of 39 Florence
Street
II G 6 St Quentin Cabaret Military
Cemetery France

V.G.A. Pickering

PICKERNELL, R.W.
Robert William
Sergeant 201372 2/4th Battalion
Devonshire Regiment
Died 6th May 1917. 32 years old
Son of Frederick and Charlotte Pickernell.
Husband of Louisa Pickernell of 12 Park
Terrace Swindon
XXI M 43 Baghdad (North Gate Cemetery)
War Cemetery
Born in Swindon

PICKETT, W.E.
William Edward
Private 20918 1st Battalion Dorset
Regiment (Formerly 3709 Wiltshire
Regiment)
Killed in Action 30th September 1918
V I D 10 Grand Seraucourt British
Cemetery
Born in Swindon

PICTOR, T.
Tom
Stoker 1st Class 278970 HMS 'Teutonic'
Royal Navy
Died 4th December 1915. 37 years old
Son of John and Emma Pictor of 39
Wescott Place
B 1812 Radnor Street Cemetery

PIDGEON, G.H.
George Harold
Driver 645278 Royal Field Artillery
Died of Wounds 28th July 1918
23 years old
XVII A II Terlincthun British Cemetery
Wimille
Born in Swindon

PIKE, C.
Charles
Private 18393 1st Battalion Wiltshire
Regiment
Died 16th June 1915. 28 years old
Son of Eliza Pike of Eastcott Hill
Husband of Francis A Pike of 63
Providence Row Regent Place
Panel 53 Menin Gate Memorial, Belgium

PIKE, E.F.
Private TR/7/25910 Royal Warwickshire
Regiment
Died 18th December 1919
562 Christchurch Cemetery Swindon

PIKE, J.
John
Private 3/500 D Company 5th Battalion
Wiltshire Regiment
Killed in Action 9th April 1916
36 years old
Husband of Elizabeth Pike of
20 Wharf Road Wroughton
Panel 30 and 64 Basra Cemetery
Born in Swindon

PILL, P.H.
Percy Herbert
Sergeant 12333 7th Battalion Wiltshire
Regiment
Killed in Action 24th April 1917
Doiran Memorial Salonika
Lived in Swindon

Lane Chippenham
Husband of Rose Gertrude of 17 Audly
Road Chippenham
Panel 115 – 119 + 162a + 163a Tyne Cot
Was educated at St Pauls School.
Attended North Wilts Technical College
in 1896 and remembered on its Stained
glass window. His brothers also served –
Pte Bernard Pinfield, L/Cpl Ernest Pinfield
and Lt Reginald Pinfield RFC.

PITT, W.J.
William James
Private 2999 1st/1st battalion City of
London Yeomanry
Died 4th June 1916. 18 years old
Son of William Pitt of 8 Chester Road
London
P20 Alexandra (Hadra) War Memorial
Cemetery

PITMAN, E.H.
Ernest Henry
Sergeant 41289 1st Battalion Duke of
Cornwalls Light Infantry
Died of Wounds 24th April 1918
20 years old
Son of Frederick Hugh and Leah Louisa
Pitman of 1 Southbrook Street
XXIX H 2 Etaples Military Cemetery
Born in Swindon Worked as a clerk in the
GWR and volunteered in 1915. He died
as a result of infection setting in from
multiple wounds.

P.H. Pill

E.H. Pitman

PINFIELD, F.B.
Frederick Bertram
L/Cpl R/38020 C Company 13th Battalion
Kings Royal Rifle Corps
Killed in Action 29th September 1917
36 years old
Son of Mr and Mrs H G Pinfield of 44 Park

PONSONBY, G.M.
Gerald Maurice
Captain 2nd Battalion Royal Inniskilling
Fusiliers 31ST August 1914
Killed in Action 1914. 37 years old
Son of Rev. Lord De Mauley 4th Baron

and Lady De Mauley of Langford House Lechlade Glos.
I Wambaix Communal Cemetery
Rev De Mauley was the Vicar of St Marks Church

PONTING, A.J.
Albert James
Acting Lance Sergeant 13507 1st Battalion Wiltshire Regiment
Died of Wounds 20th May 1916
26 years old
Son of Stephen and Eliza Ponting of Swindon
I C 8 Aubigny Communal Cemetery Extension
Born in Stratton

A.J. Ponting

PONTING, C.
Charles
Private 9956 C Company 5th Battalion Wiltshire Regiment
Died of Wounds 22 October 1915
28 years old
Son of Joseph and Emily Ponting
III C 65 East Murdos Military Cemetery Dardanelles
Lived in Swindon

PONTING, E.S.
Edwin Stanley
Private 200226 1/4th Battalion Wiltshire Regiment
Died 30th June 1916. 22 years old
Son of William and Elizabeth Ponting of 42 Gorton Road Coventry
Nisibin Memorial 245 Baghdad (North Gate) Cemetery
Born in Upper Stratton

PONTING, R.A.
Reginald Arthur
Private 8288 2nd Battalion Hampshire Regiment
Died 4th June 1915
Panel 125 134 or 223 – 226 228 – 229 and 328 Helles Memorial Dardanelles

POOLE, T.
Thomas
Private CH/12274 Royal Marine Light Infantry SS 'Northumbria'
Died 9th January 1919 . 37 years old
Son of William and Elizabeth Poole
Husband of Beatrice Fanny Poole of 50 Victoria Road
D 1023 Radnor Street Cemetery

POOLE, W.
William
Private 6968 2nd Battalion Oxfordshire and Buckinghamshire Light Infantry
Killed in Action 25th September 1915
Panel 83 to 85 Loos Memorial
Lived in Swindon

PORTER, A.J.
Arthur John
Gunner 146598 26th Anti Aircraft Company Royal Garrison Artillery
Died 21st May 1918. 19 years old
New Ground 248 Goxhill (All Saints) Churchyard
Born in Swindon

PORTER, F.
Frank
Private 10355 2nd Battalion Wiltshire Regiment
Killed in Action 15th June 1915
XVI M 13 Caberet Rouge British Cemetery Souchez
Lived in Swindon

PORTER, T.E.
Thomas Edgar
Private 7584 1st Battalion Wiltshire Regiment
Killed in Action 27th October 1914
Panel 33 and 34 Le Touret Memorial
Born in Swindon

T.E. Porter

POSTLETHWAITE, M.E.
Morton Ewart
Private 27876 6th Battalion Wiltshire Regiment (Formerly 30920 Dorset Regt)
Died 19th October 1918. 25 years old
Son of Harry Postlethwaite
Husband of Dora N Postlethwaite of 91 Victoria Road
Malbork Memorial Poland (Died in Captivity)
Born in Swindon

POTTER, J.
John
Rifleman 205041 22nd Battalion The Rifle Brigade
Died 5th October 1920. 52 years old
Husband of Elizabeth Potter of 10A Oxford Street
C 3682 Radnor Street Cemetery

POWELL, A.H.
Arthur Henry
Private 28261 1st Battalion Somerset Light Infantry
Killed inAction 4th October 1917
Panel 41 – 42 and 163A Tyne Cot
Born in Swindon

PRANGLEY, N.C.
Norman Conway
Private B/23332 23rd Battalion Royal Fusiliers
Killed in Action 17th February 1917
21 years old
Son of George Conway Prangley and Louisa Prangley of Ashton Keynes
I E 4 Regina Trench Cemetery Grandcourt
Born in Swindon

PRATT, E.
Ernest
Lance Corporal 9509 2nd Battalion Royal Berkshire Regiment
Died of Wounds 30th September 1915
I 13 147 Bailleul Communal Cemetery Extension (Nord)
Lived in Swindon

PREATER, A.B.
Arthur Benjamin
Private 23716 2nd Battalion Wiltshire Regiment
Killed in Action 18th October 1916
Pier and Face 13A Thiepval Memorial
Born in Swindon

PREATER, C.L.
Charles Lewis
Private 25900 6th Battalion Wiltshire Regiment
Killed in Action 29th April 1918
Panel 119 to 120 Tyne Cot.
Born in Swindon

PREATER, H.F.
Herbert Frederick
Lance Sergeant 203471 2/8th Battalion Worcestershire Regiment
Killed in Action 1st November 1918
I H 21 Cross Roads Cemetery Fontaine Au Bois
Lived in Swindon

PRESS, W.H.
William Henry
Sapper 520066 565th Army Troops Company Royal Engineers
Died 7th October 1917
I A 18 Malo Les Bains Communal Cemetery
Born in Swindon

PRESTON, A.E.
Albert Edgar
Driver 53397 16th Battery 41st Brigade Royal Field Artillery
Died of Wounds 10th September 1914
25 years old
Son of John Samuel and Lucy Preston of 32 Gloucester Place Cheltenham
E 843 Cheltenham Cemetery

PRICE J.
John
Gunner 3274 134th Battery 32nd Brigade Royal Field Artillery
Killed in Action 1st November 1916
Pier and Face 1A and 8A Thiepval Memorial
Born in Swindon

PRICE, J.W.
James
Gunner 1622 2nd Wessex Brigade Reserve Battery Royal Field Artillery
Died 8th February 1915 . 27 years old
Son of Mr and Mrs Fry (Step – Father)
Lived in Morris Street with his Wife and Daughter
B 1777 Radnor Street Cemetery.
His Funeral was held at St Augustines Church. The Procession took place from his house to St Augustines. A full military

burial then followed in Swindon Cemetery.

J. Price

PRICE, W.
William
Private 13456 314th Company Royal Defence Corps (Formerly 22151 Liverpool Regt)
Died 9th September 1916
V C 18 Liverpool (Anfield) Cemetery
Born in Swindon

PRIDDLE, H.J.
Henry James
Private 1524 1/7th Battalion Lancashire Fusiliers
Killed in Action 7th August 1915
Panel 58 to 72 and 218 to 219 Helles Memorial
Born in Swindon

PRIOR, G.H.
George Harry
Leading Stoker K/16131 HM Trawler 'Bombardier'
Died 27th March 1919. 25 years old
Son of John and Lilian Amy of 68 Lansdown Road
31 Plymouth Naval Memorial

PROBERTS, T.
Thomas
Private 8100 2nd Battalion Wiltshire Regiment
Killed in Action 1st December 1917
II A 12 Zandvoorde British Cemetery
Born in Swindon

PROVIS, N.
Nelson
Private 5940 1st Battalion Wiltshire Regiment
Killed in Action 20th November 1914
Panel 53 Menin Gate Memorial
Lived in Swindon

PUFFET, H.M.
Harry Macock
Private 7549 1st Battalion Wiltshire Regiment
Killed in Action 31st October 1914
27 years old
Son of Mrs Mary Ann Cave of 39 Locksbrook Road Lower Weston Bath
Panel 33 and 34 Le Touret Memorial
Born in Swindon

PULLEN, P.W.
Percy William
Acting Bombardier 860715 Attached 3rd Echelon GHQ Royal Field Artillery
Died 15th July 1917
IV F 7 Basra War Cemetery
Born in Swindon

RAISON, W.L.
William Lawrence
Corporal 265170 1/1st Bucks Battalion Oxfordshire and Buckinghamshire Light Infantry
Killed in Action 16th April 1917
Pier and Face 10A and 10D Thiepval Memorial
Born in Swindon

RANDALL, C.H.P.
Charles Henry Portlock
Private 9048 1st Battalion Wiltshire Regiment
Died of Wounds 13th October 1914
19 years old

Son of Allan and Jane Randall
Panel 33 and 34 Le Touret Memorial
Lived in Swindon

RAWLINGS, F.H.
Francis Henry
Private 9232 5th Battalion Wiltshire
Regiment
Killed in Action 31st January 1917
XVIII E 8 Amara War Cemetery
Born in Swindon

RAWLINGS, J.
James
Private 7628 1st Battalion Wiltshire
Regiment
Killed in Action 18th October 1914
Panel 33 and 34 Le Touret Memorial
Born in Stratton St Margaret

F. Rawlings

READ, A.E.
Arthur Edward
Private 10673 1st Battalion Wiltshire
Regiment
Killed in Action 5th July 1916
22 years old
Son of Edward Arthur and Annie Read of
7 Ashford Road
Pier and Face 13A Thiepval Memorial
Born in Swindon and worked in the GWR
as a boiler smiths apprentice.

REED, S.G.H.
Sydney George Herbert
Lieutenant 104th Battalion Machine Gun
Corps
Died 24th December 1918. 25 years old
Son of Thomas and Kate Reed of Sanford
House Springfield Road
B5 Kortrijk (St Jan) Communal Cemetery
Lived in Swindon and remembered on a

stained glass window in Christchurch
Swindon

A.E. Read

REES, A.C.
Albert Charles
Sapper 15105 55th Field Company Royal
Engineers
Killed in Action 3rd June 1915
I G 4 Guards Cemetery Windy Corner
Cuinchy
Born in Swindon

REEVES, F.J.
Frederick James
Corporal WR/303545 Inland Water
Transport Royal Engineers
Died 30th September 1918. 27 years old
Son of W Reeves
I N 21 Basra War Cemetery
Born in Swindon

F.J. Reeves

REEVES, R.H.
Private 19544 6th Battalion Duke of
Cornwalls Light Infantry
Died 8th October 1915. 15 years old
I H 19 Spoilbank Cemetery

REVELEY, V.M.
Vernon Melville
Private 37517 C Company 1st Battalion
Wiltshire Regiment
Killed in Action 2nd November 1918
19 years old
Son of Mr E P Reveley of 35 St Barmocks
Road Ilfracombe Devon.

I B 27 Poix Du Nord Communal Cemetery Extension
Lived in Swindon (Cheltenham Street)

REYNOLDS, H.H.
Hubert Harry
Rifleman 50295 1/8th London Regiment Rifle Brigade
Killed in Action 9th September 1918
19 years old
Son of Ernest James and Sarah Alice Reynolds of 73 Winifred Street
II A 2 Epehy Wood Farm Cemetery
Lived in Swindon

H. Reynolds

REYNOLDS, W.A.
William Arthur
Private 3/9267 2nd Battalion Wiltshire Regiment
Killed in Action 8th July 1916
28 years old
Son of Mr and Mrs Arthur William Reynolds of 6 Cardiff Road Canton Abercynon
Husband of L Reynolds of 4 Morris Street Rodbourne
Pier and Face 13A Thiepval Memorial

RHYMES, S.
Sidney
Private 9426 5th Battalion Wiltshire Regiment
Killed in Action 23rd July 1915
Panel 156 to 158 Helles Memorial
Lived in Swindon

RICHENS, G.
George
Private 21168 7th Battalion Gloucester shire Regiment
Died 31st May 1918
XX H 4 Baghdad (North Gate) Cemetery
Born in Swindon

RICHMAN, A.D.
Archibald David
Private 5185 63rd Company Machine Gun Corps (Formerly 22338 Wiltshire Regiment
Died 4th February 1918. 21 years old
Son of David Richman of 7 Devizes Road
III C 31 Hazebrouck Communal Cemetery
Born in Swindon

RICHMAN, A.G.
Alfred George
Private 26086 5th Battalion Wiltshire Regiment
Died of Wounds 19th February 1917
XXVII E 2 Amara War Cemetery
Lived in Swindon

RICKETTS, P.T.
Percy Thomas
Private 7013 1st Battalion Wiltshire Regiment
Killed in Action 19th October 1914
29 years old
Son of Philip and Frances Emily Ricketts of 12 Spring Gardens
Husband of Lily Ricketts of 11 Ponting Street
Panel 33 and 34 Le Touret Memorial
Born in Swindon

RIGHTON, C.H.
Charles Herbert
Private SPT5/1265 9th Battalion (City of London) Royal Fusiliers
Killed in Action 6th August 1916
21 years old
VIII F 13 Tincourt New British Cemetery
Born in Swindon

RIVERS, W.
William
Private 19514 B Company 1st Battalion Wiltshire Regiment
Killed in Action 20th June 1917
19 years old
Son of John and Fanny Rivers of Goat Acre Hilmarton Calne
Panel 53 Menin Gate Memorial
Born in Swindon

RIXON, W.J.
Walter John
Private 90700 23rd Field Ambulance Royal Army Medical Corps
Died of Wounds 25th October 1917
XXII A 15A Lijssenthoek Military Cemetery. Born in Swindon

D. Robbins

W.J. Rixon

C.W. Roberts

ROBBINS, D.
David
Sergeant 9085 1st Battalion Wiltshire Regiment
Killed in Action 29th July 1916
35 years old
Son of David and Sarah Robbins
Husband of Elizabeth Gertrude Robbins of 19 Britannia Place. Old Swindon
Pier and Face 13A Thiepval Memorial
Lived in Swindon

ROBBINS, H.
Henry
Lance Corporal G/21532 7th Battalion Queens own Royal West Kent Regiment (Formerly 28751 Glos. Regt)
Killed in Action 18th Sept 1918
35 years old
Husband of Phoebe Robbins of 238 Southmead Road, Westbury on Tym Bristol
Panel 7 Vis en Artois Memorial
Lived in Swindon

ROBERTS, C.W.H.
Charles William Henry
Sergeant 17417 34th Squadron Royal Flying Corps
Died 26th December 1917. 26 years old
Son of William Arthur and Eliza Roberts of Swindon
Plot 4 Row E Grave II Giavera British Cemetery Arcade Italy

ROBERTS, F.F.
Sergeant Major 8705 Ammunition Column 109th Brigade Royal Field Artillery
Died 29th March 1918
Husband of N Roberts 19 Samuel Street Woolich London

E 7368 Radnor Street Cemetery
Born in Swindon
Was an RSPCA Inspector in Swindon.
Whilst in France, Sgt-Maj Roberts wrote a letter to a Richard Passmore of Wood Str ' Dear Mr Passmore,
No doubt you think I have forgotten us and your acts of kindness to me by keeping silent so long, but such is not the case. The fact is, we have been so busy that I really have not had time for writing. Now that we have come back for a rest, I have taken the opportunity of sending a few lines to you. Before I proceed further, I hope you and Mrs Passmore are well and also your sons? As for myself, I never felt better. I must tell you, things are looking very rosy here at our quarter, and from what I can gather, it is well all along the line. I only hope the lads of Swindon will (and I have no doubt about it) respond to Lord Derby's call and come in their hundreds, and then we shall soon put the irons on 'Big Willie' and 'Little Willie' also. There is no doubt, in my opinion, they are beaten, and from conversations with the prisoners, they know it. I took part in the last great advance.

120

We had a rough time of it but they had a worse one! It was a hard time but it was a grand move, and we came out on top. I would like to tell you all that happened, but I am afraid I must not. The sights were awful, but what is that when we are fighting for our freedom and liberty? Our boys are marvels.

They seem to take trouble as if they were having a ham and egg breakfast. - Think no more of it. Our boys know they have the enemy beaten and we are now playing their game and giving them a taste of their own medicine. i.e gas, which I can assure you, they don't relish. I am with , or close to the old County Battalion, The Wilts. They too have had rough time of it, but are eager for more! A good old regiment, and the County ought to be proud of it!

I am sorry to say the weather is a great trouble to us at present. It has been raining for days and we are up to our boot – tops in mud. You can guess we look well and make a grand picture in a review at home. However, we are not down hearted, but keep pegging on. I will close with kind regards and best wishes,

Yours truly   **F F Roberts.**

ROBERTSON, F.A.
Frank Aston
Private 7476 1st Battalion Bedfordshire Regiment
Killed in Action 13th October 1914
Panel 10 and 11 Le Touret Memorial
Born in Swindon

ROBINS, H.R.
Harold Richard
Air Mechanic 1st Class F/6479 Royal Naval Air Service Dunkirk Air Station
Died 19th October 1917. 20 years old
Son of John Thomas and Sarah Jane Robins of 21 Whiteman Street
II B 10 Dunkirk Town Cemetery   France
Born in Swindon Worked as an apprentice wheelwright in the Carriage and Wagon dept GWR

H.R. Robins

ROBINSON, F.   MSM
Sergeant 386765 Royal Engineers
Died 29th December 1918. 41 years old
Son of George and Alice Robinson
C 1189 Radnor Street Cemetery
Born in Swindon

ROBINSON, F.I.
Frederick Isaac
Driver 98467 A Battery Royal Field Artillery
Died of Wounds 7th April 1917
Panel 3 and 60 Basra Memorial Iraq
Born in Swindon

ROBINSON, F.S.
Frederick Stephen
Private 19265 1/4th Battalion Wiltshire Regiment
Died of Wounds 19th November 1917
19 years old

H.R. Robins

Son of Mrs A Robinson of 17 Catherine Street
B 153 Deir El Belah War Cemetery
Born in Swindon

F.I. Robinson

ROBINSON, W.J.
Died No Details

RODBOURNE, W.T.
William Tom
Private 25811 8th Battalion (City of London Regt) Royal Fusiliers
Killed in Action 19th September 1916
Bay 3 Arras Memorial
Born in Swindon

W.J. Robinson

ROE, L.
Died No Details

ROE, T.F.
Died No Details

ROOTS, L.V.
Leonard Victor
Private G/53001 12th Battalion Middlesex Regiment
Killed in Action 23rd October 1917
Panel 113 to 115 Tyne Cot Memorial
Lived in Swindon

W. Rodbourne

ROSE, E.V.
Edward Victor
Private 20276 12th Battalion (Bristols Own) Gloucestershire Regiment
Killed in Action 3rd September 1916
19 years old
Son of Thomas and Julia Martha Rose of 11 Hythe Grove Yardley Birmingham
Pier and Face 5A and 5B Thiepval Memorial
Born in Swindon

ROWLAND, E.T.
Eli Thomas
Lance Sergeant 13566 7th Battalion Wiltshire Regiment
Killed in Action 24th April 1917
37 years old
Husband of Lily Rowland of 84 Rosebery Street
Doiran Memorial
Born in Swindon and worked as a Hydraulic Forgemans Assistant in Loco Dept GWR

E.T. Rowland

ROWLES, A.H.   MM
Arthur Herbert
Gunner 124198 Royal Garrison Artillery
Died of Wounds 23rd August 1918
30 years old
Son of Herbert John and Edith Amelia

Rowles of Trethomas Bedwas Cardiff
VII B 9A Mont Huon Military Cemetery
Le Treport
Born in Swindon

RUDDLE, H.G.
Herbert George
Corporal 10675 5th Battalion Wiltshire
Regiment
Killed in Action 25th January 1917
XVII B I Amara War Cemetery
Born in Swindon

RUSS, G.E.
George Edward
Private 9699 2nd Battalion Wiltshire
Regiment
Died 31st August 1915. 22 years old
Son of Charles and Annie Russ of 8
Regent Place
III E II Niederzwehren Cemetery
Lived in Swindon

RUSSELL, F.E.   MID
Frank Edward
Corporal 8212 1st Battalion Wiltshire
Regiment
Died of Wounds 9th June 1915
Enclosure No 2V A 17 Bedford House
Cemetery
Born in Swindon

RUSSELL, W.G.
Died No Details

SADLER, W.
Private 35281 258th Protection by Royal
Defence Corps
Died 7th June 1917. Aged 54
Husband of Hariett Sadler of 123 Albion
Street
A 709 Radnor Street Cemetery

SALOWAY, W.L.
William Luke
Signal Boy J/32006 Royal Navy HMS
'Hampshire'
5th June 1916. 17 years old
Lived at 68 Gladstone Street
15 Portsmouth Naval Memorial

SANDERS, D.
David
Lance Corporal 86976 34th Battalion
Machine Gun Corps
(Formerly 2/266123 RASC)

Killed in Action 11th April 1918
34 years old
Son of Mary and James Sanders of 83
Bright Street, Gorse Hill
Panel II Ploegsteert Memorial
Born in Swindon

D. Sanders

SANSUM, A.J.
Albert John
Private 306733 1/6th Battalion
Warwickshire Regiment
Killed in Action 18th August 1917
38 years old
Son of John and Elizabeth Sansum of 136
William Street
Panel 23/28 and 163a Tyne Cott
Memorial
Lived in Swindon

A.J. Sandum

SANSUM, F.C.
Frederick Charles
Private 19936 1st Battalion Somerset
Light Infantry
Killed in Action 25th December 1916
20 years old.
Son of Charles Frederick and Rose
Sansum of 345 Oxford Street Weston
Super Mare Somerset
VII 10 Sailly-Saillisel British Cemetery
Born in Swindon

SAUNDERS, E.
Ernest
Private 1135 6th Battalion Leinster Regiment
Killed in Action 11th August 1915
Panel 184/185 Helles Memorial
Born in Wootton Bassett, lived in Swindon

SAUNDERS, E.A.
Private 21805 8th Battalion Royal Berkshire Regiment
Died of Wounds 7th September 1916
1 I A 19 Flaitron Copse Cemetery Mametz
Lived in Swindon

SAUNDERS, S.
Samuel
Private 20881 5th Battalion Wiltshire Regiment
Killed in Action 18th April 1916
18 years old
Son of Mrs Lucy Saunders of Fore Street, Ashton Keynes, Wiltshire
Panel 30 and 64 Basra War Memorial
Lived in Swindon

SAWYER, G.F.
George Francis
Private 6384 1st Battalion Wiltshire Regiment
Killed in Action 13th October 1914
Panel 33/34 Le Touret Memorial
Born in Swindon

SCAMMELL, M.F.
Maurice Frederick
Acting Corporal 20869 3rd Battalion Wiltshire Regiment
Died 14th January 1917. 16 years old
Son of Frederick and Catherine Scammell of 147 Beatrice Street
III C 2768 Melcombe Regis Cemetery Dorset
Lived in Swindon

SCAMMELL, S.H.
Sidney Harry
Private 26160 1s Battalion Wiltshire Regiment
Killed in Action 21st March 1918
41 years old
Son of Edwin and Maria Scammell of 135 Castle Street Salisbury
Husband of Alberia Martha Scammell of 83 Montague Street
Bay 7 Arras Memorial
Lived in Swindon

SCHOFIELD, S.W.
Stanley Williams
Private 89492 Royal Army Medical Corps
Died 23rd December 1918. 24 years old.
Son of Stanley and Emily Schofield of 25 Crombey Street
213 Christ Church Cemetery

SCOTT, W.H.
Walter
Lance Corporal R/15920 17th Battalion Kings Royal Rifle Corps
Killed in Action 28th May 1917
28 years old
Husband of Lillian A Scott of 22 Gloucester Street
III D 10 New Irish Farm Cemetery Belgium
Lived in Swindon

SCRUBY, W.S.
William Samuel
2nd Lieutenant 12th Battalion Middlesex Regiment
Killed in Action 29th June 1916
Pier and face 12D and 13B Thiepval Memorial
Attended North Wilts Technical College Victoria Road 1904

SCULL, A.
Albert
Private 22706 6th Battalion Wiltshire Regiment
Died of Wounds 21st September 1917
Son of Mr C W Scull of 66 The Street Lower Stratton
I A 56 Outtersteene Communal Cemetery Extension Bailleui
Lived in Stratton St Margaret

SCULL, J.T.
James Thomas
Private 267112 2/1st Bucks Battalion Oxfordshire and Buckinghamshire Light Infantry (Formerly 3003 Wiltshire Regiment)
Killed in Action 19th July 1916
21 years old
Son of Alfred and Fanny Scull of 63 Birch Street
Panel 83/85 Loos Memorial
Lived in Swindon
His Brother Reginald also fell (below)

SCULL, R.W.
Reginald Wakefield
Private 44117 2/4th Battalion Royal

North Wilts Technical College Football Team 1908 W. Scruby seated front far left.
H. Billett also KIA standing back right

R.W. Scull

Berkshire Regiment (Formerly 46195
Hants Regiment)
Killed in Action 16th April 1918
18 years old
Son of Alfred and Fanny Scull of 63 Birch
Street
I A 6 St Venant-Robecq Road British
Cemetery
Lived in Swindon

J.T. Skull

SCULL, P.F.
Percy Francis
Private 3020 London Regiment 13th
Princess Louise's Kensington Battalion
Killed in Action 19th May 1915
Panel 10 Ploegsteert Memorial
Born in Swindon, lived in Battersea

SEAGER, E.R.
Edwin Robert
Acting Corporal 15004 54th Field
Company Royal Engineers
Died 14th July 1916. 29 years old
Son of Mr F H and Mrs E Seager of 10
Kings Cliff Terrace Bridgewater Somerset
XI B 33 Caterpillar Valley Cemetery
Longueval
Born in Swindon

SEAGER, H.J.
Henry James
Private 6731 1st Battalion Wiltshire
Regiment
Died of Wounds 19th October 1914
CE 1606 Netley Military Cemetery
Born in Swindon

125

SEAGER, J.
John
Sergeant 13596 5th Battalion Wiltshire Regiment
Died of Wounds 12th August 1915
Panel 156/158 Helles Memorial
Dardanelles
Born in Swindon
Was a striker in No 14 Shop Loco and Carriage Works GWR

SEAGER, P.
Percy
Private 7016 C Company 1st Battalion Wiltshire Regiment
Killed in Action 29th October 1914
27 years old
Son of James and Mary Seager
Panel 33/34 Le Touret Memorial France
Born in Swindon

SEALEY, J.
John
Lance Corporal 8401 1st Battalion Wiltshire Regiment
Killed in Action 22nd March 1918
Bay 7 Arras Memorial
Born in Swindon

J. Seager

SEDGWICK, C.F.
Charles Frederick
Private 1st Battalion East Kent Regiment 'The Buffs'
Died 15th September 1916
Pier and Face 5D Thiepval Memorial

SELBY, A.H.
Arthur Henry
Private 10651 2nd Battalion Wiltshire Regiment
Killed in Action 26th September 1915
35 years old
Brother of Mr F J Selby of 112 Princes Street
Panel 102 Loos Memorial
Lived in Swindon

A.H. Selby

SELLARS, A.W.
Ashley Williams
Private 202011 1/4th Battalion Hampshire Regiment
(Formerly 3419 Wiltshire Regiment)
Killed in Action 24th February 1917
Panel 21 and 63 Basra Memorial

A.W. Sellars

SELWOOD, J.R.
John Robert
Private 28914 15th Battalion Hampshire Regiment (Formerly 46222 Wiltshire Regiment)
Killed in Action 4th September 1918
19 years old
Son of Robert and Sarah Jane Sellwood of 189 Cricklade Road
Panel 88 to 90 and 162 Tyne Cot Memorial
Born in Stratton St Margaret

SELLWOOD, W.J.H.
William Joseph Henry
Lance Corporal 1104 10th Battalion Royal Fusiliers
Killed in Action 10th April 1917
22 Years old

Husband of Adelaide Sellwood of 35
Kenwood Avenue Toronto Canada
Bay 7 Arras Memorial
Born in Swindon

SELMAN, C.F.
Charles Frederick
Guardsman 5494 Scots Guards
Died of Wounds 4th November 1914
Born in Swindon

SEXTON, G.H.
George Henry
Lance Corporal 7982 2nd Battalion
Wiltshire Regiment
Died of Wounds 28th September 1915
24 years old
Son of Ellen Sexton of 45 Newhall Street
Husband of Olive E Sexton of 58
Cheltenham Street
I 26 Fouquieres Churchyard Extension
Born in Swindon

SHAKESPEARE, W.F.
Walter Frank
Acting Corporal 10553 1st Battalion
Wiltshire Regiment
Killed in Action 12th March 1915
20 years old
Son of Mr H and Mrs M Shakespeare of 11
Morris Street
Panel 53 Menin Gate Memorial

SHARLAND, J.H.
Joseph Henry
Private 20697 5th Battalion Wiltshire
Regiment
Killed in Action 5th April 1916
Panel 30 and 64 Basra Memorial
Lived in Swindon

J.H. Sharland

SHARPES, C.
Charles
Private 9055 1st Battalion Wiltshire
Regiment
Killed in Action 16th June 1915
Panel 53 Menin Gate Memorial
Born in Swindon

SHARPS, J. MM
James
Private 7135 1st Battalion Wiltshire
Regiment
Died of Wounds 26th August 1916
28 years old
Son of Mrs J Sharps of 1 Cheltenham
Street
F 22 Beauval Communal Cemetery
Born in Swindon

SHAYLOR, G.E.
George Edward
Private 25351 8th Battalion Royal
Fusiliers
Killed in Action 23rd July 1916
Pier and Face 8c 9a and 16a Thiepval
Memorial
Born in Swindon

SHALDON, W.G.
William George
Engine Room Artificer 4th Class M/7115
HMS Pathfinder Royal Navy
Killed 5th September 1914. 27 years old
Son of John and Harriet Sheldon of 18
Dean Street
3 Portsmouth Naval Memorial
He was the first Swindonian reported
casualty. HMS Pathfinder struck a mine
20 miles off the North Coast.

SHEPPARD, A.W.
Archibald Walter
Sapper 520170 455th Field Company
Royal Engineers.
Died of Wounds 18th April 1917
28 years old
Son of W S and E Sheppard of 180 Clifton
Street
II G 5 Duisans British Cemetery Extension

SHEPPARD, P.J.
Percy John
Private 29691 2/8th Battalion Royal
Warwickshire Regiment (Formerly
268018 RASC)
Killed in Action 28th September 1917
IV B 42 Browns Copse Cemetery Roeux
Lived in Swindon.

SHERGOLD, R.D.
Reginald Donald
Pioneer 43515 81st Field Company Royal Engineers
Killed in Action 26th July 1916
21 years old
Son of Herbert John and Mary Shergold of 55 Birch Street
VIII I 9 Danzig Alley British Cemetery Mametz
Born in Swindon.

A.W. Sheppard

SHERMAN, H.B.
Henry Bert
Private 6902 Royal Army Medical Corps
Attached HMS Salta
Died 10th April 1917. 22 years old
Son of James and Eliza Sherman of 39 Princes Street
Salta Memorial Ste Marie Cemetery Le Havre

R. Shergold

SHURMER, H.
Henry
Private 46456 9th Battalion Welsh Regiment
Killed in Action 1st August 1917
II C 10 Oosttauerne wood cemetery
Born in Swindon

SHERWOOD, A.
Alfred
Private 7776 1st Battalion Royal Welsh Fusiliers
Killed in Action 16th May 1915
33 years old
Son of Alfred Sherwood
Husband of Mary Elizabeth Sherwood of 1 Farm Cottage Caolway Road Penn Field Wolverhampton.
Panel 13 and 14 Le Touret Memorial
Born in Swindon

SHUTE, T.
Thomas
Private 10706 1st Battalion Wiltshire Regiment
Died 25th May 1916
Husband of J Shute of 1 Chapel Lane Wanborough
II B 14 Ecoivres Military Cemetery Mont St Eloi
Born in Upper Stratton and remembered on plaque in St Margrets Church Stratton.

SIMMONDS, W.A.
William Abner
Driver 69025 Royal Field Artillery
Died 27th May 1916. 21 years old
Son of George Henderson and Ada C Simmonds of 151 Beatrice Street
C 3370 Radnor Street Cemetery
Born in Swindon

SIMPKINS, C.H.
Charles Henry
Private 54/044419 K Supply Company Royal Army Service Corps
Died 28th March 1915. 20 years old
Son of J and E Simpkins of 181 Beatrice Street
AF I 839 Aldershot Military Cemetery
Born in Swindon.

SIMPKINS, F.A.
Frederick Albert
Driver 966449 Royal Field Artillery
Killed in Action 7th November 1917
20 years old
Son of Mr and Mrs A J Simkins of 3 Church Walk Rodbourne Cheney
VIII D 9 Gaza War Cemetery
Born in Swindon.

F.A. Simpkins

SIMS, A.   MM
Arthur
Sergeant 79035 180th Tunneling Company Royal Engineers (Formerly 7309 Gloucestershire Regiment)
Killed in Action 15th November 1918
38 years old
Son of William and Ella Sims of Laurel Cottage Redwich Pilning Bristol
II E 12 Templeux Le Guerard Brtish Cemetery
Born in Swindon.

SIMS, J.W.
James William
Private 13938 2nd Battalion Wiltshire Regiment
Killed in Action 15th June 1915
39 years old
Brother of Mrs E A Collett of 59 Hinton Street Gorse Hill
Panel 33 and 34 Le Touret Memorial
Born in Swindon.

SINGER, W.H.
William Harold
Sergeant 201034 2/4th Battalion Wiltshire Regiment
Died 5th March 1915. 21 years old
Son of Mr and Mrs Singer of 78 Cheltenham Street
Face 7 Kirkee 1914 – 1918 Memorial India
Lived in Swindon.
Worked in R Shop GWR and remembered on its memorial

SINNETT, S.A.
Sapper 520187 565th Company Royal Engineers
Killed in Action 18th September 1918
M 6 Ruigaulcourt Military Cemetery

SKINNER, W.R.
William Robert
Sergeant 53051 2nd Battalion Lancashire Fusiliers (Formerly 1430 RASC)
Died of Wounds 4th May 1918
23 years old
Husband of Ada Skinner of 'Yew Trees' Bisley Old Road Stroud Glos.
VI F 7 Lapuqroy Military Cemetery
Born in Swindon.

SKYRME, H.J.
Hubert James
Private 25463 1st Battalion Warwickshire Regiment
Killed in Action 6th October 1917
I F 8 Cement House Cemetery
Lived in Swindon.

W.H. Singer

SLADE, F.
Bombardier 38584 84th siege battery Royal Garrison Artillery
Died 13th February 1919. 23 years old
Son of Mr and Mrs Slade of 171 Beatrice Street
C3 Tourlaville Communal Cemetery and Extension

S.A. Sinnett

SLADE, J.H.B.
John Henry Bowman
Private 20079 9th Battalion Royal
Fusiliers
Killed in Action 6th October 1916
Pier and Face 8c 9a and 16a Thiepval
Memorial
Lived in Swindon.

SLATER, F.C.
Frederick Conway
Acting Corporal 7705 1st Battalion
Hampshire Regiment
Died of Wounds 3rd May 1915
I F II Bailleui Communal Cemetery
Extension (Nord)
Born in Swindon.

SLY, L.
Lemuel
Private 9845 1st Battalion Wiltshire
Regiment
Died of Wounds 30th October 1914
III A 3 Bethune Town Cemetery
Born in Wootton Bassett and lived in
Swindon

SMALL, H.H.
Herbert Henry
Private 204284 7th Battalion Somerset
Light Infantry (Formerly 5071 Wiltshire
Regiment)
Killed in Action 1st April 1918
Panel 25 and 26 Pozieres Memorial
Born in Swindon.

SMART, W.E.
William Elijah
Private 47233 22nd (Tyneside Scottish)
Battalion Northumberland Fusiliers
Killed in Action 21st March 1918
Bay 2-3 Arras Memorial
Born in Swindon.

SMITH, A.S.A.
Arthur Sidney Alfred
Private G/17455 7th Battalion East Kent
Regiment 'The Buffs'
Killed in Action 22nd August 1918
19 years old
Son of William R E and Kate Smith of 91
Eastcott Hill
II E 3 Becourt Military Cemetery Becordel
– Becourt

SMITH, A.
Archibald
Private 10444 B Company 2nd Battalion
Wiltshire Regiment
Killed in Action 8th July 1916
26 years old
Son of Frederick and Janet Smith of 132
Ferndale Road
Pier and Face 13a Thiepval Memorial
Born in Swindon.

A. Smith

SMITH, C.C.B.
Cyril Charles Bosworth
Rifleman 418001 9th Battalion London
Regiment
Died of Wounds 29th April 1918
25 years old

Frank Slade
Pictured in Jerusalem 1916

130

Son of Charles James and Esther Jane Smith of Swindon.
I D 27 Crouy British Cemetery Crouy Sur Somme
Born in Swindon.

SMITH, D.
David
Private 242844 1/6th Battalion Royal Warwickshire Regiment
Died of Wounds 18th April 1917
38 years old
Son of Samuel and Emma Smith
IV G 19 Perrone Communal Cemetery Extension
Lived in Swindon.

SMITH, F.
Frank
Sergeant 9370 61st Company Machine Gun Corps (Formerly 768 Royal Fusiliers)
Died of Wounds 10th August 1918
37 years old
Husband of Mrs A Smith of 55 Chelsea Park Dwellings Kings Road Chelsea, London
IV A 20 Aire Communal Cemetery
Born in Swindon.

SMITH, F.C.
Frederick Charles
Private 38993 7th Battalion Duke of Cornwalls Light Infantry
Killed in Action 29th September 1918
19 years old
Son of Mr and Mrs F C Smith of 42 St Philips Road Upper Stratton
Panel 6 Vis en Artois Memorial
Born in Stratton and remembered on plaque in St Margrets Church Stratton

SMITH, F.W.
Frederick William.
Private 47020 2nd Battalion Wiltshire Regiment
Killed in Action 20th October 1918
Husband of L N Smith of 326 Cricklade Road Gorse Hill
V C 13 St Aubert British Cemetery
Born in Stratton

SMITH, F.W.
Francis William.
Private 3/9500 2nd Battalion Wiltshire Regiment
Killed in Action 17th May 1915
Panel 33 and 34 Le Touret Memorial
Lived in Swindon.

SMITH, G.J.
George James
Private 14485 B Company 7th Battalion Wiltshire Regiment (Formerly 13812 Oxs and Bucks L I)
Killed in Action 24th April 1917
23 years old
Son of Frederick and Elizabeth Smith of 12 Groves Street
Doiran Memorial
Born in Swindon.

SMITH, G.J.
George John
Private 10265 2nd Battalion Wiltshire Regiment
Killed in Action 31st May 1918
Son of Mr and Mrs C Smith of 61 Medgebury Road
Husband of Mrs Smith of 2 Brunel Street
Soissons Memorial
Born in Swindon.
Formerly employed with Eastman Ltd of Regent Street

SMITH, H.
Harold
Corporal 8397 1st Battalion Wiltshire Regiment
Died of Wounds 27th October 1914
22 Years old
Son of William and Emily Jane Smith
C E 1617 Netley Military Cemetery
Born in Swindon.

J. Smith

SMITH, J.
John
Private 14210 7th Battalion Wiltshire Regiment
Killed in Action 24th April 1917
34 years old
Husband of Emily Amelia Smith of

'Ashdene' Highworth Road South Marston.
Doiran Memorial   Salonika
Born in Swindon.

SMITH, J.
John
Private 6035 1st Wiltshire Regiment
Killed in Action 19th November 1914
Panel 53 Menin Gate Memorial
Born in Stratton and remembered on plaque in St Margrets Church Stratton

SMITH, J.
John
Private 27953 9th Battalion Gloucestershire Regiment
Killed in Action 6th March 1917
F 1262 Karasouli Military Cemetery Greece
Born in Swindon.

SMITH, J.
Joseph
Acting Lance Corporal P/12417 Military Police Mounted Branch
Died 13th February 1919
Born in Swindon.

SMITH, P.E.K.
Lieutenant 31st Battalion 6th Canadian Infantry Brigade
Attended North Wilts Technical College Victoria Road and remembered on its Stained Glass window memorial

SMITH, R.R.
Raymond Reginald
Lance Corporal 12055 6th Battalion Wiltshire Regiment
Died of Wounds 8th July 1916
I F 26 Heilly Station Cemetery Mericourt L'Abbe
Born in Swindon.

SMITH, S.C.
Sapper 391 Wilts Fortress Company Royal Engineers
Died 1st July 1915. 24 years old
Son of S and C Smith of 54 Manchester Road
E 8664 Radnor Street Cemetery
Attended North Wilts Technical College Victoria Road in 1906 and remembered on its stained glass window memorial.

SMITH, G.A.
George Alfred
Private 9169 2nd Battalion Wiltshire Regiment
Killed in Action 9th July 1916. 22 yrs old
Son of Arthur William and Selina Annie Smith of 2 Cromwell Street
Pier and Face 13a Theipval Memorial
Born in Swindon. His Brother Sidney also fell (Below)

SMITH, S.W.
Sidney Walter
Private 23662 2nd Battalion Royal Berkshire Regiment (Formerly 21858 Somerset Light Infantry)
Killed in Action 5th March 1917
27 years old
Son of Arthur William and Selina Annie Smith of 2 Cromwell Street
Pier and Face 11D Thiepval Memorial
Born in Swindon. His Brother George also fell (Above)

SMITH, S.R.
Sidney Rowland
Private 18065 5th Battalion Wiltshire Regiment
Killed in Action 10th August 1915
18 years old
Son of James and Charlotte Smith of 3 Cricklade Road Purton
Panel 156 to 158 Helles Memorial

S.R. Smith

SMOKER, H.J.
Henry James
Private 9126 2nd Battalion Dorset Regiment
Died 12th September 1917
XVI N 13 Baghdad (North Gate) War Cemetery
Born in Swindon.

SNOWDEN, C.W.
Charles William.
Private G/50866 2nd Battalion Royal Fusiliers
Died of Wounds 21st March 1918
38 years old
Son of William Snowden of Ramsgate
Husband of Holly Snowden of 85 High Street Margate
II G 12 Achief Le Grand Communal Cemetery Extension
Lived in Swindon.

SOUTHWELL, H.A.
Harry A
Sapper 46274 89th Field Company Royal Engineers
Died of Wounds 13th July 1915
21 years old
Son of Henry John and Florence Southwell of 16 Park Lane
III C I Lijssenthoek Military Cemetery
Born in Swindon.
Died in Hospital of wounds received at Ypres. His Father was secretary of the GWR Mechanics Institution.

H.A. Southwell

SPACKMAN, W.E.
William Edward
Private 5776 2nd Battalion Wiltshire Regiment
Killed in Action 18th October 1916
Pier and Face 13a Thiepval Memorial
Born in Wroughton and lived in Swindon.

SPEAKE, H.V.
Harold Victor.
Private 21815 13th Battalion Gloucester-shire Regiment
Died 21st March 1918. 20 years old
Son of Mr T and Mrs M A Speake

of 92 Albion Street
V F 15 Peronne Communal Cemetery Extension
Born in Swindon.

SPECK, G.F.
George Fred
Corporal M2/151078 Royal Army Service Corps
Killed in Action 30th May 1918
V B 42 Longuenesse (St Omer) Souvenir Cemetery
Born in Swindon.

SPREADBURY, B.B.
Bertram Byron
Sapper 520034 565th Company Royal Engineers
Killed in Action 18th September 1918
25 years old
Son of Andrew and Patience Spreadbury of 106 William Street
M 6 Royaulcourt Military Cemetery
Born in Swindon.

B.B. Spreadbury

SQUIRE, F.R.
Frederick Robert
Leading Stoker 305691 HMS Queen Mary Royal Navy
Died 31st May 1916. 29 years old
Son of Frederick Robert and Bertha Squire
Husband of Florence Amy Squire of 6 Horsell Street
17 Portsmouth Naval Memorial

STACEY, E.T.
Edward Tom
Private 200285 1/4th Battalion Wiltshire Regiment
Died 31st July 1916. 22 years old

Son of Thomas and Emily Stacey of 137 Beatrice Street.
Mem. 158 Angora Baghdad (North Gate) War Cemetery
Born in Swindon.

STACEY, S.C.
Stephen Charles
Lance Corporal 23575 5th Battalion Royal Berkshire Regiment (Formerly 20341 Somerset L I)
Died of Wounds 21st July 1917
20 years old
Son of Barton Stephen and Ellen Alberta Stacey of 108 Stafford Street
I H 9 Monchy British Cemetery Monchy Le Preux.
Born in Swindon.

STAFFORD, G.
George
Private 6038 1st Battalion Gloucester-shire Regiment
Died of Wounds 5th November 1914
Panel 22 and 34 Menin Gate Memorial
Born in Swindon.

STAITE, W.
Walter
Private 10998 2nd Battalion Wiltshire Regiment
Died of Wounds 16th April 1915
22 years old
Son of Mr and Mrs George Staite of Stratton St Margret.
K 12 Bailleui Communal Cemetery (Nord)
Remembered on Plaque in St Margrets Church Stratton

STALLARD, F.
Francis
Private 1598 1/1st Battalion Hereford shire Regiment
Killed in Action 10th August 1915
Panel 198 Helles Memorial. Dardanelles
Born in Swindon.

STALLARD, W.E.
William Edward
Driver 130314 63rd Brigade Royal Field Artillery
Killed in Action 3rd December 1917
20 years old
Son of William James and Mary Ann Stallard of Jubilee Cottages Wanborough
Panel 1 Cambrai Memorial Louveral
Lived in Swindon.

STANLEY, O.J.
Oscar James
Bombardier 148378 231st Siege Battery Royal Garrison Artillery
Died of Wounds 8th August 1918
25 years old
Son of Oscar and Elizabeth Stanley of 13 Caulfield Road.
V A 19 Crouy British Cemetery Crouy Sur Somme
Born in Swindon
Formerly employed by Longs Furniture removals of Wellington Street

STAPLES, H.
Herbert
Company Sergeant Major 13600 7th Battalion Wiltshire Regiment
Killed in Action 13th October 1918
52 Maurois Communal Cemetery
Lived in Swindon.

H. Staples

STEPHENS, F.
Frank
Private 8523 2nd Battalion Wiltshire Regiment
Killed in Action 24th October 1914
22 years old
Son of Frank and Mrs E A Stephens of Didcot Berkshire
Panel 53 Menin Gate Memorial
Born in Swindon.

STEPHENS, T.S.
Thomas Stratton
Private 18372 2nd Battalion Wiltshire Regiment
Killed in Action 15th June 1915
Panel 33 and 34 Le Touret Memorial
Lived in Swindon.

STEVENS, C.
Charles
Private 7501 2nd Battalion Wiltshire
Regiment
Killed in Action 12th March 1915
Panel 33 and 34 Le Touret Memorial
Born in Swindon.

STEVENS, E.J.
Private 10582 2nd Battalion Wiltshire
Regiment
Died 12th August 1917. 22 years old
Son of Henry and Mary Stevens
C 413 Radnor Street Cemetery

STEVENS, G.W.
George W
Private 20711 1st Battalion Wiltshire
Regiment
Killed in Action 5th October 1916
Pier and Face 13a Thiepval Memorial
Born in Swindon.

STEVENS, H.A.
Herbert Arthur
Sapper 28874 2nd Field Company Royal
Engineers
Killed in Action 9th August 1916
21 years old
Son of William and Mary Ann Stevens of
18 Reading Street
III M 9 Vermelles British Cemetery
Born in Swindon.

STEVENS, W.F.
William Frederick
Private 9120 1st Battalion Wiltshire
Regiment
Died of Wounds 21st October 1914
Son of Mr W and Mrs E Stevens of
Overtown Lodge Wroughton
O I 754 Bournmouth East Cemetery
Born in South Cerney Lived in Swindon.

STINCHCOMBE, E.
Eric
Private 11331 5th Battalion Wiltshire
Regiment
Killed in Action 11th August 1915
17 Years old
Son of William and Mary Stinchcombe of
'Hillside' Deerborn Road Guildford
Sp. Memorial D 10 Embarkation pier
cemetery Dardanelles
Lived in Swindon.

STONE, C.
Charles
Private 12351 7th Battalion Wiltshire
Regiment
Killed in Action 18th October 1918
III F II Highland Cemetery Le Cateau
Born in Swindon.

STONE, F.
Frank
Private 19457 6th Battalion Wiltshire
Regiment
Killed in Action 2nd July 1916
20 years old
Brother of Maud Kimber of 479 Ferndale
Road
Pier and Face 13a Thiepval Memorial
Born in Swindon.

STONE, J.
Joseph
Sergeant 3/603 3rd Battalion Wiltshire
Regiment
Died 23rd July 1918. 43 years old
Husband of L Stone of 34 Pembroke
Street
C 1475 Radnor Street Cemetery
Born in Swindon.

STONE, W.
William.
Private 20872 2nd Battalion South Wales
Borderers
Killed in Action 11th April 1918
Panel 5 Ploegsteert Memorial
Born in Swindon.

STONE, W.E.
William Ephrame
Sergeant 8902 1st Battalion Wiltshire
Regiment
Killed in Action 22nd June 1915
21 years old
Son of William and Harriet Stone of 10
Bright Street Gorse Hill
Panel 53 Menin Gate Memorial
Lived in Swindon.

STRANGE, A.J.
Augustus
Sapper 520252 211th Field Company
Royal Engineers
Killed in Action 29th October 1918
21 years old
Son of Henry and Martha Strange of 199
Cricklade Road
II H 20 Pont de Nieppe Communal
Cemetery

A. Strange

STRANGE, J.
John
Private 19432 5th Battalion Wiltshire Regiment
Died 9th April 1916
Panel 30 and 64 Basra Memorial
Born in Swindon lived in Stratton Green and remembered on plaque in St Margrets Church Stratton

STRANGE, T.
Thomas
Private 7315 1st Battalion Wiltshire Regiment
Killed in Action 18th September 1914
La Ferte Sous Jouane Memorial
Lived in Swindon.

STRATFORD, G.W.
George Williams
Private 32097 10th Hussars
Died 2nd October 1918. 40 years old
Son of William and Sarah Stratford
Husband of Ada Louisa Stratford of 45 Union Street
504 Christ Church cemetery

STRATFORD, W.F.
William Frederick
Corporal 28469 8th Battalion Somerset Light Infantry
Killed in Action 5th April 1918
Born in Swindon.

STRATFORD, W.H.
William Henry
Driver 860750 Royal field Artillery
Died 7th May 1917
IV K 13 Basra war cemetery
Born in Swindon.

STRATTON, E.J.
Edward John
Private 19561 5th Battalion Wiltshire Regiment
Killed in Action 9th April 1916. 18 yrs old
Son of Edward J and Alice L Stratton of 58 Ipswich Street
Panel 30 and 34 Basra Memorial
Born in Stratton and remembered on plaque in St Margrets Church Stratton

STROUD, C.E.
Charles Edward
Corporal 10122 2nd Battalion Wiltshire Regiment
Died of Wounds 6th March 1916
21 years old
Son of William Henry and Elizabeth May Stroud of 41 Stanier Street
D 1501 Radnor Street Cemetery
Born in Swindon.

C.E. Stroud

STROUD, W.B.
William Bert
Private 26451 1/5th Battalion Gloucester-shire Regiment
Killed in Action 5th October 1918
Panel 6 Vis en Artois Memorial
Born in Wroughton lived in Swindon.

STURGES, E.J.
Ernest John
Lance Corporal 27770 4th Battalion
Bedfordshire Regiment
Killed in Action 27th March 1918
38 years old
Son of John Ann Sturges of 4 Birch Street
Bay 5 Arras Memorial
Born in Swindon.

STYLES, A.E.H.
Albert Edward Henry
Private 22022 5th Battalion Wiltshire
Regiment
Died 21st July 1916
VI D 21 Basra War Cemetery
Born in Swindon.

SULLIVAN, J.
Joseph
Private 20709 5th Battalion Wiltshire
Regiment
Killed in Action 25th January 1917
27 years old
Son of Patrick and Rachel Sullivan of
Deptford London
XVII B 7 Amara War Cemetery
Lived in Swindon.

SUMMERS, E.C.
Edgar Charles
Private 16190 1st Battalion Hampshire
Regiment
Killed in Action 23rd October 1916
31 years old
Son of John and Patience Summers of
Murhill Bath
Pier and Face 7c and 7b Thiepval
Memorial
Born in Swindon.

SUTTON, G.F.
George Fred.
Corporal 71029 23rd Battery 40th
Brigade Royal Field Artillery
Died of Wounds 16th September 1917
I E 38 Ypres Reservoir Cemetery
Born in Swindon.

SUTTON, W.E.G.
William Edward George
Private 27293 6th Battalion Shropshire
Light Infantry
Killed in Action 10th June 1918
19 years old
Son of W And Fanny Jane Sutton of 30
Carfax Street
V C 2 Sucrerie Cemetery Ablain St Nazaire
Born in Swindon

SYRETT, H. MM
Harry
Lance Corporal 9338 2nd Battalion
Berkshire Regiment
Killed in Action 16th August 1917
Panel 105 to 106 and 162 Tyne Cot
Memorial
Lived in Swindon, and remembered on
plaque in St Margarets Church Stratton

Old Soldiers at the Menin Gate in the 1930s.
Alfred Burton, Royal Engineers of Clifton
Street (front extreme left) spent much of his
time in the Ypres Salient.

J. Sullivan

TANNER, F.
Fred.
Private 22899 1st Battalion Wiltshire Regiment
Killed in Action 6th July 1916. 24 yrs old
Son of Mrs Ruth C Tanner Callow Hill Brinkworth
Pier and Face 13a Thiepval Memorial
Born in Swindon

TANNER, W.J.
Private 22649 No 1 Inf Works Coy Wiltshire Regiment
Killed in Action 1st July 1916. 19 yrs old
Son of E and Ada Tanner
126 ½ Kingston Portsmouth Cemetery
Born in Swindon

TARRANT, A.
Alfred
Private 200342 1st/4th Hampshire Regiment
Killed in Action 21st January 1916
Panel 21 and 63 Basra War Memorial
Attended North Wilts Technical College Victoria Road in 1907 and remembered on its Stained glass window

TAVERNER, P.
Percy
Private 268430 2/6th Battalion Devonshire Regiment
Died 20th October 1918
Son of Arthur and Sarah Taverner of 45 Gooch Street
Face C Kirkee 1914 – 1918 Memorial India
Lived in Swindon Worked as Machineman Loco and carriage dept GWR

P. Taverner

TAYLOR, C.D.B.
Coleridge David Beale
Lance Corporal 8961 1st Battalion Wiltshire Regiment
Killed in Action 26th October 1914

Panel 33 and 34 Le Touret Memorial
Born in Swindon

TAYLOR, G.
George
Gunner 314446 B Battery South Midland (Warwickshire) Heavy Battery Royal Garrison Artillery. 241st Brigade Attached 48th Division Ammunition Column.
Died 8th November 1918. 37 years old
Husband of Mrs E Taylor 50 Devon Street Saltley Birmingham
Plot 2 Row B Grave 4 Grenezza British Cemetery Vicenza Italy
Born in Swindon.

TAYLOR, G.H.G.
George Henry Green
Private 3/9713 2nd Battalion Wiltshire Regiment
Killed in Action 9th April 1917
Brother of Mr W T Taylor of 36 Archer Road Eastleigh Hants
D 5 Neuville – Vitasse Road Cemetery.
Lived in Swindon Wagon painter in carriage and wagon dept GWR

G.H.G. Taylor

TAYLOR, C.S.
Charles Stewart
Private 47131 Machine Gun Corps
Died of Wounds 14th April 1918
Son of Mrs Kate Taylor of 111 Princes Street
E 7391 Radnor Street Cemetery
Lived in Swindon

TELLING, B.C.
Bert Charles
Private 20973 5th Battalion Wiltshire Regiment
Killed in Action 9th April 1916
23 years old
Son of Albert and Caroline Telling of 14 Whiteman Street Gorse Hill.
Panel 30 and 64 Basra Memorial
Born in Swindon

TELLING, E.W.
Edward Walton
Private 99620 4th Battalion Kings
Liverpool Regiment (Formerly 62348
Royal Flying Corps)
Died of Wounds 29th September 1918
19 years old
Son of Albert and Ellen Gertrude Telling
of 128 Dean Street
I Gauche Wood Cemetery Villers Guislain
Lived in Swindon

THATCHER, W.J.
Walter John
Private 203368 6th Battalion Wiltshire
Regiment (Formerly 2190 Royal Wiltshire
Yeomanry)
Killed in Action 23rd March 1918
Bay 7 Arras Memorial
Born in Swindon

THOMAS, F.A.
Frederick Alfred
Private 19347 6th Battalion Wiltshire
Regiment
Killed in Action 21st August 1916
18 years old
Son of Francis and Emily Maria Thomas of
4 Wescott Street
L 49 Kemmel Chateau Military Cemetery
Born in Swindon

THOMAS, H.
Henry
Private 11121 2nd Battalion Wiltshire
Regiment
Killed in Action 26th September 1915
23 years old
Son of Georget Louisa Thomas of Little
Blunsdon Highworth
Husband of Annie Eliza Thomas of 33
Ermin Street Stratton
Panel 102 Loos Memorial
Remembered on Plaque in St Margrets
Church Stratton

THOMAS, J.E.
Colonial Government Service Nigeria
Remembered on the stained glass
window memorial in the Technical
College
Victoria Road.

THOMAS, W.H.
William Henry
Private 5116 A Company 1st Battalion
Honorable Artillery Company

Died of Wounds 25th May 1917
29 years old
Son of H W and Amy Thomas of 63 Bath
Road
C 24 Midel Trench British Cemetery St
Laurent Blangy
One of the bells in Christchurch, was
bought by his Father in memory of him
in 1923.

THORNBURY, H.J.
Henry John
Private 3/9856 2nd Battalion Wiltshire
Regiment
Killed in Action 21st March 1918
23 years old
Son of Maurice and Elizabeth Ann
Thornbury of 10 Portsmouth Street
Panel 64 Pozieres Memorial
Lived in Swindon

THORNE, C.   DCM & BAR   MID
Charles
Company Sergeant Major 13568 7th
Battalion Wiltshire Regiment
Died of Wounds 13th October 1918
II A 8 Homechy British Cemetery
Lived in Swindon
Had worked previously at the Swindon
employment   exchange   and   joined
up at the outbreak of the war. He was
recommended in 1918 for 'Distinction
for Gallantry'. He was killed by shell fire
that fell in the transport lines, as he was
returning from duty in the front line.

THRUSH, B.
Ben
Private 8752 2nd Battalion Wiltshire
Regiment
Killed in Action 9th November 1915
III D 6 Guards Cemetery Windy Corner
Cuinchy.

G. Thrush

THRUSH, G.
George
Private 3/8471 6th Battalion Wiltshire Regiment
Died of Wounds 5th July 1916
I C 26 Heilly Station Cemetery Mericourt l'Abbe

TILLEY, A.P.
Arthur Percy
Private 12430 6th Battalion Bedfordshire Regiment
Killed in Action 30th May 1916
IV D 8 Bienvillers Military Cemetery
Born in Swindon

TILTMAN, C.
Charles
Private 24901 14th Battalion Hampshire Regiment
Killed in Action 1st November 1916
30 years old
Son of Richard James and Ellen Tiltman of Alma Place Rye Sussex
Pier and Face 7c and 7b Thiepval Memorial
Born in Aldershot and lived in Swindon

TIMMS, P.L. *ST LUKES MEMORIAL PLAQUE*
Percy Leonard
Private 57358 3rd Battalion Worcestershire Regiment
Died of Wounds 28th May 1918
19 years old
Son of Alfred W and Kate Timms of 18 Princes Street
I E 9 La Ville Aux Bois British Cemetery
Lived in Swindon

TITCHENER, F.
Frank
Sergeant 7125 1st Battalion Wiltshire Regiment
Died 2nd January 1915
IV A 27 Valenciennes (St Roch) Communal Cemetery
Born in Swindon

TITCHENER, H.B.
Herbert Beezley
Corporal 31502 1st Battalion Northamptonshire Regiment
Died 10th July 1917. 20 years old
Son of Ambrose Richard and Annie Titchener of 6 Euclid Street
Nieuport Memorial
Attended North Wilts Technical College

Victoria Road in 1909 Remembered on its stained glass window.

TITCOMBE, J.T.
John Thomas
Private 1279 6th Battalion Royal Munster Fusiliers (Formerly 12859 Wiltshire Regiment)
Died of Wounds 17th August 1915
23 years old
Son of Mr J and Mrs K Titcombe of 23 Cambria Place
Husband of Elsie May Titcombe of 10 Council Houses Farnborough Bath
Panel 185 to 190 Helles Memorial Dardanelles
Born in Swindon

TITCOMBE, J.C.
Joseph Cornelius
Private 22416 1st Battalion Dorset Regiment (Formerly 4508 Wiltshire Regiment)
Killed in Action 11th August 1918
20 years old
Son of Joseph Cornelius Titcombe of 24 John Street
Panel 7 Vis en Artois memorial
Born in Swindon

TITCOMBE, R.E.
Rupert Ernest
Bombardier 43694 Royal Garrison Artillery
Killed in Action 23rd December 1917
23 years old
Son of Robert and Rubecca Titcombe of Haydon Wick Post Office.
III D 25 Duhallow ADS Cemetery
Born in Swindon
Worked formerly in R shop GWR and remembered on its memorial.

R.E. Titcombe

TOMBS, E.R.M.
Edward Richard Mark
Private 41305 1st Battalion Duke of
Cornwalls Light Infantry (Formerly 35159
Wiltshire Regiment)
Killed in Action 14th April 1918
19 years old
Son of Richard and Mary Tombs of 76
Beatrice Street
I AA9 Aval Wood Military Cemetery Vieux
Berquin
Born in Swindon

TOMLYN, A.L.A.
Arthur Leonard Austin
Private 42213 1st Battalion Worcester
shire Regiment
Died 12th August 1918
V C 6 Hautmont Communal Cemetery
Born in Swindon

TOMPKINS, F.J.
Frederick John
Private 30877 6th Battalion Dorset
Regiment
Died at Sea 16th May 1918. 25 years old
Son of Mrs A E Tompkins of 20 Thomas
Street
C E 1950 Netley Military Cemetery
Born in Swindon

TOMPKINS, G.J.
George James
Private 7471 1st Battalion Wiltshire
Regiment
Killed in action 13th October 1914
Panel 33 and 34 Le Touret Memorial
Lived in Swindon

TOOP, A.H.
Arthur Harold
Lance Corporal 3/306 2nd Battalion
Wiltshire Regiment
Killed in Action 9th April 1917
Lived in Swindon

TOVEY, A.A.
Archibald Arthur
Lance Corporal 84491 D Company 1st
Battalion Machine Gun Corps (Formerly
145032 RASC)
Killed in Action 24th September 1918
19 years old
Son of Arthur and Ellen Tovey of 32
Cambria Place
V D I Vadencourt British Cemetery
Maissery
Born in Swindon

TOWNSEND, C.
Charles
Driver T4/058682 296th Company Royal
Army Service Corps
Died 5th March 1915
Son of Mr D Townsend of Broad Town.
A F 1825 Aldershot Military Cemetery
Born in Swindon

TOWNSEND, C.
Charlie
Private 306600 1/8th Battalion Royal
Warwickshire Regiment
Killed in Action 15th June 1918
24 years old
Son of Edwin and Julia Townsend of
Swindon
Plot 2 Row D Grave 8 Magnaboschi
British cemetery
Born in Swindon

E.A. Townsend

TOWNSEND, E.A.
Ernest Arthur
Acting Sergeant 10690 2nd Battalion
Wiltshire Regiment
Killed in Action 12th April 1915
27 years old
Son of John and Clare Townsend of 19
King John Street
Panel 33 and 34 Le Touret Memorial
Lived in Swindon Worked as a forgemans
helper in the steamhammer shop GWR

TOWNSEND, R.G.
Reginald George
Private 55044 13th Battalion Welsh
Regiment (Formerly 24562 Wiltshire
Regiment)
Died of Wounds 18th September 1918
A 19 Thilloy Road Cemetery Beaulencourt
Born in Swindon Worked in Loco dept
GWR

R.G. Townsend

TOWNSEND, W.
William
Private 3418 1/4th Battalion Oxfordshire and Buckinghamshire Light Infantry
Killed in Action 19th July 1916
20 years old
Son of Mrs E Townsend of Cote Bampton Oxon
Pozieres British Cemetery Ovillers La Boisselle
Lived in Swindon

TROTMAN, G.H.
George Henry
Private 1417 1/5th Battalion Manchester Regiment
Killed in Action 7th August 1915
21 years old
Son of George and Maria Ann Trotman of 15 Canal Side
Panel 158 to 170 Helles Memorial Dardanelles
Born in Swindon

TRUMAN, W.C.
William Charles
Corporal 8499 1st Battalion Wiltshire Regiment
Died of Wounds 22nd October 1914
42 years old
Son of Arthur and Charlotte Truman
Husband of Ada Elizabeth Truman of 34 Bath Terrace Swindon
B10 2 210D Birmingham (Lodge Hill) Cemetery   Lived in Swindon

TUCK, F.G.
Frederick George
Private 14179 7th Battalion Norfolk Regiment
Killed in Action 20th April 1916

II K 38 Vermelles British Cemetery
Born in Swindon

TUCK, W.J.
William John
Private 23610 1st Battalion Wiltshire Regiment
Killed in Action 7th July 1916
26 years old
Son of John and Emma Tuck of The Row, Purton
Pier and Face 13A Thiepval Memorial
Born in Purton and lived in Swindon

TUGBY, T.
Private 7923 1st Battalion South Wales Borderers
Died 17th February 1915
Husband of A Tugby of 9 Gooch Street
B 1722 Radnor Street Cemetery

TUGWELL, J.M.W.
Joseph Mark Washington
Private 202658 1/4th Battalion Wiltshire Regiment
Killed in Action 9th April 1918
25 years old
Husband of M G Tugwell of 9 Whitney Street
S 66 Ramleah War Cemetery
Born in Malmsbury and lived in Swindon

TURNER, A.E.
Albert Edward
Rifleman 11249 4th Battalion Kings Royal Rifle Corps
Killed in Action 3rd March 1915
Panel 51 and 53 Menin Gate memorial
Born in Swindon Lived in Small Heath

TURTON, H.T.
Herbert Thomas
Private 201514 1/4th Battalion Wiltshire Regiment
Died 11th October 1918
Z 61 Ramleh war cemetery
Born in Swindon

TWINING, W.
Walter
Lance Corporal 23217 10th Hussars
Killed in Action 17th November 1914
Panel 5 Menin Gate Memorial
Born in Swindon

TWYFORD, J.R.
John Robert
Private 9226 5th Battalion Wiltshire

Regiment
Died 12th August 1915. 22 years old
Died at Sea
Son of Thomas William and Florence
Twyford 13 Hunters Grove
Panel 156 and 158 Helles Memorial
Dardanelles

TYLER, A.G.
Arthur George
Rifleman 3636 8th City of London
Battalion Post Office Rifles London
Regiment
Killed in Action 11th January 1916
I E 5 Ridge Wood Military Cemetery

UZZELL, W.G.
William George
Private 107355 49th Battalion Machine
Gun Corps (Formerly 3479 Berkshire
Regt)
Killed in Action 25th April 1918
19 years old
Son of William and Ellen Louisa Uzzell of
Brick yard Lane Glos.
Panel 154 and 159 and 163a Tyne Cot
Memorial
Born in Swindon

VICKERY, J.F.
John Francis
Lance Corporal 10674 2nd Battalion
Wiltshire Regiment
Killed in Action 26th September 1915
Panel 102 Loos Memorial
Born in Swindon

VINER, F.R.
Frederick Reginald
Sapper 45180 89th Field Company Royal
Engineers
Died of Wounds 9th August 1915
22 years old
Son of William John and Bessie Viner of
42 Princess Street
H 7 Ramparts Cemetery Lille Gate Ypres
Lived in Swindon

VINES, E.
Edgar
Private 8644 2nd Battalion Wiltshire
Regiment
Killed in Action 1st July 1916
IV I 23 Peronne Road Cemetery Mericourt
Born in Chippenham lived in Swindon

VINES, S.
Sydney
Private 3/731 B Company 1st Battalion
Wiltshire Regiment
Died 31st January 1916
II F 57 Outtersteene Communal Cemetery
Extension Bailleul
Born in Brinkworth and Lived in Swindon
He was the oldest man serving in the
Battalion with 22 years service

VINES, W.
William
Private 9112 2nd Battalion Dorset
Regiment
Died 31st December 1916
Panel 22 and 63 Basra Memorial
Lived in Swindon

VIVASH, J.B.
Jacob Bunce
Lance Corporal G/4145 6th Battalion
Royal West Kent Regiment
Killed in Action 26th February 1916
F 16 Quarry Cemetery Vermelles
Born in Swindon and lived in Bickley Kent

VOKINS, B.
Bernard
Private 90708 Royal Army Medical Corps
Died of Wounds 31st March 1918
26 years old
Son of William and Mary Ellen Vokins of
Oxford Street Ramsbury
VIII I 175 Bologne Eastern Cemetery
Attended North Wilts Technical College
in Victoria Road in 1903 and
remembered on its Stained Glass
Window memorial

WADE, F.
Private 32945 10th Battalion Somerset
Light Infantry
Died 17th February 1918
C 965 Radnor Street Cemetery

WAITE, A.G.
Albert George
Private 7436 2nd Battalion Wiltshire
Regiment
Killed in Action 16th October 1914
27 years old
Son of Robert Waite of 40 Union Street
27 Kruiseecke German Cemetery
Memorial Zantvoorde British Cemetery
Lived in Swindon

WAKELING J.V.
James Victor
Private 39190 1st Battalion Royal
Berkshire Regiment
Died 25th July 1918. 19 years old
Son of Leslie James and Sarah Wakeling
of 5 Western Street
H 8 St Hilaire Cemetery Extension
Frevent

WALDRON, A.H.
Alfred Harry
Private 19520 5th Battalion Wiltshire
Regiment
Killed in Action 9th April 1916
17 years old
Son of Walter and Amy Beatrice Waldron
of Eastcourt Swindon
XVI K 14 Amara War Cemetery
Lived in Swindon

WALKER, G.E.
George Edward
Lance Corporal 7741 2nd Battalion
Wiltshire Regiment
Killed in Action 9th April 1917
34 years old
Son of Abner and Eliza Walker of 90
Beaufort Terrace Rodbourne Road
VI G 26 Wancourt British Cemetery
Born in Swindon

WALKER, H.J.
Henry John
Sergeant 8037 6th Battalion Wiltshire
Regiment
Killed in Action 7th July 1916
Pier and Face 13a Thiepval Memorial
Lived in Swindon

WALSTOW, W.H. MM
William Henry
Lance Corporal 15646 23rd Field
Company Royal Engineers
Died of Wounds 20th May 1918
A I 4 Wormley (St Laurence) Churchyard
Born in Swindon

WALTERS, E.C.
Ernest Charles
Rifleman 4273 8th City of London
Battalion Post Office Rifles
Killed in Action 15th September 1916
VII A 33 Catapillar Valley Cemetery
Longueval
Lived in Swindon

H. Walton

WALTON, H.
Harry
Private 10245 1st Battalion Wiltshire
Regiment
Killed in Action 18th June 1915
20 years old
Son of William and Harriet Walton of 15
Drew Street
Panel 53 Menin Gate Memorial
Born in Swindon

WARBURTON, H.J.
Herbert James
Engine Room Artificer 4th Class HMS
Carnarvon
Died 17th October 1919
Son of Manoah and Marion Warburton
Husband of Mabel Warburton of 61
Morris Street
E 4549 Gibraltar (North Front) Cemetery

WARHAM, A.G.
Alfred George
Private L/10042 1st Battalion Queens
Royal West Surrey Regiment
Killed in Action 14th September 1914
Born in Swindon and lived in Godalming
Surrey

H. Warman MM

WARMAN, H.V. MM
Corporal M2/118949 'P' Seige Park
Attached XI Corps Heavy Artillery
Died 15th November 1918 Influenza
25 years old
Son of Albert Edward and Annie Warman
of Swindon
Husband of Ruby Warman of 29
Richborough Road, Cricklewood London
XI A 18 Terlincthun British Cemetery
Wimille France
He was assistant trainer in Swindon Town
FC

WARNER, S.J.
Stephen James
Sergeant 4674 1st Battalion Kings Royal
Rifle Corps
Died of Wounds 6th March 1917
31 years old
Son of Stephen J and Mary Warner of
Portsmouth
Husband of Dora Warner of 46
Kingsdown Road Stratton
O VII G 6 St Sever Cemetery Extension
Rouen
Lived in Swindon

WASLEY, W.G.
William George
Driver TS/027446 15th Divisional Train
Army Service Corps
Died 7th August 1916. 21 years old
Son of Frederick W and Ellen Wasley of
61 Newcastle Street
V H 28 Bethune Town Cemetery

WATLING, H.W.
Corporal 138557 Southern Command
Labour Centre Labour Corps (Formerly
Pte 35961 Devonshire Regt)
Died 2nd November 1918. 22 years old
Son of Mrs H E Watling 157 Beatrice
Street
C 868 Radnor Street Cemetery

WATTS, I.C.
Isaac Charles
Private 7210 2nd Battalion Wiltshire
Regiment
Killed in Action 17th May 1915
Panel 33 and 34 Le Touret Memorial
Lived in Swindon

WATTS, W.
William
Lance Corporal 3/303 5th Battalion
Wiltshire Regiment

Killed in Action 10th August 1915
Panel 156 to 158 Helles Memorial
Born in Hungerford and lived in Swindon.
He worked as a Labourer in the Loco and
Carriage dept GWR

WEAVER, W.R.
William Reuben
Private 22065 6th Battalion Wiltshire
Regiment
Killed in Action 2nd July 1916
23 years old
Only Son of Reuben and Mary Jane
Weaver
Pier and Face 13a Thiepval Memorial
Born in Swindon

WEBB, A.
Arthur
Private 94669 74th Battalion Machine
Gun Corps
Killed in Action 1st November 1918
V K 7 Tournai Communal Cemetery Allied
Extension
Born in Swindon

WEBB, C.G.
Cyril Gordon
Private Trg/9145203 52nd Battalion
Bedfordshire Regiment
Died 7th June 1918
D 402 Radnor Street Cemetery
Born in Swindon. He attended North
Wilts Technical College in Victoria Road
in 1911 and remembered on its Stained
Glass Memorial

WEBB, M.T.
Mewyn Thomas
Driver 10453 186th Brigade Royal Field
Artillery
Died of Wounds 5th October 1918
23 years old
Son of James and Sarah Webb of Purton
IV E 41 Terlincthun British Cemetery
Wimille
Born in Swindon

WEBB, T.G.
Thomas George
Private 16694 5th Battalion Oxfordshire
and Buckinghamshire Light Infantry
Killed in Action 27th July 1915
Panel 37 and 39 Menin Gate Memorial
Born in Swindon

WEBBER, A.H.
Albert Henry
Lance Corporal 20793 2nd Battalion
Gloucestershire Regiment
Killed in Action 1st September 1918
30 years old
Son of John Cleave Webber of Tiverton
Devon.
Husband of Evelyn A Webber of Park
Lane
D 954 Karasouli Military Cemetery
Born in Swindon

WEEKS, F.
Frederick 6120 1st Battalion Wiltshire
Regiment
Killed in Action 19th October 1914
29 years old
Husband of Mrs Weeks of 41 Edinburgh
Street Gorse Hill
VII A 23 Ration Farm Military Cemetery
La Chapelle D'Armentieres

WELLS, H.G.L.
Herbert George Long
Private 50229 9th Battalion North Staff-
ordshire Regiment (Formerly 204103 RE)
Died of Wounds 14th May 1918
Husband of Melinda Ethel May Wells of
12 Redcliffe Street
P VII O IA St Sever Cemetery Extension
Rouen
Born in Swindon

H.G.L. Wells

WESTALL, T.C.
Gunner RNB – 1289 HMS President 3
(Formerly RMA 110313)
Died 10th August 1918
United Free Church yard Isle of Islay
Argyllshire
Joined the Royal Marine Artillery in 1914,
serving on board HMS Illustrious for 12
months. He was then drafted for service
in German East Africa and invalided
home.

He volunteered for a posistion in the
Mercantile Marine as a gunner. His ship
encountered and sunk a U boat that
fired a torpedo at them. While the ship
was in dock to be repaired, he was
walking along the deck and stumbled
over some obstacles which caused him
to fall into the hold. He later died of his
injuries.

WESTBROOK, A.G.
Alfred George
Private 25966 12th Battalion (Bristol
Battalion) Gloucestershire Regiment
Killed in Action 23rd August 1918
Panel 6 Vis en Artois Memorial
Born in Swindon

WESTLAKE, A.L.
Alfred Longhurst
Ordinary Seaman Bristol 2/2777 Royal
Navy Volunteer Reserve HMS Victory
Died 7th October 1918. 17 years old
Son of Alfred W and Annie Westlake of 27
Cambria Place
D 1021 Radnor Street Cemetery
Died of Pneumonia

WESTON, A.
Arthur
Sergeant 12051 6th Battalion Wilt
shire Regiment
Killed in Action 12th June 1917
31 years old
Son of Francis M and Emma Weston of 42
Whitehead Street
Panel 53 Menin Gate Memorial
Born in Chiseldon and lived in Swindon

A. Weston

WHALE, A.
Arthur
Lance Corporal 10262 1st Battalion
Wiltshire Regiment
Killed in Action 16th June 1915
Panel 53 Menin Gate Memorial
Lived in Swindon

WHATLEY, F.C.
Air Mechanic II 234368 No 1 School of Navigation and Bomb Dropping RAF Died 12th October 1918. 19 years old
Son of Mr and Mrs W G Whatley of 29 Broad Street
B3111 Radnor Street Cemetery

for his country, and along with countless thousands, paid the Supreme Sacrifice. Tranquil you lie your knightly virtues proved. Your memory hallowed in the Land you Loved'

F.C. Whatley

WHEATCROFT, F.G.
Frederick George
2nd Lieutenant 5th Battalion East Surrey Regt (Attached B Company 13th Battalion).
Killed in Action 26th November 1917
35 years old
Son of James and Mary Wheatcroft
Husband of Susan Jesse Wheatcroft of 18 The Mall
I F 12 Anneux British Cemetery France. Born in Derbyshire in 1882. He was a school teacher but much better known as an amateur football player. He played for Swindon in 1904-5 season and 1914-15 season making 23 FA cup appearances and 215 Southern League appearances scoring 92 goals. He had 2 spells with Derby County making 21 appearances and scoring 5 goals. He moved to London for a while where he played for Fulham and Reading. He was also an amateur England International. A memorial to him in his birthplace of Alfreton was unveiled in 1927.
'Not merely a player of great merit but was one to whom his fellow players looked up. His influence and inspiration brought about the best team work and all that lended to a teams success . He played the game for his Town and he also played the game for his country and in that greatest of all duels, he fought

F.G. Wheatcroft

WHEELER, F.J.
Frederick James
Private 6274 1st Battalion Wiltshire Regiment
Killed in Action 31st October 1914
Panel 33 and 34 Le Touret Memorial
Lived in Swindon

WHEELER, W.
Walter
Private 320003 2nd Battalion Royal Wiltshire Hussars
Died 13th December 1917. 53 years old
Son of William and Dinah Wheeler
Husband of Jane Wheeler of 24 Lansdown Road
553 Christ Church Cemetery

WHETHAM, C.E.
Charles Edward
Private 3/8810 2nd Battalion Wiltshire Regiment
Killed in Action 26th September 1915
23 years old
Son of Charles and Emma Whetham of 17 Merton Street
Brother of George Joseph Whetham
Panel 102 Loos Memorial
Born in Guernsey and lived in Swindon

WHETHAM, G.J.
George Joseph
Private 10626 C Company 2nd Battalion Wiltshire Regiment
Died of Wounds 22nd November 1915
18 years old
Son of Charles and Emma Whetham of 17

Merton Street
Brother of Charles Edward Whetham
Lived in Swindon. Formerly a waiter in
the GWR refreshment rooms.

WHITE, E.G.   MC
Edwin Gordon
Captain 8th Battalion Devonshire
Regiment
Killed in Action 7th May 1918
26 years old
Son of Mrs S White of 61 Graham Street
Plot I Row C Grave 2 Montecchio
Precallino Communal Cemetery
Extension
Attended North Wilts Technical College
Victoria Road in 1904 and remembered
on its stained glass memorial.
In November 1914 he received his
commission and was sent to the 8th
Battalion Wiltshire Regiment. In August
1915 he went to the Dardanelles as a
draft conducting officer, between
Lemnos and the Peninsular, to both
Sulva Bay and to Anzac. By November
he was invalided home suffering from
dysentery.
He rejoined his battalion in February
1916, until July when the 8th was broken
up. He was gazetted to the 1st battalion
and sent to France. In October of the
same year , he was wounded at the
Ancre.
In July 1917 after recovery, he was sent
back to France, where he saw service
with both the 1st and 6th Battalions
Wiltshire's. In October he was sent to
Italy where He was attached to the
Devons receiving a Captaincy . He served
with the Italian Expeditionary Force, until
he was wounded in action , dying later of
his wounds.

WHITE, W.H.
Private 179080 Training Battalion
Machine Gun Corps.
Died 5th November 1918. 18 years old
Son of Mr and Mrs W White of 102
Kingshill Road
E 8452 Radnor Street Cemetery.

WHITMAN, E.R.
Edwin Riley
Private 18481 1st Battalion Wiltshire
Regiment
Killed in Action 6th July 1916
18 years old

Son of Mr and Mrs L Whitman of 4
Linslade Street
Pier and Face 13a Thiepval Memorial
Born in Swindon

WIGGINS, W.
Wilfred
Gunner 126022 Royal Garrison Artillery
Died of wounds 24th July 1917
28 years old
Son of Charles and Emily Wiggins of 2
Union Place Marlborough
B 22 Hospital Farm Cemetery
Lived in Swindon

WILDMAN, A.J.
Alfred James
Gunner 128231 190th Brigade Royal
Field Artillery
Died of Wounds 28th September 1917
26 years old
Son of James Frances and Ellen Emma
Wildman
IV N IJ.B Mont Huon Military Cemetery
Le Treport
Born in Swindon

WILDMAN, F G
Francis Geor.e.
Lance Corporal 7623 2nd Battalion
Wiltshire Regiment
Killed in Action 12th March 1915
29 years old
Brother of Mrs M E Brown of 1 Argyle
Street
Panel 33 and 34 Le Touret Memorial
Born in Swindon

WILKS, C.P.
Charles Peter
Sergeant 100213 1/3rd Field Ambulance
Royal Army Medical Corps
Killed 16th June 1918. 38 years old
Son of William and Mary Wilks
Husband of Alice Celia Wilks of 48
Winstonian Road Cheltenham
IV C 12 Anzia St Aubin British Cemetery
Born in Swindon

WILLIAMS, A.E.
Arthur Edmund
Private 10238 1st Battalion Wiltshire
Regiment
Died of Wounds 18th May 1916
I M I Ecoivres Military Cemetery Mont St
Eloi
Born in Swindon

WILLIAMS, E.A.
Edward Albert
2nd Lieutenant Royal Flying Corps
(Formerly 2nd Regt Egyptian Labour
Corps)
Died 31st December 1918. 24 years old
Son of James Samuel Williams and
Elizabeth Annie Williams of 142 Beatrice
Street
B 88 Ismalia War Cemetery Egypt
Attended North Wilts Technical college
Victoria Road 1907 Remembered on its
stained glass window

WILLIAMS, E.J.
Edward James
Private 25383 8th Battalion Gloucester-
shire Regiment
Killed in Action 25th March 1917
19 years old
Son of Mrs C Williams of 53 Telford Street
Rodbourne
I D I Klein Vierstraat British Cemetery
Born in Swindon

E.J. Williams

WILLIAMS, F.S.
Francis Sydney
Lance Corporal 32648 1st Battalion
Wiltshire Regiment
Died of Wounds 12th August 1917
28 years old
Son of W S and S A Williams of Calne
VI C II Brandhoek New Military Cemetery
Born in Swindon

WILLIAMS, H.
Hubert
Private 8789 C Company 2nd Battalion
Wiltshire Regiment
Killed in Action 10th November 1914
20 years old
Foster son of Mr and Mrs Heath of 34
Newhall Street
I A 7 Lancashire Cottage Cemetery
Born in Battersea London Lived in
Swindon

WILLIAMS, H.H. MID
Herbert Henry
Captain 6th Battalion Wiltshire Regiment
Killed in Action 20th September 1917
23 years old
Son of Mr and Mrs Thomas Williams of 85
Curtis Street
H 23 Kemmel Chateau Cemetery
Born June 22nd 1894, only Son of Mr
and Mrs Thomas Williams. He was
educated at Sanford Street School,
attended North Wilts Technical College
Victoria Road in 1907. He then went to
St Pauls College in Cheltenham, before
working as a teacher in Ferndale Road
School. He joined the army on 11th
September 1914. He went on to become
commanding officer of C Company 6th
Battalion Wiltshire Regiment
The 6th Battalion was heavily involved
in the 3rd Battle of Ypres in 1917. On the
20th September, the battalion attacked
on the right flank of Passchendaele ridge.
The attack was deemed a success,
though they suffered heavily from
machine gun fire. All the company CO's
were lost including Captain Williams.
He had been mentioned twice in
despatches. In April 1917 by Sir Douglas
Haig and again in this last battle 'For
gallant and distinguished service in the
field'
He is remembered on the plaque in
Sanford Street School (Education Dept)
on the Stained Glass window in the
Technical College Victoria Road and on
the plaque in Christ Church.

149

WILLIAMS, W.J.
William James
Private 201524 1/4th Battalion Wiltshire
Regiment
Died 9th December 1918. 21 years old
Son of John and Esther Williams of 28
Albion Street
F 225 Kantara War Cemetery Memorial
Lived in Swindon

WILLIAMS, W.J.
William James
Private G/27450 13th Battalion
Middlesex Regiment
Killed in Action 11th June 1917
Panel 49 and 51 Menin Gate Memorial
Lived in Swindon

WILLIAMS, W.J.H.
W John Harris
Gunner 9102 7th Reserve Battery Royal
field Artillery
Died 16th March 1915
OCE 738 Preston (New Hall Lane)
Cemetery
Born in Swindon

WILLIS, A.E.
Albert Edward
Private 19000 5th Battalion Wiltshire
Regiment
Killed in Action 29th March 1917
Panel 30 and 64 Basra Memorial
Born in Swindon

WILLIS, A.H.
Albert Harry
Private 3/9939 2nd Battalion Wiltshire
Regiment
Killed in Action 9th April 1917
VI G 30 Wancourt British Cemetery
Lived in Swindon

WILLIS, F.J.
Francis James
Private 201549 1/4th Battalion Wiltshire
Regiment
Died 20th November 1917
Egypt
Lived in Swindon

WILLS, W.H.
William Henry
Private 7967 1st Battalion Gloucester
shire Regiment
Died 29th October 1914
Panel 22 and 34 Menin Gate Memorial
Born in Tiverton Devon lived in Swindon

W.H. Willis

WILSON, C.S. MC MID
Cyril Spencer
Major Wilts Fortress Engineers Royal
Engineers
Died 27th October 1918. 36 years old
Son of Mr J H Wilson Mrs E Wilson of
Woodville Lansdown Bath Charlcombe St
Mary Churchyard Somerset (In West Part
of Churchyard) Died of Pneumonia
(Spanish Flu).
He was awarded the Military Cross for his
long record of devotion and ability in
June 1917. He was also mentioned in
despatches 31st December 1915. He had
trained the company, known as the
Swindon Company and had led them
with much courage and showed
devotion to his men, who were
particuarly saddened by his death.
The Swindon Company Wilts Fortress
Engineers were one of the most hardest
worked units of Engineers on the
western front. Known for their bridge
building skills, they were mainly
recruited from men from the rail-works
in Swindon. He was assistant manager of
the Carriage and wagon works .

Major C.S. Wils

WILSON, E.J.
Edwin John
Private 203054 2nd Battalion Wiltshire
Regiment (Formerly 5063 Somerset Light
Infantry)
Killed in Action 31st July 1917

19 years old
Son of Alfred and Bessie Mary Wilson of
41 Bright Street
Panel 53 Menin Gate Memorial
Born in Swindon

WILSON, H.D.
Henry Day
Private 203612 1/4th Battalion Wiltshire
Regiment (Form.1709 Wiltshire
Yeomanry)
Killed in Action 2nd November 1917
21 years old
Son of Robert and Alice Wilson of 26
Taunton Street
XIII C 3 Gaza War Cemetery
Born in Swindon

H.D. Wilson

WILSON, J.
James
Private 5728 2nd Battalion Wiltshire
Regiment
Died of Wounds 19th May 1918
II F 14 Le Touret Military Cemetery
Richebourg
Born in Swindon

W.H.R. Wilson

WILSON, W.H.R.
William Henry Richard
Lance Sergeant 200215 1/4th Battalion
Wiltshire Regiment
Died of Wounds 11th May 1918
Son of Mr and Mrs Wilson 41 Bright
Street. Brother of F J Wilson
Buried in Egypt.

C.H. Wiltshire

WILTSHIRE, C.H.
Charles Henry
Air Mechanic 1st Class F/13545 Royal
Naval Air Service
Died 16th October 1918. 21 years old
Son of William and Mary Ann Wiltshire
A 2459 Radnor Street Cemetery

WINCHCOMBE, S.W.
Sydney Wilfred
Sergeant 50531 124th Brigade Royal
Field Artillery
Killed in Action 3rd May 1917.
29 years old
Son of Charles and G M Winchcombe of
38 Winifred Street
D 53 Cojeul British Cemetery St Martin
Sur Cojeul
Born in Swindon

WINCHURST, B.
Bert
Private 3/9826 2nd Battalion Wiltshire
Regiment
Killed in Action 26th September 1915
19 years old
Son of Mrs Winchurst of 13 Havelock
Street
Panel 102 Loos Memorial
Born in Swindon

B. Winchurst

WINSLOW, J.F.
James Frederick
Corporal 12358 7th Battalion Wiltshire
Regiment
Killed in Action 24th April 1917
18 years old
Son of James Winslow (Lt RAF) and
Fanny Winslow of 164 Pitt Street Sydney
New South Wales Australia
Doiran Memorial   Salonika
Born and Lived in Swindon

WINTER, C.
Charles
Private 18269 2nd Battalion Wiltshire
Regiment
Killed in Action 18th October 1916
C 6 Valley Cemetery Vis en Artois
Lived in Swindon

WOODHAM, J.H.
James Herbert
Private 201513 1/4th Battalion Wiltshire
Regiment
Died of Wounds 1st November 1917
19 years old
Son of Mr and Mrs John Woodham of 21
Cross Street
XIII C 10 Gaza War Cemetery
Lived in Swindon. He attended Sanford
Street School

In a letter Mr and Mrs Woodham
received from Captain T N Arkell they
were informed that - James was
'Standing To' in the trench with 3 others
with rifle grenades when a Turkish shell
landed on the trench. All 4 were
wounded and James died shortly after.
Another who was wounded was Private
R M Wills also from Swindon.
They also received a letter from Lt Col A
Armstrong of the Wilts Regt who
explained that James had been buried
next to a comrade,
                                    Pte Goodall.

WOODLEY, W.H.
William Henry
Private 32688 8th Battalion Cheshire
Regiment
Died 5th September 1917. 29 years old
Son of John and Edith Woodley of 17
Maidstone Road
XVI D 12 Baghdad (North Gate) War
Cemetery
Lived in Swindon

WOODMAN, A.F.J.
Albert Frederick James
Private 4857 1/8th Battalion Royal
Warwickshire Regiment
Killed in Action 1st July 1916
20 years old
Son of Frederick and Mary Jane
Woodman of 15 Davis Street
I A 28 Serre Road Cemetery No 1
Born in Swindon

WOODWARD, A.V.
Albert Victor
Private 11116 2nd Battalion Wiltshire
Regiment
Killed in Action 15th June 1915
27 years old
Son of Mrs Mary Ann Woodward of 155
Beatrice Street
Panel 33 and 34 Le Touret Memorial
Lived in Swindon

WOODWARD, G.W.J.
George William John
Private 56509 15th Battalion Royal
Welsh Fusiliers (Formerly 32200 Wiltshire
Regiment)
Died of Wounds 2nd August 1917
19 years old
Son of Frederick William and Clara Ann
Woodward of 101 Eastcott Hill
II J 3 Dozinghem Military Cemetery
Born in Swindon

WOODWARD, H.H.
Harry Hall
Corporal 8382 2nd Battalion Hampshire
Regiment
Killed in Action 8th August 1918
II G 5 Borre British Cemetery
Born in Swindon

WOOLFORD, A.E.
Albert Edward
Sergeant 21871 C Battery 83rd Brigade
Royal field Artillery
Died 27th October 1917. 35 years old
Son of George and Alice Woolford of 25
Albion Street
III A 19 Duhallow ADS Cemetery
Born in Swindon Brother of Sidney
Woolford (below)

WOOLFORD, S.F.
Sidney Frank
Private 8794 1st Battalion Wiltshire
Regiment
Killed in Action 7th June 1917

28 years old
Son of George and Alice Woolford of 25 Albion Street
Panel 53 Menin Gate Memorial
Born in Swindon Brother of Alber (Above)

WOOLFORD, F.W.
Drummer 370816 288th Area Employment Company Labour Corps. (Formerly 8171 6th Battalion Wilts Regt)
Died 27th January 1919   26 years old
Son of William Woolford of 13 Cross Street
C 99 7 Radnor Street Cemetery

WOOLFORD, J.J.
Joseph John
Driver 261778 312th Brigade Royal field Artillery
Died 8th November 1918. 19 years old
Son of Arthur J and Clara F A Woolford of 1 Stanley Cottages Pavehill Purton
C 12 Maubehqe Centre Cemetery
Lived in Swindon

WORDLEY, G.
George
Lance Sergeant 8205 2nd Battalion Wiltshire Regiment
Killed in Action 24th October 1914
25 years old
Son of David and Emma Wordley of 24 Newport Street
Panel 53 Menin Gate Memorial
Lived in Swindon

WRIGHT, A.T.   DCM
Alfred Thomas
Company Sergeant Major 200546 1/4th Battalion Royal Berkshire Regiment
Died 1st November 1918
Son of Mr and Mrs Wright of Swindon
Plot 1 Row F Grave 3 Granezza British Cemetery Italy
Born in Swindon

WRIGHT, E.C.
Ernest Chivers
Sergeant 6391 2nd Battalion Wiltshire Regiment
Killed in Action 24th October 1914
28 years old
Son of Joseph and Ruth Wright
Panel 53 Menin Gate
Born in Swindon

WRIGHT, F.J.
Frederick Johnson
Sergeant 200690 1/4th Battalion Berkshire Regiment
Died 15th June 1918. 25 years old
Son of Mr and Mrs G Wright of Swindon
Plot 1 Row D Grave 10 Boscon British Cemetery
Born in Swindon

WRIGHT, H.F.
Harry Francis
Private 6118 1st Battalion Wiltshire Regiment
Killed in Action 31st October 1914
29 years old
Son of William Wright of Swindon
Husband of Kate Wright of Carlingcott Bath
Panel 33 and 34 Le Touret Memorial
Born in Swindon

WYATT, H.
Harry
Private 14233 8th Battalion Royal Berkshire Regiment
Killed in Action 25th September 1915
33 years old
Son of Mrs S Wyatt 248 Cricklade Road Gorse Hill
Panel 93 – 95 Loos Memorial
Born in Swindon

WYLEY, J.J.
John Joseph
Lance Corporal 10113 2nd Battalion Connaught Rangers
Killed in Action 26th August 1914
23 years old
Son of L F Wyley of 134 Chapel Street Gorse Hill
3 Grand Fayt Communal Cemetery
Born in Bantry Co Cork Lived in Swindon

YEO, T.D.
Thomas David
Private 19174 5th Battalion Wiltshire Regiment
Died of Wounds 1st May 1916. 20 yrs old
Son of George William Yeo
Panel 30 and 64 Basra Memorial
Lived in Swindon

Those Who Served and Survived

Old Soldiers Never Die They Simply Fade Away

ACKHURST, Arthur Charles Ackhurst. 40 Albion Street. Served throughout the war. He died in the 1920s never fully recovering from his ordeals.

ACKRILL, Ernest Frank Ackrill. Son of Frank Ackrill. 120 Cricklade Road.

ADAMS, Sergeant F. Adams DCM Somerset Light Infantry. Awarded DCM for rushing a German trench with a small number of men. Son of George Adams a police officer in the Bath Police Force. He had 3 Brothers, 2 serving in the Somerset Light Infantry and another in the North Somerset Yeomanry. Lived at 12 Belgrave Street.

ADAMS. William J Adams. Was a porter in the passenger dept GWR. Enlisted in the army 1914 aged 23.

ALDRIDGE. Arthur Aldridge served with the Army Service Corps.

ANDREW. George Edward Andrew. Engineer Commander on HMS Kent. The son of Donald MacDonald Andrew of Swindon. He was awarded a CBE for his work on board Kent, in the Falk land Islands.
He had been educated in Swindon, and afterwards went on to the GWR Technical Classes. He went later to Greenwich College later becoming a draughtsman in the GWR works in Swindon. He served in the Navy for 22 years.

APPERLEY. 2nd Lieutenant W H Apperley Served in Army Service Corps. Lived at 97 Edinburgh Street Gorse Hill. Formerly worked in the GWR.

Arthur Aldridge ASC

APPLEGATE. Lieutenant W H Applegate served with the Royal Berkshire Regiment. He was the son of Mark Applegate of the Victoria Inn 88 Victoria Road.

ARMAN, Sapper W. Arman 'B' Coy 6th Btn Royal Berkshire Regt. Attached to the R E. Lived at 15 Lowestoft Street.
The following is a letter he sent to his parents in September 1915 from France.
'Dear Father and Mother,
I am writing you a few lines hoping you are in the best of health. It is grand weather out here at present, though rather cold nights and mornings. We have been in action. Last Wednesday night, our battalion, the Royal Berks had it pretty warm, for a lot of the Germans started shelling us in all directions for about an hour. The Germans, thinking we were all done in, started to advance towards our trenches in massed formation. They came within 20 yards of our trenches and they had it hot from our rifles, machine guns and artillery. You ought to have seen them falling down like chaff before the wind. There were not many that escaped. It was like hell for a short time. We had a few casualties, but the Germans lost nearly a battalion of men. We called them the Saxons. They are half German and half English. They have been very quiet since that night. They thought they had a soft job on, but they were mistaken for once. I am getting used to bully beef and biscuits now. I am getting short of a razor. I can't get one for love or money. You ought to see my face! I have not had a shave for three weeks. We get a pay this week – 15 francs, that is about 4s 2d to a franc. If God spares me, I will send it home because I can't spend it out here. Could you send me a razor out? It looks so bad asking everyone for the loan of a razor. It would not cost much for postage. We are sleeping in old dug-outs what the French used to sleep in. We never have our clothes off, but always sleep in them. I have not much more to say at present. I wish you all good luck and good-bye for the present. Remember me to Will and tell him I wish him a safe and speedy passage across the water.'

ARNOLD. Sergeant W E.Arnold DCM Somerset Light Infantry. Awarded the DCM for escaping a German patrol in France, while wounded on 30th August 1916. Son of Mr J Arnold who was manager of Swindon Corporation Sewage Works. Four Sons of Mr Arnold served. All four had been wounded in the war. His eldest son Percy, also won the DCM. His Four son in law also served as well as eight nephews.

ASHTON. 2 brothers – Arthur Reginald Ashton and John Gordon Ashton served in the Wiltshire Regiment. Arthur was captured in August 1914 (see POW's section) Their parents lived at 54 Graham Street.

BADEN. Edward Baden was a Gunner in the Royal Field Artillery and served in India. He was a Son of Frank Baden of 60 Kingshill Road. His brother Pte Frank Baden served in the 5th Btn Wiltshire Regt and was killed in Gallipoli. (see roll of honour for details)

BAKER. Frederick Richard Baker of 32 Edinburgh Street, born January 1899, enlisted into the Wiltshire Regiment. He saw service in India with the 2/4th Battalion. He emigrated to Australia after the war, serving in the Australian defence forces as a sergeant in WW2. His sister married a chum of his Frank Edward Jones from Gloucestershire who served with him in the Wilts. They continued to live at 32 Edinburgh Street.

Frederick Baker

F. Baker 2/4th Wilts India

F. Baker with 2/4th Wilts (Middle row 2nd left)

BALDWIN. Sidney Baldwin of 5 Church Walk, served in the Royal Field Artillery, the same unit as Frederick Simpkins of 3 Church Walk, who was Killed in Action in 1917. Sidney bought Frederick's personal effects back home for his Mother

BALCH. Lieutenant J Balch, son of Mr A Balch of Swindon. He was on board the transport Ship 'Cameroria' when it was torpedoed by a German U Boat. Lieutenant Tuckey was another Swindon man present on board. (see details under his name)

BARTLETT. Trooper 2106 George Bartlett Born in 1890, he enlisted with the Royal Horse Guards on 28th October 1914. He transferred later to the Guards Machine Gun Regiment, as a Machine Gunner. He was transferred to the reserve 15th April 1919.

BARNES. Private Edgar Barnes MM Son of John Barnes, Painter and Decorator of 5 Tennyson Street. He attended Swindon's Higher Elementary School (Euclid Street School) Then served an apprenticeship with Mr Crowdy at the Quan took Motor Works Devizes Road. He joined the army early in the war. He was awarded the Military Medal for repairing a motor under fire and bringing 3 wounded safely to hospital.

BEASANT. Private 36506 Albert Beasant of 88 Crombey Street, served with the Royal Army Medical Corps.

George E Bartlett

BEZER. Driver 616562 Reginald Ewart Bezer Royal Army Medical Corps. Born in 1893 He joined the Territorial army in 1912 He was transferred from the RAMC to the Royal Horse Artillery in January 1917. He lived at 8 Church Walk, Rodbourne Cheney. Besides the war, he also survived the Spanish Flu which he contracted afterwards. He was demobilised 8th March 1919 going back to his job in the GWR as a painter. His brother, Walter, a barber in Rodbourne Road, also served. On enlistment, however, he was detained for 6 weeks as his name raised suspicion, despite his brother already serving in the army!

Reginald Ewart Bezer

Reginald Ewart Bezer (seated on bench front right)

BILLETT. 3 Brothers served – Thomas served with the Royal Fusiliers. Arthur, with the Royal Engineers and Harold, who had emigrated to South Africa, served with the South African Infantry.

Harold was Killed in Action (see roll of honour) Arthur served in the RAMC and was soon promoted to Sergeant. He later transferred to the Royal Engineers, where he was sent to train in the use of gas. He eventually went to Officers training school to obtain a commission. After the war he became a teacher, living in Bath Road.

Tom   Harold   Arthur

Arthur Billett RAMC

Arthur Billett (2nd row down 4th from right)
Officers Training School

Arthur Billett (4th from left seated) R.E. Special Bridge Gas Training

BIRT. Brothers of 30 Avening Street served – Private J Birt 6th Leinster Regiment Private S Birt 1st Battalion Wiltshire Regiment.

S. Birt   J. Birt

BIZLEY. Harold Bizley Royal Army Medical Corps of 34 Ashford Road

Harold Bizley RAMC (second from left)

BLAKE. Private 18125 H Blake M.M 2nd Btn Wiltshire Regt.. Was awarded the Military Medal, for, despite being wounded in the shoulder continued his work as a stretcher-bearer. His brother served in the Tank corps. Their father was Mr M Blake, a builder, Lived at Rushey Platt House.

BLUNSDON. Eight sons of Mr and Mrs Charles Blunsdon of 62 Edinburgh Street served.-

William Blunsdon Formerly served with the 1st Battalion Wiltshire Regiment. He had seen service in India and the South African Campaign. He worked for the GWR in A&E shop after army service. In 1913 he emigrated with his brother Albert, to Australia. He rejoined his old regiment on the outbreak of war.

Frederick Blunsdon was married and lived with his wife at 56 Argylle Street. He had seen previous military service with the Wiltshire Regiment in South Africa. Worked in GWR as a striker in No 14 shop, and re-joined his old battalion of the 2nd Wiltshires at the outbreak of war. His first child, a daughter was born soon after he left England for active service. Unfortunately he was never to see her as he was killed in September 1915 in Belgium. (See roll of Honour)

William   Frederick

Albert Blunsdon also saw previous service in the army during the South African campaign with the 1st Wilts. He also worked in the Carriage shop GWR then emigrated to Australia. Again he returned to rejoin the Wiltshire Regiment.
John Blunsdon He previously saw service with the Army Service Corps. Working in the Loco shop GWR he rejoined the army at the outbreak of war, but was eventually rejected on medical grounds.
Charles Blunsdon Saw previous service with the 1st Wilts and worked as a Mason in the GWR. Rejoined his battalion and was wounded at Mons. He returned to the battalion after recovery.
Reginald Blunsdon A regular soldier with the 2nd Wilts. He formerly worked in the boiler shop GWR. He was captured in October 1914 and spent the war in captivity (See POW's details)

| Albert | John | Charles |

Frank Blunsdon Joined at the outbreak of war and served with the 7th Battalion Wilts.
Arthur Blunsdon Joined at the outbreak of war at 16 years old and served in the Royal Field Artillery.
The boy's father,Charles Blunsdon also worked in the GWR. He had also seen army service, serving with the Royal Engineers for 8 years. At the outbreak of war, he offered himself for service with the army but was turned down, much to his disappointment. He had 2 daughters whose husbands also served. One in the 6th Battalion Wiltshire Regiment, the other an ex-soldier engaged in Coastal defence duties.

| Reginald | Frank | Arthur | Charles |

Swindon Volunterr Training Corps on Parade 1915

BRAY. 3418 Private Jesse Bray served with the 4th Battalion Wiltshire Regiment and was attached to the Signal service Royal Engineers. Living at 59 Avenue Road, he enlisted aged 17 years. He kept a diary of his movements during his war service.

Diary of Jesse Bray. Wilts Regt 1915-1919

First No. 3418
201550 Private J Bray 4th Wilts. Attached Signal Service Royal Engineers. 1917 – 1919
Indian Army

April	24th	1915 - Enlisted in 4th Wilts.
"	25-27th	Holiday in Aldbourne
"	28th	Sworn in at Princes Street, Swindon.
"	29th	Issued with uniform at Trowbridge. Returned to Swindon until 1st May
May	1st	Reported to Trowbridge and sent to Coombe Down,Bath. Put in Billett with Mrs Powney at 'Williamstrip'
"	4th	Inoculated
"	7th	Inoculated
June	14th	Issued with Leather equipment
"	19th	Moved to Chedder under canvas
"	23rd	Sick with measles. Regeneration for 21 days, then seven days leave.
Sept.	3rd	Joined Signal Service.
"	15th	Moved to Winton, Bournemouth. Billetted with Mrs Best 33 Somerly Road Winton
Nov	13th	18th Birthday
Jan	7th	1916 - To billetts in Hamsworthy, Poole, for a course of firing. Billetted with Mrs Brown at Saw Mills
Feb	7th	Returned to Winton.
Mar	10th	Dad and Sid came to Winton.
"	13th	On parade at Wallis Down and instructed to pack and move off at 8pm.
"	14th	Embarked on HMS Saturnia at Devonport. Set sail at noon. Destination unknown.
"	18th	Passed through Straits of Gibraltar.
"	20th	Isolated at rear of ship with fever.
"	21st	Inoculated. Passed the Minniapolis at 4.30. It was torpedoed and sunk at 8pm.
"	28th	Second burial at sea. Through Suez Canal.
April	3rd	Arrived Alexandra Docks. Bombay Camped at Colaba
"	6th	Entrained Victoria Station Bombay en route Barrielly
"	12th	Arrived Barielly. Changed to narrow gauge for Kathgodam
"	13th	Arrived Kathgodam and marched to Jelicote rest camp. 13 miles
"	14th	From Jelicote to Bowali marched 12 miles.
"	15th	Bowali to Ratighat. Marched 10 miles
"	16th	Ratighat to Bonshon Marched 9 miles
"	17th	Bonshon to Chanbattia. Marched 17 miles
May	4th	Joined Signal Section.
July	7th	Visited Ranikhet 4 miles
"	9th	Left Chaubattia with seven other ranks for Chakrata signal school Arrived Bonshon via short cut. Marched 5 miles. Left Bonshon arrived Ratighat Marched 9 miles
"	10th	Left Ratighat for Bowali. Marched 10 miles.
"	11th	Bowali to Jelicote Marched 12 miles. Good views of Mai-a-Tul e Biotal
"	12th	Jelicote to Kathgodam Marched 13 miles. Narrow gauge railway to

July	12th	Barrielly arriving 5pm. Entrained for Dera-Dun arriving 9pm and stayed in rest camp.
"	19th	Dera -Dun to Saharanpur marched 12 miles
"	20th	Saharanpur to Kalsi Marched 9 miles
"	21st	Kalsi to Seih marched 15 miles
"	22nd	Seih to Chakratu Marched 15 miles
"	25th	Commenced three months course at signal school.
Aug	10th	Climbed Deoban via the lower Simla Road
Nov	6th	Visited Kailana
"	9th	Left Chakrata en route to Delhi Arrived Lieh Marched 15 miles
"	10th	Lieh to Kelisi Marched 15 miles
"	11th	Kelisi to Saharanpur Marched 9 miles
"	12th	Saharanpur to Dera-Dun Marched 12 miles
"	14th	Entrained at Dera-Dun for Dehli
"	15th	Joined Regiment at Dehli
"	21st	WBattery RHA 1/5 Somerset Light Infantry 2/2 Gurkhas and Nepalese Regiment
Dec		Orders as having passed first class at school of signalling
Jan	1st 1917	Tired. Leiu-de-jai outside Delhi Fort and Jamma Musjid
Feb	14th	Struck off strength of Regt and joined Signal Service Depot at Poona
"	15th	Law Jag-Mahal waiting for train connection. Changed trains at Manmad and Dhand
Mar	31st	Inoculated Went to Kirkee
April	27th	Warned for German East Africa
"	29th	Warned for Mesopotamia
May	2nd	Left Poona for Mesopotamia
"	3rd	Embarked at Bombay on HMS Mutlah
"	8th	Crossed Bar into Shat – el -Arab
"	9th	Disembarked at Manyuhi
"	11th	Sent to Basra
"	17th	Joined 14 Division
"	18th	Arrived Qurnah
"	19th	Advanced to Amara
"	29th	Passed Ctesiphon
"	31st	In Bagdad
June	2nd	Arrived at Hinaidi on the Dialah
"	3rd	To Collinghams Port
"	4th	To Cassels Port
"	5th	To Bakuba
"	11th	Joined 2/2 Gurkhas
July	4th	To Mahnut
"	5th	Beled Raiy Linperate 130′
Oct	10th	Advanced to Mendali with 7th Cavalry Brigade
"	19th	To Jebel Hamnin Hills
"	22nd	Bad day. Several Gurkha's killed and wounded
"	26th	Small wound in left forearm
Nov	10th	To Seria.
Dec	4th	Occupied Kirzil Robah Crossed Dialah River
Jan	1918	Attached to the 1st/2 Gurkhas 35th Brigade
Feb		To Kuddarah with 1st/2 Gurkhas To Mirjana with 37th Brigade
April	4th	Advanced towards Kifri
"	7th	Occupied Kifri. Large number of prisoners. Population without food
May	4th	Joined 14 Divisional Headquarters
June		To Quashi Shris Persia Sand Fly Fever

Oct	16th	Last Action
"	20th	Poisoned arm
Nov	1st	Armistice with the Turks
"	11th	Received message 7 minutes past midnight. Armistice signed by Germany.
Jan	1919	Regiment withdrawn
Feb	24th	Joined Divisional Headquarters
"	26th	To Baghdad for stores
Mar	4th	Left for England via Bombay
"	15th	Arrived Baghdad Left for Kut same evening.
"	19th	Arrived Kut. Arrived Amara
"	26th	Arrived Basra
"	27th	Ammunition handed in
"	28th	Kit fumigated and took creosote bath
April	2nd	Transferred to demob camp
"	8th	Embarked on HMS Stephanta
"	9th	Crossed Bar to the Persian Gulf
"	12th	Armed Alexandra docks and left for Deolali to await ship for England
"	13th	Warned that Martial law had been proclaimed in the Punjab. No troops are to be allowed to leave India.
"	14th-15th	Provisional Battalion formed and warned to proceed to Calcutta.
"	16th	Cancelled.
"	17th	Issued with Ammunition
May	2nd	Warned the ex-Mesopotamian troops would embark for England on 8th May
"	7th	Serious Situation on the Afghanistan frontier
"	8th	Warned for long train journey
"	17th	Sent to Poona to join Signal Depot
June	4th	Arrived Hisar Arrived Delhi
"	9th	Arrived Lahore
"	11th	Arrived Royal Hindi and left for Kohat
"	13th	Left for No4 Lines of Communication Arrived Hangai 8pm
"	15th	Arrived Thal Fort then on to Peshawar on the Afghan Frontier
"	30th	Returned to Kohat
July	4th	Joined 46th Brigade at Thal Fort
Aug	1st	Afghan signed armistice
"	5th	Returned to Kohat
"	6th	Warned for demobilization
"	14th	Left for Royal Hindi
"	15th	Arrived Royal Hindi
"	16th	Left for Deolali Attack of Sand Fly Fever
"	17th	Passed Lahore
"	24th	Arrived Deolali
"	25th	Kit Inspection
"	26th	Change of Rifles from short Enfield to long Enfields
"	29th	Transferred to departure camp
Sept	22 1919	Warned for England
"	23rd	Left Deolali
"	24th	Arrived Bombay and set sail midday on the Merkara
Oct	1st	Arrived Aden
"	3rd	Passed Port Suez Arrived Port Said
"	5th	Left Port Said for Marseilles and Straits of Bonifacio between Corsica and Sardinia. Left Marseilles for Gibralter.
"	14th	Arrived Plymouth and entrained for Fovant
"	16th	Handed in rifle and left for Swindon

163

Oct	17th	Commenced 28 days demobilization leave
Nov	13th	22nd Birthday
"	15th	Transferred to class 2 reserve
Jan	1st 1920	Disembodied
April	1st	Final Discharge

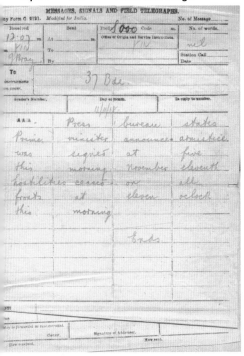

A telegraph taken down by Jesse Bray as signaller for 37th Brigade HQ.
'Armistice is signed, Hostilities to cease.'

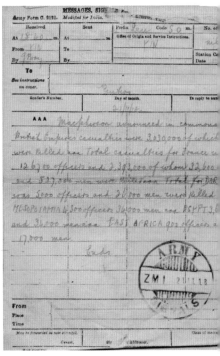

Another telegraph taken down by Jesse Bray on the 21st November 1918. It states the number of the Commonwealth casualties.

Total casualties of the British Empire numbers 3,030,000
France – 126,700 officers and 2,393,000 Other Ranks of which 32,600 Officers and 527,000 Other ranks were killed
Dardanelles – 5,000 Officers and 26,000 Other Ranks Killed
Mesopotamia - 4,300 Officers and 34,000 Other ranks Killed
Egypt – 3,600 Officers and 34,000 Other ranks Killed
East Africa – 900 Officers and 17,000 Other ranks Killed
Total 684,400.

BROOKS. 2nd Lieutenant Charles A H Brooks Wiltshire Regiment. Was wounded in March 1915

BURGE. Sergeant E E Burge MID. served in the Royal Dublin Fusiliers. One of three sons who served, of Mr and Mrs Burge of 29 Omdurman Street. Joining up in September 1914, he was sent out to the Dardanelles with his battalion where he was wounded. He returned to active service to France. He was Mentioned in Despatches in Mid November at Cambrai. He was awarded the 'Ginchy Diamond' the highest distinction available in the Irish Division. (It came in the form of a green diamond shaped ribbon

164

worn on the right arm.) He worked formerly in the GWR as a painter. His two brothers were Edward Guy Burge and Harry J Burge.

BURGESS. J. Burgess   Engine Room Artificer Royal Navy. Served on board HMS Benbow

BURTON. Sapper Alfred Edward Burton. Royal Engineers, of 75 Radnor Street. His brother Owen Edgar RN was killed at the Battle of Jutland (see roll of honour)

Armistace day 1930. GWR works band in front of one of the many Great War memorials.Alfred Buton is 3rd from left

Old comrades crossing the channel on their return to the battlefields. A Burton is front right

Alfred Burton (with wreath) in Ypres

BUTLER. Lt Col. Ralph William Butler Royal Engineers, son of Mr T Butler, a JP in Swindon, became a Lieutenant-Colonel in command of the Road Board Section RE in Flanders aged 33 years old. He was educated at Swindon Elementry and Secondary Schools, before moving to Plymouth to train as a Civil Engineer.

BUTT. Sapper R Butt Royal Engineers Lived at 2 Turle Street.

BUTTLE. Bombardier A A Buttle MM served with the Wessex Brigade Royal Field Artillery. He had enlisted with his brother in February 1915, and left for France with a contingent of 30 others including VC winner Sergeant W Gosling of Wroughton. He had 2 brothers who served. One a sergeant in the Royal Field Artillery and another in the Motor Transport Army Service Corps.

BUTTON. Four sons of Mr W Button of 91 County Road served. Charles, Percy, John and Thomas. Thomas a private in the Wiltshire Regiment was captured in 1918. (See POW's details)

Sapper R Butt

CANDLE. Private Leonard Candle 5th Wiltshire Regt. Son of John Candle of 15 Prospect Place. Whilst serving in the Dardanelles, was seriously wounded, when a Turkish bullet struck him in the face just below his right eye and became embedded in his right shoulder. The bullet was extracted and he was returned to England to recover.

CHAPPELL. 3 brothers, William, Albert and George Chappell of 1 Marlborough Street served. All 3 were territorials and worked in the GWR works. William and Albert served with the Wiltshire Regiment. Albert served in India with the 4th battalion and later transferred to the Royal Navy to HMS Maidstone a Submarine repair depot. George served with the Royal Navy. All three survived, both Albert and George returned to work in the GWR. William emigrated to Australia. He would not have been able to return to the GWR, because on leaving the works for active service, he 'sorted out' his foreman who had 'had it in for him'!

Frederick J Chandler
A Coppersmiths
Apprentice GWR

The Chappell family. Marlborough St. William Albert and George

Alberts wedding 14th July 1917. His brother George is standing behind him in Naval uniform

4th Battallion Wilts Regt. India. Albert Chappell is sat on chair on left

4th Wilts India. Albert Chappell is seated in the centre

CHURCH. 3 brothers served. -
Lieutenant Jack Church, served
with the Canadian Infantry. He
had been a trooper D Squadron
Wiltshire Yeomanry. Had served
an apprenticeship in the GWR
and emigrated to Canada in
1912. He was badly wounded at
the Battle of St Julien on April
23rd 1915. Christopher Church
who was a Gunner in the
Machine Gun Corps.
Brad served in the Engineers as
a Signaller.

CLEMENTS. Harry Clements of
120 Redcliffe Street, served in
the Royal Marine Light Infantry
on board HMS Bellerophon.

Albert Chappell 4th Wilts

Albert. Royal Navy

Francis J H Chirgwin
Royal Engineers

Pte J Cockell RAMC
173 Manchester Road

Ernest Coleman
Worked in No 21a Shop GWR

COLLETT. Mr and Mrs W Collett of 13 Page Street, had 7 sons. 5 of which served in
the army.
Sidney Collett Wiltshire Regiment. He was wounded and lost an eye as a result. He
was a PT instructor in Marlborough College after the war, eventually emigrating to
Australia.
Bert Collett served with the Royal Engineers after being transferred from the East
Kent Regiment (The Buffs) He worked in the GWR as a plumber.
John Collett 8108 Sergeant D Company 2nd Battalion Wiltshire Regiment. Killed 1917
(see roll of honour) Ben Collett was a Corporal in the Wiltshire Regiment.
Ernest Collett a Private in the 1st Battalion Wiltshire Regiment was killed in 1915 (see
roll of honour) The 2 remaining sons, Frank and Alf, were too young to serve.

COLLEY. S W Colley served in the Royal Navy on board HMS Zealandia. He wrote the
following letter in 1915 to his Father, Mr J S Lovelock of 93 Stafford Street.
"Dear Dad, Just a few lines in answer to your most kind and welcome letter, hoping,
this will find you all in the best of health. Well, Dad, this time last Sunday, we were
close on the heels of the Germans and everyone was merry and bright at the thought
of it. If their ships had not been so close to their own port, Admiral Beatty would have
cut them off and they would have been straight into us, or our squadron and there

would have been no retreat for them. But, anyhow, they were lucky in getting back again! Have you started digging trenches in the back garden yet? The cellar is very handy! What I can see of it by ....'s letter, people are getting a bit nervous in Swindon, which I think is rather silly!

As the Germans would not get that far in land. Of course, one never knows! But seaside towns are quite handy. It is not quite so risky. But I think Dad, if you buy a bow and arrow and supply the family you will be safe. So poor old Town went under the hammer. It is what I expected! I don't think there is anything else I can write about, only that I am of the same opinion as you and that is, I trust, I shall come out and home again quite safe "

Sidney   Bert   John   Ben   Ernest (Inset)

COOK. Lance Corporal Reginald A Cook, Army Ordnance Corps. Enlisted at 16 years old,he had worked as a clerk in the accounts dept of the Loco and carriage dept GWR. He was commended by his Major General for 'snatching from another man, an enemy stick grenade that had become ignited and throwing it into a shell hole saving the mans life at grave risk to his own'

L/Cpl R A Cook

George Cook Wilts Regt
A labourer in No14 Shop GWR

S T Corner RN
Apprentice Boilersmith GWR

COUSIN. 3 brothers who all held a commission.

A J Cousin, a Major 3rd East Anglian RFA. He was previously in the Royal Navy Volunteer Reserve. He had attended the North Wilts Technical College, Victoria Road.

D P Cousin, a 2nd Lieutenant 2nd East Anglian RGA. He served previously in the 5th Btn Wiltshire Regt.

F J Cousin a 2nd Lieutenant 2nd East Anglian RGA. He had also attended the North Wilts Technical College. Their Father, Mr J Cousins, left Swindon to move to 41 Camden Road Tunbridge Wells.

COX. A J. Arthur Cox. Worked as a Machine Man in the Loco and Carriage dept and served in the Royal field Artillery.

C. Cowley   Arthur J Cox

Albert Crewe (standing left)

CREWE. Arthur Albert Crewe of Swindon, had emigrated to Canada before the war but returned to England to enlist. He 'signed up' at the Lacarno in Old Town and served as Private 221287 Army Service Corps. He remained in England after the War and lived at 22 Caulfield Road.

CRUSE. Brothers John and Sid Cruse of 7 Albert Street both served. Their nephew, William of Horsell Street also served. He suffered from shell shock and died in Netley Hospital after the war, and is buried in Radnor Street Cemetery.

CULLING. L/Cpl 520106 Ernest Frank Culling MM 565th AT Coy RE, of 60 Exmouth Street, worked in R shop GWR. He was a member of the Wilts Engineers Territorials. (Wilts Fortress Engineers.) Born in 1893, he was called up on 16th September 1914. Serving with the Fortress Engineers, he would have seen service in all British held areas in France and Flanders. As with most veterans, he rarely spoke of his experiences. Winning the Military Medal in 1918, he returned to England being discharged June 1919. He was based for a short time in Germany with the victorious allied forces and billeted with a German family. The owner of the house had served with a Prussian regiment. Ernest said that he was treated well by the family but just as he was leaving them, the German called his young son over, looked at Ernest and spoke the chilling words 'Revenge'! He returned to work in the railworks where he was very active in creating R shop's war memorial which included the 10 men who never returned.

Ernest Culling MM   E Culling (back right)

Wilts R.E.(J) Home Service Section. 1914.

Ernest Culling MM (back row 2nd from right)

Canal du Nord Sept1918. The largest military bridge built on the western front.
by Wilts Engineers and New Zealand engineers

Royal Engineers Comrades Association Genral Committee 1925-1926
F W Haines   F Fricker   C Chown   E F Culling   F Maskell   T Baker
Yarnton   E Marsh MM   M Jones (Pres)   A Last   S Bellinger
V Morgan   R Butt   C Taylor   F G Perry DCM

Unveiling the R Shop Memorial GWR in the mid 1920's:
Memorial is now on display in 'Steam'

CULLINGFORD. Mr and Mrs F T M CULLINGFORD of 95 Victoria Road, had 8 Sons who served, and their 9th son worked in a munitions stores -

Frederick, served in the RNVR. He died in 1918.(see roll of honour for details)

Frank, a teacher, served in the Dorset Regt as a Sgt-Major.

William, a solicitors clerk, served as a corporal in the 11th Field Ambulance RAMC.

Tom, a printer, served in the RGA as a telephonist.

James, formerly an ambulance man living in Yorkshire, served in the RAMC.

Jack, a butcher, was rejected 3 times on enlistment. He finally was accepted into the ASC.

Robert, a clerk, served in the RFA.

Richard, served as a signaller in the RFA in India.

Ernest, the eldest son, though not in the army, was a superintendent foreman in a Munition stores.

Tom Cullingford

Sir, would some of your readers kindly send us a football as it is very lonely out here after we have finished work. We should be very pleased if you could send us one. We are Swindon Boys, all of us and are doing our bit for our King and country.

Signed. Spr. H N Harris, Spr E G Purnell, L-Cpl. W J Pike, Spr, A W Sheppard, Spr H C Taylor, Spr,T W Mitchell, Spr D Moore.

1st Wilts R E BEF

A letter sent to the Swindon Advertiser, August 1915

Sapper A W Sheppard of Clifton Street was killed in April 1917 (See Roll of Honour)

DAVIS. Private F C Davis of Rose Cottage Drove Road, served with the 6th Battalion Gloucestershire Regiment. The following is an extract from a letter that he'd written to his parents at Rose Cottage.

'The Parcel which you kindly sent to me came the very day we moved in to the firing line, and my friends and I devoured the contents there and then. The only thing I took with me was the tin of milk. We had to march six miles to the trenches and as you know, our packs, rifles, ammunition, etc are no light weight and I did not feel equal to carrying the additional weight of the parcel. The trenches we held, once occupied by the French, who have queer kind of customs of their own. The thing that struck me most was the strange practice of burying their dead in the parapet. Not three yards from my dug out, there was one grave in the parapet, with a small roughly made wooden cross bearing an inscription in French, which interpreted read, 'Here lies a French soldier, a brave man, killed whilst doing his duty'.

We were in the trench for four days and had a rather exciting time, but although the trenches are fairly close together, very little rifle is done,and the occasional sniping. Most of the work is done by the artillery, who are at it all day and at frequent intervals, during the night. We have both French and British guns behind our lines, and I can assure you that our gunners always give the 'Allemands' one worse than they give us. Sometimes, the enemy send high explosives and sometimes shrapnel, but we do not get a very large number of casualties in comparison with the amount of shelling which goes on.

The second day we were in, one poor fellow in my ompany 'D' was struck with shrapnel and received 11 wounds. I have not told you before, but for some weeks, I have been attached to our company of brigade grenadiers whose special duty is to throw bombs, hand grenades etc. Whenever such a time arises that the use of these are found more effective and will do more damage than a rifle. In the case of our trench being attacked, or in case we make an attack, then the grenadiers play an important part.

The Germans are also very handy with bombs and three nights following, the rascals threw bombs at our listening post. Fortunately, none of our men were knocked out, and we had orders to fire two rifle grenades into their trench to every one bomb they threw at our listening post. The rifle grenade, unlike all the other grenades or bombs, is fired from the rifle, and of course, travels much further than those thrown by hand. The average distance of the rifle grenade is 200 yards. It has shrapnel casing which splits and scatters into about 75 pieces the instant the thing explodes. Whilst in the trenches the grenadiers are split up into parties of five or six men, who are stationed at various points along the line.

One NCO, three privates and myself, formed our party. In our dug out, was kept the chief supply of bombs etc, including boxes of rifle grenades, hand grenades, shrapnel coated bombs, high explosive bombs, detonators etc. As was , of course, necessary, the dug out was very dry and strong, with a shell proof top. I say 'Shell proof" but I'm afraid that if a Jack-Johnson had landed on top, it would have meant Golden Gates for the lot of us! However, we were very lucky to have a dry dug out. Hundreds of our poor fellows were washed out of theirs, owing to the heavy rain we have had. One night, whilst on sentry, I got wet through to the skin, but I was dead tired, so turned in, and I can honestly say, that I never slept better in my life. A foolish thing to do, you will say but what was I to do? Why , it was about the only thing I could have done. I couldn't change into dry clothes because I had none. One thing I wished I had and that was an extra pair of socks! We left the trenches about three days ago, and you would have screamed with laughter had you seen us. To enter or to leave the front line trenches it was necessary to come through a communication trench about 2 or 3 miles long and the greater part of this was flooded so badly that we took off our socks and puttees, turned our trousers up well over our knees, and waded through it as best we could.

My word , didn't we have a time! I remember once I forgot myself for a moment and thought I was on Weston sands again. It was of course a very unpleasant journey, but every now and again we were bound to stop and have a good laugh. We really looked very funny, knee deep in water, and splashed up to our neck with mud. When at last, we reached our billet, we took off our kit went straight to the nearest pond, washed our boots inside and out, and removed the mud from our legs and after drying our feet we turned in and slept well all night.

Our billet is a kind of jerry built farm arrangement, but we have some hay to sleep on and are quite lousy. The Germans shell the village every day and its a miracle that our billett has not been struck. Some shells have only missed the roof by inches. For last two days, the enemy have sent over quantities of shells, dozens of which have not exploded. I hope they have thousands more which will not explode!'

DAVIS. Sergeant Oswald Davis DCM Wilts Fortress Engineers. He worked in the Loco dept GWR and lived at 154 Redcliffe Street. He was awarded the DCM for his heroism in repairing a bridge under heavy fire on the Yser Canal Ypres in May 1915. On leave in Swindon, in the Lecture Hall in the Mechanics Institute,his workmates presented him with a marble clock. Afterwards he gave a graphic description of the events at the front.

Sgt Oswold Davis

DAY. Four sons of Henry Day, Headmaster of Even Swindon School, served.-

Laurence, served throughout the war. Became a teacher afterwards eventually starting up a private school, The Reading Collegiate School. He retired before WW2, during which he served as a special constable.

William, served with the Wiltshire Yeomanry. He was wounded after 3 months active service. After recovery, he was transferred to the Machine gun corps. He worked in the GWR, to which he returned after the war until he retired. During WW2 he served, as a Sergeant, in the Home Guard.

Lesley, served from the outbreak of war till the end, coming through unscathed. He worked for the GWR becoming the works chief chemist. He suffered from cancer during WW2, eventually dying from the disease before the end.

Frank. Served from the outbreak, serving in the Dardanelles campaign and being wounded twice. He went into teaching and moved to a London school eventually becoming headmaster.

Arnold. Due to an accident as a younger man, he lost an arm so could not enlist.

Lawrence Arnold William Lesley Frank

DERRICK. Walter Frank Derrick, served with the Machine Gun Corps. He tried to enlist again at the outbreak of the 2nd World War but was turned down on health reasons.

DIXON. Alfred Dixon of 13 Colbourne Street worked in the GWR when he enlisted aged 15. After the war he served in Northern Ireland as a member of the Black and Tans.

Arthur Dobson. Was a Machinist Loco & Carriage dept GWR

Lieutenant L Dobson 4th Wilts Worked Loco & Carriage dept GWR

Walter Frank Derrick

Sidney Dowse

Sidney Dowse (in raincoat) with
Toc H 'Deaf & Dumb Club'

DOWSE. Sidney Dowse of Kent Road served with the Wiltshire Regiment. After the
war he helped out with the Swindon 'Toc H'.

The Toc H movement was begun by the Rev Philip Byard 'Tubby' Clayton in 'Pop' in Belgium, 1915 when he opened a rest home for soldiers.He named it 'Talbot House', after Gilbert Talbot, the son of the Bishop of Winchester, who was killed in the Ypres Salient. (Buried at Sanctuary Wood Cemetery) The name Talbot House was shortened in the Army signallers language to 'Toc H'. This wonderful house is still there today, hardly changed, and welcomes the 'Pilgrim' to the Western Front. Everyone who visits, comments on the atmosphere that exists in this home. Thousands of soldiers passed through this house during the war, many never to survive the front. They enjoyed the peace the house offered them. This peace remains there still.

DUNN. Four members of the Dunn family from Beatrice Street served.Herbert Hillier Dunn – Royal Marine Light Infantry. William Dunn – Royal Engineers and John and Fred Dunn, Regiments unknown.

Unknown Army Chaplin

Herbert was born on 6th April 1884, he joined the Royal Marines 29th July 1901, enlisting as John Hillier Royal Marine Light Infantry – Ch/12740. He declared his real name a few years later.

Herbert Dunn 17 years old

Herbert Dunn in 1924

HMS Encounter 1908. Herbert Dunn (on floor with arm around his left shoulder)

They were mobilised for war on August 2nd 1914, the Royal Marines taking part in the early action at Ostend and the defence of Antwerp in October. In February 1915 he sailed for the Dardanelles. He was mentioned in despatches in November 1917, finally leaving the Marines on 15th May 1919.

Marine Artillery chums of Herbert Dunn

William Dunn was born in 1890 and enlisted in 1907 into the Royal Army Medical Corps. He married Florence Ellen Godfrey in 1912 in Warwick, where she continued to live at their address of 48 Castle Lane.In the Great war, william was transferred to the 118th Railway Company Mining Engineers, of the Royal Engineers.He served throughout the war in France and Flanders, being discharged on 21st March 1919. He continued to live with Florence in Warwick, working as a Railway Engine Fitter. Unfortunately, little is known of their brothers John and Fred, other than they both survived the war.

William Dunn and his wife Florence (Godfrey) married 1912

William Dunn Royal Engineers

ROYAL MARINES, CHATHAM DIVISION.

On your leaving the Chatham Division, Brigadier-General H. M. C. W. Graham, C.M.G., Commandant, Chatham Division, wishes to present you with a small souvenir of your service, ashore and afloat, and can think of no more suitable gift than the following extracts from the stirring speech on the 19th November, 1918, by His Majesty the KING, our Colonel-in-Chief, after the signing of the Armistice.

"Now that the clouds of war are being swept from the sky, new tasks arise before us. We see more clearly some duties that have been neglected, some weaknesses that may retard our onward march. Liberal provision must be made for those whose exertions by land and sea have saved us. We have to create a better Britain, to bestow more care on the health and well-being of the people, and to ameliorate further the conditions of labour.

May not the losses of the war be repaired by a better organisation of industry and by avoiding the waste which industrial disputes involve? Cannot a spirit of reciprocal trust and co-ordination of effort be diffused among all classes? May we not, by raising the standard of education, turn to fuller account the natural aptitudes of our people and open wider the sources of intellectual enjoyment?

We have also, in conjunction with our Allies and other peace-loving States, to devise machinery by which the risk of international strife shall be averted and the crushing burdens of naval and military armaments be reduced. The doctrine that Force shall rule the world has been disproved and destroyed. Let us enthrone the rule of Justice and International Right.

In what spirit shall we approach these great problems? How shall we seek to achieve the Victories of Peace? Can we do better than remember the lessons which the years of war have taught and retain the spirit which they instilled? In these years Britain and her traditions have come to mean more to us than they had ever meant before. It became a privilege to serve her in whatever way we could; and we were all drawn by the sacredness of the cause into a comradeship which fired our zeal and nerved our efforts. This is the spirit we must try to preserve. It is on a sense of brotherhood and mutual goodwill, on a common devotion to the common interests of the nation as a whole, that its future prosperity and strength must be built up. The sacrifices made, the sufferings endured, the memory of the heroes who have died that Britain may live, ought surely to ennoble our thoughts and attune our hearts to a higher sense of individual and national duty, and to a fuller realisation of what the English-speaking race, dwelling upon the shores of all the oceans, may yet accomplish for mankind.

For centuries past, Britain has led the world along the path of ordered freedom. Leadership may still be hers among the peoples who are seeking to follow that path. God grant to their efforts such wisdom and perseverance as shall ensure stability for the days to come.

May goodwill and concord at home strengthen our influence for concord abroad. May the morning star of peace which is now rising over a war-worn world be here and everywhere the herald of a better day, in which the storms of strife shall have died down, and the rays of an enduring peace be shed upon all the nations."

May you uphold the honour of your Country in Civil Life as well as you have in Military Life.

The Commandant wishes you every success in your future, and trusts you will make His Majesty's Speech the keystone of your future welfare.

H. Graham

Charles Dunn Royal Field Artilery

Jack Dunn with his wife Elizabeth &
daughter Philis of Caufield Road

EDWARDS. 3 brothers from 32 Thomas Street served. Albert (a sergeant in the Wilts Fortress engineers) Charles and Harry. Harry joined under age and his Mother went to the drill hall to bring him out. On reporting him to the Sergeant, she was told that he would attain the right age in a few weeks anyway! So the army kept him.

ELLISON. Sergeant Wilfred Ellison Croix De Guerre of 13 Lorne Street, served in the Royal Flying Corps. He was awarded the French Croix De Guerre in 1916, which was presented to him by Sir Douglas Haig.

ESAU. Corporal William Esau DCM served in the Royal Field Artillery. His brother - Corporal Ted Esau DCM served with the Royal Engineers. Their Father was a a blacksmith in T shop GWR.

EVANS. Sergeant 8870 Frederick Arthur Evans MM + Bar 2nd Battalion Wiltshire Regiment of Chapel Street. Son of William and Elizabeth Evans of 18 Caulfield Road. He died from the effects of the war on April 24th 1928 in Roundway hospital Devizes, aged 35 years.
He is buried in Radnor Street Cemetery.

H Elderfield Worked in the Stores Dept GWR

EVANS. Brothers Thomas and Hubert Evans of Dean Street served. Hubert went on to serve in Northern Ireland after the war as a member of the Black and Tans.

Lt C F Faith
Army Ordanance Corps

2nd Lt G W Ferguson

FERGUSON. 2nd Lieutenant G W Ferguson MC. The nephew of Sir Daniel Gooch, served in the Army Service Corps and was in France by August 1914. He later was posted to Egypt. He was commissioned in February 1917 after his transfer to the Royal Flying Corps. He worked formerly, in the drawing office of the Loco & Carriage Dept GWR.

FERRIS. Company Sergeant Major George Ferris Wiltshire Regiment. Lived at 11 Westcott Place.

Cpl 70666 James Patrick Farrell
Royal Field Artillery

FISHER, Driver Thomas F Fisher. MM Royal Field Artillery An apprentice in the GWR, he lived in Beatrice Street. He won his Military Medal for bringing in a wounded man from no mans land under fire. His brother also served.

FLEMING. Captain Harold J Fleming. Wiltshire Regiment.of 1 The Knoll. Born in Down ton in 1887 he became a PT instructor stationed in Cambridge. He played for Swindon Town FC from 1907 – 24 and was an England international, being capped 11 times. Fleming Way was named after him.

FLUCK. Albert E S Fluck served as a Captain. He was Commanding Officer of 52nd Graduated Battalion Royal Warwickshire Regiment.
He lived in Marlborough Road and worked previously in the Accounts Dept GWR. Returning to his job after the war, he was a well known piano player in Swindon and took part in local shows around the town. He was described by people who knew him as 'A perfect Gentleman' Father of Diana Dors.

Harold Fleming

FOWLER. Hubert William Fowler. Royal Engineers. Born in 1896, he lived at 10 Horsell Street. Served in Salonika. He died in 1978 living at 103 Drove Road.

Albert Fluck

FOX. Driver MS – 154 John Arthur Fox 621 Company MT Depot Army Service Corps. 1st Cavalry Division HQ Worked in Loco shop GWR. He Enlisted 9th August 1914. He was wounded on May 21st 1916 and honourably discharged.

FRANKLIN. Mr and Mrs FRANKLIN of 4 Poulton Street, Gorse Hill, had 5 sons who served -
David, was a Sergeant in the Royal Engineers
Bernard, a Corporal in the RAMC. He won the DCM on September 29th 1915 at Loos. He served an appren ticeship in the GWR. Moved to Tyneside where he worked in a ship building yard
Alan, was a sapper in the Royal Engineers
William, a Private in the Canadian Forces. He was wounded when he was shot by a sniper.
However,after recovery, he returned to the front.
Oliver, served as a stoker in the Royal Navy.

Hubert Fowler

FREEBURY. John. of Stratton St Margaret, had 4 Sons who served in the army.
William, John, Johnathon and Edward. 3 served in the Wiltshire Regt and 1 in the Welsh Fusiliers.
Edward served as a Pte in the 1st Wiltshire Regt. He was called up at the start of the war as he was a reservist. He was Killed in Action 27th December 1914. His body was not recovered until 27th August 1915.
A letter was sent to his Sister, Mrs F Daniels, who lived at 14 Union Street, by Sgt W Smith, who found his body between British and German lines. -

" Just a few lines to notify you of the death of 7159 Pte E Freebury, who was killed in action, when? I cannot say. How I came to know it was Pte Freebury, was by his pay book and an envelope with F Daniel 14 Union Street Swindon, on it. I thought it no harm in letting you know about it. I can safely say it must have been a 'bottled hell let loose' for there were 17 bullet holes in his clothes! Now to how I found him. There were several dead bodies in front of our trenches and we were about 60 yards from the Germans. I got out into the open and crawled to the first body I came across, which proved to be that of Pte Freebury. I got his pack and bought it in and found your address. That is how I came to send you this letter. A Lance-Corporal and myself brought him in during the night and buried him in a place in the back of the trench and made a rough cross for it. I have handed in all particulars to my orderly room and the orderly Sergeant will report the matter to other quarters.
I should say he was killed in December 1914, for that was the last pay he had on the 14th December 1914.I have a pair of gloves which I took out of his pack. If you want them, I shall be only too glad to forward them to you. And I may say, with all due respect to my fallen comrade, - He died facing the foe. I hope you know who his parents are. Please let them know, as I could only make out a few words in his pay book, and that was "Father -" the name was faded and I could not read it. The next was "Wroughton Wiltshire" Please Let me know. - I remain yours. 4037 Sgt. W Smith, A coy, 2nd Btn. The Kings Own Regiment, 83rd Brigade, 27th Division BEF France. Please write back and let me know if you know his friends. I found him on Friday 27th August 1915.

Private John W Fuller Royal Berks Regt worked in No 21a Shop GWR as a Frame Builders assistant

FULCHER. Private G H Fulcher of 63 Ponting Street served with the 7th Battalion Wilt shire Regiment.

GAGE. Sapper A E Gage. DCM   32nd Motor Air Line Section Royal Engineers.
The Son of Sarah Jane Gage of 51 Havelock Street. He was awarded the DCM for 'Conspicuous Gallantry' at Vlamertinge in Belgium on December 19th 1915. He assisted in repairing telephone lines under heavy shell fire.

He described the incident – 'The Germans attempted to make an attack on Sunday morning,December 19th, using gas. We were in an area which was being very heavily shelled. A route of five wires were broken in several places by shells, and of course someone had to go out and restore them. My Sergeant asked me if I would go with him, as some of the wires were working important circuits. We started out about seven o'clock, got them through with a lot of patience, and arrived back at half past one. I think we had to repair them 14 times. We would just get them through in one place and then see a shell come over and break them in another. Still, we stuck at it and tried them out, for they gave us a rest on that route, in the afternoon. I just had time for a bit of dinner, when we had to go out again on another wire, a cable, and found that broken in five places. Put that through, got back, had to hop off once again on another route, an open wire, which had been cut to pieces by shell fire, for about half a mile. Had quite a busy day of it. This was the first attack and bombardment for us to go through. Too many shells buzzing around for my liking. The noise of the guns was deafening. What the poor fellows in the trenches had to go through must have been terrible. If we earned DCM's, they earned VC's. What with the gas creeping over to them and knowing that the trenches they were in were the actual targets for the guns. Our guns roaring away behind, tis a marvel any of them kept in their right minds. Yet the spirit of the men is marvellous. Some of them really enjoy it and are very disappointed when they are not allowed to have a go at the Germans. Still, I think everybody will be glad when it is all over!"

Men of the Wilts Company Fortress Engineers in France

W W Gale
Formerly a Labourer in the Loco and Carriage Deot GWR

GARNER. Private Ernest Garner 2nd Battalion Wiltshire Regiment. An 'Old Contemptible' Buried in Whitworth Road Cemetery.

GARRETT. Frederick Richard Garrett. Royal Engineers. Of Gladstone Street. Worked as a Foreman Coach Body Maker No 4 Body Shop GWR

Frederick Garrett Royal Engineers   William Garrett

GARRETT. Private William Garrett No 171030, a Rodbourne Lad, served with the Machine Gun Corps as part of the 13th (Western) Western Division, one of 'Kitcheners' new divisions. They fought in the Dardanelles, then after went to Egypt and Mesopotamia. This division included the 5th Battalion Wiltshire Regiment, which 'Bill' Garrett was a member of. (Note Horseshoe Divisional sign on his upper arm.) He worked in the GWR and lived in Turner Street after the War.

GIBBS. 3 brothers, Walter Ernest and Sidney of 22 William Street served. All three were territorials and worked in the Rail works.

This photograph shows Walter, Ernest and Sidney Gibbs, all signallers in the Wiltshire Regiment (Trawsfynydd Camp July 1913)

All three served in India with the 4th Battalion Wiltshire Regt. Sidney later transferred to the Royal Field Artillery. They all survived to return home and to the railworks after the war.

GILMORE. Mrs GILMORE of 4 Oxford Street, had 7 Sons who served,
J G Gilmore Colour-Sgt.
T W Gilmore L/Cpl Signals RE
F L Gilmore Pte ASC
Albert Richard Gilmore Pte 1st Btn Royal Berkshire Regt
Lancelot Charles Gilmore Bmdr 3rd Wessex Brigade RFA
Harry Edgar Gilmore L/Cpl 1st Btn Somerset Light Infantry
A E Gilmore ERA Royal Navy
Mrs Gilmore also had 2 Grandsons, 2 Son-in-Laws and 8 Nephews serving.

GODWIN. Mr and Mrs C D GODWIN, lived at 21 Redcliffe Street. They had five sons who served -
Edward, was a corporal in the regular army at the outbreak of war. He served with the Royal Field Artillery. He gained promotion finishing the war as a Captain. He served for several years afterwards.
T D Godwin a Lance Corporal in the Royal Engineers
W H Godwin a Sapper in the Engineers. Served in the Telegraph dept.
E W Godwin, a private in the Army Veterinary Corps.
Albert a Sapper in the Royal Engineers.

Sidney Gibbs in Meerut
India 1916

Godwin Family

T C Gillett

QMS E J Godwin (seated left)

184

RODBOURNE ROAD WORKING-MENS CLUB
Winners of the Nomination Cup 1923

Albert Godwin (seated left) wearing his silver war badge as are 2 other veterans
Arthur Payne (centre back) & next to him William Ricks

STFC 1911-1912 season
Smiling Fleming and Wheatcroft (seated 2nd and 3rd from left)
Harold Warman MM Assistant trainer is stood middle row 2nd from left.

Wheatcroft and Warman did not live to see the end of the war (See Roll of Honour).
Their names along with 3 other players were commemorated on a brass tablet which
was displayed in the dressing rooms. It 'dissapeared' when alterations were carried
out to the stand in recent years.

SWINDON TOWN FOOTBALL CLUB

COUNTY GROUND, SWINDON

Saturday, Sept. 16th, 1916,

SWINDON

Versus

FLYING CORPS

(Farnborough)

Kick-off 3-30 p.m.

Flying Corps—	Swindon—
Kempton (Arsenal)	Matthews
Bettridge (Chelsea)	Kay
Macconnachie (Everton)	Weston
Butterworth (Millwall)	Archer
Russell (Fulham)	Stoneman (Cyclists)
Jennings (Bolton W.)	Walker
Ford (Chelsea)	Jefferson
Brown (Maryhill)	Smith
Ford W. (Chelsea)	Williams
Freeman (Chelsea)	Davies
Walters (Oldham C.)	Ing

Prices of Admission, including Tax—
Ground, 4d. Boys 2d.
Stands, Unreserved and Ring Seats. 7d
Grand Stand (RESERVED CENTRE) Gents 1/2. Ladies. 7d

John Drew (Printers) Ltd., Swindon

186

GODWIN. Company Sergeant Major 21541 William Godwin. DCM MM 57th Btn Machine Gun Corps.
London Gazette 3rd Sept 1919
For 22 months the conduct of this W/O has been exemplary. He is very cool under shell fire. In the attack on Schaap Baille on 26th October 1917, he did excellent work controlling ammunition supply under heavy fire. In the attack in the Drocourt Queant line on the 2nd September 1918. He did most valuable work arranging ammunition supply and also when his C/O was badly wounded, not only saved him by his prompt assistance, but also by his excellent reports, enabled the C/O to keep in touch with the situation and to arrange for a successful carrying out of the operation.

GRAY. Private 130974 Lawrence Gray of Swindon, served with the 45th Battalion Royal Fusiliers. He served in France and Flanders as a Lewis gunner. In July 1919 he went with his Battalion to Russia, as part of the Russian Relief Force until 30th September 1919.

Lawrence Gray above, in Uniform and in 'civvies' He is pictured wearing on his lapel, a 'Comrades of the Great War' Badge. This was the fore-runner of the British Legion. The Swindon Branch of the Comrades, used to meet at No 25 Milton Road in what is now The Milton Road Club.

GREEN. Private Roy Green DCM Royal Inniskilling Fusiliers. Son of Mr and Mrs Green of 21 Colbourne Street

He was awarded the DCM for Conspicuous Bravery. 'He went directly in to the enemy's barrage on October 15th and under heavy shell and machine gun fire, bandaged and dragged into the cover of shell holes, three severely wounded men. Also on September 29th he and his Platoon officer, rushed an enemies machine gun nest and bayonetted a German who had shot at the officer and wounded three others. It resulted in the capture of three German officers, 36 other ranks and 4 Machine guns.'

Private Green had two brothers who all joined in 1914. Private Archibald Rowland Green of the 6th Wilts died of wounds 11th October 1915 (See roll of Honour) Lance Corporal E G Green served in France and Mesopotamia and survived the war.

GREEN. Charles Green, ex Berkshire Regiment, of Green Lane Upper Stratton had 8 sons who served.

James Green	Royal Berkshire Regiment
Albert Green	Cheshire Regiment.
William Green	Cheshire Regiment
George Green	Wiltshire Regiment.
Charles Green	Kings Royal Rifle Corps
Edward Green	Wiltshire Regiment.
Arthur Green	Warwickshire Regiment
Thomas Green	Royal Flying Corps

A Grandson of Charles served in the Wiltshire Regiment.

HAINES. Brothers George, Fred.and Albert Haines served. The family lived in Ipswich Street. George married after the war and lived at 33 Kent Road.

George Haines

The Haines Family Ipswich STreet.
Back row Fred, Albert and George served

HANCOCK. Sergeant Archibald Percival Hancock of 16 Hunt Street served in the Royal Horse Artillery.

HART. Charles.W. Hart. Royal Naval Air Service. Lived at 108 William Street. He received the distinction of his name being brought before the Secretary for War by Sir Douglas Haig, for ' Gallant and Distinguished Conduct in the field.'

George Haines 10th London Regt

HAWKETTS. Private 43876 Frederick Edwin Hawketts the son of Edwin and Ruth Hawketts was born in 1898 in 79 Cromby Street. He enlisted 21st January 1917 at South Farnborough in to the Essex Regiment. He later went into the Royal Flying Corps before returning to the 1st Battalion Essex Regiment. He was severely wounded in August 1918. He was discharged on 22nd April 1919. He returned to his job as a upholsterer in the GWR. He married Clara Smith on the 8th May 1920 and lived at 8 Alfred Street. He passed away in his house at 27 Merton Ave on 8th October 1966.

Gnr George Hawkins RFA (seated) Frederick Hawketts

HAWKINS. Gunner 190708 George Edward Hawkins. Royal Field Artillery Born January 19th 1886 in Upper Stratton. Died 16th April 1952 in Roundway Devizes.

HAZELL. 54847 Harold Wilfred Hazell Royal Flying Corps. Lived at 255 Ferndale Road. He enlisted 11th January 1917 and served as an armourer until his discharge on 30th April 1920. He was on Class E reserve until 1929, and worked in No 15 Shop as a machine man in the GWR. He was called up again on 1st July 1939, when he served in India as a Sergeant in No 99 Squadron RAF. He died on Active service on 12th August 1942 and is buried in Karachi Military Cemetery.

Harold Wilfred Hazell

HEATH. Frederick George Heath, 2nd Battalion Wiltshire Regiment, lived at 34 Newhall Street. Serving with the battalion in France and Flanders he was wounded 3 times. His Foster Brother Herbert Williams also served in the same Battalion. He was Killed in Action 1914 (see Roll of Honour)

HISCOCK. Mrs Hiscock of Dean Street had 2 Sons who joined together - Alfred Norman and Arthur William, both joined the Wiltshire regt.
Arthur was wounded and invalided out of the service in 1916. Alfred who previously lived in Prospect Hill, was Killed in Action 13th January 1917. (see Roll of Honour for details)

George Heath

HILL. Private 7825 Harry Hill Wiltshire Regiment. (Though a Highworth man, he is included on Swindons Roll of men who served. Also, personal connections, as he is the Grand father of a good friend of mine!) Working as a wheelwright in Highworth, he walked, as many did, to Devizes to enlist. In 1915, he was wounded and as a result was blinded. Whilst living in St Dunstans home for the blind, he advertised in the local press for a wife. It was answered by a young widow, Elizabeth. He told the reporter, that he had gone, with a nurse to meet Elizabeth at the Railway Station. He confessed, he fell in love with her voice. They were married and lived in Highworth. Elizabeth helped him regain his trade. Unfortunatly, they did not have a long life together as Elizabeth contracted TB and died in the early 1920s. He eventually re-married and moved to live in Salisbury.

Harry Hill

BLIND SOLDIER'S ROMANCE: FELL IN LOVE WITH A VOICE.

rs. Hill helps her husband over a stile.

How to use the saw.

Teaching him the carpentry trade.

The marriage of Private Hill, who was blinded through wounds received earlier in the war, is one of the most touching romances of modern times. While at the Home for the Blind Private Hill advertised for a wife. The advertisement was answered by a young widow. The two met on a Thursday and were married by special licence on the Monday. He fell in love with his wife's voice as soon as he heard it. She is now teaching him the carpentry trade.—(*Daily Mirror* photographs.)

C Coy 2nd Wilts 1914

190

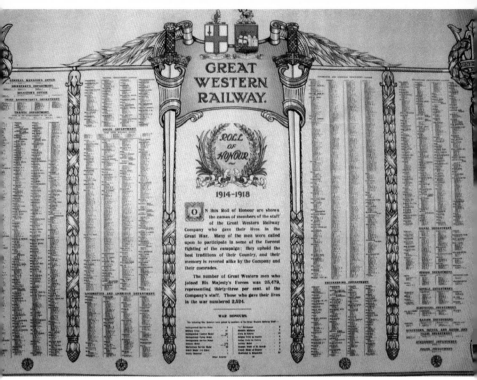

The Roll of Honour for the GWR. It contains the names of 2,524 members of staff, who gave their lives in the Great War. The total number of staff who served was 25,479. The memorial to these men is at Paddington Rail Station London.

Your King and Country Need You.

A CALL TO ARMS.

An addition of 100,000 men to his Majesty's Regular Army is immediately necessary in the present grave National Emergency.

Lord Kitchener is confident that this appeal will be at once responded to by all those who have the safety of our Empire at heart.

TERMS OF SERVICE.

General Service for a period of 3 years or until the war is concluded.

Age of Enlistment between 19 and 30.

HOW TO JOIN.

Full information can be obtained at any Post Office in the Kingdom or at any Military Depot.

God Save the King!

HOBBS. Private W Hobbs of 20 Bright Street served with the Dorset Regiment.

Pte W Hobbs Dorset Regt

Lt. E J Hodsell RNAS Formerly worked in the Drawing office Loco & Carriage Dept GWR

HOLLISTER, W. Pte. 1st Btn Wiltshire Regt. From Prospect Hill, he left for the front in August 1914 and was an avid writer of letters, both to his relatives in Swindon and also to the Advertiser. One of his letters, written in August 1915 gives a typical description of life at the time - "A few weeks ago , our regiment, in fact the whole brigade, were in some very severe fighting and we were called upon to do two charges in a few days, which were a success , especially the first. But of course we had a good many casualties, and day after day, there were terrific bombardments. So it was decided to give us a 'nerve tonic' namely, a rest. We were taken to a place where we were well out of the sound of the guns. This seemed to relax our minds. A six a side football tournament was arranged, also a concert in which both officers and men took part. We were also going to have some sports, but circumstances prevented it, for we were called away very suddenly for 'sport' else where!

Where we have been lately, we have had some very anxious times, especially with mines. On one occasion, several of us were on a listening post down in a sap, and whether it was fancy or not, I cannot say, but anyhow we reported to one of the Engineer Officers, that we could hear a kind of hammering. He also thought he could hear the Germans sapping.

The next morning, we had our beliefs confirmed. Anyhow, our engineers blew it up. Since then we have been very near to quite a number of mines, which the Germans have blown up, and I can assure you, it is not a very nice feeling which comes over you when near to one of these. The ground shakes for miles around, and your trench, even though it is not the one intended to be blown up, rocks like a boat!

The Germans are using a new shell now which we have named 'Whiz – Bang!' These come very suddenly and explode as soon as they strike the parapet of your trench, which means you have to build it up again as soon as possible. We have had several casualties by these lately, but generally they do not do much damage if you are in a good trench. A little while ago, we were able to witness the Germans using the burning liquid on some of our trenches, as it was not very far from the trenches we were holding. The trench that I am in, while writing this letter, is the best we have ever been in! As we are getting so used to the comfortable little dugouts and as we get all our mail bought right up to the firing line, we don't seem to care when we get relieved! We have already done twelve days . The worst part of it, is that we have got to keep our equipment on all the time, and of course never dream of taking off our boots.

There is only one of our number which is exempt from wearing his equipment and that is out little rabbit who is our sections mascot. He goes every where we go, whether it is in the firing line or back in the billets and he has just the same rations, for he enjoys a bit of bully beef and a biscuit, and he will also be contented with bread and cheese or a bit of jam. In the daytime "Bunny" will of his own accord, leave the trench and run about the long grass, but he always returns to our section. When we are moving from place to place, he does not object to being tied up in a sandbag and carried. When any shells came handy he ears go up and he seems more contented when they stop. Our Officer thinks it will be advisable to get a respirator for him in case we are gassed.

Well, I suppose most of you would think that "Tommy" is in the best of spirits when returning from the firing line but often when returning from the trenches we are too tired to talk much. But if you could walk by the side of any regiment going to the firing line you would hear a conversation similar to the following: - "March at ease! Pass it down, you can smoke – Got a match lad? - Here you are – Thanks".

Song - "You take the high road and I'll take the low".

"Hello, is that the Wilts going up again? Hello, they have dropped a few more in the old church; Look Jack!

Sling the ration bag over Harry – Here you are, I was just beginning to find it a bit lumpy. Hello, do you know who that is, well I'm blessed – Fancy the Swindon Engineers out here. Hey Bill, how you going on lad? A-1 I've heard you have had a pretty rough time lately – Not half - Well good luck, might see you again later. When do you think you will be coming out of the trenches? - Well, in about 6 days time – Right I'll look out for you – Goodnight – Well, give us a light lad, lets have another draw – Pass it down, no smoking – Just my luck, never mind in about half an hour we shall be in the trenches – 'Bang, Bang, Bang' – That's the stuff to give em – Not Half – Look at the star shells over yonder, the Germans got the wind up. 'Ping, ping, ping' – Mind the Johnsons – Holes on the left and right, pass it down to keep close up and walk quickly. Hello, we are close to the sniper – 'Ping', keep down! Star shells going up, ping, ping – Pass it down to mind the overhead wire. Bang, bang, bang – Keep your heads down, mind that wire underfoot, here is the trench just here. Ping, ping, keep down – Hello, they have spotted us, anybody hit? - No, good – Hello, is that the Wilts? - Yes – Cheero Wilts – Cheero HAC – What sort of time have you had HAC? - Not too bad you know. They persist in sending those trench mortars over – Any casualties? - Only a couple wounded yesterday – That's good! - Well, goodnight Wilts and good luck – Goodnight HAC."

WILTSHIRES IN FRANCE

Sir, allow me to venture on a little of your valuable space to voice the opinion, not only of myself but of many of the lads, who have left dear old Swindon and desired to make future history, and to do their bit to bring about the freedom of the world. Many of us have read your paper regularly during the weary years, months or weeks we have been away, but we look in vain for the one thing we most want to see. For months we read in your columns, of how the New Zealanders took Messines, but not a word about your own county regiment. Do you know, it is a fact, that no regiment in the battle covered itself with more glory than the 'Springers' your old county regiment. And yet their names only appeared in the casualty lists.

Only once, when with the good old Worcestershire's, they fought and defeated the Prussian Guard at Theipval in 1916, did you blow their trumpet? But then every paper was doing the same.

Now I come to the biggest battle in the history of men. Will you try to find what part your county regiment played and is still playing in that? Surely it should be as easy to find out the doings of the same as it is to find out the glorious deeds of the New Zealanders at Messines!

Think of the relatives of those in your county and town and think how they would appreciate the knowledge of how their husbands, sons, brothers or lovers paid the supreme sacrifice on the alter of patriotism. Would it not renew the hopes of those at home to learn the story of how Lt-Col Ogilve, DSO with bar, although surrounded by hordes of the enemy, acted with such cool determination and courage, that he inspired his men to fight and win and today live in thanks for his great leadership? Will you ever try to find out how the gallant Wiltshires repeatedly repulsed swarms of the enemy hoards who were cut down like blades of grass by our Lewis gunners? I am but an ordinary Tommy and this may never reach you, but, if it does, I hope you will want it in your columns. Believe me to be one, who is proud to wear the badge of the Wiltshire Regiment!

PTE W Hollister 1st Btn Wiltshire Regt.

A letter to the Swindon Advertiser printed April 10th 1918.

HOWSE. Sergeant 200229 Archie Howse 4th Battalion Wiltshire Regiment. Born in 1893, He lived at 73 Purton Road 'Veronica' (now the site near the Vets on round about at Akers Way) He became a Blacksmith before enlisting into the Wilts Regt. He served in India, where he later suffered from Malaria. He returned to England after the war and suffered illness due to malaria.After hearing from someone that to fully recover he should return to India for a while, he re-enlisted into the army, and served in the Rifle Brigade, 1st/13th Battalion Great Indian Peninsular Railway Regiment. He remained in India, with his wife, finally returning to England in the 1930s.

HUMPHERIES. William Henry Humpheries of 65 Princes Street served with the Royal Engineers.

Archie Howse 4th Wilts India

Archie Howse as Sergeant 4th Wilts

Archie Howse Rifle Brigade 1920 Outside 'Veronica' 73 Purton Road

HUNTCHINGS, J. Chief Engine Room Artificer Royal Navy Served on HMS Benbow

HUTT. Private 71214 Victor George Hutt MM. Enlisted under age in 1914, but was sent home after his true age was revealed. He enlisted again in 1916, joining the 2nd Battalion Devonshire Regiment. He saw action on the Somme that same year. He finished the war in the Worcester Regiment. He won the Military Medal and was Gazetted on 23rd June 1919. He later married Fathering 5 children, passing away in 1966. He suffered from the effects of Gas for the remainder of his life.

HYDE. Mr and Mrs E W Hyde of The Fox Tavern in Regent Street. Had 3 sons who served - Jack served with the Wilts Battery Royal Field Artillery, in India.Charlie served with the Royal Army Medical Corps.Robert was a Gunner in the Royal Field Artillery. He joined at 17 years old. Transferred to the Ammunition column 51st Highland Division, he was wounded in 1915 He wrote the following letter to his parents from the hospital he was recuperating -

Victor George Hutt MM

"Dear Mother and Dad, Just a few lines to let you know how I am going on. I received your letter at 9 o'clock this morning and at 11 o'clock, I had your parcel. What a treat the cake and bread pudding was! Please thank 'Jocks 'for sending apples. I had 8 letters this morning and shall have some work to answer them all. I was pleased to see that brother Charlie has been made a corporal. I said in the first instance, that he would have some stripes and I can venture to predict that he will soon be promoted to sergeant. I expect you feel proud to know that you have 3 sons in the army and 2 of them with stripes!. I have twice been complimented by the colonel – one while in the firing line and later at the base. The colonel said he was proud of such lads at my age (17) to have the pluck and courage to come out here. On another occasion the colonel complimented me on going and fetching his horse and sticking to it when the Germans were shelling us. The horse took fright at the shells dropping around us. I caught the animal and rode it back, but we had to shoot the poor animal because it was badly wounded. We also lost some of our mules the same evening. ....

JAMES, W. James. Chief Engine Room Artificer. Royal Navy. Served on HMS Benbow.

JOHNS. Brothers Frederick and Stanley Johns served. Frederick, a fitter and turner in the railworks, served with the Kings Royal Rifle Corps. Stanley, a machine man 'inside' served with the Hampshire Regiment.

Fred Johns

Stanley and Frederick Johns

Stan Johns

JOHNSON. Harold G Johnson, of Oriel Street, served in the RAF. He worked in the GWR and went on to management in the works after the war. He lived at 139 Drove Road in later years, where he remained until his death.

The wedding of L/Cpl Tony Grande RE to Elsie Johns
Fred Johns and his wife. Stan Johns and his wife   Billy and Rena Johns
Gladys Johns

KANE. William Kane, a Lay Preacher of 26 Ford Street, enlisted on 12th October 1915 aged 47 years. He insisted that if his Son served, then so would he. His Son George enlisted at the same time aged 16 years.

William had worked as a timber porter GWR, and his skills were used by the army as he served as a Private 296807 994th AS Coy Labour Corps Army Service Corps serving in France.Private 41157 George Kane was sent for training with the 5th Battalion Wiltshire Regiment. He received all his innoculations along with the rest of the Battalion in readiness for service in the Dardanelles. Because of his young age, the army held him back when the battalion left. He was later transferred to the Duke of Cornwalls Light Infantry when he 'came of age' Serving in France,he achieved his Snipers qualification.During an attack on German lines, he was wounded in the leg and crawled for cover in a shell hole, where he remained for 13 hours using his bayonet as a tourniquet. He was finally rescued by a Canadian Officer who helped him back to allied lines. His leg was removed by field surgeons. He worked after the war in the GWR and became a foreman in 'T' Shop in the Brass foundery shop.

William Kane

George Kane

KENT. Private F G Kent MM. Served with the Army Service Corps. His Father C G Kent of the Rifleman's Hotel, received the following letter from him.-
'Just to let you know I have got out of the line on a short rest after the worst two months I have ever experienced, which finished up with me getting my car blown up! You will be surprised to hear I was recommended twice. The last time for bringing in wounded under heavy shell fire and I have been awarded the Military Medal, for which I am wearing the ribbon. But still, I have been lucky getting through without a scratch. If you'd had seen my bus before it went up, you would have thought it was a pepperbox! There were about half the drivers wounded the last time we were in. So I have something to be thankful for getting out with a whole skin. You must remember me to all the boys who come into the Billiard room and Bar.'
Harry F Kent, his brother also served.

KENT. Brothers Ernest and William Thomas Kent served. Ernest in the Royal Field Artillery, who served in India, and William in the Royal Flying Corps

Ernest Kent

Ernest Kent India 1916

William Kent

William Kent (front reclined)

William Thomas Kent RFC

KING. Lieutenant B King, Warwickshire Regiment. He had previously worked in the Stores Department of the GWR.

GWR men of the 111th Railway Company Royal Engineers   Lt. B King

LACEY. Thomas Lacey of 24 Lorne Street served with the Royal Flying Corps.

LANG. Private John. F. Lang. MM Wiltshire Regiment. Son of Mrs Lang of 46 Havelock Street. Won the Military Medal for conveying messages and doing useful work during the advance of September 29th. He was educated at Sanford Street School and was a member of St Johns Church Choir. He worked previously as an apprentice in the Carriage and Wagon dept. His brother Cecil Lang also served but was killed at Hooge in 1915 serving also with the Wilts. (See Roll of Honour)

J F Lang MM   Thomas Lacey

LEACH. Sergeant F. Leach. DCM Wiltshire Regt. His parents lived at 30 Westcott Place. His wife and 2 children lived at their home in Andover. He was a regular soldier and had served in South Africa before the war. He won the first DCM of the regiment in the war. He was commended for several acts of bravery. He won the DCM for saving a comrade. 'He was in a trench when a shell exploded on the parapet. One of his comrades was buried in the debris and was in a dangerous position being directly in the line of fire. Sgt Leach, despite the hail of bullets being directed on the trench, dug his pal out and bought him to cover.'

LEGG. Private 3-7253 Albert (Bertie) Legg 1st Battalion Wiltshire Regiment. Born in Wroughton in 1887. He Lived in 64 Haydon Street. He was a Regular Soldier, joining the army 20th August 1903 he went into the 2nd Battalion Wiltshire Regiment.

He was wounded in August 1915, later returning to the front. He served 17 years 10 months with the army, being discharged in 1921. He married in 1919 at Christ church. He died aged 70 on 20th November 1957, and was interned in Whitworth Road cemetery.

LINDSEY. John Lindsey MM of 130 Beatrice Street, born in Holt, Trowbridge in 1891, served in the Royal Engineers. Transferred later to the 231st Light Railway Operation Company R E serving throughout the War in France, he went on to win the Military Medal. His sons William, Ernest Albert and Frederick also served. William and Frederick both returned safely. Ernest who served with The 6th Battalion Wiltshire Regiment was killed on the second day of the Battle of the Somme aged 19. (see roll of honour for details)

MARTIN. Brothers Dan and Tom Martin served with the 21st Lancers. Dan survived the war and emigrated to Canada afterwards. Tom died in India in 1915 (see Roll of Honour)

MASON. Driver John William Mason MM 'He along with a corporal extinguished a fire that broke out in an ammunition dump under heavy enemy shell fire. He was wounded in the course' 2 of his brothers also served, one was discharged from the army after being invalided home, the other served in Mesopotamia. All three were the Sons of Mr and Mrs A L Mason of 16 Byron Street.

MASSEY. Gunner Wilfred Raymond Massey, Royal Garrison Artillery. Lived at 17 Car fax Street he worked in the GWR works. He died in an accident in the works during an air raid warning in 1940.

MATTHEWS. Private S W Matthews 1st Battalion Wiltshire Regiment. Telford Road Club.

MAYELL. Sidney Ernest Mayell 405875 Wilts Battery and his brother William Mayell Royal Field Artillery, enlisted 8th August 1914 and served in India and Palestine. They both later transferred to the Royal Flying corps.
Sidney returned to his job in the coppersmiths shop GWR and William to his as a boilermaker. Sidney retired due to ill health and died aged 67 in 1961.

Dan Martin

William Mayell RFA India

Sidney Mayell (seated)

STANDING

199

'A' Sub Wilts Battery RFA North Wales 1914
Sidney Mayell is standing back row 2nd in from left

William Mayell RFC (back row 4th from left)

MENHAM. Reginald W Menham, of the Castle Hotel, North Street, had 3 sons who served. Reginald and Archibald and his Step-Son Alexander McKay.
Both Reginald and Alexander were killed. (See Roll of Honour for details)
Archie, the youngest son, enlisted in the Royal Field Artillery. He survived the War and went on to work in the GWR works. The following is an extract from a letter he wrote home in 1915.
'I am a Gunner on the 18 pounders, but would rather be on the Howitzers. It is very dangerous where we are, shells falling everywhere and sometimes you have to look out. I have seen some awful sights already. One day a shell burst in the street not far from us, killing a woman and her 2 children. We are where the Jack Johnsons burst and the scrapping is at its full height. It is a pity to see the place in ruins'

MILLS. Albert Mills served in the army. He was Licensee of the Ship Hotel Westcott Place.

MORRIS. Lieutenant Harry Morris served in the Wiltshire Regiment. He formerly worked in the GWR.

MORSE. Regimental Sergeant Major Harry Jacob Morse MM 4th Battalion Wiltshire Regiment. He left England for service in Egypt and India, returning March 1919. He was married and lived with his wife in Cheney Manor Road. After his discharge, they lived in William Street. He returned to his job in the GWR where he worked as a clerk. During the Second World War, he served as an officer in the GWR Home Guard. He died aged 81 on 7th September 1967.

RSM. H J Morse.   Harry Morse India
MM 4th Wilts

NCOs 2/4th Wilts India: H M orse (2nd from right back row)

NEABARD. Dennis John Neabard of Northbrook Road, enlisted, under age, in the Royal Marine Light Infantry. He survived the war, but was committed to Roundelay Hospital in the early 1920s. His sad story was unfortunately so common with many other Swindon men. So many became 'institutionalized' in these psychiatric units as Dennis did. He remained in the hospital up until his death in the early 1950s.

NEVILLE. Reginald Neville worked in the GWR Swindon works and served as a Lieutenant in the 1st Battalion Bedfordshire Regiment

D N Neabard

GWR Home Guard WW2 Harry Morse is the officer (centre front)

NEW. 3 brothers of 101 Ferndale Road served -
Trooper A J New 11th Hussars, Private F W New 4th Battalion Wiltshire Regiment,
Driver H T New Royal Field Artillery.

A J New 11th Hussars   F W New 4th Wilts   H T New RFA

'C' Coy 2nd Wilts 1914

2nd. Wiltshire Regt. Parkhouse Camp. Salisbury.

Swindon Recruiting Staff 1917
L/Cpl Williams, S/Mjr J Fry,F M Bizley,J Coleman, R E Wilton,E Hearnell, A A Nelson,
Peggy? M Simmons, Lt/Col W Johnson,   Capt Russell, F E Wilton, M T Wilton,W H
Bagnell, M M Joller, L/Cpl A Chapman.

NICHOLLS. Mr and Mrs T Nicholls of 24 Newport Street had 5 sons who served. -
Private Roland Nicholls 1st Battalion Wiltshire Regiment.A reservist called up at the
was wounded in January 1915. He was paralysed in both legs.
Driver Alfred Nicholls Royal Field Artillery also worked in the GWR
Private Frank Nicholls a Signaller with the 3rd Wessex Brigade Royal Field Artillery
Private Jesse Nicholls served with the Royal Welsh Fusiliers
Private David Nicholls served with the South Wales Borderers.

'Sir, Will you kindly ask any of your readers if they could supply our chaps with a hair
cutting machine, as it is difficult to get your hair cut where we are. We should be
very thankful if you could. I am sending this letter by a man on leave.
My home is in Swindon.' Yours truly. Arthur Oxley

A letter received by the Swindon Advertiser in 1915, written by Private Arthur Oxley of the Army Ordnance Corps, Travelling Workshop. BEF France.

ODEY. 2 brothers of 63 North Street served.
William Odey Royal Field Artillery and Albert Daniel Odey served in the Royal Marine Light Infantry. Both survived to return home. Albert again served in WW2 with the RAF.

Bill Odey   Albert Odey   A Odey RAF WW2

OSMAN. Frederick Percy Osman of Kingdown Road, Stratton, born 1885, enlisted as Private 12273 Osman 'B' Company 7th Battalion Wiltshire Regiment. He went with the battalion for training at Sutton Veny, as part of the 26th Division. They left for France September 1915 and were in the reserve lines for the Battle of Loos. On October 29th, they were removed from the line, and entrained for Marseilles, destined for Salonika. The Battalion fought with distinction in a 'forgotten' campaign. They returned to France in July 1918 and fought there untill the end of hostilities.

Frederick Osman (kneeling extreme left) 7th Wilts

Frederick was batman to Company Comander of 'B' Battalion Capatain G K Hulbert MC. He received many letters from his officer after the war, two of which are as follows.-

Bodenham, Salisbury. 20th November 1918

Dear Osman,
I am sending a line to your home hoping it will be forwarded, as I should much like to hear how you are getting on.
It was bad luck your getting hold of that Malaria as you did and I was sorry to be able to do nothing for you when you came to Le Cateau. But I was very busy and I sent Pratley up in the evening to enquire about you, but you had gone off to hospital. I unfortunately fell ill with flu just before going into the next attack. It was bad luck leaving the company just at the last, for they sent me down to Rouen and then back to Blighty and now home for a month.
I am much better but still have a nasty cough. Did you hear, that Captain Law died. I am dreadfully sorry about it, for I liked him more than any other officer. I think he was so full of spirit and so cheerful. I felt the loss of Cpl Goodman almost as much. He was such a sportsman and such a good soldier too. I don't know whether I shall get back to the battalion, or when, but I want to see B company demobilised, although, I am so sorry there will be so many not with us to say good – bye to one another. Let me know how you are and where.
Lieutenant Byrne lost his arm and leg (amputated) Lieutenant Stanford is going on well. Lieutenant Maskell still has no use in one leg. Lieutenant Goldie has lost a finger or two.
Yours truly   **GK Hulbert**

Captain 'Jimmy' Law MC. Was wounded leading a gallant attack against German positions at Le Cateau. He died later of his injuries. Lt Goldie, was promoted to Captain. He had made quite a reputation of himself from his actions in Salonika.

Another letter received several months later read:

Dear Osman, 23rd July 1919
I never thanked you for the photo which I was very glad to have to remind me of the old days, when you looked after me so well. You never failed to get my 'biviy' up or my dug-out comfortable, when we moved in to the line or on the march, and I guess you felt a bit weary some nights. I really feel very grateful to you. I am glad to hear you are back at work again and I wish you luck.
Yours truly   **GK Hulbert**   Frederick Osman

PAINTER. Mrs R Painter of 65 Winifred Street had 6 sons who served.
R. Painter Royal Marine Light Infantry HMS 'Empress of India'
Private T Painter C Company 1st Battalion Wiltshire Regiment. Wounded in the severe fighting near La Bassee October 14th 1914. He returned to active service after recovering and survived the war.
Private 7833 Edwin C Painter 2nd Battalion Wiltshire Regiment captured during First Ypres in October 1914
Private Mervyn Painter Army Service Corps
John Painter Australian Imperial Forces
Albert Painter Australian Imperial Forces.
Two of Mrs Painters Son in Laws Served as well
F G Whitford Royal West Kent Regiment. And Arthur Threadfold RAMC

PAKEMAN. Oscar Henry Pakeman MM of High St, served in the Wiltshire Yeomanry. He won his Military Medal in 1917.

PATTERSON. Cyril J Patterson served with the Wiltshire Yeomanry. He lived at 68 Red cliffe Street and worked in the Loco and Carriage Dept GWR as a Painter.

PAUL. 2 brothers served Charles T Paul. Frederick George Paul MM. Of 18 Gladstone Street. The latter served in the Royal Army Medical Corps winning his Military Medal in December 1916. Both brothers formerly worked in the GWR.

PAYNE.
Lance Corporal 5423 G F Payne Wiltshire Regiment. He was wounded on March 1915

Sgt Arthur G J Pelling Wilts Regt

PERRY. 4 Sons of Mr and Mrs W H Perry of County Road served Francis Perry, Frederick G Perry DCM, Frederick C. Perry and John L Perry. Frederick G Perry, who was a Corporal in the Army Troops Coy, Royal Engineers attached to the 1st Btn Wiltshire Regt. He won the DCM in 1915. He was the Inspector of School Buildings under the Swindon Education Committee before he joined up.

PIFF. William Harold Piff MM Royal Engineers. Was a painter in the Loco and Carriage Dept GWR. He enlisted on 2nd September 1914. He won his Military Medal for 'Gallant Conduct and Devotion to Duty in the Field'

PITT. Harold J. Pitt A cooks mate in the Royal Navy aboard HMS Warspite. He had worked previously for J W Cowley of Gorse Hill. He was present at the Battle of Jut land.

7th Battalion Wiltshire Regt. Memorial in Marlborough

GWR Yard Inspector Mr Perry with his wife and 4 sons

PLOWMAN. Albert Plowman Royal Engineers. Lived at Butts Depot, Evelyn Street.

Albert Plowman (centre 2nd in front right)

Sub Lt Walter William
Peters. RNR

POWELL. Private 1994 Reginald Powell of 5 Ferndale Road,
served in the Royal Army Medical Corps. His Brother Private
28793 W J Powell served with the Gloucestershire Regiment.

Albert Plowman

Wounded in Italy R Powell
(in Pith Helmet 2nd from left)

Pte R Powell RAMC

Royal Army Medical Corps serving in Ita
Reginald Powell is standing extreme le

H G Provis Wilts Regt
worked in Loco & Carriage Dept
GWR

R Powell (left) in Italy

PROBETS. Mrs Probets, of 42 Gooch Street, had 7 Sons who served -
Dvr W Probets, Died.
Pte J Probets, Dublin Fusiliers (Formerly 1st Btn Wiltshire Regt).
Pte Alfred F Probets, 1st Btn Wiltshire Regt. Was Invalided.
Dvr F Probets, 1st Btn Devonshire Regt. (Formerly 1st Btn Wiltshire Regt).
Pte Herbert Probets 2nd Btn Wiltshire Regt. Was Invalided.
Pte T Probets, 2nd Btn Wiltshire Regt. Killed in Action 1917. (see roll of honour for details)
Dvr A Probets, Wilts Battery Royal Field Artillery.

PUFFETT. Private Sidney Puffett. 1st Battalion Wiltshire Regiment. Lived at 232 Ferndale Road. On December 28th 1914, he wrote home to his Mother -
" Some people say that the Germans can't shoot, but take my word for it, they can!.......... It is awful out here. I have been in action but now am enjoying a well earned rest for a few days. I went into the trenches on Christmas eve, but I feel too full to tell anything about it. I have pulled through and that is good enough. I am sorry to say that we lost 4 killed. 2 of them were fellows who came over with me, on Christmas day too! It seems terrible to think that football and all such amusements are going on at home, when fellows are giving their lives for their country out here "
He went on to say that he received his Princess Mary's Gift box and prizes the letter from the King. He said that he would keep them and bring them home when the war is over, which he thought would be soon!

RANDELL. Reginald Randell of 6 Taunton Street, was one of 3 Brothers who fought. -
Frederick, served with the Royal Field Artillery
Walter served with the Wiltshire Regt.
Reginald, aged 15, enlisted into the 3rd Btn Wiltshire Regt at the War's Outbreak. He served a month before his Mother caught up with him and reclaimed him! He ran away again, this time he went to Bristol and joined the Navy. He joined his ship HMS Warrior in June 1915.His Ship was part of the 1st Cruiser Squadron of the British Grand Fleet, and with the fleet he participated in the Battle of Jutland in May 1916. The following is of an account he gave when he returned to Swindon on leave.

"In company with the 'Black Prince' 'Lion' 'Tiger' 'Defence' and 'Edinburgh'. The Warrior left on May 30th, and it was off the coast of Denmark that we sighted the German fleet. After they had been pursued, the enemy turned round and opened fire at 15,800 yards. The Warrior was hit about 5 minutes after it had been in action , but it kept on firing until about mid-day.

After sinking one ship and setting another on fire, we caught fire and had to be towed out of the firing line. We lost a great many men through poison gas from the shells. We tried to get our vessel along but it was no use as she was sinking fast and we had to leave her. A ship that was running about with aeroplanes upon it, picked us up and bought us to land. We proceeded to Edinburgh, where we were given cake, bread and butter and tea. Our Captain gave us a very good name and is trying to get us on another ship together. He said that we were one of the best crews he had ever had and that he was more than satisfied with us.

I was engaged in supplying ammunition for the 7.5 in. gun turret. This was the first action I had been in and it came off greatly, but none the more for that. I don't want to see any more like it. Of the ships boys, only one was shot. As we were leaving the scene, we were chased by 4 German destroyers, but some of our destroyers came up and drove them back. As we were leaving our vessel for the one that took us off , a man with a leg off fell between the 2 ships, but another jumped in after him and fetched him up unconcious. He was bought round but he died on the way to land. One man was left on the Warrior. We only lost one officer , the Chief Carpenter. We had respirators made of cotton and filled with Oxygen, tied around our mouths and noses. It was through this that I was saved from being gassed. We also had lifebelts around our waists.

A comrade called Mildenhall who served with our crew, is also from Swindon and lives in Westcott Place."

Of the Squadron, which consisted of Defence, Black Prince Duke of Edinburgh and Warrior, only Duke of Edinburgh remained.

REED. David C. Reed of 80 Clifton Street, served with the Wiltshire Regiment. He previously worked as a clerk in the GWR.

RICE. Private Eric Thomas Rice. Wiltshire Regiment. Lived at 37 Havelock Street. Enlisted at 16 years old. He worked in Wills after the war. Those who knew him often comented on his 'wicked' sense of humour!

Pte E Reed. 1st Battalion
Wiltshire Regt. Lived at 103
Manchester Road

Eric Thomas Rice.
Both Photographs clearly
show his youth

RICHENS. Sergeant J W Richens of the 2nd Battalion Wiltshire Regiment, wrote the following letter from the Western Front. It was written to Mr H Spackman, who was Superintendant of Swindon Law Institution.
30th July 1915.
'Mr Burgess, (The Vicar of Wanborough) wrote to me to say that he thought perhaps you would care to hear from me, so I hope the card I sent the other day did not surprise you. Someone kindly sends me out the local papers every week and in last weeks issue, I saw that you had 11 of your boys in the army and 10 in the navy. I will try and give you a few particulars of each of your old boys.
First of all, I must tell you, that, my brother Jack has enlisted in the Army Service Corps as a driver and expects to be coming out here shortly. In this Regiment, there are 4 of us Sergeants, 1 Corporal and 1 Lance/Corporal. Charlie Love was a Sergeant and I think he was either killed or made a POW at Ypres, I am not sure, but I believe he was captured. Bill George is another Sergeant, and only rejoined us this week after being twice wounded. Bert Hill is a Machine gun Sergeant still out here with us and I am the other Sergeant.
I was slightly wounded in the hand in the hand last November, but I am quite well again now. The Corporal is Bert Button who was wounded at Ypres last October and is at present waiting at Weymouth for his turn to come out here again. William Giddings is the Lance Corporal. Private Ted Ellison is a POW and Burt Norton another Private was seriously wounded in October and is at present, in England. The only other fellow I know is Tom Cook who is a drummer in the Dorset Regiment.'

ROBINS. Frank Robins lived in Caulfield Road, served with the Wiltshire Regiment. He was entually commissioned and held the rank of Captain. His brother Harold Robins, lived in Whiteman Street and served with the Royal Naval Air Service. He was killed in 1917 (see roll of honour)

ROBINSON. Private F Robinson MM Welsh Regiment of 7 Beatrice Street, won the Military Medal in 1917. His brother Driver 98467 Frederick Isaac Robinson Royal Field Artillery, died the same year in Iraq. (see roll of honour)

ROBERTS. Alfred L Roberts, lived in Rodbourne. He later became Mayor of Swindon.

ROBERTS. Mrs Roberts of 38 Cambria Place had 6 sons who served.
Gunner 340888 J A Roberts No 1 section 2nd Canadian Div.
C L Roberts HMS 'Drul Castle'
Bombardier 42535 Roberts Royal Garrison Artillery.
Private 92585 L Roberts Royal Army Medical Corps.
Sapper 2858 W N Roberts 77th Field Company Royal Engineers.
Driver 51447 Harold David Roberts. RA Section Royal Horse Artillery.

Frank & Harold Robins

RODDA. LIEUTENANT H C Rodda MC of 86 Broad Street, served with the Wilts Fortress Engineers Royal Engineers. He had served previously in the South African campaign as a stretcher bearer in the Medical Corps. He worked in the GWR as a draughtsman. He was awarded the French Medaille Militaire on 6th November 1915 for his work on a survey near Verbranden-Molen. He was Gazetted 31st December 1915, 'for Gallant and Distinguished Conduct in the field'. Awarded the Military Cross 2nd June 1919.

ROGERS. Mr and Mrs Rogers of 1 South Street, had 6 Sons. -
Pte 7989 W J Rogers 2nd Royal Welsh Fusiliers. He was wounded and later honourably discharged
Pte 10515 Thomas Rogers 2nd Btn Royal Welsh Fusiliers. Also wounded, twice, in October 1914 and April 1917. Served the remainder of the war in England.
Pte 16087 Herbert Rogers Royal Marine Light Infantry. Served on HMS London later on HMS Suffolk.
Bdr 94081 Lewis Rogers Royal Field Artillery. He was wounded in April 1917.
Pte 131998 Edward Rogers 597th Coy MT Army Service Corps.
Pte M.339945 J Rogers 302 Section MT Army Service Corps.

A soldiers war medals. 1914 Star known more commonly as the 'Mons Star'. War Medal and Victory Medal Old soldiers referred to these medals as 'Pip, Squeak and Wilfred' Many proudly wore their medals on Armistice day and other special occasions. Others put them away in a drawer to be forgotten. Common medals but hard won!

Silver War Badge.
This was awarded to the soldiers who had been wounded and invalided out of the services. It was worn on the lapel of civilian clothes to prevent men, not in uniform being harassed by women giving them white feathers

ROWLAND. John Burnell Rowland served with the Wiltshire Yeomanry, later transferring to the Royal Engineers. Born in West Hartlepool he moved with his family to Swindon where he worked in the GWR as a fitter and turner living in Carr Street. (photo shows him with his wife Mary in 1920).

A cheerful John Rowland in later years. An unsung Hero

SAVILLE. Percy Sidney.Saville DSM Chief Stoker Royal Navy Submarine.
Son of Mrs Saville of Hinton Street Gorse Hill.

SCOTT. Lance-Corporal A G Scott DCM. 5th Battalion Wiltshire Regiment. He worked in the GWR works as a Machine man in the Wagon Frame shop, before enlisting. He was sent with the 5th Battalion to the Dardanelles, where he won a DCM. He was one of a party outside British lines at Chunuk Bair for over a fortnight, at the end of which time, greatly exhausted and weakened, he, with the greatest bravery, made his way in, and so bought about the rescue of his comrades. He was constantly under heavy fire and succeeded, with utmost difficulty. He did not hesitate, however, to return at once, to act as a guide to the relieving party.

Corporal A G Scott DCM

SHACHEL. Reginald George. Shachel 2nd Lieutenant Royal Flying Corps.
A teacher in Clifton Street Boys School. He enlisted in September 1915. He was one of 50 men to be asked by the RFC to take up wireless training. He went to the British school of Telegraphy in London for 4 months, then was sent to France in February 1916. In October he received his commission in the field.

SHEPPARD. Four brothers from the SHEPPARD family of 86 Cheltenham Street served -
Sgt 5701 Ashley Francis Sheppard 1st Btn Wiltshire Regt. Killed in Action April 1918. (See roll of honour) He lived in Bristol and was mentioned in despatches
Sgt 94214 E Sheppard Royal Field Artillery.
Pte 19397 F Sheppard Wiltshire Regt.
Pte 18307 S E Sheppard Royal Marine Light Infantry. On board HMS Vindictive.

SHEPPARD. William Charles Sheppard of 76 Clifton Street, served in the Royal Field Artillery. He suffered as many old soldiers from the effects of Gas.

SHURGOLD. Corporal Ernest W Shurgold, of Hythe Road, served with the 2nd Battalion Wiltshire Regiment.

'Six weary days, six dark, long nights, D Company's held the trenches tight. Stand too! At dawn, Stand down at seven, up comes the rum and we're in Heaven. Sometimes we think that we're in hell when the Hun sends his shrapnel shell Some scream on high, some fall quite low. Then into the old dug-outs we go'

Ernest Shurgold 1916

SIMPKINS. Ernest Simpkins of Church Walk Cheney Manor, attempted to enlist under age. He succeeded, but, by chance, he arrived at the same camp as his elder brother, Frederick, who reported him as being under age, which resulted in him being returned home. He re-enlisted later in the war. Frederick, who served in the Royal Field Artillery, was killed in Action in 1917. (see roll of honour)

SLADE. 5 brothers of the Slade family from Hythe Road served.
Frank, served with the Royal Garrison Artillery. He served in the Middle East and France. He died in February 1919 (see Roll of Honour)
Albert, also served with the Royal Garrison Artillery.
Jack, served in the Royal Field Artillery.
Richard, with the Royal Navy on board the dreadnought HMS Ramillies.
James, also with the Royal Navy. He stayed on with the navy after the war. He became a chief petty officer serving on HMS Hood, Courageous and Glorious. All three ships were destined to be destroyed in WW2. James was serving on Glorious in 1940 and went down with her when she was sunk 8th June 1940. He is remembered on the Plymouth Naval Memorial Panel 36 Column 3.

Albert Slade Pictured in the corners are his Sisters left, his Mothers right

Jack Slade France 1918

Albert Slade at 17 years old Pictured at Burdrop Park

Albert Slade (extreme left) Egypt 1916

Richard left and James Slade right

Richard Slade

James Slade in WW2

SMITH. Private Alfred Smith Wiltshire Regiment. Born in 1899 He is buried in Whitworth Road cemetery. His grave has no headstone, but has a brass marker from The Old Contemptibles Association.

SMITH. Mr and Mrs Arthur SMITH of 2 Cromwell Street had 4 Sons. Sydney, volunteered in the Royal Berkshire Regt in November 1915. He worked at Harding and Co in Fleet Street. He was wounded 3rd August 1916 but returned after he recovered in December 1916. He was Killed in Action 5th March 1917. (See roll of honour for details)
Arthur a Private in the Wiltshire Regt, was wounded in Mesopotamia 5th April 1916 But survived and returned safely.
Henri also a Private in the Wiltshire Regt served in India and also returned safely.
George a Private in the Wiltshire Regt, was Killed in Action on 9th July 1916 (See Roll of Honour for details)

SMITH. Private G J.Smith 5th Btn Wiltshire Regt. Son of Charles Smith of 61 Medgbury Road.
He was serving with the battalion in the Dardanelles, when he was wounded. He was hit several times. One bullet hit him in the breast and perforated a pocket book, a small diary he had kept since starting from Avonmouth. The same bullet also shattered a Turkish knife that he kept in the pocket. As he made his way back, he came across a wounded sergeant, who had received an injury to his eyes and could not see. So they helped each other back. The sergeant was unfortunately hit by another bullet in the leg. As Pte Smith could not carry him he had to be left where he was.

Walter Smith Royal Engineers

SPARKES. Trooper Frederick Charles Sparkes, of Ashford Road served in 'D' Squadron Royal Wiltshire Yeomanry. He was invalided out in 1915 following an accident during training in Eastbourne. He worked for the rest of the war for the Aviation manufacturers Avro in London, living in Seven Sisters Road.

'D' Squadron Wiltshire Yeomanry. Frederick Sparkes (back row extreme right)

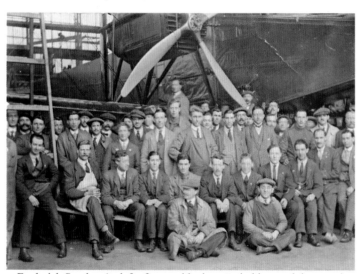

Frederick Sparkes (to left of man with cigarette in his mouth in centre)
Avro Aviation works London

A cousin of Frederick Sparkes, was William Gosling of Wanborough. He had enlisted with the Royal Field Artillery and whilst serving in France, attached to a Trench Motor battery of the 51st Highland Division, he won the Victoria Cross. William lived and ran his own dairy in Wroughton after the war. He is now buried in St Helens and John the Baptist Churchyard in Wroughton.

TAYLOR. Two brothers who served, Jack and Gilbert, the sons of Mrs R Taylor of 27 Manchester Road. Jack had been a Tram conductor with the Swindon Corporation, before trying his luck in Canada where he moved to in 1912. When the War broke out, he joined the 92nd Canadian Contingent. He served in France and Belgium with distinction. At Vimy, in 1917, he won the Military Medal. Later,that same year, during 3rd Ypres (Battle of Passchendaele) he won the DCM. He wrote to his wife, back in Toronto, describing to her, the battle, in which he had been wounded. - " We went into the line on the Ypres front, directly in front of Passchendaele on the night of October 30th, being told it was only for 48 hours, as it was such a hot place. On the night of November 2nd, instead of being relieved, we were to make an attack at 2am, without a barrage, making it a surprise attack. My platoon had to take a farm. Well, we took it, then Fritz threw some bombs in amongst the bunch of us, but he did not get me, but I noticed, there was only my officer, Lt Cohen and myself left. Before we had time to think, Fritz counter attacked, but I got most of them with the Lewis gun. Lt Cohen went to see if he could find any of the fellows around. Finding 3, he sent 2 up to me and then started to come back himself, but a

The Taylor Brother
Jack (sitting) & Gilbert

sniper got him about a yard from me. So I was left in charge of the objective with 3 men. Any way , I picked off as many Huns as I could and then had to retire as I only had 10 rounds of ammunition left. It was while getting back that I got this piece of shrapnel from one of his heavies. I walked about 2,000 yards got a drink of rum and then walked another 4,000 yards to a casualty clearing station From there we went through Ypres to Proven, another casualty clearingstation and from there got a hospital train to Rowan, reaching there on the 6th of November. By then my leg had swollen quite a bit as I had it soaked in mud when coming out. The doctor cleaned the wound off then pulled some bandages through it to clean it inside. Since then it has been much easier. When making the attack I was up to my knees in mud and water nearly all the time and quite a number of times I had to crawl out on my knees a my feet were stuck fast!"

G Taylor (back right) 16th Div R E

TAYLOR. Private R E Taylor of 182 Redcliffe Street served with the 1/4th Battalion Wiltshire Regiment

R E Taylor

Gilbert Taylor (front)
with pal Sid Smith

THATCHER, S. Thatcher Engine Room Artificer. Royal Navy. Served on HMS Benbow

THORNE. Charles Aldridge Thorne. DCM Company Sgt/Maj. 7th Btn Wiltshire Regt. A clerk in the Labour Exchange. Lived at 27 Stanier Street. Joined at the outbreak of War.On April 27th, 1917 he took command and rallied his company after they had sustained heavy casualties, and kept them together.

THORPE. 5 Son's of Mr and Mrs J Thorpe of 94 Commercial Road joined up.
Frederick. A Lance-Corporal in the Army Ordnance Corps
Charles, a Trooper in the Royal Gloucestershire Hussars
Arthur, a Gunner with the Royal Field Artillery.
William, a Private in the Wiltshire Regt.
Ernest, tried 8 times to enlist. Finally joining the Wiltshire Regt. He was wounded and discharged.

TOWNSEND. Lance-Corporal G Townsend MM Machine Gun Corps. Formerly worked at J E Antis Drapers of Regent Street. His work colleague, Port, also served, as a Rifle man in the Kings Royal Rifle Corps

TUCKEY. Lieutenant J Tuckey of 99 Goddard Avenue, survived the sinking of the transport ship 'Cameroria' after it was struck by a torpedo fired from a German U-boat.
Another Swindon Officer, Lieutenant Balch was also on board and survived.

Our system of leave is by length of service in France,and as they have not finished the members of the original 7th Battalion, they have not yet started on the draft men. So, it looks like being some time yet before my turn comes around.
We have some fellows who have been out here nearly eleven months and had not yet had any leave! So you can see how things stand. I have every reason to believe that our rest is soon coming, and, by all accounts, we shall be out for Easter Monday. Of course, Easter and other holidays, didn't make much difference to me when I was on the Underground, as I always worked. So I shall not be missing much by being out here. Shall not be sorry to get out of this show, as they are developing mining too much! And every day, we get a mixture of mines, rum jars and shells, and I can tell you, its not healthy! I saw a mine go up yesterday. I believe it was a German one, and you would think it was the lid of hell its self! Picture an explosion, like thunder.

The earth opens and a huge sheet of flame shoots up and the debris and plenty of smoke. After that the pantomime starts, with bombs, trench mortars and shells and it is pandemonium for an hour or so. If you are in a dug – out when a mine is put up, the earth rocks backwards and forwards once. It is a peculiar sensation.

April 17th 1916. A letter written by Private Frederick Tuck 7th battalion Norfolk Regt. To his brother – in – Law Mr Donald Andrew. Pte Tuck was killed 3 days later on the 20th. (Details in Roll of Honour)

TURNER, T H. Lieutenant M.C. .Royal Engineers. Attached 23rd London Regt. Formerly a clerk in the GWR.
Son of Mr Herbert Turner of 56 Newhall Street.

TYLER. Sapper Richard Tyler, Royal Engineers. Born in London and moved to Swindon to work in the GWR No 19 Shop.

A Swindon wedding, between Sapper Richard Tyler, nephew of Mr & Mrs R E Smith of the Masons Arms Newport St and Ethel Bizley of 34 Ashford Road. (sisters of Harold Bizley RAMC)

2nd Lt T H Turner

Richard Tyler

Ethel Bizley with her brothers Harold, Wilf & Roy
(see Harolds details under Bizley)

VIVEASH. 5 brothers of the Viveash family from 45 Ipswich served.
Frederick John, born in 1893.
Thomas James, born in 1894, served with the Royal Horse Artillery.
Cecil, born 1895 and served with the 2nd Battalion Wiltshire Regiment.
He was captured in the German offensive of spring 1918. (see POWs details)

William Percy, born 1898 and served with the Royal Marine Artillery.
Leonard, born 1899, served with the 15th Hussars.

E Walton 6th Leinster
Regiment of 138 Beatrice
Street

Leonard Viveash (centre standing)

WAIT. Mr and Mrs Wait of 104 William Street had 5 sons who served.
Private H A Wait Somerset Light Infantry
Petty Officer A E Wait HMS 'Inflexible'
Private A Wait 2nd Battalion Coldstream Guards
Sapper 46308 Samuel Wait Royal Engineers He enlisted on 3rd September 1914 qualifying with the trade as a carpenter. He was transferred to Army reserve June 1919.
Gunner 128611 Charles Wait MM 77th Brigade Royal Field Artillery Won the Military Medal 1st June 1917

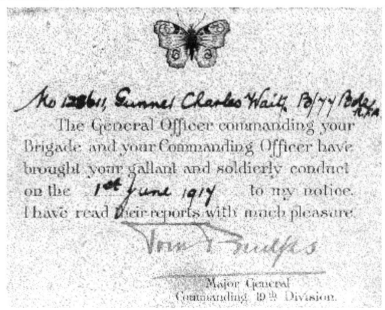

WALTER. 3 Sons of Mr and Mrs Walter of 10 Poulton Street Gorse Hill served.
Robert John Walter. Private 202974 4th Battalion Wiltshire Regiment. Was born in 1895 enlisted 1914 for service. Transferred to 1/4th Dorset regiment. Spent the war in Middle east and India. Discharged 14th March 1919. From 1928 till his death in 1979, he lived at 69 Plymouth Street.
Edward Joseph Walter. Lance Corporal Inniskilling Fusiliers. Born 1899. Lived at Chiseldon when he married a few years after the war. Raised 5 children. As with so many of the men, he was deeply affected by his experiences of the war. In old age, he returned to Swindon to live with one of his daughters, till he died in 1988.
Frederick Walter. Royal Marine Artillery. Born in 1900, served with the Marines till long after the War. In the 1920s, he served on HMS Hood. He lived in Deal, Kent during WW2 and later, in 1950 employed as a dockyard policeman at Sheerness, Kent. He retired to Harlow in Essex and passed away in 1983.

The Walter Family

Robert in India

Robert with the 4th Wilts   Men of the 1/4th Dorsets in India Robert Walter is sat in the middle

1/4th Dorsets India

Robert in Barracks

Robert, Edward and their
younger sister....'in uniform'

Frederick & Edward Walter

WATTS. Brothers Benjamin Thomas Watts and William Walter Watts of 7 Page Street served. Benjamin was in the Army Veterinary Corps. William, Wiltshire Regiment served in the Dardanelles.

WEBB. Sapper A Webb MM Royal Engineers and his brother served. Sons of M A Webb of 1 Durham Street.

WEIGHT. Mr B C WEIGHT of Wood Street, had 3 Sons 'doing their bit'
Reginald, a Corporal in the North Somerset Yeomanry. He was on the staff of the Swindon Education Dept.
Arthur, a Driver in the Army Service Corps He worked in the Swindon Rates office Town Hall
Bertie, a Private in the North Somerset Yeomanry. Tried to enlist in 1914, under age at 16, but his father re-claimed him. He re-enlisted in 1916.

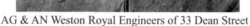
AG & AN Weston Royal Engineers of 33 Dean Street

WESTALL. 2 Brothers served. F G Westall (Pictured above) and his brother Sidney Westall of 112 Beatrice St. Both served in the Royal field Artillery. Sidney was captured and held as a POW (See details in POWs Section)

WHEELER. Thomas M Wheeler a newsagent of 78 Victoria Road had 3 sons who served - 2nd Lieutenant W H Wheeler. Private C J Wheeler Wilts Regt who became a Prisoner of War. (See POW's details)   F E Wheeler DCM Company Sergeant Major Royal Fusiliers. He had served previously in the South African Campaign and the Tibet Expedition.

WHETHAM. F. G. Wiltshire Regt. Son of Charles Whetham of 17 Merton Street. One of 3 brothers who joined up. Both his Brothers Charles and George were Killed. Charles in September 1915, George, died of wounds November 1915. (See roll of honour for details)
A letter was sent home from Lieutenant Badgley of 'C ' Coy 2nd Btn Wiltshire Regt, after the death of George. -
' Dear Mr Whetham, I am sorry I am the bearer of bad news, but I thought you would like some further particulars, beyond the bare facts from the War Office. That your son has been killed, or rather died of wounds on the 22nd November. He was a good lad and died doing his duty. All his comrades speak well of him and I know he will not be forgotten. He was so willing and always bright and cheery and ready to help others. I sympathise with you and yours in your sad loss. If there is anything I can do for you I shall be glad to help you in any way possible '

WHITE. Private Harry Charles White of 10 Dover Street served with the Wiltshire Regiment. Formerly employed in the GWR he enlisted at the outbreak of the war. He was later badly wounded in the arm and leg.

WHITEMAN. Gunner 1700 J E F Whiteman, Wilts Reserve Battery 3rd Wessex Division, RFA. Of no. 13 Belgrave Street, wrote this letter home to his parents. " We are experiencing beautiful weather and the scenery is lovely. I have been inoculated a second time, but, going on well. The food is good some days, but not every day. One day we had for dinner, beef, beans,potatoes and pickled cabbage. While for tea we had bread and butter and marmalade. Another day we had to exist on biscuits, - and they were hard, just like dog biscuits. I should be glad if you would send a Christmas pudding."

WHITEMAN. Lancelot Charles Whiteman of Curtis St served. He worked as a cabinet maker for Pooles and Butler of 81 Regent Street.

WICKS. Joseph William Wicks of 40 Haydon Street served in the Royal Flying Corps. His Son Frank Wicks also served. First in the 4th Battalion Wiltshire Regt, transferring later to the Royal Engineers.

Joseph William Wicks

Frank Wicks

(Above) Shows Joseph Wicks wearing his enlisted armband. Inset is (left) His Son – in – Law, Herbert Edwin Tarrant who became a POW (See details in POW section) Inset right is Frank Wicks 4th Wilts.   (Photo below shows Frank with his daughter.)

A E Wilkins
Formerly a Labourer Loco &
Carriage Dept GWR

2ND Lt David Williams R E
Wilts Fortress Engineers.Formall
worked in the Drawing office Loc
& Carriage Dept.

WILSHIRE. William Wilshire of 48 Newhall Street served with the 5th Battalion Royal Welsh Fusiliers.

WILTSHIRE. Percy Wiltshire of Regent Street served. As did his brother Charles, Royal Naval Air Service, who died (see roll of honour).

Group of RWF in Egypt William Wilshire is 9th from left at back

WRIGHT. Major F G Wright of 52 Bath Road, was commanding officer of the Wilts Fortress Royal Engineers. He was Assistant Superintendant of the GWR works in Swindon

WYATT. Mr and Mrs E Wyatt, of 248 Cricklade Road, had 7 sons who served, -
Harry, a private 8th Btn Royal Berkshire Regt. He was Killed in Action 1915 in the Battle of Loos. (See roll of honour for details)
Alfred, a private in the 281st Infantry Btn Canadian
Forces.
James, Submarine Depot, Royal Navy
Frank, a Driver, Motor Transport, Army Service Corps.
David, a Sapper Royal Engineers.
William, HMS Leonidas Royal Navy Edward, a Sapper Royal Engineers.

William Wilshire   Major F G Wright

2nd 4th BN. THE (DUKE OF EDINBURGH'S)
WILTSHIRE REGIMENT

'C' Platoon 2/4th Wilts.
Fred Baker of 32 Edinburgh St (middle row 2nd from left)

India F Baker (left) 2/4th Wilts

'Calne boys Poona India

2/4th Wilts Regt No 10 platoon. Winners of 'C' Company Challenge Cup

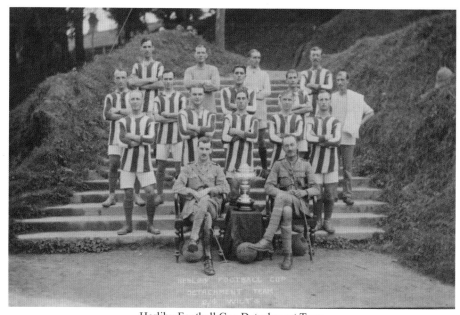

Herlihy Football Cup Detachment Team
2nd/4th Wilts

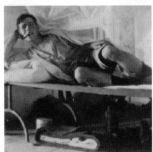

3 men from the Wilts Regt. Note the bugle hanging from the Lady's shoulder.

Prisoners of War

BOROUGH OF SWINDON.

TOWN HALL,
SWINDON, February, 1917.

DEAR SIR (MADAM)—

WILTSHIRE REGIMENT.

Prisoners of War in Germany.

As you are no doubt aware, there are about 700 men of the Wiltshire Regiment who are prisoners of war in Germany, and about 100 of these men belong to Swindon. Owing to the insufficient food supplied to these men by the Germans, it has been absolutely necessary to send food from here to save them from starvation.

A committee of ladies (Chairman, Miss Slade; Hon. Sec., Miss Handley) have been devotedly carrying out this work for nearly two years, the funds having been generously provided by the public of Swindon. Since the 1st December last, parcels have had to be sent in accordance with a scheme settled by the War Office, and the parcels are sent under the joint auspices of the British Red Cross Society and the St. John's Ambulance Association.

The cost of sending these parcels to the men of the Wiltshire Regiment who are prisoners of war will be about £17,000 per year, some small part of which will be contributed by relatives of the men and adopters.

To provide parcels for the Swindon men will cost about £3,000 per year, in addition to which comforts (woollen socks, mittens, helmets, etc) are required, particularly in the winter months, for the men in the Battalions at the "Front." It has, therefore, been decided to make an appeal to all sections of the community on behalf of this noble work.

Weekly or fortnightly subscriptions, however small, are invited, and any person may become an "adopter" or "joint adopter" of any particular prisoner of war. Three parcels are sent to every prisoner of war every fortnight, and the cost of these is about 25s.

Regular weekly or fortnightly contributions are respectfully invited, and if you will kindly state on the annexed slip the amount you can kindly see your way to give, collectors will call for it weekly or otherwise as may be desired.

I would like earnestly to appeal for your sympathy and support of this most deserving fund.

I am, Yours faithfully,

A. J. GILBERT,
MAYOR.

In October 1914 a committee was formed in Swindon. Its purpose was to provide ' Comforts for the troops of the Wiltshire Regiment' Mary Slade of 63 Avenue Road, was elected as Chairman. Miss F K Coleman was secretary up till March 1915, when, due to ill health, she was forced to resign, dying shortly afterwards. Kate Handley of 50 the Mall, succeeded her. Miss Gover of 28 The Mall,was elected as Treasurer.

Their aim was to collect items such as gloves, socks scarves etc, then to send them to the Wilts Regt depot at Devizes, ready to be despatched to the front.The Mayor made a public appeal for items which was answered immediately. He made another appeal in 1915 for money, which would be spent on food to aid the starving prisoners of war being held in German and Turkish camps. From letters the committee had received from these men, it was clear that without this aid, many would die of starvation and exposure. Parcels were packed, each carried a Red Cross label and distributed to men of the Wilts being held in the various camps.

From the amount of correspondance the committee received from these men, thanking them for the parcels, demonstrated what these meant to the hundreds who were being held in some really appalling conditions.

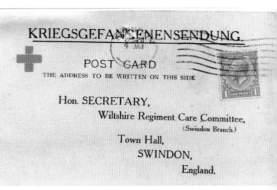

All these letters and postcards, were carefully recorded, as were all items that were sent out by the committee. By October 1915, they were sending out parcels to over 650 men. They encouraged Schools, business's and many individuals, to 'adopt' a soldier held as POW. The idea was for the guardian to sponser a regular supply of items to their soldier.

An example of the details of this scheme was as follows. Entries were listed -

5826 Sergt W.G. Bull	8265 Pte B. Bolter	8609 Dvr R S Blunsdon
Home Address - 6 Cross Street Swindon	33 North Street Swindon	63 Edinburgh Street Swindon
Adopters - Miss F.M. Goss Little Sneyd. W' Bristol	Mr E Robsom and Boys, Fossdene LCC School. Charlton, London SE7	Gorse Hill Girls School
Prisoners Address. Comp 46 Group 3 Dulmen	Hameln.	Langensalza Comp 6

By the end of 1916, because of the expense of sending parcels to now, 700 men, it was decided to share out the responsibility to each district in Wiltshire. The Swindon branch was to carry on sending aid to the 100 Swindon men now held. By then there was 32 members on the packing committee.

On March 21st 1918, disaster struck on the Western front, when the Germans, aided by many fresh divisions, freed up after the collapse of Russia, broke through in a huge offensive. The 1st 2nd and 6th Battalions of the Wiltshire Regiment, was in the direct path of the advancing German army. Many of them who survived, found themselves completely surrounded and were forced to surrender.

Over 200 Swindon men became prisoners to add to the 100 already held. The work of the committee became ceaseless. There is no doubt, that without the aid that was sent out to these men, the numbers that died in captivity would certainly have been a lot higher.

At the wars end, many men were not returned home immediately. Due to the shocking state of them, they were kept in France or Holland for recuperation. The last prisoners returned to Swindon as late as March 1919. Some men such as Pte C Haggard, returned so weak, that he died in Swindon just 3 weeks after his return. Others that survived, were damaged physically and mentally. Some would take years to recover. Some died at an early age as a result. Many displayed odd characteristic's. Depression, mood swings or loss of temper, dislikes of certain food's. A common occurrence was for the man to leave the house saying that he was going for a walk, for example, returning after 2 or 3 days with no recollection of where he had been.

The committee of Comforts for the troops, who worked so hard during the war years, continued to aid the returned service men and their families long after the wars end. In fact, the committee was not finally dissolved until after another World War in 1946.

The men who had joined up in 1914 and after, did so with the knowledge that they were fulfilling the ideal that they were upholding justice and freedom. Many who fought, did so for the reason, that their sons should not have to go through what they had. They had completed their job. The bitterness set in when they returned. Had the world changed, or had they? Many could not cope.

An entry in the committees minute book, for the date 3rd July 1919 was as follows -

" The war pensions committee applied for help for Mrs M J Walker, whose husband, late of the 1st Somerset Regt and the 1st Wiltshire Regt, is in the Devizes asylum, as a result of his war service. A grant of £4.10.0 was made to assist Mrs Walker temporarily on the proposition of Mrs Morris seconded by Miss Gover.

The Hon. Secretary also bought forward from Mr Dean, the case of Mr J D Jones, late of the 3rd Wiltshire regt. Who through ill health, has been unable to meet his expenses and is in debt to the amount of £7.6.6. On the proposition of Miss Slade, seconded by Mrs Morris, the amount of £6 was granted for his relief."

Another for 9th August 1921 -
" The case of Mrs E Groves of 33 Regents Place, a widow of the late Sgt William A Groves Wiltshire Regt, whose pension is 6/- per week. She has poor Law Relief of 12/6 per week for her 2 children. She has been very ill and unable to work and is now in great distress until she is well enough to work again. Temporary assistance was asked for. The committee decided to grant £2.10 for Mrs Groves to be distributed at 10/- per week for 5 weeks by the Hon. Secretary. (Kate Handley)   The second case is that of William Bizley of 9 Medgbury Road, who was a shoe smith in the RFA and served in the army from 23rd May 1915 until 18th November 1919. He is suffering from paralysis of the right arm and leg. He was recommended by the Medical board for

100% pension. This was not accepted by the Ministry. He has only 10/6 Insurance and sick club money. His mother, aged 60, has a pension of 5/- per week for another son who was killed in the war (Arthur Bizley KIA 5.12.17) and except for what she can earn by laundry work. This is the whole income of the family. Application is being made by the Swindon War Pensions Committee, to augment this pension to 15/- per week and meanwhile, temporary assistance is needed. The committee granted temporary assistance of £5 to be paid by the secretary at 10/- per week."

These are just two examples of the many appeals the committee had. Another appeal was made from a Lady with a young family, who could not afford a funeral for her late husband in 1921, an ex- soldier who died as a direct result of his war service.

A land fit for heroes and a grateful nation!

Field Marshal Haig, received £100,000 plus an Earldom. Other army commanders received around £30,000 and were made Viscounts. Politicians on the war cabinet were given huge grants of thousands of pounds as gratuity. Returning soldiers were paid anything between £10 to around £35. If he handed in his greatcoat he would receive a further £1. Mrs Bizley of Medgbury Road received a pension of 5/- a week for her loss of her Son.

Thankfully for many families, they survived through help they received from the committee. Mary Slade was awarded the MBE in later years. She became the headteacher at King William Street School.

oooo**O**oooo

November 25th 1918.
To Miss K Handley. Secretary. Town Hall
Swindon.

Dear Madame,
I am writing on behalf of D company 1/4th Battalion Wiltshire Regiment, to thank you and the supporters of your fund in Swindon, for the very generous and welcome present of socks, which you sent out to us, for the Swindon men.

I have distributed them in the company and also among the Swindon men at the battalion HQ. I can assure you, that the socks themselves and the kind feelings which prompted gifts, are equally appreciated. I am sure that you in Swindon will be proud to learn, that the Swindon men played a very auditable part in the recent victory in Palestine and they are hoping that it will not be long before they are back home again.

We would be glad if you would tell all those who have contributed to send these socks out, how greatly they are appreciated.
Belive me to be yours truly

J G Lockhart Captain. C/O   D Company 1/4th Wilts

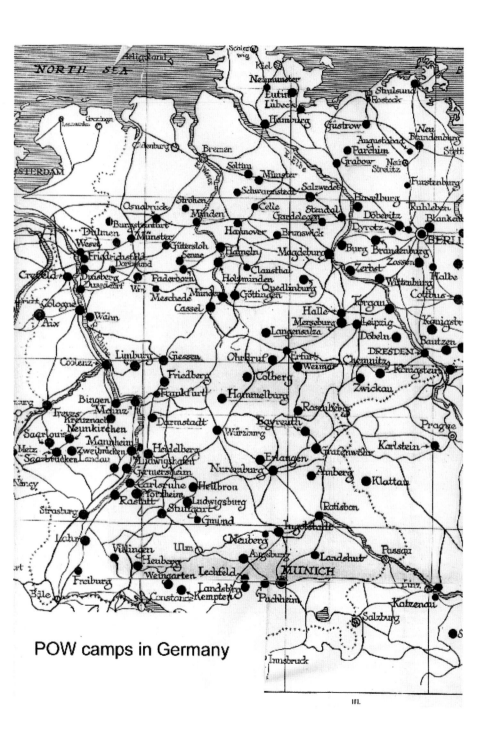

POW camps in Germany

ABBOTT, R
Pte. 38420 8th Btn. Royal
Berkshire Regt. Captured 26th October
1918. Held in Limburg. Returned to
Swindon 5th December 1918. Lived at 3
Deacon Street

ADDISON, A A
L-Cpl. 29839 2nd Btn
Wiltshire Regt.

ALEXANDER, C
Pte 27430 1st Btn
Wiltshire Regt.

ANGELL, V C
Pte 18458. 2nd Btn
Wiltshire Regt. Held in Soltau Z 995

APSEY, J G
L-Cpl 34804.

ASHTON, A E
Pte 7579 1st Btn Wiltshire
Regt. Captured 24th August 1914 Held in
Sennelager. Exchanged to Switzerland.
Returned to Swindon 30th January 1919.
Lived at 64 Dryden Street.

AVERY, H
Pte 36555 2nd Btn Wiltshire
Regt.

AYERS, F
Pte 9202 2nd Btn Wiltshire
Regt. Captured 21st March 1918. Held in
Gustrow. Returned to Swindon 11th
January 1919 Lived at 21 Morse Street.

BACK, H
L-Cpl 27486.

BACON, W E
Pte 27437

BAKER
H V Pte 21505 2nd Btn Wiltshire Regt.

BAKER, W
Pte 11887

BANCROFT, E
Pte 10502

BARKER, H, J
Cpl 33111 1st Btn Wiltshire Regt.

BARUARD, J
Tpr 18th Hussars.
Captured 24th August 1914. Held in
Lamstead. Returned to Swindon 6th
February 1918. Lived at 52 Rodbourne
Road.

BEALE, A
L-Cpl 13937 2nd Btn Wiltshire
Regt. Captured 21st March 1918. Held in
Cottbus. Returned to Swindon 5th
January 1919 Lived at 44 Haydon Street.

BEARD, A
Pte 31850 2nd Btn Wiltshire Regt.

BEASENT, G S
L-Cpl 20925 1st Btn Wiltshire Regt.

BEASLEY, B
Pte 10031 Wiltshire Regt.
Held in Camp 1 diat 5855 Zerbst. Anhalt

BEAUMONT, E A
Pte 8323 Wiltshire Regt.
Held in Cassel Comp 1. Lived at Slade's
Building Upper Stratton

BECK, A
Pte 35300 2nd Btn Wiltshire Regt

BELLEMY, L
Pte 27440

BEST, J
Pte 203597 1st Btn Wiltshire Regt.

BIRD, B W
Pte 27324

BISHOP, E M
Pte 8200 2nd Btn Wiltshire Regt.
Captured 24th October 1914. Held in
Friedrichsfeld. Returned to Swindon 1st
December 1918. Lived at 115 Beatrice St.

BLACKFORD, C
Pte 26339.

BLAKE, A
MM. Pte 18125 2nd Btn
Wiltshire Regt. Captured 21st March
1918. Held in Hameln. Returned to
Swindon 1st January 1919.

BLAKE, H V
Pte 18125 Wiltshire Regt
Held at Hameln Prisoner No
86500. Lived at Rushey Platt
House

BLAKE, W D
Pte 21776 2nd Btn Wiltshire
Regt.

BLOUNT, E
Spr Royal Engineers.
Captured 25th April 1918. Held
at Limburg. Returned to
Swindon 5th December 1918
Lived at 78 Manchester Road.

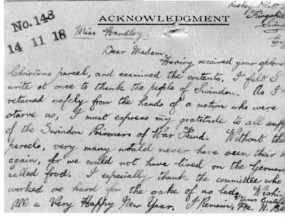

BLUNSDON, R S
Dvr 8609 Wiltshire Regt.
Captured 24th October 1914 Held at
Langensalza, Comp 6 No 7743
Returned to Swindon 20th December
1918 Lived at 62 Edinburgh Street.

Reginald Blunsdon

BOLTER, B
Pte 8265 2nd Btn Wiltshire Regt.
Captured 24th October 1914. Held in
Hameln. Prisoner No 33972.
Returned to Swindon 14th January 1919
Lived at 33 North Street.

BOSWELL, W
Pte 202100

BOULTER, C
Pte 35543 2nd Btn Wiltshire Regt.

BOURDEN, C
Pte 27045 2nd Btn Wiltshire Regt.
Reginald Blunsdon

BOURTON, F J
Pte 2238

BOWDEN, F G
Pte 204306.

BOWLY, P A
Pte 22596 2nd Btn Wiltshire Regt.
Captured 26th April 1918.
Held in Marpent, France. Returned to
Swindon 24th November 1918 Lived at
24 Gladstone Street.

BOWN, V
Pte 39624

BRAY, L
L-Cpl 7341

BRITTEN, F G
L- Cpl 8716

BRIDGES, C
L-Cpl 7082 1st Btn Wiltshire Regt.
Captured 24th October 1914. Held in
Munster Returned to Swindon 2nd
December 1918.

BRINE, E W
Pte 29924 6th Btn Wiltshire Regt.

BROMLEY, J T
Pte 3/194 6th Btn Wiltshire Regt.

BROOKS, Charles
A H. Pte 8239 2nd Btn Wiltshire Regt.
Held in Langensalza, Comp 6 No 4853.
Lived in 7 Cambria Cottages. Wounded
March 1915.

BROOKS, H
Pte 25531 2nd Btn Wiltshire Regt.

238

BROOKS, J
Pte 27961

BROWN, C A
L-Cpl 8814 2nd Btn Wiltshire Regt.
Captured 24th October 1914. Held in Soltau: Bar14. Z 3010.
Returned to Swindon 22nd November 1918 Lived at 24 Colbourne Street.

BULL, J H
Pte 2/4th Royal Berkshire Regt. Held in Freiburg. Returned to Swindon 27th November 1918. Lived at 10 Spring Gardens.

BULL, W G
Sgt 5826 2nd Btn Wiltshire Regt. Minden. Returned to Swindon 22nd November 1918 Lived at 6 Cross Street.

BUTTON, T R
Pte 19434 6th Btn Wiltshire Regt. Captured 10th April 1918.
Held in Friedrichsfeld Returned to Swindon 2nd December 1918. Lived at 91 County Road.

CAMILLE, G H
L-Cpl 22417 2nd Btn Wiltshire Regt. Captured 21st March 1918 Held in Cassel, No 964 Comp 1
Returned to Swindon 8th January 1919 Lived at 6 Handel Street.

CARPENTER, C H
Pte 2nd Btn Royal Irish Rifles. Captured 24th March 1918.
Held at Quedlinburg. Returned to Swindon 1st January 1919. Lived at 49 Ipswich Street.

BURDEN, A
Pte 20020 2nd Btn Wiltshire Regt.

BURGE, E
Sgt 15705 2nd Btn Royal Dublin Fusiliers. Captured March 21st 1918 Held in Quedlinburg. Returned to Swindon 2nd January 1919 Lived at 29 Omdurman Street

BURGIN, A
Pte10596 2nd Btn Wiltshire Regt.

BUTCHER, T
Pte 5408 Wiltshire Regt.
Held at Langensalza. D Comp. Lived at 4 Lansdown Road

CARTER, P
Pte 7th Btn Wiltshire Regt. Captured 4th October 1914 Held at Dulmen Released 28th December 1918 to Holland

CASTLE, W R
Pte 8015 2nd Btn Wiltshire Regt Captured 24th October 1914 Held in Cassel, Comp 1. Returned to Swindon 2nd January 1918. Lived at 87 Bright Street.

CATER, H
Pte 35649 Wiltshire Regt.

CAVALO, C A
L-Cpl 11283 6th Btn Wiltshire Regt. Captured 23rd March 1918. Held at

Rennbahn, Munster II, Working party 10. Returned to Swindon December 1st 1918. Lived at 179 Westcott Place.

CHANDLER, A E
Pte 6685 1st Btn Wiltshire Regt.

CHARD, G E
Pte 33938

CHIVERS, J
Pte 18111 2nd Btn Wiltshire Regt. Held at Langensalza Comp VI 8903

CHUN, E
Pte 1st Royal Marine Light Infantry. Captured 24th March 1917 Held at Cottbus II Returned to Swindon 10th December 1918 Lived at 125 Morrison Street.

CHURCHER, T G
Pte 37273.

CHURCHILL, A A
Pte 1st Btn Royal Warwickshire Regt. Captured 9th August 1918. Held at Gardelegen. Returned to Swindon 22nd November 1918. Lived at 60 County Road.

CLAPP, J W
Sgt 203044 2nd Btn Wiltshire Regt.

CLARGO F
L-Cpl 8810 2nd Btn Wiltshire Regt. Captured 24th October 1914. Held at Hameln 17. Returned to Swindon 23rd November 1918. Lived at 5 John Street.

CLARKE, J
Pte 8643 2nd Btn Wiltshire Regt. Captured 24th October 1914. Held at Langensalza. Returned to Swindon 2nd January 1918. Lived at 78 Gladstone Street

COLBORNE, L D
Leonard, L-Cpl 8638 2nd Btn Wiltshire Regt. Captured 24th October 1914. Held in Cassel, Comp.I Section 66. Returned to Swindon 19th October 1918 Lived at 21 Goddard Ave.

COLE, J E
Gunner 10396 Royal Field Artillery. Captured 30th November 1917. Held at Dulmen Returned to Swindon 9th January 1919. Lived at 36 RedcliffeStreet.

COMPTON, G
Pte 7931 Wiltshire Regt. Held at Chemnitz,
No 1597, Comp 7. Lived at 30 Newhall Street.

COOK, F
Pte 18523 2nd Btn Wiltshire Regt Captured 21st March 1918. Held at Rastatt. Baden, Offiziers Kompagnie, Block 2. Returned to Swindon 21st December 1918. Lived at 15 Kingshill Road.

COOK, F
Sgt. 6416 DCM Wiltshire Regt. Held at Cottbus, Comp 18.

Pte James Clarke (seated 4th from left) at Langensalza

COOK, F G
Sgt 6122 1st Btn Wiltshire Regt.
Captured 24th March 1918. Held at
Cottbus Returned to Swindon 9th
January 1919. Lived at 3 Western Street.

COOK, H
Pte 4844. 2nd Btn Wiltshire Regt
Captured 24th October 1914 Held at
Langensalza, Comp 6. Returned to
Swindon 14th January 1919 Lived at 51
Taunton Street. Died 6th May 1919 (see
roll of honour)

COOK, W H
Pte 2nd Btn Wiltshire Regt, Captured
24th October 1914. Held at Cassel, Comp.
7 Detach. 1023.
Released 19th December 1916 to
Switzerland. Lived at 8 John Street.

COOMBS, A J
L/Sgt 8168 2nd Btn Wiltshire Regt.
Captured 24th October 1914. Held at
Soltau, Z 3036 Barracks 4. Returned to
Swindon 22nd November 1918.

COOMBES, A
Pte 25602 6th Btn Wiltshire Regt Held at
Munster II Block IV Lived at 170
Westcott Place.

COOMBS, P
Pte 8904 1st Btn Wiltshire Regt.
Captured 29th August 1914. Held at
Munster I, Corvee 14, Lager II. Returned
to Swindon 22nd November 1918. Lived
at 35 Avening Street

COOPER, F
Pte 27108

COUZENS, F
Pte 32208 1st Btn Wiltshire Regt.

COWLARD, W J
Pte 203258 6th Battalion Wiltshire Regt.

COX, W C
Pte 8664 2nd Btn Wiltshire Regt.
Captured 24th October 1914. Held at
Munster I, Detach. 4 Lager I. Returned to
Swindon 5th December 1918. Lived at
37 Iffley Road.

CRITCHLEY, H M
L-Cpl 1st Btn Worcester Regt. Captured
4th October 1916. Held at Friedrichsfeld.

Returned to Swindon 26th November
1918. Lived at Carr Street.

CURTIS, W J
L-Cpl 9709 2nd Btn Wiltshire Regt
Captured 8th May 1918. Held at Doberitz.
Returned to Swindon 16th January 1919.
Lived at 16 Holbrook Street.

DASH, A N
Pte 8736 2nd Btn Wiltshire Regt.
Captured 24th October 1914 Held at
Wittenburg, Post Kleinwittenburg, (Elbe)
Arbeits Kommando No 14. Returned
28th December 1918 Lived at 11 Market
Street.

DASH, E
Pte 8941 2nd Btn Wiltshire Regt.
Captured 21st March 1918 Held at
Giessen. Returned to Swindon 14th
December 1918

DAVIS, B
Pte 128370 Machine Gun
Corps.(Transferred from Warwickshire
Regt.) Captured 28th April 1918. Held
at Gustrow Returned to Swindon 1st
December 1918 Lived at 13 Dowling
Street.

Bertram Victor Lawrence Davis
Enlisted at Chiseldon Camp into the Royal
Warickshire Regt at 17 years old.

DAVIS, T H
Pte 6157 1st Btn Wiltshire Regt.
Captured 27th October 1914 Held at
Limburg, Filiallager 243. 5561 E.
Returned to Swindon 14th December
1918 Lived at 17 Holbrook Street.

DIXON, R P B
Pte 9152 2nd Btn Wiltshire Regt.
Captured 24th October 1914 Held at
Hameln Returned to Swindon 14th
January 1919 Lived at 60 Summers
Street.

DOBSON, B
Sgt 5461 2nd Btn Wiltshire Regt.

DREW,T
Pte 9289 2nd Btn Wiltshire Regt.
Captured 24th October 1914. Held
at Langensalza, Comp 6 Returned to
Swindon 23rd December 1918 Lived at 8
Oxford Street.

DRISCOLL, J W
Pte 7226 2nd Btn Wiltshire Regt. Held
at Chemnitz, Comp 7 No 21. Lived at 20
Argyle Street.

EAMER, W
Pte 21102 2nd Btn Wiltshire Regt.
Captured 21st March 1918 Held at
Mannheim. Camp 12 No 60810
Returned to Swindon 17 December 1918.
Lived at 67 Bruce Street.

EATWELL, A E
Pte 21245 2nd Btn Wiltshire Regt.
Captured 21st March 1918 Held at
Hameln Returned to Swindon 4th
January 1919. Lived at 5 Kitchener
Street.

EATWELL, G
Pte 5113 Wiltshire Regt. Held at
Chemnitz, No 1605 Camp 7
Gefangenenlager. Lived at 12 Cambria
Cottages.

EDMONDS, J
Pte 6193 1st Btn Wiltshire Regt.
Captured 27th October 1914 Held at
Limburg Returned to Swindon 7th
December 1918 Lived at 145 Beatrice
Street.

ELLISON, E.
Pte 8202 2nd Btn Wiltshire Regt.
Captured 24th October 1914 Held at
Langensalza Returned to Swindon 28th
December 1918 Lived at 3 South Street.

EMBLING, H
Pte 13017 5th Btn Royal Berkshire Regt.
Captured 30th November 1917 Held
at Munster. Returned to Swindon 26th
November 1918 Lived at 72 Hinton
Street.

ENSTONE, F J
Pte 203058 Wiltshire Regt. Held at
Langensalza, Camp 6 No 8915. Lived at
Myrtle Villa Rodbourne Cheney.

EVANS, G
L Cpl 2nd Btn Wiltshire Regt. Captured
24th October 1914 Held at Langensalza
Returned to Swindon 24th November
1918.

FALLEN, H W
Pte 35709. Wiltshire Regt.

FELL, A
L-Cpl 21549 Machine Gun Corps.
Captured 21st March 1918. Held at
Soltau Returned to Swindon 29th
December 1918. Lived at 19 Albion
Street.

242

FERRIS, E G
L-Cpl 9650

FIELD, E F
Pte 26959. 2nd Btn Wiltshire Regt.

FLETCHER, J H
Pte 204235

FOREST, J
Pte 4222 1st Btn Wiltshire Regt.
Captured 26th August 1914. Held at
Hameln, No 4441 Kom Leese Stolzenau.
Returned to Swindon 31st Dec 1918.

FOWLER, T
Pte 7275 1st Btn Wiltshire Regt.
Captured 26th August 1914 Held at
Gustrow. Camp 3. Returned to Swindon
5th February 1919. Lived at 36 Hawkins
Street.

FOYLE, H E
Pte 60518 2nd Btn Wiltshire Regt.
Captured 12th March 1918. Held at
Hameln, No 66367. Returned to Swindon
30th December 1918 Lived at 122
Chapel Street.

FRANKLIN, A H
Cpl. 27272 2nd Btn Wiltshire Regt. Held
at Heuberg. Comp 5 Lived at 124
Kingsdown Road

FRENCH, F
Pte 10614 Wiltshire Regt.

FROST. F H
Pte 8225 2nd Btn Wiltshire Regt. Held in
Limburg a Lahn Filiallager 924. Died in
Belgium 20th December 1918 (see roll of
Honour for details)

FRY, F
Pte 52319 2nd Btn Wiltshire Regt. Held at
Soltau Z3348

FURZE, C
Pte 26154 2nd Btn Wiltshire Regt. Held
in Hammelburg

GALE, S N
Pte 8639 2nd Btn Wiltshire Regt.
Captured 24th October 1914 Held at
Langensalza, Camp 6 No 7348 Returned
to Swindon 13th January 1919 Lived at
170 Manchester Road.

GALLICHAN, P J
Pte 8388 Wiltshire Regt. Held at Fried
richsfeld. No 55757 Detach 204 Bar 32
Lived at Beatrice Street.

GEE, C C
Pte 8657 2nd Btn Wiltshire Regt.
Captured 24th October 1914 Held at
Chemnitz, Co 7 No 1591 Returned to
Swindon 17th December 1918. Lived at
63 Newport Street.

GIBBS, A R
Pte 8802 2nd Btn Wiltshire Regt.
Captured 24th October 1914 Held
at Limburg, No 5597 Filiallager 1584.
Returned to Swindon 8th February 1919
Lived at Coate.

GIBBS, C W J
Pte 21921 1st Btn Wiltshire Regt
Captured 24th March 1918 Held at
Dulmen, Camp 5 Returned to Swindon
6th December 1918 Lived at 20 Argyle
Street.

GILES A J
Pte 4th Btn Northamptonshire Regt.
Captured 24th March 1918 Held at
Bayreuth Returned to Swindon 5th
December 1918. Lived at 18 Quarry Road.

GILL, W F E
Pte 24577 6th Btn Wiltshire Regt. Lived
in Kent Road.

GOODENOUGH, H
Pte 20737 2nd Btn Wiltshire Regt. Held at
Cassel Kom 1259 No 668.

GODWIN, H J
Sgt 203174 6th Btn Wiltshire Regt. Died
in captivity 10th August 1918. (see roll of
Honour for details)

GODWIN, W
Pte 8067 2nd Btn Wiltshire Regt.
Captured 24th October 1914 Held at
Friedrichsfeld, Detach. J O 32, Returned
to Swindon 12th December 1918. Lived
at 14 Hughes Street.

GOLDING, A
Pte 204272 6th Btn Wiltshire Regt
Captured 23rd March 1918 Held at
Sennelager, No 33457, Block 2 Returned
to Swindon 19th December 1918 Lived
at 44 Whiteman Street

GOSLING, R E
Gnr Royal Field Artillery. Captured
30th November 1917 Held at Munster
Returned to Swindon 5th December
1918

GRACE, A
Sgt 3/291 2nd Btn Wiltshire Regt.
Captured 21st March 1918 Held at
Mannheim Returned to Swindon 17th
December 1918. Lived at 50 Prospect
Hill.

GRAY, C H
Pte 22013 6th Btn Wiltshire Regt.
Captured 23rd March 1918 Returned to
Swindon 3rd December 1918 Lived at 16
Haydon Street.

GREGORY, E J
Pte 10296 2nd Btn Wiltshire Regt.

GUY, J C W
L-Cpl 220004 2nd Btn Wiltshire Regt.

HABGOOD, R
Pte 32991. 2nd Btn Wiltshire Regt. Held
at Langensalza. Co.6

HAGGARD, C E
Pte 8380. 2nd Btn Wiltshire Regt.
Captured 24th October 1914. Held at
Krossen-on-Oder Returned to Swindon
12th January 1919. Lived at 60 Stafford
Street. (Pte Haggard died within 3 weeks
of his return home, due to starvation and
exposure. See roll of honour for his details

HALL, W F
Pte 5445 2nd Btn Wiltshire Regt.
Captured 24th October 1914 Held at
Hameln, Comp I 14092. Returned to
Swindon 2nd January 1919. Lived at 35
Haydon Street.

HALL, W H
Pte 8062 2nd Btn Wiltshire Regt.
Captured 24th October 1914 Held at
Munster, Lager I Detach 4.Returned to
Swindon 6th December 1918 Lived at 89
Westcott Place.

HAMLEY, A
Pte 13786 2nd Btn Wiltshire Regt.
Captured 21st March 1918. Held at
Parchim Returned to
Swindon 15th December 1918 Lived at
97 William Street.

HARDING, G A
RAF Captured 16th October 1916 Held
at Minden Returned to Swindon 9th
December 1918.

HARMAN, G H
Pte 22869 1st Btn Wiltshire Regt.
Captured
24th March 1918 Held at Parchim,
Arbeits Batt, Vogt Stammlager. Returned
to Swindon 10th December 1918. Lived
at 22 Dixon Street.

HARRIS, A W
Pte 9661 1st Btn Wiltshire Regt. Held at
Rennbahn, Munster. Detach 414 Camp III.
Lived at 2 Gordon Road.

HARRISON, E
Pte 34th MGC Captured 26th March
1914. Held at Dusseldorf Returned to
Swindon 3rd December 1918. Lived at
the Queens Hotel.

HARVEY, P J
Pte 71208 2nd Btn Devonshire Regt.
Captured 27th May 1918 Held at Namurs.
Returned to Swindon 20th November
1918 Lived at 70 Bruce Street

HAYWARD, F E
L-Cpl 22486 1st Btn Wiltshire Regt. Held
at Paderborn

HAYWARD, F
Pte 242592 1/5th Btn Kings Own Royal
Lancaster Regt. Captured 30th November
1917 Held at Friedrichsfeld Returned to
Swindon 30th November 1918. Lived at
122 Cricklade Road

HAYWARD, S
Pte 44830 5th Btn Royal Berkshire Regt.
Captured 27th May 1918 Held at
Meschede Returned to Swindon 14th
December 1918 Lived at 27 Guppy
Street.

HAZELL, A J
Pte 23068 2nd Btn Wiltshire Regt.
Captured 21st March 1918 Held at Cassel
Returned to Swindon 16th March 1919.
Lived at 15 Villett Street.

HERBERT, H V
Pte 20783 1st Btn Wiltshire Regt.
Captured 24th March 1918 Held at
Rennbahn, Munster. Lager 2 Com 85.
Returned to Swindon 6th December
1918. Lived at 80 Radnor Street.

HILL, F
Pte 37511 1st Btn Wiltshire Regt.
Captured 28th May 1918 Held at

Friedrichsfeld Returned to Swindon 23rd
November 1918 Lived at 27 Westcott
Place.

HILLIER, S D
Pte 7392 2nd Btn Wiltshire Regt.
Captured 24th October 1914. Held at
Cassel No 10325 Sect X1/1 71 – 10
Detach 1213.Returned to Swindon 11th
March 1919 Lived at 32 Havelock Street.

HINCHCLIFFE, J
Pte 6th Btn Wiltshire Regt Captured
10th April 1918 Held at Altdamm
Returned to Swindon 26th November
1918 Lived at 262 Cricklade Road.

HINTON, F J
Pte 203295 6th Btn Wiltshire Regt. Held
at Schweidnitz.

HOBBS, A P
Pte 26462

HOBBS, R
Pte 1st Btn Dorset Regt Captured
22nd October 1914 Held at Merseburg.
Returned to Swindon 9th January 1919.
Lived at 2 East Street.

HOLLAND, J
Pte 7538 2nd Btn Wiltshire Regt
Captured 14 October 1914. Held at
Langensalza, No 6729 Comp 6. Returned
to Swindon 6th January 1919. Lived at 48
Bright Street.

HOLLEY, H C
Pte 19143 1st Btn Wiltshire Regt.
Captured 24th March 1918. Held at

Munster II Returned to Swindon 1st December 1918 Lived at 2 Gordon Road.

HOLLIDAY, H J
Pte 22079 1st Btn Wiltshire Regt. Captured 11th April 1918. Held at Hassalt Returned to Swindon 4th December 1918. Lived at 121 Morrison Street.

HOOPER, G
L-Cpl 8329 2nd Btn Wiltshire Regt. Captured 24th October 1914 Held at Friedrichsfeld, No 9749.Barrack 9B.Returned to Swindon 21st November 1918. Lived at 64 Rodbourne Road.

Cpl. G Hooper

HOPKINS, F
Gnr 3363 RFA Captured 21st March 1918 Held at Munster III Returned to Swindon 4th December 1918 Lived at 20 Ford Street.

HOPKINS, F G
L-Cpl 8731 2nd Btn Wiltshire Regt. Captured 24th October 1914. Held at Lechfeld, Bavaria. No 21726 Comp 2. Returned to Swindon 21st November 1918 Lived at 25 Deacon Street.

HOWLETT, A
Pte 5418 2nd Btn Wiltshire Regt. Captured 26th October 1914. Held at Friedrichsfeld Returned to Swindon 24th November 1918. Lived at 16 Hughes Street.

HUGHES, A
Cpl 203192 6th Btn Wiltshire Regt. Captured 23rd March 1918 Held at Schwarmstedt Returned to Swindon 29th December 1918 Lived 63 Ashford Road.

HUNT, J W
Pte 9883 Wiltshire Regt. Held at Soltau. Mat. 1162 Z3008. Lived at Victory Row.

HUTT, C
Pte 8720 2nd Btn Wiltshire Regt. Captured 24th October 1914 Held at Langensalza Mat 6016 Comp 6.Returned to Swindon 23rd December 1918. Lived at 39 Catherine Street.

ILES, H C
Pte 7674 1st Btn Wiltshire Regt, Captured 26th August 1914. Held at Doberitz, Block 9/4, Camp 4 Returned to Swindon 20th December 1918. Lived at 16 Granville Street.

ILES, W
Pte 8433 2nd Btn Wiltshire Regt. Captured 24th October 1914 Held at Langensalza , Coy 6 No 2829 Wolkra mahausen. Returned to Swindon 28th December 1918. Lived at 7 Exeter Street.

JERRAM, A
Sgt 204307 6th Btn Wiltshire Regt. Captured 10th April 1918 Held at Limburg Returned to Swindon 5th November 1918 Lived at 42 Prospect Place

JOHNSON, A J
Pte 8813 2nd Btn Wiltshire Regt. Captured 24th October 1914 Held at Mannheim Returned to Swindon 28th December 1918 Lived at 73 Chapel Street.

JONES, A J
Lt. 3rd Btn Royal Berkshire Regt. Captured 15th April 1918. Held at Philip popolis, Bulgaria. Returned to Swindon 29th December 1918. Lived at 137 County Road

KANE, A O
Sgt RFA Captured 27th May 1918. Held at Cottbus, Returned to Swindon 8th January 1919 Lived at 52 Morse Street.

KEEN, A C
Tpr. 13321 Inniskilling Dragoons. Captured 25th March 1918 Held at Sennelager Returned to Swindon 17th December 1918 Lived at 4 Avening Street.

KENT, F
Pte 7569, 2nd Btn Wiltshire Regt
Captured 24th November 1914 Held at
Munster, Comp 2 Lager 1.Returned to
Swindon 2nd December 1918. Lived at
49 Salisbury Street

KENT, R F
L-Cpl 8984 1st Btn Wiltshire Regt.
Captured 26th July 1914 Held at
Doberitz, Comp 4 Returned to Swindon
14th January 1919 Lived at 40 Brunswick
Street.

KETHERO, W J
MGC Captured 11th April 1918. Held at
Gardelegen Returned to Swindon 5th
December 1918. Lived at 33 Eastcott Hill.

KILMINSTER, H
Pte, 204176. 6th Btn Wiltshire Regt. Held
at Munster, Camp III Lived at 11 Carlton
Street

KING, F
M427 Royal Navy, HMS Aralis Captured
11 February 1916 Held at Soltau
Returned to Swindon 29th November
1918 Lived at 27 Ipswich Street.

KING, G E
Pte 4332 15th Btn Australian Imperial
Force. Captured 18th August 1917 Held
at Meschede Returned to Swindon 16th
December 1918. Lived at 27 Deburgh
Street.

KING, F S
Pte 26753 2nd Btn Wiltshire Regt.

KING, V W
Pte 32637. 2nd Btn Wiltshire Regt. Held
at Limburg, No 109298. Lived at 145
Albion Street.

KIRBY, L
Pte 8696 2nd Btn Wiltshire Regt,
Captured 24th October 1914 Held at
Rennbahn,
Munster. Lager 2 Detach 23. Returned to
Swindon 17th December 1918. Lived at
103 Eastcott Hill.

KITCHING, A
Cpl 9935

KNIGHT, W E
Pte 35536 2nd Btn Wiltshire Regt.

LAMPORT, W A
Pte 33538 2nd Btn Wiltshire Regt.
Captured 21st March 1918. Held at
Heuberg. Returned to Swindon 21st
December 1918. Lived at 69 Gladstone
Street.

LANSDOWNE, V
Pte 23770

LANG, J F
Pte 10970 MM 6th Btn Wiltshire Regt
Captured 23rd March 1918. Held at
Rheinhaussen Returned to Swindon 26th
December 1918 Lived at 30 York Road

LAVINGTON, W O
Pte 27392 6th Btn Wiltshire Regt.
Captured 24th March 1918. Held at
Munster II Returned to Swindon 1st
December 1918. Lived at 5 East Street.

Pte W O Lavington

LAW, B
Pte 6164 Wiltshire Regt. Held at Limburg.
Filiallager No 1594 5633 E Bar 29
Stammlager. Lived at 3 Deburgh Street.

Pte Ben Law

LAWRENCE, E W
Pte 8526 Wiltshire Regt Held at Hameln Gef No 41771. Lived in Gorse Hill.

LAWRENCE, W
Pte 18671

LEACH, F G
Pte 10293 1st Btn Welsh Regt. Captured 3rd October 1915 Held at Stuttgart Returned to Swindon 23rd December 1918. Lived at 20 Marlborough Road

LEONARD, S A
Cpl. 10213. 2nd Btn Wiltshire Regt. Captured 26th April 1918. Held at Fried richsfeld. Returned to Swindon 1st December 1918 Lived at 54 Iffley Road

LESTER, W J
L-Cpl 7192 1st Btn Wiltshire Regt. Captured 28th October 1914. Held at Cassel, Comp 1 Sec. 54/16. Returned to Swindon 15th November 1918. Lived at Broome Cottages.

LEWIS, A J
Pte 76772 11th Btn Durham Light Infantry. Captured 24th March 1918 Held at Chemnitz Returned to Swindon 26th December 1918 Lived at 6 Maidstone Road.

LLEWLLYN, W A
Pte 18563 2nd Btn Wiltshire Regt. Captured 21st March 1918 Held at Hameln Returned to Swindon 7th January 1919 1 St Paul Street.

LOVE, T J
Pte 8147 2nd Btn Wiltshire Regt. Captured 24th October 1914. Held at Langensalza. Comp. 6 No 4876. Returned to Swindon 21st December 1918. Lived at 55 Hinton Street

LOVELOCK, F A J
Pte 204071.

LOVERIDGE, E
Pte 2nd Btn Royal Marine Light Infantry. Captured 28th April 1917 Held at Munster III Returned to Swindon 14th December 1918 Lived at 1 Ferndale Road.

MAHONEY, D
Pte 10th Btn Royal Warwickshire Regt. Captured 10th April 1914. Held at Limburg. Returned to Swindon 16th November 1918 Lived at 67 Westcott Place.

MALIN, C
Pte 9607 2nd Btn Wiltshire Regt. Captured 24th October 1914 Held at Cassel. Comp 8 Sect 104/15 Returned to Swindon 12th January 1919. Lived at 13 Byron Street.

MATTHEWS, J
Pte 1575 2nd Btn Wiltshire Regt. Captured 21st March 1918 Held at Mannheim, Camp 12. No 60080. Returned to Swindon 17th December 1918 Lived at 3 Folkstone Road

MATTHEWS, P
Sgt, 8233 1st Btn Wiltshire Regt
Captured 26th October 1914 Held at
Soltau. Bar1 Z 143 Returned to Swindon
1st March 1919. Lived at 6 Union Street.

MATTHEWS, W
Royal Air Force. Captured 8th August
1918. Held at Holzminden Returned to
Swindon 15th December 1918. Lived at
48 Radnor Street.

McLOUGHLIN, W L
Cpl 7883 1st Btn Wiltshire Regt
Captured 26th October 1914. Held at
Altdamm, No 35198 Returned to
Swindon 19th November 1918 Lived at
33 Albert Street.

MEAD, C
Pte 8687 Wiltshire Regt. Captured 1914
Held at Friedrichsfeld, Mat, 79050. Lived
at 11 Haydon Street.

MILES, F V
Cpl. 18526 1st Btn Wiltshire Regt.
Captured 10th April 1918 Held at Cassel.
Returned to Swindon 23rd December
1918 Lived at 23 Curtis Street.

MILLS, H G
Pte 202815 1st Btn Wiltshire Regt. Held
at Limburg. Died 15th July 1918 (see Roll
of Honour)

MOBEY, F R
Dvr. 8698 2nd Btn Wiltshire Regt.
Captured
24th October 1914 Held at Cassel, Comp
1. Returned to Swindon 4th January
1919. Lived at Temple Street.

MORSE, A
Pte, 37498.1st Btn Wiltshire Regt.
Captured 27th May 1918 Held at
Rennbahn. Room 10 Block 4 Lager.II
Returned to Swindon 16th November
1918 Lived at 84 Albion Street.

MORSE, W
Pte 6390 1st Btn Wiltshire Regt. Captured
24t August 1914 Held at Hameln. No
24840 Wispenstein. Returned to
Swindon 15th January 1919 Lived at 23
Page Street

MULLIS, W
Pte 8236 1st Btn Wiltshire Regt

Captured 24th October 1914 Held at
Langensalza Comp 6 No 2941. Returned
to Swindon 26th December 1918 Lived
at 36 Ipswich Street.

NASH, A
Cpl 9320 2nd Btn Wiltshire Regt.
Captured 24th October 1914 Held at
Rennbahn. Room 14 Block 4 Lager 2
Working party 84.Returned to Swindon
9th December 1918 Lived at 36 Thomas
Street.

NASH, F H
2nd Btn Devonshire Regt. Captured 24th
May 1918. Held at Friedrichsfeld
Returned to Swindon 23rd November
1918. Lived 8 Westcott Place.

NEATE, F
L-Cpl 25895. Wiltshire Regt. Held at
Parchim. No 805.

NORRIS, C
Pte 8690 Wiltshire Regt. Held at Munster.
Detach 4 Lager 1. Lived at 27 Granville
Street.

NORRIS, R S
Lt 11th Btn Royal Sussex Regt. Captured
22nd March 1918 Held at Clausthal.
Returned to Swindon 23rd January 1919.
Lived at 26 Kent Road.

PAGE, H S
Pte 7950 2nd Btn Wiltshire Regt.
Captured
24th October 1914 Held at Munster.
Lager II Block 4 Det 84. Returned to
Swindon 2nd December 1918. Lived at
87 Ponting Street.

Pte H S Page Le Marchant Barracks

249

PAINTER, C H
Pte 7114 1st Btn Wiltshire Regt. Captured 27th October 1914 Held at Friedrichsfeld. Bar. 24A Corvee 5, No 17754. Returned to Swindon 10th November 1918. Lived at 99 Hyde Road.

PAINTER, E.C.
Pte 7833 2nd Btn Wiltshire Regt. Captured 24th October 1914. Held at Soltau. Z VII. Mat 3036. Returned to Swindon 3rd January 1919. Lived at 65 Winifred Street.

PAINTER, E.G.
Pte 8316 2nd Btn Wiltshire Regt. Captured 24th October 1914. Held at Cassel. Lager 1. Returned to Swindon 2nd January 1919. Lived at 96 Cricklade Road.

PICKETT, A R
Pte 2nd Btn Royal Berkshire Regt. Captured 27th May 1918 Held at Giessen. Returned to Swindon 8th December 1918 Lived at 23 North Street. (Brother of E H Pickett Below)

PICKETT, E H
Pte 10230 1st Btn Wiltshire Regt. Captured 16th June 1915 Held at Giessen. Comp X Bar B No 4890 Det 2082. Returned to Swindon 14th December 1918 Lived at 23 North Street.

PIKE, E.A.
Pte 8602 2nd Btn Wiltshire Regt. Captured 26th October 1914. Held at Wittenburg. 17252 Arbits Kom 138. Returned to Swindon 28th December 1918. Lived at 50 Summers Street.

PINNIGAR, P
Pte 8593 2nd Btn Wiltshire Regt. Captured 24th October 1914. Held at Chemnitz. Co.7 No 58. Returned to Swindon 1st January 1919. Lived at 36 Jennings Street.

POSTLETHWAITE M E
Pte 27876 6th Btn Wiltshire Regt. Died in Captivity Remembered on Malbork Memorial in Poland (see Roll of Honour)

PRESTON, J
Sgt 15302 7th Btn Somerset Light Infantry. Captured 30th November 1914. Held at Soltau. Returned to Swindon 8th December 1918. Lived at 27 Ripley Road.

PRINCE, G
Pte 18126 1st Btn Wiltshire Regt. Captured 11th September 1918. Held at Sagan Returned to Swindon 8th January 1919 Lived at 5 Albion Street.

PUFFETT, S
Pte 11033 2nd Btn Wiltshire Regt. Captured 21st March 1918 Held at Parchim. Returned to Swindon 16th January 1919 Lived at 232 Ferndale Road

PURDUE, E
Pte 8041 2nd Btn Wiltshire Regt. Captured 24th October 1914. Held at Hameln 5. No 41798. Returned to Swindon 2nd January 1919 Lived at 10 Marlborough Road.

RAZEY, G E
Pte 8423 Wiltshire Regt. Held at Holzminden. Lived at 26 Davis Street.

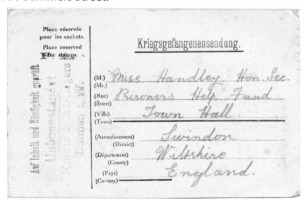

REYNOLDS, W A
Pte 28983 7th Btn Somerset Light Infantry. Captured 23rd March 1918 Lived at Merseburg Returned to Swindon 9th January 1919 Lived at 13 Deburgh Street.

RICHENS, J
Pte 85415 1/6th Durham Light Infantry. Captured 27th May 1918 Held at Doberitz Returned to Swindon 4th December 1918 Lived at 84 Edinburgh Street

ROCHESTER, H
Pte 7478 2nd Btn Wiltshire Regt. Captured 24th October 1914. Held at Cassel Returned to Swindon 14th January 1919 Lived at 61 County Road

RYMILLS, W A
Sgt 1189 9th Btn East Surrey Regt. Captured 26th March 1918 Held at Stendal Returned to Swindon 11th January 1919 Lived at 20 Havelock Street.

SADDLER, T
Pte Royal Irish Fusiliers. Captured 20th October 1918. Held at Dulmen Returned to Swindon 2nd December 1918.

SANDLE, A O
Pte 31736 6th Btn Wiltshire Regt. Captured 23rd March 1918 Held at Munster Returned to Swindon 9th December 1918 Lived at 71 Whiteman Street.

SAUNDERS, J O
Pte 41692 2/8th Worcestershire Regt Captured 21st March 1918 Held at Grabow Returned to Swindon 16th January 1919 Lived at 75 Ponting street.

SCHORN, S J
Pte 3rd South African Infantry Regt. Captured 19th July 1915 Held at Munster III returned to Swindon 17th January 1919 lived at 91 Kent Road.

SELLWOOD, A
L-Sgt 8237 2nd Btn Wiltshire Regt. Captured 24th October 1914 Held at Soltau Z3036. Returned to Swindon 25th November 1918 Lived at 18 Western Street.

SHARPE, W G
Sgt 7189 6th Btn Wiltshire Regt. Captured 20th March 1918 Held at Cottbus. Returned to Swindon 11th January 1919 Lived at 11 Carlton Street.

SIMMONDS, C
Pte 13th Btn Royal Scots. Captured 1st August 1917 Held at Munster II Returned to Swindon 29th November 1918. Lived at 8 Beatrice Street.

SKINNER, E H
Pte 33218 2nd Btn Wiltshire Regt. Captured 21st March 1918 Held at Heuberg. Returned to Swindon 19th December 1918 Lived at 30 Pembroke Street

SMART, A E
Pte 22628 3rd Btn Somerset Light Infantry. Captured 18th March 1918 Held at Heuburg. Returned to Swindon 21st December 1918 Lived at 44 Elmina Road.

SMITH, F
Pte 9435 2nd Btn Wiltshire Regt. Captured 24th October 1914 Held at Cassel Detach. 1737 Comp 5 Group 100/16 Returned to Swindon 13th January 1919 Lived at 9 Little London

SMITH, G F
Pte 6232 Wiltshire Regt. Held at Dulmen Lived at 106 Stafford Street.

SMITH, T F
Pte 7515 Wiltshire Regt. Held at Dyrotz. Comp 5. Lived at Eastcott Hill

SMITH, W H
Pte 6th Btn Shropshire Light Infantry. Captured 21st April 1918 Held in Strassburg Returned to Swindon 19th November 1918 Lived at 11 North Street.

SOLOMON, B J
Cpl. 10580 1st Btn Wiltshire Regt. Captured 24th March 1918 Held at Cottbus. Returned to Swindon 16th December 1918. Lived at 4 Beatrice Street.

SPACKMAN, G
Pte 7324 1st Btn Wiltshire Regt. Captured 27th October 1914 Held at Limburg. Bar.29 Mat. 5742E Stammlager.

Returned to Swindon 6th December 1918. Lived at 3 Summers Street.

SPACKMAN, H
Pte 8729 2nd Btn Wiltshire Regt. Captured 24th October 1914. Held at Cassel. Returned to Swindon 2nd January 1919. Lived at 25 Lansdown Road.

STEVENS, A.E
Pte 3709 2nd Btn Wiltshire Regt. Captured 24th October 1914. Held at Langensalza. Comp 6. No 6634. Returned to Swindon 23rd December 1918. Lived at 27 Theobald Street.

STONE, W
Pte RAMC, Captured 9th April 1914 Held at Limburg. Returned to Swindon 2nd December 1918 Lived at 7 Argyle Street.

STRANGE, R C
Pte 34817 6th Btn Wiltshire Regt. Captured 10th April 1918 Held at Hameln Returned to Swindon 19th December 1918 Lived at 60 Rodbourne Road.

STRATFORD, A G
Pte 424430 1st Btn East Yorkshire Regt. Captured 27th May 1918 Held at Ohrdruf. Returned to Swindon 2nd January 1919 Lived at 122 Manchester Road.

STRATTON, E
Pte 8203 2nd Btn Wiltshire Regt Captured 24th October 1914 Held at Langensalza. Co. 6 No. 2911. Returned to Swindon 23rd December 1918 Lived at 53 Rosebery Street.

STUART, E F
Pte 9054 2nd Btn Wiltshire Regt. Captured 24th October 1918 Held at Gardelegen 6. Mat. 947, Comp. W. Returned to Swindon 26th Swindon 1918. Lived at 89 Rosebery Street.

STURGESS, E A
Pte 10233 2nd Btn Wiltshire Regt Captured 21st March 1918 Held at Gustrow. Returned to Swindon 9th January 1919. Lived at 25 Florence Street. (Edward kept a diary of his time in captivity, which appears later in this chapter.)

SUTTON, J.E
Pte 8109 2nd Btn Wiltshire Regt. Captured 24th October 1914. Held at Hameln. Mat. 41810 Co,4. Returned to Swindon 29th December 1918. Lived at 11 Kingshill Road.

SUTTON, S W
Pte 24588 6th Btn Wiltshire Regt Captured 23rd March 1918 Held at Dulmen. Returned to Swindon 9th December 1918 Lived at 10 Princes Street.

SWAN, W D
Pte 1681 Middlesex Regt Attached 2nd Norfolk Regt. Captured 29th April 1916. Held at Kedos Anatolia (Turkey) Returned to Swindon 20th December 1918 Lived at 51 Farnsby Street.

SYLVESTER, W
Pte 9002 Wiltshire Regt. Held at Doeberitz Comp 5 Block 9-4. Lived at 108 Kingshill.

TALBOT,
E J L-Cpl 2nd Btn Wiltshire Regt. Captured 24th October 1914 Held at Hameln. No 34529. Returned to

Swindon 17th November 1918. Lived at 46 Gooch Street.

TARRANT, A
L-Cpl 27297 6th Btn Somerset Light Infantry Captured 22nd March 1918 Held at Saaralben Returned to Swindon 4th December 1918 Lived at 16 County Road.

TARRANT, H E
Pte 7115 Wiltshire Regt. Held at Limburg Filiallager 1069, Lived 4 Bathampton Street.

H E Tarrant

TITCOMB, J
Pte 1688. Wiltshire Regt Held by Turkish Forces Bagtche. Lived at 12 Whiteman Street

TITCOMBE, W E
Pte 6935 Wiltshire Regt. Held at Limburg. Filiallager 261. Lived at 174 Ferndale Road.

TOWNSEND, E.J
Sgt-Maj 29809 13th Btn Yorkshire Regt. Captured 22nd March 1918. Held at Limburg. Returned to Swindon 22nd December 1918. Lived at 87 Medgbury Road.

TRUEMAN, H
Pte 1st Btn Wiltshire Regt. Captured 24th March 1918 Held at Hameln Returned to Swindon 10th December 1918 Lived 50 Havelock Street.

TURTON, F C
Pte 8167 2nd Btn Wiltshire Regt Captured 24th October 1914. Held at Langensalza. Co. 6 No 4851. Returned to Swindon 14th December 1914. Lived at 13 Henry Street.

TURYFORD, T W
Sgt 7th Btn Royal West Kent Regt.

Captured 8th January 1918 Held at Sennelager Returned to Swindon 27th January 1919 Lived at 13 Hunters Grove

TYLER, W
Pte 18474 2nd Btn Wiltshire Regt Captured 21st March 1918 Held at Heuberg Returned to Swindon 21st December 1918. Lived at 1 Warwick Road.

UNDERHILL, W
Pte 42422 1st Btn East Yorkshire Regt. Captured 27th May 1918 Held at Dortmund Returned to Swindon 22nd November 1918 lived at 35 Avening Street.

UNDERWOOD, W
Pte 60 2nd Btn Wiltshire Regt. Captured 24th October 1914 Held at Munster. Lager II Block 4 Working Party 84 Returned to Swindon 4th February 1919 Lived at 26 Churlady Stratton.

VENNING, W
Rflm Rifle Brigade. Captured 21st March 1918 Held at Quedlinburg Returned to Swindon 3rd January 1919. lived at 53 Curtis Street.

VIVEASH, C
Pte 18440 2nd Btn Wiltshire Regt. Captured 24th March 1918. Held at Giessen. Returned to Swindon 18th December 1918. Lived at 45 Ipswich Street.

WAKEFIELD, W
Pte 31275 1st Btn Northampshire Regt. Captured 10th July 1917 Held at Bayreuth. Returned to Swindon 23rd December 1918. Lived at 22 Lucerne Terrace.

WALKLATE, E
Pte 8406 2nd Btn Wiltshire Regt Captured 24th October 1914 held at Hameln 5 No 41814 Returned to Swindon 2nd January 1919. Lived at 2 New Station Road

WALTER, W H
Pte 2nd Btn Wiltshire Regt. Captured 26th April 1918 Held at Friedrichsfeld Returned to Swindon 4th December 1918 Lived at 16 Farnsby Street.

WAREHAM, C
Pte 8794 2nd Btn Wiltshire Regiment. Captured 24th October 1914. Held at Stendel. No 4890 Comp 6. Returned to Swindon 28th December 1918. Lived at 71 Rodbourne Road. (Brother of J Wareham below).

WAREHAM, J
Sgt 2876 2nd Btn Royal Munster Fusiliers. Captured 22nd March 1918. Held at Soltau. Returned to Swindon 30th December 1918. Lived at 71 Rodbourne Road.

WEBB, C E
Pte 18115 2nd Btn Wiltshire Regt. Captured 26th April 1918. Held at Fried richsfeld Returned to Swindon 17th December 1918. Lived at 22 Queens Villas Gypsy Lane.

WEBB, W
Sgt 9th Royal Welsh Fusiliers. Captured 23rd March 1918. Held at Franfurt. Returned To Swindon 14th February 1919. Lived at 28 Brunel Street.

WESTALL, S
Cpl 8931 1st Btn Wiltshire Regt Captured 11th April 1918 Lived at Cottbus Returned 8th January 1919 Lived at 112 Beatrice Street.

Sidney Westall

WESTON, B W
Pte 9102 2nd Btn Wiltshire Regt Captured 24th October 1914. Held at Chemnitz. No. 1703 Comp.7. Returned to Swindon 26th December 1918. Lived at 42 Whitehead Street.

WHEELER, C J
Pte 7770 Wiltshire Regt. Held at

Sennelager. Mat.32380. Lived in Victoria Road

WILLIAMS, A
Pte 1st Btn Lincolnshire Regt. Captured 16th October 1914 Held at Chemnitz. Returned to Swindon 28th December 1918 Lived at 74 Bright Street.

WILLIAMS, F.J
Pte 8511 2nd Btn Wiltshire Regiment. Captured 24th October 1914. Held at Minden. No 37196. Returned to Swindon 21st December 1918. Lived at The Lodge, GWR Park.

WILD, A.E
Pte 31780 2nd Btn Wiltshire Regt. Captured 21st March 1918. Held at Cassel. Returned to Swindon 10th January 1919. Lived at Union Row.

WILTSHIRE, W G E
Pte 1/4th Royal Berkshire Regt. Captured 16th May 1916. Held at Giessen. Returned to Swindon 11th December 1918. Lived at 27 Gordon Road.

WINDSLOW, A.E
L-Cpl 7244 1st Btn Wiltshire Regt. Captured 24th August 1914. Held at Merseburg. Comp 4 No 6435a. Returned to Swindon 6th January 1919. Lived at 2 New Station Road.

Pte Woodward 1st Wilts

WINTER, H
Pte 10th Btn London Regt Captured 21st September 1918 Held at Doberitz Returned to Swindon 14th December 1918 Lived at 21 Queens Terrace.

WITTS, A J
Pte 6126 1st Btn Wiltshire Regt Captured 27th October 1914 Held at Gardelegen. Co. 4 Mat. 1355 Mannischafts Gef Lager. Returned to Swindon 1st January 1919

WOODWARD, W
Pte 6134 1st Wiltshire Regt Captured 25th October 1914. Held at Mannheim. Returned to Swindon 21st June 1918. Lived at 9 Carlton Street

Pte Ben Law 1st Wilts 3 Deburgh St

WOODWARD, W
Pte 10th Btn Worcestershire Regt. Captured 10th April 1918. Held at Cassel. Returned to Swindon 14th January 1919 Lived at 28 Western Street.

WOOF, F
L-Cpl 7432 2nd Btn Wiltshire Regt. Captured 24th October 1914 Held at Langensalza. Comp 6. No 4566. Returned to Swindon 17th November 1918 Lived at 6a Westcott Place.

WOOLFORD, W T
Pte 7030 1st Btn Wiltshire Regt Captured 24th August 1914 Held at Minden. Returned to Swindon 21st November 1918 Lived at 40 Windsor Terrace Rodbourne
Pte Woodward 1st Wilts

YEO, F C
Pte 8761 Wiltshire Regt. Held at Franfurt on Oder.

YOUNG, C F
Pte 7797 1st Btn Wiltshire Regt. Captured 26th August 1914 Held at Doberitz. Block 9-4 Returned to Swindon 8th January 1919. Lived at 49 Summers Street.

Many of these men listed, who spoke of their experiences to friends or relatives, mostly, long after the war, mention the moment of capture. Often they expected to be killed outright by their captors which happened frequently on both sides.

For the many men of the Wiltshires, who were captured during the First Battle of Ypres in October 1914, four, long, hard years, lay ahead.

Some men were luckier. In May 1916, an agreement between Britain and Germany was signed, to exchange wounded prisoners of war via Switzerland. On 29th May, the first 300 British prisoners arrived in Switzerland, many badley wounded. On 1st June a second batch of around 150 arrived. The Swiss welcomed their 'guests' warmly. Many POWs were overwelmed by the welcome that greeted them. One such man was Pte Arthur Ashton, of the 1st Btn Wiltshire Regt. He wrote to his parents in 54 Graham Street in June 1916, from Chateau d'Oex in Switzerland.

" I expect you will think I am on a holiday tour. It's very like it, but I have no wish for any one else to go through the first half of it. Thank God we are clear of that low – down, dirty, rotten sausage – land. I expect you know a little of the treatment of prisoners, but the old country has no idea how the poor wounded (I say the majority are wounded, or they would not be there.) captives are living. It makes one's heart ache to think of those unfortunate ones we left behind. I could write a lot about it, but really, it's better to try and forget a little.
Another 12 months and I am sure I should have been properly daft!

I cannot express my feelings now, but it is simply like being born again! Straight from hell to heaven! The reception given to us by the Swiss people, will never be forgotten, banquets, bands, speeches and everything. The way they look after us here is everything to be desired, nothing short of royalty themselves.

We are staying in hotels. Each man has his own room, good food and very few restrictions. Of course, things must have time to get into working order. What do you say of a holiday over here? It would do you all the world of good. It's a splendid country and the view from my window is great, the tops of the mountain's being snow – covered. But still the view's I have been accustomed to was barbed and electric wire, rifles, bayonets, helmets and a lot of cursed pigs! But that has changed, thank God. We are to be allowed our wives and friends over here if possible. The passage, half rate is something like £3. Then there's the hotel expenses. I have so much to tell you now which I could not before. As you may guess, the German censor was quite good at tearing up our letters, but that is a thing of the past now. I suppose you thought my letters and post card's peculiar? Well I hoped you would try and understand a thing or two by reading between the lines. The tonic I asked for was a newspaper. Oh, you are slow, but we have English papers here, what a luxury! You can knock off sending parcels now. Of course, should I want any little odd thing I will let you know.

I am sent here as disabled, but it is nothing to cause you alarm. I have tried time after time to pass for exchange to England, but with no luck, and I have tried without permission, but got captured! I shall have such a lot to tell you some day.

Not much sign of the war ending yet, I think. My word, wern't they prepared? But the state of Germany today is awful. I mean in the way of food, the poor downtrodden women and children. Of course, we always have kept our hearts up and know who will come out on top, but it's a damned long way to Berlin, as a square – headed German told me once!
I have been through no end of things and had quite a large piece of bone removed. It is wonderful how I can use it now. I am expecting another operation when I get home, but it's quite alright, you don't have to worry.

My greatest regret, is that I had a short career – Monday, August 24th 1914, 8.30 am.
Cheer up! Are we down – hearted?

The Swiss army took over medical care for these men, as well as security issues. As Arthur Ashton explained, the men were put up in chalets and hotels and the wounded recovered very quickly as a result of the care they received and the surroundings they now lived. Once recovered, the men needed to be kept busy, so schools were arranged for them to learn various trades.
By the second half of 1917, there were just under 2,000 POWs in Switzerland. An agreement was reached, that some could be repatriated. In September, 850 men were returned to the UK. Others returned in March 1918. The last ones, were not returned until 1919.

FORTFIELD TERRACE,
SIDMOUTH.

As Colonel of the Wiltshire Regiment, (which I first joined nigh 67 years ago) I beg to offer you on behalf of all the surviving Officers, N.C.Os., and Men, who have ever served in the Regiment up to the end of this great War, our most grateful thanks for your patient and self-denying work in helping to provide comforts for our comrades during all the long fighting.

May the memory of it cheer the rest of your days.

John Hart Duane gen.
Colonel of the Wiltshire Regt.

To *Mrs Slade*

THE
YOUNG MEN'S CHRISTIAN ASSOCIATION
WITH THE
BRITISH PRISONERS OF WAR INTERNED IN HOLLAND.
UNDER THE AUSPICES OF THE
BRITISH NATIONAL COUNCIL OF YOUNG MEN'S CHRISTIAN ASSOCIATIONS.
NATIONAL SECRETARY - SIR ARTHUR K. YAPP K. B. E.

REPLY TO 2562 L/Cpl. E J Tallot
2nd Bttn Wiltshire Regt.
British P.B. Dt. interned in Holland
House 75
Group 4
Scheveningen. Holland
18. 3rd 1918.

Dear Mrs Handley
No doubt you will be surprised and pleased to hear that I have arrived in Holland after 3½ years in Germany. I wish to thank you & the committee for the great kindness you all have shown to me during the time I have been in Germany & if it was not for the parcels you sent to me, I would have had a very hungry time indeed, in fact I think I would have starved to death if I had to live only on German rations and I am sure you cannot realise how thankful I am to you all. We cannot realise our good fortune in being here, after so long a time in Germany, where we have being continually punished because we were Englishmen because the Germans hate us more than any other nation. Well I must not bore you with our misfortunes so I will close now again thanking you all for your great kindness to me. I remain
Yours Sincerely. E J Tallot L/Cpl.

257

Wiltshire Regimental Care Committee.

DEVIZES.

The War Office has sanctioned the sending of a "Personal Parcel" to prisoners by the relatives under the following conditions :—

1. Any of the articles noted below may be included — **but nothing else.**

Pipe	Handkerchiefs (one a quarter)	Cloth Brushes
Sponge		Buttons
Pencils	Shaving Soap (one stick a quarter)	Chess
Tooth Powder		Draughts
Pomade	Insecticide Powder	Dominoes
Cap Badge and Badges of Rank	Braces and Belts (provided they are made of webbing and include no rubber or leather)	Dubbin
		Hobnails
Shaving Brush		Sweets (½lb.)
Safety Razor		Medal Ribbons
Bootlaces (Mohair)		Brass Polish
Pipe Lights	Combs	One Woollen Article either Muffler, Mittens, or Socks (one pair each every quarter)
Housewife	Hair Brushes	
Health Salts	Tooth Brushes	

2. The "Personal Parcel" may be sent once a quarter only. It should not weigh less than 3 lbs. (so as to minimize the risk of loss in the post) but must not weigh more than 11 lbs.

3. It must be packed and sent through the POST OFFICE, (addressed to the Prisoner, **not** to this Committee) by the friend or relative of the Prisoner who receives the coupon from us, and the coupon must be affixed to the parcel.

4. A coupon will be furnished by us in the case of each Prisoner once a quarter on application. (Stamped envelope must be enclosed.)

5. The next-of-kin has the right to the coupon, or to name the person to whom it is to be given.

6. No letter or printed paper must be enclosed. Postage is free. If any article not mentioned in the above list is enclosed, the parcel will not reach the Prisoner.

7. Pack in strong cardboard box and wrap in brown paper.

Pte 9338 Edward William Shilton
Enlisted 12th August 1914 Wiltshire Regiment

Private Shilton on his return to England after the war, was one of those who felt compelled to put down in writing, his experiences during the 'Great Adventure' whilst serving with the 5th Wiltshires in the Dardanelles, then with the 2nd battalion in France and Flanders. The following is copied from his handwritten story, written whilst recuperating in hospital on his return to England.

MY LIFE STORY DURING THE GREAT WAR

" It was on the fourth of August in the year of 1914 that England declared war with Germany. So it was on the tenth of this same month, that I enlisted in the army, to do my best for the old country. First of all, we went to the Wiltshire Regimental depot, which was at Devizes, where we first put on a uniform of Khaki. So we stayed here for about one month and then we moved on to Tidworth, which is a large training depot for all troops of his Majesty's Forces. We remained in training for two months. From here, we went to Cirencester. We were billeted in private houses in the town. While staying here, we won a good name from the town's people. We remained for three months. Then on the first week of February, we left here and went to Woking, in Surrey, where we were camped out under canvas and remained till the end of April. We boarded a train and went to Avonmouth docks. Here we boarded a ship called the 'Franconia' which sailed away the following morning of the first of May 1915, to Alexandria in Egypt. On our way out here, we had a fine voyage, although we were dodging submarines most of the time,so it took us nearly three weeks.

So on arriving here, we were put onto a destroyer for Gallipoli, which is in the Dardanelles. But before going here, we went to the Greek Islands, where we were put on to a smaller boat, then went on to Gallipoli. It was in the evening when we reached the entrance of the bay that took us into where we were to land. Well, it was close on midnight when we got into the middle of the bay, so now we could hear the rumbling of the guns and we were now under shell fire. The shells were falling all around the boat and every now and then one would just miss us or would fly close, across the top of the boat, so we could see we were in for a rough time. Well, while all this was going on, we were all busy packing a lot of rations and ammunition and lots of other things that would be required, for we knew too well that we should want all we could carry and more. So while we were doing this, our boat was drawing nearer to land. So the time came for us to land and on landing we had to climb over barges, boxes and planks. This was no easy job, for it was dark, shells and bullets were flying all around us.

Every now and again, some poor fellow would slip over into the sea and had to get out the best they could, or drown. So all this went on till at last we got on land, on the beach under some high cliffs. Now here we were all wondering what might happen next. We were all loaded up like a lot of pack mules and had to climb up through one cutting on to the top of the cliffs which we went along only to go down again to the bottom back under the cliffs. After a march of about ten miles, we halted, for every man was about done in. We felt as we didn't care what would happen to us as we were ordered to rest as best as we could till morning. Though the ground on which we had to sleep, was made up of rocks and stones, we still slept soundly.
We awoke in broad daylight to find that the sea had been washing over our feet while we were sleeping. As we looked round at our surroundings, we noted, that all over the place and all down the sides of the cliff, were scattered rifles, ammunition and dead men and mules.

We had breakfast that consisted of bully beef and a few hard biscuits. Then we set to work to clear and bury the dead. We had a week of this before moving into the front line trenches. We remained for 14 days in which we had a rough time and lost a lot of our men. After we were relieved, we were taken from Cape Helles to one of the Greek Islands for a rest.

We returned after 4 days to the trenches, where we stayed until ordered further up the beach to 'Shrapnel Gully' where we had rather a rough time. We made an advance on the Turkish positions. Owing to heavy machine gun fire, we had to dig in. It was not easy trying to dig in laying flat on our stomachs. We suffered heavy casualties. After a few days we were moved back to the beach, further along than we were before. We stayed here for sometime, living in dugouts we created in the cliffs.

Our Battalion was bought up to strength.

We were to be in the third line of fire for the battle of a hill, more towards Sulva bay. It was on 9th August that we were laying close to the bottom of the hill that we were going to take from the Turks on the following morning. The big navel guns began the battle, other guns and machine guns all opened up. The din was terrible. We advanced steadily and began to climb up the slope of the hill. It was awful to see men dropping like flies, they were laying everywhere, blown to pieces. We managed to drive the Turks off the hill. Here we were relieved and we moved back to the bottom of the hill for a rest but it was not long before we had an order to move again. We moved in single file across a gully and climbed a steep slope which was covered with thick bushes and trees. The only way to climb this was to catch hold of the roots of the trees and bushes and pull one another up – no easy job in the dark!

We reached the summit and found that as we were walking we were walking on the bodies of the dead Turks who were laying in huge numbers. We came to a big hollow between two slopes where we had to dump our machine guns, ammunition, rations and cans of water that we had been carrying. We settled here for a days rest so we set to work to dig in and make ourselves comfortable. Trouble came at first light, shots came at us from the top of the slopes so we took cover as best as we could but we were ordered by the Officers to carry on digging in but many of our men were killed. We came under machine gun fire, the Officer ordered us to retire so we made for a big gully thinking we should get out of it,but to our surprise we found when we had gone someway down we had fallen into a trap that the Turks had set up for us.

They had surrounded us from all sides and opened fire with machine guns. The only way out was to go back the way we came, back down the sleep slope. I only have God to thank that I am still alive now, I was only one of seven survivors. We stayed under some very thick bushes and lay still for the great part of the day in the burning hot sun. There were two wounded men, we managed to bandage them up as best as we could, but we had no water to give them. We remembered passing a water spring further up the gully, but it meant a certain death in an attempt to get some. One man had an empty water bottle on him and volunteered to try and get some. He had not gone far when he came rushing back to inform us that the Turks were coming down the gully towards us, we had to get out of there. We struggled down the slope, two at a time, with the wounded men. The Turks kept firing at us but we managed to make it back to the beach without any casualties. We were still alone and managed to get down between some bully beef boxes as the night set in we and lay down to get some rest. In the morning we managed to find some of our battalion. Our clothes were tattered and torn from our quick decent and we were covered from head to foot with scratches that bleed profusely. We were called together for a role call with the remnants of our battalion. It was found that 120 men and 1 Officer was left out of the whole battalion so we were sent back to base camp that was on one of the Greek islands.

After a week we returned to Sulva Bay where we remained for some time. It was here in November that the winter set in. One evening it came over dark and black and it rained in torrents. We were in the front line trenches at the time, and in less than half an hour, we were up to our knees in mud and water. It rained all night and all throughout the next day. The following evening it turned to snow and began to freeze. We had to endure this for three days. No food was bought to us, so we had to make the best of what little we had! Many men died in these freezing conditions. I had to be carried out as I could not feel or move my limbs. I ended up in hospital on the Greek Island, and remained there for a fortnight. I was put on a hospital ship called the Etquitaina, which bought us back to England, where we arrived on the second of January 1916. This ended my story of the Dardanelles.

After my release from hospital, I was given a spell of home leave, before having to report back to our depot again, later that January. Our new destination was to be

France. We arrived at Rouen, and moved to a base camp , where we remained for about three weeks in training. We then moved out to join up with the 2nd battalion of the Wilts. It was not long after till we moved up the line. We went into the reserve trenches and found some old dugouts. The trenches were filled with mud and slush. Within three days I was knocked out again and taken back to hospital. I ended up at Boulogne. I stayed here for just over a month, then sent back to Rouen, where I met my brother. I was so pleased to find out, that he was in the same camp as I, and we had a jolly good time together! All too soon, we both had to go our separate ways to join our regiments.

I joined my battalion just in time to go on a long forced march to our new positions, on one side of the Ypres canal. We were to make an attack on the Huns and take a wood. It was no easy job, as they were well dug in and concealed. Still, we made the attack, under heavy enemy shell fire. Many men were lost. We were ordered to dig in at the wood and make a stand. We were in small sections and dug in as fast as we could. The trouble was with the water. We did not have to dig to far before we were flooded with water. Still we lay in this mud as deep as we could and waited for the inevitable Hun counterattack. We fixed up the machine gun we had. It was a quiet night. The following day dawned bright and clear. The Germans sent aeroplanes over to search for our positions. They were flying over very low, when some of our planes made an appearance. An exciting air fight took place above us. First to fall was a Hun plane which turned upside down and then burst into flames and came down right behind our lines. This was soon followed by one of our planes which suffered the same fate. Two more planes were destroyed before the Germans broke off and turned towards their own lines. They had spotted our positions because later on the German gunners began to shell our positions. We were in for a hot time! They shelled us all day long. The position next to us had a direct hit, so we expected our turn to be next, but miraculously, we were spared. As night fell, they began shelling the positions behind us, effectively cutting off supplies to us and making any reinforcement of our lines impossible. I joined a team of men who was to try and get back to our supply lines to fetch up rations. We managed to get back to the canal and pick up supplies, but we had to stay put at the canal, as our own guns started up and a massive artillery duel took place. We had to stay put till morning when the gunfire died down. We moved out to the wood knowing now it was daylight, the Germans would be able to see us. We moved through the wood in single file, then the Germans opened fire on us. Myself and two others were bringing up the rear and a shell dropped among us. My chum and I were blown clear into a shell hole, ('the better ole' as they call it!) and we found ourselves completely unhurt but up to our necks in slime.

The poor third man though had been hit and was badly hurt.
We picked him up and made our way back to the canal. After dropping him with the medics, we began our journey again. We found our supplies and managed to reach our positions again. We were famished and dived into our rations. I was sorry to hear two of my chums had been killed in this action. We had to bury them where we were. I was so upset. It was one of the hardest things I have ever done. All we could do was to drop them into a shell hole and cover them over. They deserved so much better than this, but it was the best we could do. We were relieved the following night and moved back to rest.
We moved back up the line a week later. We were to remain in the Ypres sector for some time. It was by far, the worst place on the whole front. Early one morning, an attack on the Hun lines was made on our left. Our gunners opened a barrage to support them, but the shells began falling short, falling straight onto our lines. We were loosing so many men that we were ordered to clear out of the trenches till the barrage moved on.
Some time later, orders came through to us to move on. We were to move down to a new sector in France. With a combination of train journeys and route marches, we arrived at our new front at Longueval where we stayed for some time. It was a lot more pleasant here, than at Ypres.

The following month, in January 1918, I was given 14 days home leave. It was a relief to see England again. After a seemingly short time, it was time to return. I rejoined the battalion at St Quentin. It was 19th March, that we were in the front line trenches. We knew something was about happen. The Germans were expected to launch an attack. On the evening of the 20th, my section was moved out to listening posts. These were positions, well forward in some old German trenches. There was 6 of us,staying in pairs. We were to whistle if anything could be seen happening. The morning began very misty. At 5am all hell broke out. We took shelter where we were as we could not move back as our guns had started up along with machine gun fire. We were in the middle of it all. The shelling was tremendous. We sheltered in some old dugouts when we could smell gas. We got our gas masks on when a shell landed directly on our dugout. The roof collapsed partially burying us. We struggled out to find ourselves surrounded by Germans. They were pointing rifles and revolvers at us. One German, who spoke English, asked us if we had any money or valuables on us. When we said no and after them searching us, 2 of them marched us to the rear behind their lines. What a mess! Our gunners had given them a rough time. There were bodies and wounded everywhere, and everything had been blown to pieces. We came across a wounded German, only a young lad like ourselves. Our guards ordered us to pick him up and carry him. We went into the town of St Quentin, where we dropped him off at a first aid station. We remained here for most of the day under guard. Throughout the day, we were joined by a growing number of our side. Late in the afternoon, we were ordered to march, which we did for about 20 miles. We rested for the night, but we had not received any water or food. The next morning they served us up some soup, or I called it warm water. But we wolfed it down. Afterwards, we marched again, till we came to a camp where we stayed for 3 days. After moving on again. This carried on for well over the next week. They fed us nothing except for the occasional warm water soup. Many men dropped of exhaustion on this march. We grew so weak. I don't know what became of those who fell by the wayside.

Edward Shilton marked with a cross, in camp at Gustow

We came to a large French town, where they put us into a large camp. There was no shelter at all. We were just left in the open. That night was very cold and there was a frost. In the morning, after our warm water, we were taken to a railway station and herded into cattle trucks. We were given a loaf of black bread between 2 of us and remained on the train for 3 days. We arrived at a place called Cassel, where there was a large camp.

Here we stayed for around 6 weeks. A lot of our men were dying, from starvation and exposure. We were again moved further into Germany to another place at Gustrow Mecklenburg. We were sent from here to places of work. I was lucky, I was sent to work on a farm where I met another Englishman. He had been a prisoner for the last 14 months and he told me how pleased he was to talk to another Englishman. We were lucky, other men were sent to terrible places to work. Our farm was not a bad place to work, but the German farmer did not like us. He did everything to make things unpleasant for us. But everytime he tried to play one of his little games with us, we would play them right back by causing some damage to his wagons or his farm in some way.

This went on for the 9 months. When we heard that the armistice had been signed, that was it! We pleased ourselves with what work we should do, and what times we should get up in the mornings and took no notice of what the old farmer said to us. About a fortnight later we were told to return to camp. It was nearly a month later myself and 5 others left this camp by train. We stopped first at Lubeck. Stayed here a night in a large school room. Next day we went on to Rostock. We boarded a Danish ship. A good old English tea was waiting for us as we steamed away from that damned country of the Huns. We were taken to Copenhagen where a warm welcome was awaiting us. Here we stayed for a week. We were well looked after. We finally boarded a ship for England. We learnt we were on the last ship to leave Denmark, and they gave us a good send off! The King of Denmark's own Life Guards band played us out. How the people cheered us!

We had a good voyage across the North sea. We landed in Leith in Scotland, where we had a fine reception. A train took us, then to Ripon in Yorkshire, where we stayed for 2 days. I was given 2 months leave then to await discharge. I went home, where I am staying now. Life in time, I hope, will settle down and I hope to live in peace and happiness ever after.
So now this is the end of my adventures during the Great War.

Written by the adventurer E W Shilton Late of the 2nd Wiltshire Regiment. January 1919

Another soldier from the same battalion and captured at the same time was Edward Sturgess. Formerly a tram driver for Swindon corporation, living at 25 Florence Street, he had enlisted into the Wiltshire regiment at the outbreak of war. He served with the 2nd battalion in France and Flanders. He was wounded when a bullet struck him in the head. The bullet, struck his cap badge and was deflected, thus saving his life! He kept the badge, which is now in the possession of his grandson, who is himself in the army. After a spell recovering in hospital, he returned to his battalion.

He was captured during the great offensive of the Germans on the 21st March 1918 at St Quentin. From this time, he also kept a diary -

Diary of Pte 10233 E A Sturgess 2nd Battalion Wiltshire Regiment.

On the 21st day of March 1918, the German barrage started. At 2.30am Thursday morning,on the British line near St Quentin, there was found to be gas floating in the air. At 4.15 we were compelled to wear our gas helmets, also ' Stand to ' through a heavy shell fire from Fritz, having reached our trench in support, which at this time was occupied by HQ coy, and a part of A coy.

We were severely shelled by Fritz, who saw us take up our positions in the line from 4.30 am to 3.30 pm. We were now ready for any attack, which we thought really would never come off , but we spotted some black objects running about so we let fly with all we had, which was really affective on the foe. But the mis – fortune now must come and at a quarter to twelve, the Germans made an attack, but was forced to go back. They came again and out – numbered us.

At 3.30pm we were surrounded and captured, but not before we had spent all our ammunition and destroyed our guns, which would have been used by the enemy. We were then taken through the German lines under very heavy fire from our own guns which were very effective on the German transport which was coming up in the rear, but moving very quickly. We at last got to St Quentin and was marched about until dark, not knowing what to do with us, they put us into a big mill, where we slept till daylight the next morning.

We then started marching to a place called Aisonville about 30 miles, without food of any kind and it was very hot. We at last arrived and was put in a large hut and we got settled down. We were given one piece of black bread, about one inch thick and four inches long. This had to last out our following march through Belgium, which lasted nearly 3 days. When we finally reached a place called Landeccies on the border of Belgium. We slept there one night in a field with machine guns all around us and very cold and wet. Here we got a bowl of soup, which consisted of hot water and bad vegetables, but we were that hungry we were forced to eat it. After this we started for our main camp at Cassel, but having a 2 day train ride, we were stopped at a place called Hessen for food, which was about the same, maybe a little better. At last we arrived at Cassel on the morning of the 27th day of March.

We were told, we had to be punished for the treatment to their soldiers in France. This punishment was 3 weeks starvation, which we were forced to have and over 300 of my comrades died for want of food at this place.

We were then sent to Gustrow, which when we landed, we thought it was heaven, for the food was much better, also we had a little work to do. We stayed in Gustrow, until we were strong enough for work, then we were sent to a wood yard at Wismar. Here we got on well until we left for Gustrow and stayed for 4 days, then went to Lunow, on a farm. We had to work very hard, but the food was a little better and we got on well with the people. While I was at this place, I received a letter from my darling Mother, but with some bad news enclosed. I took all for the best and remembered the old saying, that there are just as good a fish in the sea as ever been caught. So I left it at that and thank God, I found her out before she became my wife. (Referring to his fiance who had met another man)

I stayed at Lunow till October 10th and we had to walk over 10 miles to Hessen. Here we had some very hard work indeed, for it was a sugar factory. I was unloading sugar beat for 10 days. We had very bad food, little money and long hours, 7 till 7 and no time for food. After the 10 days I was sent inside the factory, stoking.

I did not stay here long, for I lost my temper and struck my guard, so I was sent to Gustrow under arrest. I was very lucky here for I only spent 10 days in a control camp under a strong guard and I was allowed my parcels. On the 10 days being over, I was put into cells for 14 days on a slice of black bread and cold water. But luck came my way, for I only spent 4 days in cells and was released by a civilian, who told me that the war was over. Of course I was overjoyed.

I then went into camp and here we did well for food, for we had a large amount of English red cross parcels in stock, so we were OK. I stayed here till January 1st 1919, then took a train for Lubeck, a German port, but after staying here for 3 hours, we found our boat was at Willummunds, so we left by train for the same. Here we got on a ship called Hyalmo and had a jolly good sea trip to Denmark. What a release! We found plenty of good food and I had my first piece of fresh meat since I was taken prisoner.

We stayed here and had a real good time, until January 3rd 1919, when we left for dear old Blighty and landed at Lieth near Edinburgh and what a joy to see dear old faces faces after so long.
We landed on the 6th day of January and stayed until the morning of the 7th. We felt overjoyed, had a real good concert on board, then had the bagpipes to play us to a real good English feed, good cigs, sweet meats etc. Then took train for Gippin where we stayed for a day or so, then back to dear old Swindon, to where all my dear people still well and happy. I had 2 months leave, so made up for all what went on. I then went to my depot, got my discharge and started on the SCT once more.

A photograph of Gustrow. Showing the photographers shop.

I am a poor Keiedfangenon, I wish that I was dead.
I'm tired of drinking German soup and eating mouldy bread.
I sleep in a drafty corner, my bed is on the floor.
My back is nearly broken and my ribs are very sore.
About 5am each morning, I wake up with a fright.
A German standing over me shouts
"Upstine loose arbite"

I don't know what it's all about, I must have done some kind of crime,
When I hear that one eyed sentry shout "Loose you English swine"
At evening when my work is done I sit beside no fire.
I sit and think of those I love and those I admire.
When I read the German papers, its full of tales of woe.
It say's there's no more England and Lloyd George has to go.
Packets arrive once a week, they are too few by far,
and once they land they don't last long
As we do like our char.

Edward Sturgess

Edward Sturgess (standing 3rd in line) 2nd Wilts

e following, list's, all the Swindon men who served in the Great War. There may still many names to add to this list, but it has not been possible to find every single me..Those who have been omitted, have not been so, intentionally.

he following section is dedicated to all those men from Swindon, who served and whose names do not appear alongside their comrades.

Those names marked + did not survive and appear in the Roll of Honour.

ert Edward Abbott,+; R. Abbott, (3 Deacon Street, Pte Royal Berks Rgt); Jason bbott; R. Abbott; Alfred G. Abrahams; Thomas S. Absalom; Albert Absalom; hur Charles Ackhurst (40 Albion Street); William Ackling; Ernest Frank Ackrill 0 Cricklade Road); George, A. Ackrill; Leonard F. Ackrill; Arthur Acott; Herbert orge Acott+; David Acott; Frank Adams, DCM (12 Belgrave St, Sergeant merset Light Infantry); Lionel N Adams; Graylon B Adams; Alfred J Adams; orge V Adams; Bertram Adams; Isaac Adams; Thomas Adams; C L Adams; lliam J Adams; A A Addison; Walter B Addison; Ernest G Adkins; Reginald lam; N J Ainsworth, MC (Captain Worcestershire Regt 103 Bath Road); Thomas ers, MM (Sergeant Army Service Corps :36 Linslade Street); Albert Ernest der,+; Frederick E E Alder; Walter Gee Alder+; Walter J Alder; Arthur dridge; William Aldridge; Alfred G Alexander; Arthur D Alexander; George exander; Charles E Alexander; Stanley J Alexander; Charles R Alexander; uis Alford; Frederick Allard; Walter Frank Allard+; Alfred Henry James away+William C Allen; William Allen; Dennis Allen; Edward William Allen; arles Allen; George Allen; Jesse Allen+; Edgar Alley; Jesse Alley; Roy sopp (25 Argyle Street); Bertie Amor; Edgar Amor; Alex Anderson; H derson; George Edward Andrew CBE (Engineer Comander HMS Kent); William ndrews; Alfred C Andrews; William H Andrews; Walter G H Andrews; Frank ndrews; John Andrews; Tom Angell; V C Angell; S E Angold; Frank L gold; Vernon G Annett; E J Ansty; H Ansty; George Amor+; Edwin ginald Amos+; Horace Frank Anderson+; Stewart Annand+; Frederick cil Ansty+; W H Apperley, (97 Edinburgh St, 2nd Lt ASC); W H Applegate; nest H Aplin; J G Apsey; Arthur Edwin Archer,+; Clarence George Edward her,+; Francis John Archer,+; Thomas Archer; William H Archer; William her; William James Archer; John Archer; J V Archer; Ernest G Archer; n Owen Archer; Frederick J Archer; Leonard J D Archer; Robert Archer; A her; Thomas Arkell; Albert Arkell; B J Arman; Charles E Arman; H Arman; red R Arman; Reginald A Arman; W Arman, (Berks Regt, 15 Lowestoft Rd); rcy Arnold,DCM; W E Arnold, DCM; William James Arshur; Francis Ash+; rk Ashby; B G J Ashfield; Cyril T Ashfield; James W Ashman; Ernest ,S hman; John Gordon Ashton; Arthur Reginald Ashton; Bernard H Atkinson; tkins; H M Attrill; Arthur Attwood,+; Harry Aubertin; Charles Ausden; R usden; John C Ausden; Geoge E Ausden; Arthur George Austin,+; Francis arles Austin,+; F H Austin; George Austin; Thomas Austin; H W Avenell; c Avenell; William James Avenell; Edward Thomas Avenell; H E Averay; very; Harold Averies,+; Stanley J Averies; William Ivor Avern; J W Avern; Avern; A E Avery; H Avery, (Wilts Regt); S G Avery; Arthur William James ford,+; A E Axford; Frederick Axford; R C Ayliffe; Thomas W Ayres; H J res; Ernest J Ayres; Ernest A Ayres; F Ayers;

Back; W E Bacon; Edward Baden; Frank Baden,+; John Badminton; hur Baggs,+; H Baggs; Clifford Bailey,+; Ernest G Bailey; Fred Bailey,+; derick Bailey, +; Frederick Thomas Bailey,+; H Bailey,+; Harry Bailey; S ley; T W Bailey,+; Alfred Baker; Albert J Baker; Arthur M Baker; Charles A ker; Edgar Frank Baker +; Edward L Baker; Ephram John Baker +; Edward B

Baker; Frederick Baker,+; Frederick H Baker; Frederick N Baker: H V Baker;
Reginald A F Baker; Thomas Baker; Victor C Baker; W Baker; William J Baker;
A J Balch; Frederick Arthur Balch,+; J Balch; A E Baldry,+; F C Balcombe; A E
Baldwin; C E Baldwin; G Baldwin; Sidney Baldwin; Sidney A Ball; W H Ball;
M W Ball; Charles Ball; G W A Ball; Albert Ball; AE Ball; F A Ball; Fred Avery
Ball,+; Frederick Ball,+; Frederick E Ball (TheQuarries. Royal Field Artillery);
George G Ball,+; G Ball,+; J H Ballard,+; B W Ballinger,+; Thomas Balsdon;
Charles H Bambridge; A E Banbury; E Bancroft; Nicholas Banner; A V Bannister;
H Bannister; Alfred J Banyard; Arthur E Banyard; Edward H Barber;
William Joseph Barber; H H Barber,+; Ernest Barefoot; Alfred Joseph Barford;
Edwin Barke; A J Barker,+; H J Barker; Robert Barkham; H Barling,+; Harry
Barnard; Johnathon Barnard; A A S Barnes,+; A J Barnes; Charles P Barnes;
E A T Barnes; Edgar Barnes MM; E G Barnes; F T Barnes; H H J Barnes; Tom
Barnes; W Barnes; W A Barnes; W H F Barnes,+; A E Barnett; A H Barnett;
H Barnett; R T F Barnett,+; W J Barnett; H S L Barrat; George Barrett; Fred
Barrett; Harry G Barrett; J Barrett,+; Jesse Barrett; J F Barrett,+; J H Barrett;
George H Barrett; M Barrett,+; Norman Barrett; P S Barrett,+; W F Barrett,+;
W J Barrett; W J Barron; Percy Barter; H Bartlett; Albert R Bartlett; Charles
Bartlett; F Bartlett,+; Frank Bartlett; George Bartlett; John Bartlett;
T E Bartlett,+; William Alfred Bartlett; E Barton,+; J Baruard; Charles A Basden;
J Basing; W Basing; P J Batchelor; John Batchelor; Ernest J Bateman; A J
Bates (Royal Marine Light Infantry. 20 Bristol St); A W Bates; H A Bates; A C Bath
St John; G Bathe,+; William H Bathe; Sydney Bathe; Stanley Batt; Henry Batt;
Vincent Batt; Charles Baycroft; Charles Bayley; Albert P Baylis; F J Bayliss;
W E Baylis; Albert J Bayliss; Arthur J Bayliss; Horace Bayliss; Alfred Bayliss;
E C Baxter; F C Baxter; James Baxter; Edward Charles Baxter; Albert E Beames;
C T Beames,+; W H Beames; Albert Beale; E N Beales,+; G F Beales; A Beard;
F Beard,+; Albert Beasant; Ernest Beasant; Edward A Beasant; F T Beasant;
H E Beasant; Jack Beasant; John Beasant; M G Beasant,+; R F Beasant;
Frederick G Beasant; F A Beasent,+; G S Beasent; W F Beasent; B Beasley;
T M Beasley; E A Beaumont; C P Beaven; H W Beaven; S Beaver; A Beazley;
V Beazley; F Beazley; J J Beazley; A Beck; V Beck. MM (L/Cpl Wilts Fortress
Engigeers R E); H Beckett,+; Christopher C Beckinsale; L F Beddon; O R
Bedford; R Bedwell,+; Robert Bedwell; W G Bee; W Beechey; P Beechey;
A E Bees; E J Beint: W E Beint; E J G Belbin,+; C Beltcher,+; C M Belcher
(Page St); W H Belcher,+; Harold J Bell; Robert L Bell; A C Bell; William E Bell;
Arthur Bell; Charles Bell; L Bellemy; Arthur Belsham; Stanley C Bellinger. (L/Cpl
Wilts Fortress Engineers. Special mention in Despatches); J L Benbow,+; James
Bendall; William Henry Bendell; William F Bendell; James A Bennell; Walter
Bennell; Alfred C Bennett; Albert H Bennett; F Bennett; William H Bennett;
Robert Berry; N A Berry; Walter C Berry; William H Berry; W W Berry,+;
R T Berwick,+; Trevor Steven John Besant; George A Besant; Benjaman Besant;
J Best; Alfred E Bevan; E W R Bevan,+; F H Bevan,+; G Bevan,+; Albert W
Bevington; Thomas H Bevington; Ernest A Bevington; A G Bezer; Reginald
Ewart Bezer; Walter Bezer; A F Bezzant,+; John W Bezzant; James Bezzant;
C A Bick,+; E L Biggs,+; L Biggs,+; Sidney Biggs; S Bignall,+; Arthur Billett;
Harold Billett,+; Thomas Billett; William Billingham; Frederick W Billingham;
Frederick Billinghurst; William Binding; Sam G Bingle; G Harry Bingham;
James E Bingham; Royston L Bingham; William C Bingham; Walter Bint; W H
Bint ,+; B W Bird; F Birkett; George A Birks; Jesse C J Birt; Sydney C V Birt;
William G Birt; Arthur Bishop; A E Bishop; E Bishop; Edward G Bishop;
E M Bishop; F E Bishop; Frederick Harry B Bishop; Herbert G Bishop;
R F Bishop; Thomas H Bishop; A Bizley,+; Albert Henry Bizley; Harold Bizley;
R C Bizley,+; William A H Bizley; William Bizley; Harold Blackall; C Blackford;
J B Blackford,+; Arthur E Blackman; A H Blackman; Joseph John Blackman;
Alfred E Blackwell; Thomas H Blackwell; A Blake MM; Albert Blake; F A Blake;
F B Blake,+; D C Blake; H V Blake; Harold Blake MM; R A Blake,+; W G Blake;

William Blake, William Blanchard, Bert Blanchard, Reginald Blanchard
William R Blankey; F T Bliss; Albert E Blossom; Edgar Blount; F Bloxsom,+
H Bloxsom,+; Albert Blunsdon; Arthur Blunsdon; Charles Blunsdon
Frank Blunsdon; Frederick Blunsdon,+; John Blunsdon; Reginald S Blunsdon
F Blunsdon; William Blunsdon; John Henry Boden; William H Bodman
Christopher J Boffin; S C Bolding, (Bmdr RFA); Thomas Bolland (16 Morrison
Street); B Bolter; John Henry Bond; John Sidney Bond; Walter J Bond; Charles
Bond (Essex Regt),+ Son of William Bond (Rifle Brigade),+; Edgar T Bond
George H E Bond; Francis W Bond; Henry Booker; J Booker; Frederick C Boon
W Boswell; John E Bottomley; William Henry Boucher; C Boulter
Alfred J Boulton; Elijah Boulton (Painter Loco & Carr Dept GWR); Ernest Rice
Boulton,+; Reginald Cyril Boulton,+; Thomas Boulton; Edward T A Boulton
Albert E V Bouran; C Bourden; F J Bourton; William George Bourton; J H
Bowbrick; F G Bowden; G T W Bowell; Alfred G Bowen; D J Bowen
Edward Bowen,+; F W Bowen; Reginald W Bowen; Walter Bowen,+; John
Edwin Bowering,+; F G Bowerman; Kenneth J Bowles; William Henry Bowles.+
R Bowly; Edward Bowley,+; P A Bowley; William Henry Bowman,+
Albert N Bown; Harold A Bown; Norman H Bown; Sidney C Bown; Stanley
Bown; Thomas Bown; V Bown; William T Bown; H Bowns; S B Bowrne,+
Ernest A Bowron; Frank Bowron,+; Percy Bowron,+; William Bowron; J A
Bowyer; Thomas Henry Boyles,+; Ernest Bradbury; F W Bradbury; Thomas
Henry Bradfield,+; Henry C Bradford; Frederick Bradley; Hubert E Bradley
Horace W Bradley,+; W H V Bradley; Charles Henry Bradshaw; Henry H
Bradshaw; William H Brace; George Braid; George Braid; Arthur E Brain
William Thomas Brain,+; Stanley W Brake; Francis C Bramble; George Bramble
Johnathon J Bramble; William Bramble,+; L V Brasington; Jesse R Bray; L Bray
George Brakspear; George H Brealey; Albert Breewood; L G Bretsch; Arthur
Brett; Edward F Brettell; Vernon E Brewer; F R H Brewer; J E Brewer; Sidney
George Brewer,+; F Bridge; Charles Bridge; Arthur A Bridgeman,+; Charles
Oliver Bridgeman,+; F Bridgeman; George Bridgeman; George E Bridgeman
Henry Bridgeman,+; John Bridgeman; William G Bridgeman; Arthur A
Bridgeman; C Bridges; Ernest W S Bridges; Frank Bridle; Alfred John Bright,+
T Bright; Joseph Charles George Bright,+; P N Bright; J W Bright; A B Bright
C S Brimson; Joseph B Brind; Albert E Brindle; Alfred M Brine; E W Brine
John M Brinkworth; H Brinkworth; J V E Brinsdon; Clayton Briston,+; Bert H
Bristow; H E Bristow; Charles Brittain; Frank Brittain; Harry Varney Brittain,+
Johnathon Britten; Benjamin Broadhurst,+; Thomas Henry George Brockway,+
Henry Thomas Bromage; Austen M Bromley; John T Bromley; Reginald A
Bromley; Sydney R Bromley; Alfred E H Brooks; Charles A H Brooks; George
Brooks; H Brooks; Harold R Brooks MM; J Brooks; James Brooks; John T
Brooks; R J Brooks; Ralph R Brooks; William H Brooks; Richard Brookes,+
F Brookham,+; Herbert Broom; J Broom; Richard McAllister Broomfield,+
William Brotheridge,+; R Brow; Arthur Brown; C A Brown; Charles George
Brown,+; Edward Henry Brown; Ernest J Brown; Ernest V Brown; F Brown
Francis S Brown; F Brown (Royal Field Artillery); George Brown; George H
Brown; H Brown; Henry Brown,+; Henry Brown; John Edwin Brown,+; John
W Brown; Norman Frederick Theodore Brown,+; Oliver C Brown; Percy A Brown
Percy Osman Brown,+; Philip Brown; Robert Brown; Thomas Brown; William
Alfred John Brown,+; William G Brown; William Brown; W D Brown; William
James Brown; Wilfred E Brown (Royal Flying Corps, 34 Montague St); William
Brown; W A J Brown; William H Brown; Stan T Browning; Royston L
Brunsdon; Walter Thomas Brunsdon,+; Allan Edgar Bryant,+; Arthur Reginald
Bryant,+; Gilbert Edward Bryant,+; Oswald Bryant; Reginald Walter Bryant,+
A J H Bubb; H J Buckingham; Archibald Buckland; Horace Buckland; Francis
Buckland; Percy F T Buckland; Reginald Buckland,+; William Henry Buckland
Alfred J Buckland; Frederick W Buckland; Reginald C Budding; Frederick Bugg
George Bugg; Alfred Bull; Arthur Bull,+; Edgar A Bull; Daniel Edward Bull

Edward L Bull; Ernest E Bull; George T Bull; W J Bull; J H Bull; James Bull,+;
Walter G Bull; William G Bull; Arthur C Bullock; George R Bullock; Walter F
Bullock; William F Bullock William I Bullock; William J Bullock; Alfred H Bunce
Francis H Bunce; Frederick John Bunce,+; George H Bunce; John
Burbridge,+; William G Burbridge; George O Burch; Frank Burchell; H H
Burchell; A W Burchell; William Eli Burchell,+; William George Burchill;
Burden; Edward Burden; Edward J Burford; E E Burge MID; Edward Guy Burge
Henry J Burge; A G Burgess; Francis John Burgess,+; Henry Burgess; J Burgess
William G Burgess; A Burgin; Daniel A Burke; John T Burn; Charles Stewar
Burns,+; William John Burness,+; John R Burnett; George Burns; Henry Burns
Martin J Burns; Micheal Burns; Stanley Burns; Thomas P Burns (Sergeant 1/4th
Btn Wiltshire Regt); Bert H J Burry; J Burry; George Burson; Robert R Burson
Christopher Stigant Burt,+; Samuel E Burt; Alfred Edward Burton; Owen Edga
Burton,+; Wilfred R Burton; W Burton; Frederick G Bush; Albert Edward
Butcher,+; Arthur Stewart Butcher,+; D Butcher; Fred Butcher; George Edward
Butcher,+; George J Butcher; Leonard Butcher; Percy Butcher; Reginald
Butcher; T Butcher; Albert D Butler; Edward John Butler,+; Francis Butler
Fred Butler; Frederick Charles Butler,+; Frederick Thomas Butler,+; John
Butler,+; Ralph William Butler (Lt-Col); Robert Herbert Butler,+; H Butlin
Robert Butt; William E Butt; William Frederick Handley Butt,+; A A Buttle MM
Charles E Button; Percy A Button; Herbert C Button (2nd Btn Wiltshire Regt)
Herbert J Button(2nd Btn Wiltshire Regt); John N Button; Thomas R Button
Reginald C F Button; Reginald Buy; James Bye; Henry Byett; H G Bygate
Rev. L Calway; J R Cambourne; H Camden; G H D Camille; A A Campbell
Leonard Candle; R Cann; Richard George Fred Cann,+; Victor W Cann
A Cannings; Ernest Cannings,+; Sidney Cannings,+; Tom Canter,+; O J Caple
A H Capper; James Carey; John Carey,+; Leonard E Carew; Walter J Carnell
F J Carner; A Carpenter; C H Carpenter; F G Carpenter; G E Carpenter
Harold F Carpenter; Henry James Carpenter; Henry Joseph Carpenter
Thomas Carpenter; William Edwin Carpenter,+; Allen Carter; B H Carter
B L L Carter; Bertram Carter,+; C H Carter; Charles Carter; Frank Carter
F G Carter; Herbert Carter; Henry Carter,+; Issac Carter; Jonathan Carter
Leonard Carter; P Carter; Percy Charles Carter,+; William C Carter
William Carter,+; W J Carter; John Carmody; Percy R Carr; W J Carrivick
J C Carver; A E Carvey; Charles Carvey; C F Carvey; Edward Carvey,+
William Carvey; E J Case; Charles H Castle; E Castle; Ernest George Castle,+
John Castle; L C Castleman; Ernest Edward Caswell,+; Walter Caswell; H Cater
E H Cathcart; L Candle; C A Cavalo; George F Cave; George F J Cave; Ernest
Cavey; E J Cavey; H Cavey; William Cavill,+; A J Ceutler; George Challis
G J Chamerlain; A J Chambers; E J Chambers; E O Chambers; George Austin
Chambers,+; J W Chambers; P H Chambers; S W T Chambers; Sydney William
Chambers,+; A E Chandler; Charles E Chandler,+; E R Chandler; E W Chandler
E G Chandler; Frederick J Chandler; H G Chandler; Samuel Thomas Chandler,+
Thomas Chandler; W Chandler; W C Chandler; James Channon,+; Sidney
Harold Chanter,+; Cyril L Chaplin,+; Edward Chapman; Frederick Chapman
E Chapman; G W Chapman; James George Chapman,+; Robert Chapman
William James Chapman,+; W P E Chapman; Albert Charles Chappell; George S
Chappell; George S Chappell; H J Chappell; William Chappell; G E Chard
H Chard; Stanley Chard; E A H Chegwidden; Clarence N Chequer; F Chequer
Herbert Jeffrey Chequer,+; William A Chequer; G N Cherry; A F Chesterman
H Chesterman; Percy Thomas Chesterman,+; Alfred Chew,+; A George Chew
A James Chew; Frederick Chew; Albert J Child; Alfred Robert Child,+; John
Child; William A Child; Ernest G Chilton; Samual Chilton; Sidney R Chilton
A Chirgwin; Francis J H Chirgwin; J G Chirgwin; Herbert Chirqwin,+
Alfred Chitty; E T Chivers; Joseph Chivers; John A Chivers; W L Chivers
A W H Christian; Edward Chubb; Edgar Chun; George Chun; Wilfred R Chun
Brad Church; Christopher Church; G Church; H Church; Jack Church

G Churchel; Alfred Churchill; A H Clack; Gerald Lipfinistone Clack,+; Herbel
G Clack; Hubert G Clack; Ronald R P Clack; Robert Clack; Sidney A Clack
Stanley Clack; William G Clack; Frederick Clapham,+; F W Clapham
G F Clapham; Jonathan F Clapham; J W Clapp; Francis Clargo; A Claridge
F Claridge; F E Claridge; Cecil Clark MM,+; Frank Clark,+; John Clark
Army Service Corps); Reginald Clark; William M Clark; Ernest Clarke; Frederick
H Clarke; Frederick S Clarke; Henry Clarke,+; Hubert J Clarke; James Clarke
James Clarke,+; John Clarke,+; Jonas Clarke; P B F Clarke; Walter Clarke
Walter S Clarke; William Clarke; William E Clarke; William G Clarke; William
Henry Clarke,+; T O Claughan; G H Cleave; F C Clements; G T Clements
H Clements; William Clements; H G Cleverley; O W Cleverley; Walter Cleverley
Albert Clifford,+; Albert Godfrey Clifford,+; Alfred Clifford; E K Clifford
G H Clifford; H J Clifford; William Clifford; William George Clifford,+; W
Clifford; W N Clifford; W S Clifford; H C Clinkscales; H A Clissold; C J Cockbill
M Cockell; J E L Cockey; James Cockhead; William Cockhead; Ernest Coker
Arthur R Colbourne; F P Colbourne; Leonard D Colbourne; Albert E Cole
Arthur Cole MM; C E S Cole; Ernest Cole; E G Cole; F W Cole; Henry Cole
E Cole; James Cole,+; R J Cole; Walter H Cole; W F Cole; A H Coleman
C J Coleman; Ernest Cleman; F Coleman; Frederick Charles Coleman,+
C Coleman; A K Coleridge; Charles Coles,+; C H Collard; J W Collard
F Collard; A J Collett; Ben Collett; Bert Collett; Ernest George Collett,+
E L Collett; Frederick Collett; H R Collett; John Collett,+; Nelson Collett
Sidney Collett; Thomas G Collett; S W Colley; Charles Collier; W E K Collier
A E Collins; A T Collins; Ernest Collins; Frank Collins; Gilbert Collins,+
N H Collins; W S Collins; Harry Collyer,+; F C Comely; John Comley,+
Percy Harold Comley,+; A J Comer; W J Comer; Albert Comley (Rosebery St)
Albert Clarence Comley (Wilts Regt); C A Comley; F Comley; F W Comley
R Comley; Thomas William Comley (1st Wilts); T J Comley; W H Comley (R F C)
George Compton; Stanley Compton; George Connett; J C Conway
Albert Cook,+; Albert Edward Cook,+; A J Cook; C H Cook; Charles Cook
Edward Frank Cook,+; Edward Joseph Cook; Frederick I A Cook; F Cook DCM
Frederick E Cook; F G Cook; H Cook,+; Hubert James Cook,+; Jesse Cook
Joseph T Cook; Percy Cook; Percy A Cook; Ralph Joseph Cook,+; Reginald A
Cook; Stuart Cook,+; William A Cook; W C Cook,+; William G Cook
N H Cook; William H Cook,+; William Cook; Walter F C Cook; Walter James
Cook,+; William John Cook,+; Frank Cooke,+; A E Cooksey; Charles Frederick
Cooksey,+; P A Cooksey; A Coombes; A J Coombs; A T Coombs; Frederick
Coombs; P Coombs; Arthur |Cooper,+; A Cooper; Charles George Cooper
Ernest Cooper,+; Frederick John Cooper; F Cooper; George Cooper; G E
Cooper; Henry G Cooper; Hubert Cooper,+; K Cooper; William A Cooper
H J Coote; Samual Copp; E H Coram; Arthur Corbett,+; Edward Corbett,+
William Corbett; P A Corbyn; P D Corbyn; G H Cording; G H Cording (Junior)
N H Corgrove; F P Cork; Arthur Cornish,+; W J Cornish; Charles Cornley
Charles Corpe; Horace Corser,+; H Corser (Dorset Regiment); Reginald Corser,+
Cyril Cotton,+; Fred Cotton; Ralph Cotton,+; C F Cottrell; E G Cottrell
W Cottrell; Jacob Cottrell; John Cottrell; Walter Cottrell; P Coughlin
Horace Arthur Couldrey,+; J H Couling; T F Court; D Cousens; A J Cousin
D P Cousin; F J Cousin; A H Cousins; E J Cousins; S C Cousins; F Couzens
Ernest Cove,+; E A Cove; Henry Cove,+; Thomas Cove; F Covey; H Covey
E Covey; David Cowan; W Cowan; W J Cowlard; A J Cowley; A W Cowley
C E Cowley; E W C Cowley; Frederick William Cowley,+; H J Cowley; H F
Cowley; H W Cowley; James Cowley,+; James Frederick Cowley,+
William Cowley; Walter Cowley; Victor Cowley; Albert H Cox; Alfred T Cox
A E J Cox; A E Cox; A W Cox; Alfred Cox; A James Cox; Albert Harry Cox,+
Alfred John Cox; Ernest George Cox; Ernest James Cox; George Cox
Isaac Cox,+; J E G Cox; L J Cox; Thomas Cox,+; William Charles Cox
William John Cox; William Percival Cox,+; A W Cozens; F H Cozens

Charles William Craddock,+;   E H Craddock;   L J Craddock;   G H Craven; J S Crawford;   G J Crayford;   W Crayford;   Stafford William Vernon Creber,+; Sidney Creighton,+;   A Creswell;   A S Crew;   Albert Arthur Crewe;   D R Crewe; V C Crewe;   Philip Crewe,+;   Geofrey Crippen;   P J Crippen;   A E Cripps; A G Cripps;   C H Cripps;   G O Cripps;   H Cripps;   L G Cripps;   Reverend K N Crisford;   Thomas Crisp,+;   H M Critchley;   A Crocker;   George Augustus Crocker,+;   G F Crocker;   Ralph Henry Crocket,+;   S Crockett;   J F Croft; W J Crompton;   Arthur Crook,+;   A J Crook;   E J Crook;   Henry Crook,+; H J Crook;   John James William Crook,+;   C E Cross;   William Cross; George Crossley;   C Crumbie;   John Cruse;   Sidney Cruse;   William Cruse; F E Cryer;   R W Cudmore   William Cuff;   W G Cull;   Jacob Culley;   Frederick E Cullingford,+;   Frank Cullingford;   Jack Cullingford;   James A Cullingford; Richard C Cullingford;   Robert Cullingford;   Tom W Cullingford;   William Cullingford;   G W Cullip,+;   W H Cummins;   O G Cumner;   Victor George Cumner,+;   William Cumner;   Charles Curle;   B W Curtis;   E G Curtis;   F W Curtis; H F Curtis;   P G Curtis;   S E Curtis;   Sydney Herbert,+;   William George Curtis,+; W J Curtis;   W T Curtis;   T A Cusner;   A E Cuss;   Cyril Cuss,+;   E J Cuss;   F G Cuss; Frederick George Cuss;   W H Cuss;   Charles Cussons;   E C Cussons;   H W Cusworth;   A J Cutler;

A Dabbs;   F Dadge;   Gilbert George Dadge,+;   George J Dadge;   Henry Edward Dafter;   Harry R Dafter;   George Dainton;   Arthur Dance;   Frank Dance; Francis J Dance;   Henry Dance;   Herbert C Dance;   W H G Dance (South Wales Borderers);   Fred Dangerfield;   George P Dangerfield;   Frank W Daniell;

Memorial now in the outlet village

Cyril H Daniels;   George Daniels;   John Edward Charles Daniels;   Thomas Dark; Albert Lancelot Darling,+;   F W Darling;   Charles Darlington;   A N Dash; Everett Dash;   Herbert George Dash;   Henry R Dash;   John Dash,+; Percy Edward Dash,+;   Charles A Dashfield;   Frederick Dattin;   Harold Davenport,+;   Zakariah Bartley Davenport,+;   Walter Davey;   Archibald H Davidson;   Clements L Davies;   Edwin Davies;   Frank Davies;   George R Davies; Herbert Davies;   Johnathon Davies;   J Edward Davies;   William J Davies; Alfred O Davis;   Arthur E Davis;   Albert Davis;   Arthur Herbert Davis; Albert Edward Davis;   Alfred Davis;   Arthur Thomas Davis;   Archie Frank Davis; Bertram Davis;   Cyril George Davis;   Charles J Davis;   Charles E Davis;   Ernest Davis;   Edgar F Davis;   Ernest J Davis;   F C Davis;   Frederick George Davis;

George Davis; Herbert Henry Davis; Harold C Davis; Henry Victor Davis,+; F Davis; Joseph George Davis; John J Davis; James H Davis; Lewis Denni; Davis,+; Oswald Davis DCM; S J Davis,+; Samual Davis; Thomas Henry Davis; William John Davis,+; Walter Davis; William P Dawe; Arthur R Dawes; Charles Dawes; C P Dawkins; Arthur Herbert Day,+; Alfred John Day; Edward Walter Day; Ernest A Day; Frank Day; Herbert Thomas Day; Jack F E Day; J H Day; Leslie Day; Lawrence Day; Maurice Day,+; William Day; William Edward Levi Day; William Henry Day; Charles Godfrey Montague Deacon,+; E S Deacon; Frederick S Deacon; Thomas Deacon; William Henry Deacon; William James Deacon,+; Clarence L Dean; George Frederick Dean,+; Dean; Thomas Dear; Arthur George Deave,+; J W Deeth; Charles William Deller; H V Dennis,+; A E C Dent; Bertram Robert Dent,+; Charles Frederick Dent; Richard John Dent; Harold Dennet; Walter William Denton,+; Walter Frederick Derrick (MGC); Albert Dew; Albert V Dew; Eli Edward Dewe,+; Frederick Henry James Dewe,+; Reginald Dewe; Stanley Dewe; Henry G Diamond; R J Dibben; W H Dibben; D H R Dibbs; F A Difford; George Dickenson; Alfred Dickson; Aubrey J Dickson; Charles William Dickson; Ernest F Dickson; George Dickson; Henry Dickson; Jonathan R Dickson; P E Dickson; Robert Dickson; Raymond Dickson; William Dickson; William Dickson; William T N Dickson; William Membry Difford,+; Alfred Dixon; Edgar Arnold Dixon,+; Norman Reginald Walter Dixon,+; R P B Dixon; William James Dixon,+; Arthur James Dobson,+; B Dobson; E H G Dobson RFA); William Charles Dobson; Frederick William Dodd; Herbert W Dodgson; Lawrence O Dodgson; Frederick J Dodson; Francis William Dodson; Leonard J Dodson; Percivale Dodson; Samual Doell; Henry Dolan; James Dolman; William Charles Dolman; Charles Done; Ernest Done; Herbert Charles Done; Joseph Jesse Dore; Frederick Edwin Doughty; A W Douglas; Joseph Dowd; James Dowdell; Frederick R Dowding; George Henry Dowding; William Edward Dowding; Christopher George Dowell; Francis John Dowers,+; Robert H Dowers; Edwin Dowling; F H Draper; G Draper; Johnathon William Draper; Percy W Draper; T J Draper; C T Drew,+; E S Drew; H Drew; T Drew; Frank Drewett; Stanley George Drewett,+; W Drewett; J W Driscoll; W G Driver,+; Frederick L Drury; Henry Philip Drury,+; Leonard Drury; Phillip Charles Drury,+; W Drury,+; E W Dry; F J Dry; Frederick Ernest Duck,+; James Edwin Duck DCM Sgt/Mjr Wilts Engineers); John William Duck; William Arthur Duck; Walter E Duck; Ernest A Duffill (RE); Harry F Duffill (RE); William Walter Motta Dulin,+; Arthur J Dunford; John Henry Dunford; Arthur Dunmore; Frederick Dunmore; William Joseph Dunmore; Charles Dunn; Fred Dunn (Ferndale Road); Fran Dunn; Henry Dunn; Henry Charles Dunn; Herbert Hillier Dunn (RMLI); Jack Dunn; John Dunn (Westcott Place); H W Dunn,+; William James Dunn (RE) William Dunscombe; Percy Dunsdon,+; Henry Dunsford; Richard Dunstan; Albert Edward Durbridge; John Durbridge; Edward Durham; Frank Durham; Thomas J Durham; Hugh Durnford; Harry Durrant; J Dutton; Thomas Dutton; Arthur Dyball; Frank Edward Dyer,+; Lewis Edwin Dyer; Percy W Dyer,+; Sidney A Dyer; William Upfold Dyer; Fred Dyke,+; Harold Dyke;

E A Eagleton; F W G Eagleton; Charles Eagles; Archibald C Ealey; Herbert D Ealey; William Henry Ealey; B Eames; William Eamer; Cyril Earnshaw; Richard James East; W C Easter; C Eastbury; George Henry Eaton; Walter Eaton; Albert E Eatwell; Albert Eatwell; B J Eatwell; Charles Eatwell; G Eatwell; Henry Eatwell; John Eatwell; Ernest Eborn; R Ebrey; George Eburne; W H Edens; Charles Edge,+; G F Edge; V J Edge; Thomas Edgington; A J Edmonds; F Edmonds; F J Edmonds; Henry S Edmonds; J Edmonds; Edmonds (RN); Walter Edmonds; William Francis Edmonds; William I Edmonds; William R Edmonds; Fred Edmunds; Arthur Edwards,+; Arthur Frederick; Edwards; Albert W Edwards (Segt Wilts Fortress Engineers); Charles F Edwards; Frederick Edwards; Harry Edwards; Henry James Edwards; John Edwards,+

ames Henry Edwards; Samuel Edwards; William G M
Edwards; Henry James Pitt Eggleton MM,+; Joseph Eggleton; Thomas Edward
Eggleton,+; Frederick Henry Eldridge; James Eldridge; Jesse E Eldridge
W Elford; Harold Joseph Elines; Alfred Harold Ellen; B Ellen; Thomas Frederick
Ellen; George Ellery; Henry Ellicott; William Ellicott; Percy Elliot; H R Elliott
Hubert Joseph Elliott; L D Elliott; Percival Elliott; Arthur Cecil Ellis,+; F E Ellis
Sidney Ellis; A Ellison; E Ellison; Gerald Ellison; Sidney George Ellison
Thomas Ellison; Wifred Ellison Croix de Guerre; Henry James Elston
ames Elton; Mark Elton; Oliver Elton; Albert E G Embling; E L Embling
E T Embling; F H Embling; Francis George Embling,+; Henry Embling
Sidney George Embling; Thomas Henry Embury,+; Charles F W Emery
Percy Charles Emery,+; Francis James English,+; I H English; F J Enstone
Cyril Frances Eois,+; Edward (Ted) Esau DCM; William Esau DCM; Stuart
Etherington; Arthur A Evans; Bert W Evans; Daniel J Evans; Frank Evans
Frederick Arthur Evans MM,+; Bar; F H Evans; G Evans; Henry Johnathan
Evans; Henry Evans; Harold F Evans; Hubert Evans; James Evans; Johnathan
M Evans; Thomas Evans; Thomas David Evans,+; Walter Evans; William Evans
William H Evans; Leonard G Eveleigh; William Charles Eveleigh,+; M F Evemy
Arthur Everett; Edward George Everett; Francis Aubrey Everett,+; George
Everett; Johnathan A Everett; Henry Joseph Exton; Wallice B Exton; William
Albert Exton; D G Eyres; Edward Eyels,+; L L Eyres; Reginald Johnathan Eyres

C F Faith; William Faithfull,+; H W Fallen; Henry E Faning; Francis Henry
Farmer,+; Frederick R Farmer; James Farmer; Johnathan H J Farmer; Walter
Farmer,+; Frederick W Farncombe; Charles Farndell,+; James Patrick Farrell
B Farrow; Albert Charles Fell; Charles A Fell; Colin Garret Fell,+; Stanley L Fell
Thomas Curtis Fell,+; William J Fenemore; Charles Fenner,+; G W Ferguson
MC; Charles G Ferris; E G Ferris; Edward M Ferris; F J Ferris,+; George Ferris
George B Ferris; H G Ferris; Maurice V Ferris; R Ferris; S A Ferris; William
Ferris; William Johnathan Ferris; Joseph B Fessey; Robert James Donald Few,+
F Fiddes (Curtis Street); L H Fiddes (Curtis Street); Arthur A Fido; Charles
Field,+; E F Field; F J M Field; Grantley Field; Jacob Field; Percy R Field
Henry G Finch; Albert Fincham; Douglas G Fincham; George Findlay; Robert
A Findlay; Charles J Finn; Christopher A Finn; Reginald F M Finn; Thomas F
Finn; Robert J Finney; William H Finney; Arthur E Fisher; Ernest Fisher,+
Frederick A Fisher; Fred Fisher; F J Fisher; G W H Fisher; Harold Ernest Fisher,+
Henry Fisher; James Charles Hugh Fisher,+; Thomas Fisher; Thomas F Fisher
MM; Albert Victor Fishlock,+; W Fishlock; F J Fitchett; George Flay; Harold
F Flemming; Robert Flemming; Frederick Fletcher; J H Fletcher; Johnathan
Reginald Fletcher; T Fletcher,+; Wilfred Fletcher; Edward Flint; Henry
Florey,+; Arthur Regnald Flower; Edwin Brian Flower,+; Albert E S Fluck
Robert Fluck; Arthur H Follit; Albert E Ford; Dan Ford,+; Ernest G Ford

...nest J Ford; Kenneth E Y Ford; Richard L G Ford; Victor Reginald Ford,+;
William E Ford; William Frank Ford,+; William Frederick Ford; I W Foot; Jame
Herbert John Forest,+; Walter Forest,+; Fred Forrest; Joseph Forrest; Alber
E Forsey; Bertram Forsey; F H Forsey; George Henry Forster; Robert Forster
W V Forteath,+; A E Fortune; John Fortune,+; Ernest Foster,+; Harold Foster
S F Foster,+; Herbert James Fowler,+; Hubert William Fowler; Harry Fowler
Herbert Henry Fowler; Stanley G Fowler; T Fowler; Thomas Fowler,+; H E
Foyle; Albert Henry Fox; Charles E Fox; Frederick F Fox; John Arthur Fox
Johnathan C Fox; Johnathan W Fox; Joseph William Fox,+; Leopald C Fox
Percy Fox; Stanley T Fox; William A Fox; William Henry Fox,+; Henry Edward
Foyle; F C Frampton; A H Francome; C R Francome; A H Frankis; H R Frankis
W E Frankis; Albert Franklin; Alan Franklin; Arthur Franklin; Bernard Franklin
Charles Stanley Franklin,+; David H Franklin; George Franklin,+; Henry Franklin
Hollister Clare Franklin,+; Henry Thomas Franklin,+; Leonard Franklin,+; Olive
Franklin; Stafford William Franklin,+; V G Franklin; William Franklin
B H Frearson,+; Edward Freebury,+; John Freebury; Johnathan Henry Freebury
Reginald Edward Freebury; William Freebury; Harold W Freegard; Thomas A
Freeman; Donald M Freeth; Hubert Freeth; William T Freewin; F French
Albert Charles Fricker,+; A G Frost; Albert Frost; Charles J Frost; Frank Frost
Frederick Harold Frost,+; Robert William Frost; A Froud; Albert Froud; Charle
E Froud; Edward George Froud; Ernest Froud; Sidney Froud; F Fry; William
Fry,+; G H Fulcher; James N Fulker,+; William John Thomas Fullaway,+
Edward Fleetwood Fuller,+; F Fuller; George C Fuller; John W Fuller; L T Fuller
F W Fulton; G Fulton; C Furze;

Francis Thomas S Gabb; William Gadd,+; A E Gage DCM; G E V Gale; Herber
William Gale,+; Johnathan Gale; Johnathan S R Gale; Percy Herbert Gale
Robert C B Gale; S N Gale; Wilfred Sydney Gale; William J Gale; Henry Game
Henry Edward Gammage; James William Gane; Edmund John Gapp,+; A D
Gardiner,+; Charles William Gardiner,+; George Henry Gardiner; Herber
Gardiner; P J Gallichan; Archibald Garlick; Maurice Garlick; Ashley Fred
Gardner; Albert E Gardner; Charles E Gardner; Dan Gardner; Harold Gardner
H E Gardner; Maurice Gardner; Ernest Charles Garland,+; Ernest Garner (2nd
Wilts Regt.); J Garratt; Ernest George Garrett; Frederick Richard Garrett
Richard I Garrett; W Garrett; Walter Johnathan Garrett; George Eward Garroway
Reverend J H Gavin (Army Chaplins Dept. Trinity Presbyterian Church Swindon)
Thomas George Gay; R Gealer; Sydney Johnathan Gealer; Albert George Gee,+
C C Gee; Charles H J Gee; Francis Sidney Gee; Fred James Gee; George Wilfrec
Gee,+; O F Gee; William Henry Gee,+; George Alfred Gent,+; Edward George
Herbert Gladstone George,+; Henry Samuel George; William Edward George,+
William Ernest George,+; Alfred Charles Gerring; William Johnathan Gerring
Isacc Johnathan Gerrish; Leslie G Gerrish; Reginald J Gerrish; A R Gibbs
L W J Gibbs; Edward Alfred Gibbs; Frederick Gibbs; F Gibbs; Frederick John
Gibbs; George Gibbs; Henry Charles M Gibbs; Robert Harold Gibbs
Harry Gibbs,+; J Gibbs,+; Sydney R Gibbs; W Gibbs; Thomas Gibbons
George Gibson MM (Australian Forces, Son of Mrs Gibson, 5 Holbrook Street)
Albert William Giddings; Johnathan Giddings; William Henry Giddings (2nd Wilt
Regt.); Archie Gilbert; C M Gilbert; Johnathan Clifford Gilbert; George Gilbrey
Albert Edward V Gilby; Herbert W Gilder; A J Giles; Frederick W Giles
George William Giles; J T Giles; L G W Giles; William Andrew Giles
Edward Gilfoyle; Richard Gilfoyle; William Gilfoyle; Francis W Gill; Giles Gill,+
W Gill; Samuel Tyler Gillard,+; Alfred Howard Gillespie,+; F C Gillett; A Gillman
Frederick Alexander Gillman; Walter Johnathan Gillman; Albert Richard B Gilmore
A E Gilmore; Harold Edgar Gilmore; Lancelot Charles Gilmore; F L Gilmore
G Gilmore; T W Gilmore; Edward Johnathan Gingell; Fred Gingell
William Gingell; W H M Gladwin; Albert Glass,+; Ernest Glass; Herbert Stanley
Glass,+; Alfred Gleed; Alfred F Gleed; Francis James Gleed,+; Frederick Gleed

T Gleed; Ernest Glover; William Glover; William James Glover; George Goatly;
George E Gobey; Albert George Goddard; Arthur W Goddard; Bertram
Goddard,+; Charles W R Goddard; E G Goddard; Frank Goddard,+;
Francis Ernest Goddard; Frederick Charles Goddard; James Nelson Goddard;
Stuart G W Goddard; William Frederick A Goddard; Walter John Goddard,+;
John Godden; William Godding; Edward Frederick Godsell; George Frederick
Godsell; Percy Godsell; William Charles Godsell; Albert Godwin; Arthur Godwin;
Alfred H Godwin; Edward James Godwin; Ernest Walter Godwin; Harold John
Godwin,+; James Godwin; Thomas D Godwin; William Godwin DCM MM;
William Henry Godwin; Ernest A Golby; Horace Lett Golby,+; James John Golby;
John Henry Golby,+; A Golding; William Golding; Charles John Goldsmith;
Ernest Walter Goldsmith; Sidney William Goldsmith; Tudor Johnathan Goodall;
Albert Jesse Goodenough,+; Frederick Goodenough; H Goodenough; Sidney
Thomas,+; Albert George Goodman; C Goodman; Ernest William Goodman;
Harold Goodman,+; John Wilfred Goodwin,+; Philip Godman; Arthur James
Gore; Charles H Gore; Frederick Elijah Gore; Frederick Woolford Gorton,+;
Arthur Everett Gosling; Cecil Henry Gosling; Cecil Walter Gosling; Harold Austin
Gosling,+; Reginald Charles Gosling; R E Gosling; William Frederick Gosling;
William Henry Gosling,+; Frederick Goss; Percy Frank Goss,+; C W G Gough;
Cyril W Gough; F E Gough; Frederick George Gough,+; F J Gough; F W Gough;
Frank Gough,+; Francis Henry Gough; H H Gough; Henry Maurice Gough;
John Leonard Gough; William Johnathan Gough; William Scott Gough;
H Goulding; Alfred J Govier,+; Edgar Albert Govier; Walter John Govier,+;
A Grace; Edward Grace; George Henry Grace; Thomas Grace; William George
G Grace; W H W Grace; William James Grace,+; William Thomas Granger,+;
Alexander Victor Grant; John Grant,+; William Grant,+; William H Grant; Alfred
Ernest Graves; Frederick G Graves; Albert J Gray ('A J'); Bert H Gray; Charles
Albert Gray; Charles Herbert Gray; Ernest Charles Gray; Frederick James Gray,+;
Percy Frederick Gray; Sidney James Gray (RFA); Thomas Charles Gray,+; Wilfred
Johnathan Gray (RFA); William James Gray (RFA); Alfred Grayhurst; Albert Green;
Archibald Rowland Green,+; Arthur Green; Arthur Edward Green (RFA); Arthur
Leonard Green,+; Charles Green; Edward Green; Edward Reginald Green,+;
George Green; Henry Arthur Green,+; Horace James Green; Hubert S Green;
Henry Wilfred Green; James Green; John Green,+; John Henry Green;
Joseph Green; Reginald Frederick Green; Roy Green DCM; Stanley H Green;
Thomas Green; William Green; William E R Green (ASC); William James Green;
H C H Greenaway; Ashley J Greening; Frederick S Greening; Leonard Harvey
Greening,+; Wilfred Manley Greenman,+; W E Greenwood; E J Gregory;
Frederick John Gregory,+; Thomas Albert Gregory; William Henry Gregory;
E Gribble,+; F C Griffin; Hugh Griffin; J H Griffin; Mervyn Granville
Griffin,+; Percy Charles Griffin,+; Stanley V Griffin; William Griffin; Albert E
Griffiths; Alfred Edward Griffiths; A G Griffiths; Charles Frederick Griffiths;
Frederick Griffiths; Frederick A Griffiths; Gordon Griffiths; Henry Griffiths;
Henry C Griffiths; L A Griffiths; Albert H Grist; William George Grist;
Arthur John Grover; Ernest William Groves,+; William Alfred Groves,+;
Charles Grubb; Edward W Grubb; Jesse Gubbins MM,+; Edward George Guley
+; H C Guley; A H Gullis; William Gullis,+; Francis Thomas Gunner; Francis
H Gunston; R C Guthrie,+; J C W Guy; Victor William Guy (RE 26 York Road)
Percy William Gwillim; James H Gwyther; Leonard W B Gylby;

R Habgood; Percy Habgood; Robert Habgood; William Habgood
Albert Hacker; Arthur Hacker,+; G T Hacker,+; Harry Hacker; Harold Hacker
Herbert Hacker; L T Hacker,+; Oscar C Hacker; Reginald A Hacker; William
N Hacker; Clifford Hackman,+; George Haddrell; Charles E Haggard,+;
Frederick V Haggard; Samuel J Haggard; Albert Haines; Frederick W Haines
James Haines,+; George Haines; William Haines; Lionel E Haire; A Hale,+
Alfred Hale,+; A W Hale; Charles Hale; Frederick William Hale; Henry Hale;

Richard Hale; William Hale; George Hales; H J Halestrap; S J W T Halestrap;
Arthur Hall; Albert William Hall,+; Charles Hall; Edwin Hall; E G Hall,+; H Hall
H W Hall; S Hall; Thomas Hall: Walter Hall: W F Hall: William Jasper Hal
DSM,+; Harry Hallett,+; William Hallett; E T Hallewell; W J Hallewell
E Halliday; R H Hamber; F A Hamblin; H W Hamblin; Richard G Hamblin
A S Hambidge; G Hambidge; Ernest Frederick Hambidge,+; William Arthu
Hambidge,+; W F Hambidge; Albert Hamley; Arthur Hammond
George Hammond; James Hammond; Albert F Hancock; Archibald Perciva
Hancock; Charles J Hancock; E G Hancock; Edward F Hancock; Ernest William
Hancock,+; F C Hancock; Frederick J Hancock; Frank Hancock; Harold F
Hancock; HaroldJ Hancock; William A Hancock; Arnold William Handel
F V Handel; Joseph Handy; C V Hanks; Percy Hanks; Walter Charles Hanks
Albert R Hanley; Thomas Hanson; W E Harfield; H Harding; Thomas Neate
Harding,+; Henry Edgar Hardyman,+; Charles Harman,+; G H Harman
Frank Harper; G A Harper; William Harper; William Edgar Harper; A Harrington
Ben S Harris; Clarence Harris; Charles W Harris; Colin Harris; Charles Harris
Ernest Harris; Frederick Harris; George D Harris; Geofrey Harris; Henry Harris
James E Harris; James Henry Harris,+; Joseph H Harris; Leonard Harris
Rawley Harris,+; Samual Harris; Walter R Harris; Walter Harris; W E Harris
William J Harris; W C Harris; W I Harris; Arthur Harrison +: Charles Harrison
E J Harrison; F G Harrison; George Henry Harrison; W Harrison; W F P Harrison
W George Harrison; Edward Harrod; Frederick John Harrod; Harry Harrod
A V Hart; Charles W Hart; John Henry P Hart; Reginald Percy Hart ,+; W G S
Hart; Walter Henry Hart; R Hartless; Thomas Haskins; Tracy V Hastings
Johnathan Haslam; Charles W Hartley; Frederick A Hartley; Harold Ernes
Hartley,+; William Hartley; William Walter Hartwell,+; Charles A Harvey; James
E Harvey; William Harvey; Charles S Harwood; Charles Hatcher; George
Leonard Hatcher,+; W Hatcher; Henry Wilfred Hathaway; A Hatherall
G W Hatherall; Sidney E Hatherall; John Hatherall; Albert Prior Hatherell,+
Arthur H Hatten; C J Hatton; Frederick A Hatton; F Haward,+; F J Hawkes
Frederick E Hawketts; Albert Edward Hawkins,+; Alfred Hawkins; Charles
Hawkins; Frederick Hawkins; George Edward Hawkins; James H Hawkins
John Hawkins; Walter F Hawkins: William Charles Hawkins; Walter Henry
Hawkins,+; William H Hawkins; E F E Hawksbee; Stanley F Hay; Thomas
Haydon; Walter H Haydon; Edward Hayes; E H J Hayes; F W Hayes; Herber
E Hayes; Frederick C Haylock,+; Arthur Henry Haynes; Bert Haynes; Frederick
A Haynes; Oliver Mark Haynes,+; William Haynes; Ernest Johnathan Haysom
Ernest C Haysom; Reginald A Haysom; Albert Thomas Hayward,+; Alber
R Hayward; Francis H Hayward; George Samual Hayward; H G Hayward
J G Hayward; Joseph Hayward; James E Hayward; Nelson Hayward
Robert W Hayward; S Hayward; Thomas Hayward; William Alfred Hayward,+
Alfred Thomas Hazel; H C Hazel; W J Hazel; Edward James Hazell,+; Harold
Wilfred Hazell; Charles Hazzard; H Hazzard; Harry Hazzard; Cornelius Head
Edgar E Head; Francis W J Head; G Head; Robert J Head; S A Head (25530 Wilts
Regiment); William Head,+; Charles Heath; E C Heath; Frederick Charles
Heath; Frederick George Heath; Fred Heath; George Heath,+; Harry Thomas
Heath,+; Joseph William Heath,+; P J Heath; Reginald Heath; Clarence
W Heath; Wilfred P Heath; Arthur Heavens; Ernest Heavens; Raymond F
Heavens; Sidney H Heavens,+; F C Heaver; Richard William Heap,+; Henry
James Hedges; George Hedges; William Edward Hedges,+; William James
Hedges; George Williams Hemming; Robert Hemmings; William James
Hemmings,+; Reginald T C Hemmins; Roy Allnutt Hemmins,+; Ernest Edward
Hendon,+; Frederick C Hendy; Joseph Hendy; P G Henley; W F Henley; Edga
B Henly; Albert Henstridge; Reginald Robert Henstridge,+; Henry G Henty
Edwin Herbert; Frederick H Herbert; Henry V Herbert; W F Herbert; Walter
Herbert; Jesse Herman,+; James Hermon; Thomas Henry Hern; Ernest Edward
Herring; Henry Hester: Alfred James Hewer; Cyril Hewer; George Hewe

John Henry Hewitt; Jonathan William Hewer; Thomas Hewer; Wilfred Hewer; Hewitt; A M H Hewlett; Frederick Thomas Hewlett; P F Hibbard; Alfred Edward Hibberd,+; Ernest George Hibberd,+; G Hibberd; J T Hibberd; William Hibberd; William G Hibberd; John Hibbert; William G Hickmott; Edward Hicks; Francis Harold Hicks,+; Frederick Hicks; John Hicks; Thomas Hicks; William Hicks; Henry Charles Hiett; George Frederick Hiett,+; George J Higgins; Herbert Frederick Higgins; Reginald Higgins; William G Higgins; George Henry Higgs; James W Higgs; William E Higgs; William George Higgs,+; William George Hilborne; Arthur Hill; C H Hill; Charles J Hill; Edward Hill; F Hill; Frederick Charles Hill; Harry Hill; James Hill,+; Johnathan Thomas Hill; P A C Hill; R J Hill; Richard G Hill; Samual Hill; Stephen Hill; Thomas A Hill; Herbert Charles Hillard,+; Albert Hillier; Archibald G Hillier; C S Hillier,+; Christopher Thorpe Hillier,+; George Hillier; Harold Hillier; Henry George Hillier; R R Hillier,+; Sidney David Hillier; Thomas Hillier; William Hillier; William James Hillier; Edward Hillman; Roland Henry Hills; S Hilton; F W Hind,+; Arthur F Hinder; Christopher George Hinder,+; E J Hinder; Harold Hinder; Harding J E Hinder; Percy Hinder,+; Richard John Hinder,+; Thomas William Hinder; A Hinton; Charles George Hinton; Harry Hinton,+; I H Hinton; Alfred Norman Hiscock; Arthur William Hiscock; Fred Hiscock,+; Valentine Hiscock; F Hiscocks; George Hiscocks; Henry S Hitchcock; Ronald Frederick Hitchman; Alfred Henry Hobbs; Albert Edward Hobbs; Albert William Hobbs; Charles Henry Hobbs; Ernest R Hobbs; Ernest Hobbs; Ernest E Hobbs; Frederick George Hobbs; Charles Henry Andrew Hobbs,+; Henry James Hobbs; Reginald Charles Hobbs; Thomas Hobbs; Wilfred Hobbs; William Hobbs; W P Hobbs; Arthur Henry Hodges; Ernest H Hodges; Herbert Stanley Hodges; Reginald Victor Hodges; Sidney Philip Hodges,+; Henry William Holder; Charles Henry Hole,+; E W Hole; Johnathan Edward Hole; Francis Thomas John Holley,+; H C Holley; Stanley Percy Holley,+; Wilfred Holley; Arthur E Hollick; Edward William Hollick,+; Eric C Hollick; F G Hollick; H J Holliday; James Holliday; F Hollier; Charles C Hollister,+; William Edward Hollister; A P Holloway; George Holloway; William Thomas Holloway; William Holman; Albert Holmes,+; William Joseph Holmes; C Holt; Harold H Holt,+; Albert Homer; S Honey; Frederick E Hookings; Henry Thomas Hookings; Arthur Hooper; George Hooper; Sidney Richard Hooper; John Hopgood; Ernest G Hopkins; F Hopkins; F G Hopkins; James Henry Hopkins; Johnathan Henry Hopkins; Percy william Hopkins; Frank Horan; Edwin Horler,+; Andrew James Hornblow; Frederick H Hornblow; Walter C Hornblow; David Horne; Francis H Horne; Charles Henry Horrell; Horton,+; T Howard; J Howard,+; Ernest Albert Howe; John Henry Howe; Alfred James Howell; George Howell,+; George Thomas Howell; W H Howell; W J Howell; A Howlett; Cecil Howlett; Ernest Howlett; Archibald Howse; E Howse; Henry Howse; James Howse; William G Howse,+; W J Howse; Ernest Huband; N Huck; Howard Huckson; Albert Hughes; Arthur Hughes; Arthur Stanley Hughes,+; Charles Normandale Hughes,+; Charles E Hughes; Ernest Reginald Hughes; George Henry Hughes; George A Hughes; George James Hughes,+; H F A Hughes; Henry James Hughes,+; Johnathan E Hughes; Stephen John Arthur Hughes,+; T Hughes; Walter George David Hughes,+; William Hughes,+; W H Hughes; Walter Johnathan Hughes; Charles N E Huggins; Frederick Hulbert; George R Hulbert; Henry Hulbert; Sidney G Hulbert; William James Hulbert; Percy James Hull; Frank Hulme; Albert William Humphries; Albert S Humphries; Charles Humphries; Ernest Charles Humphries,+; George Humphries; Henry James Humphries; Jesse Humphries; Levi John Humphries,+; Percy E Humphries; Sidney Johnathan Humphries; Thomas James Humphries; William Henry Humphries; Wilfred J Humphries; William Stanley Humphries; Frederick Humphrey; Alfred W C Hunt; Albert Hunt (8 Page Street); Albert Victor Hunt,+; Charles Percy Hunt; E F Hunt; Ewart Hunt; Edwin J Hunt; George Hunt; Herbert William Hunt; Henry Hunt; Henry C J Hunt; John William Hunt,+; K R Hunt; Samual Hunt; Thomas David Hunt; Wallace Samuel Hunt,+

CORRECTIONS

Page 157 Caption should read – 'George Bartlett'

Page 166 CANDLE should read – 'CAUDLE'

Page 199 Sidney Mayell (Seated) Should read – (Standing)

Please accept my sincere apologies for these mistakes and other printing errors that appear in the book. They are no reflection on my proof readers as they were made after their checks. I alone take full responsibility for these.

Sincerely

Mark Sutton

CORRECTIONS

Walter Hunt; William Frederick Hunt (8 Page Street); Ralph Hunter; A J Huntley;
Herbert Charles Huntley; John Henry Huntley MM,+; Richard W Huntley; Victo
Huntley; Johnathan Hunter; F S Hurcom; George Hurcome; Reginald E J Hurn
George Hurrell; T H Hursey,+; Johnathan George Hurst; W J Hurst,+; G
Hutchings; J Hutchings; John Frederick Hutchinson,+; C J Hutt; Victor George
Hutt; Charlie Hyde; Henry Hyde; Jack E Hyde; Oliver E Hyde; Robert E Hyde

Bert Iles,+; Charles E Iles; Edward Iles; Ernest A Iles; Ewart S Iles; Hubert C
Iles; Percy E Iles; R Iles; Walter J Iles; William James Iles; Sidney Iles; Alber
W T Illett; D N Imms; William Imms; Frederick C Inge; Frederick A Ingram
George H Ingram; James H Ingram; R K Innes (RFC); Henry G Instone; A H Irish
Ireland; H W T Ireland; Reginald Pearse Ireland,+; Walter E G Ireland (Page
Street); James W Ireson; Frederick Hollaway Issacs,+; FC J Isgar;

Frederick Henry Jackson; George F Jackson; Johnathan Jackson; Joshua Jackson
T B Jackson; Reginald John Jackson,+; T G J Jackson; William J Jackson
Charles Jacobs; F E Jacobs; Harry Jacobs,+; William Jacobs; Reginald Jago,+
A H H James,+; Alfred W James; Frederick A James,+; George W James; Harold
F James; Herbert James,+; Jonah C James (Tailor of 41 Regent Street); Richard C
James; Samuel James,+; Wilfred James; William E James; William H James
A Jannaway; Reginald Lethbridge Pleydell Janaway,+; Harold Jarman; J S
Jarman; J W Jansen; Albert G Jarvis; George Jarvis; Henry R Jarvis; Samue
Jeffcutt,+; Albert E E Jefferies; Albert Henry Jefferies,+; Charles A Jefferies
Edward Jefferies; James S Jefferies; Johnathan Jefferies; William E Jefferies
William John Bennett Jefferies,+; William Henry Jefferies,+; Alfred Jeffery
William Jeffery,+; Frederick Jefford; Leslie Arthur Jefford,+; Sidney Jelly
K Jenkins; Arthur John Jenner,+; J W Jennings; Sydney R Jennings (ASC)
W E J Jennings; A Jerram; John Jermy; William Jerome; Albert Edward Jew,+
E F W Joachim; Percy Jobbins,+; William Jobson; Leonard Johnsey,+; T
Johnsey; W L Johnsey; Albert Johnson,+; Alfred Johnson; A J Johnson
A N Johnson; Edward Johnson; Ernest H Johnson; Frederick Johnson; George
E Johnson; Henry Edward Johnson,+; Henry J Johnson; Harold G Johnson
John Johnson,+; Norman Johnson; Reginald Johnson,+; William Johnson
Cecil William Johnston,+; Augustine Jolliffe,+; Albert A Jones; A B Jones
A J Jones; Alfred S Jones; Arthur W Jones; A W E Jones,+; Bert W Jones
Charles Edwyn Jones,+; Edward R Jones; Edward G Jones; Edwin P Jones
Francis Walter Jones,+; Frank Jones; Frederick George Jones,+; Fred W Jones,+
George Thomas Jones,+; Gordon Jones; George E Jones; Harry Harold Jones
+; Horace C Jones; John D Jones; J C Jones; Lambert Jones; Norman W
Jones; Owen H Jones; Oswald F Jones; Richard E Jones (Page Street); Richard
M Jones; Robert E Jones; Robert G Jones; Thomas C Jones; Thomas Jones DCM
+; William Jones,+; William G Jones; William Henry Jones,+; William R Jones
Wilfred R Jones; Wilfred Arthur Jones,+; Albert Victor Jordan,+; Edgar J Jordan
F Jordan; H H Jordan; Frederick H Journet; A Joyce; J J Joyce; William Henry
Joyce,+; Albert Joynes;

Archibald O Kane; Frederick C Kane; George W Kane; William Kane; A M
Keating; Albert Keefe; Frank Keefe (Rodbourne Road); Thomas Keefe; H A
Keel,+; Hubert J Keel; Lawrence H Keel; Norman R Keel; Andrew U Keen
Arthur C Keen; George Keen; Hurbert S Keen; Percy George Keen,+; Walter
Keen; Wilfred H Keen; William G Keen; Arthur Daniel Keene,+; Bert Keene
Charles F Keene; H J Keene; Jesse Keene; John Keevil,+; Percy Kelly
A Kemble; Arthur A Kemble; W H Kemble; C Kempster; Percy J Kendall
Arthur H Kennett; George R Kennett; Harold James Kennett; William Kennett
Alfred T Kennea; Edward Kennyfec; C Kent,+; Charles Henry Kent; Charles
S Kent; Ernest Henry Kent; F G Kent; F J Kent,+; G W Kent (Wilts Regiment)
Henry E F Kent; Henry James Kent (Wilts RFA); Herbert Henry Kent; Herber

Kent; R F Kent; William George Kent,+; John James Keogh; Charles Edward Kerridge; C G Kerslake; Charles Edwin Kethero,+; Ernest Henry Kethero; William John Kethero; William C Kewell; Albert J Key; George Key; Thomas Key; William H Keylock; E H Kibblewhite (4 Medgebury Place); G Kibblewhite,+; John Kilby,+; William Kilby; William James Kilford (11 Page Street); H Kilminster; Albert S King; A King; A J King; Albert King; Alfred King; Basil King; C J King; Dennis H King; E H V King; Edward E King; Ernest V King; Frederick W King; Francis King; Frederick James King; Frederick Richard King,+; G E King; George Henry King; George Thomas King; Henry James King; H J King; Johnathan King; Joseph Henry King; Peter King; Robert King; V W King; William A King; William C King; William James King; Walter King; Wilfred E King; W J A King; Charles Kingston; Charles Parker Kirby,+; Christopher Kirby; Harold P Kinneir; Douglas William Kirby; Frederick Kirby; John Edward Kirby; John Hopkins Kirby,+; L Kirby; Manfred Kirby,+; Wilfred Henry Kirby; Johnathan William Kirk; R Kirk; Richard William Kirk; William Kirk; A Kitching; Charles Kitching; Edward A Kitson; Charles Edward Knapp,+; Archibald Edward Knee,+; Dennis Arthur Knee,+; Arthur H Knight; Charles Knight; Frank Knight,+; G R Knight; George Edward Knight,+; W E Knight

Leslie Lacey; Charles R Lainchbury; William T Lake; Charles Lamb; Victor E C Lamb; Reginald George Lambdin,+; Ernest A Lambert,+; Frederick Charles Lambert,+; Albert Henry Lambourne,+; Douglas R Lambourne; E Lambourne,+; Frederick Lambourne; William Lambourne; W E Lambdin; Wilfred Edward Lampard; Frederick Percy Lamport; William Albert Lamport; William Lamprey; A Lancaster; J L Lancaster (ASC); C C Lander,+; William John Landfear,+; William Alexander Gunning Lane,+; Alfred Edward Lanfear,+; Cecil Lang,+; John F Lang MM; Albert V Langcaster; Albert Henry Langdale; L J Langdale; R C Langley; R C Langley; Arthur Edward Lander; Arthur Ernest Lander; Charles G Lander; Bucklee Landon; Charles Lane; David A Lane; Frederick Thomas Lane; Harold S Lane; Jack Lane; William James Lane; Thomas Percy Lanham (British Red Cross); V Lansdowne; Frederick Johnathan Lapworth; John Lapworth; Joseph Lapworth,+; S H Largent; A S Last; W J Last; Victor Latter; G H La Touche; Charles Edwin Launchbury,+; James C Lavington; W O Lavington; W E Lavis; Ben Law; Ernest Godfrey Law; Frederick J C Law; Harold George Law,+; John William Arthur Law,+; Mark M Law; William Law; Albert Geoffrey Lawes,+; Alfred J Lawes; Albert Edward Lawrence; Charles Lawrence; E W Lawrence; Frederick Cyril Lawrence,+; Francis Johnathan Lawrence; Frederick William Lawrence; George Thomas Lawrence; George Wellman Lawrence,+; Harry Lawrence,+; Henry Charles Lawrence,+; Jesse Lawrence,+; Joseph Lawrence; Samual Lawrence; Thomas Valentine Lawrence; William John Lawrence,+; William Joseph F Lawrence; W Lawrence; Charles Lay; Edward William Lay; Frank Lay; John H V Lay; Arthur William Lea; David Lea; Thomas Lea,+; F Leach DCM; F G Leach; Reginald Bery Leach; W E Leach; George Henry Le Cappelai (RE); Michael J Ledwidge; George Lee,+; Graham Lee; Reginald Lee; Stanley Lee; S G Lee,+; Wallice Lee; A Legg (Wilts); Arthur Legg; Albert Edward Legg; Arthur Richard Legg; George Legg,+; Henry John Legg; John Henry J Legg; Septimus Henry Legg,+; William Legg; Ernest George Leggett,+; William Stephen Leggett,+; A Leighfield; Isaac James Leighfield,+; Mark James Leighfield; Reginald Albert Leighfield; Sydney Francis Leighfield,+; William Charles Leighfield; R Lenham; Johnathan Fleming Lennie; Arnold James Leonard; E J Leonard,+; Frederick Charles Leonard,+; George Herbert Leonard; Percy Harold Leonard,+; Reginald Leonard; Sidney Alfred Leonard; A H Lester; Albert Henry Lester; Herbert A Lester; Joseph Lester; Reginald W Johnathan Lester; Thomas Frederick Lester: W Lester; Wallice Lester; William James Lester; John Leveson; Kenneth M L L'Evine; Stanley Lewington; Alan J Lewis; Albert Sidney Lewis; Charles Lewis,+; Charles Albert Lewis; Edgar Lewis; Edward Lewis,+; Frederick James Lewis,+; Frederick

William Lewis; George J V Lewis; Harry Lewis,+; Harold Augustus Lewis,+;
Henry George Lewis; H G Lewis; Henry Stephen Lewis,+; John William Lewis,+
Reginald Walter Lewis; Robert Lewis; Robert Johnathan Lewis; Robert Thomas
Lewis; Thomas Arthur Lewis Croix de Cuerre (Bel),+; William Christopher Lewis
William Oliver Lewis; W E Lewis; Arthur C Liddamore; Albert Lidbury; F S
Lidbury; Edward Liddiard; Albert Edward Liddington; Johnathan H Liddington
Percy Harold Liddington; Wilfred Edmund Liddington,+; Walter Lidden,+;
John Henry Liddon,+; Ernest Albert Lindsey,+; Frederick Charles Lindsey
H L Lindsey; William John Lindsey; Walter T Lindsey; Guy Lintern; P F
Lintern; Harry Linnegar (Oxs and Bucks LI – Park Hotel); George Edward Lilly
Herbert W Litten; Alfred W R Little,+; H G Little,+; Melton Little; P Little;
Little; W R A Little; H Llewellyn; Harold Llewellyn; Herbert Edgar Llewellyn
Thomas Alfred Llewellyn; Thomas J Llewellyn; W A Liewellyn; Edward Henry
Lloyd; Frederick Lloyd; Reginald P J Lloyd; B Loader; Frederick H Lock
Frederick C H Locke; Albert George Lockey; Thomas Lockey,+; W Lockey,+
Joseph E Lockyer; Reginald Arthur Loder,+; John Logan; William A Loker
George Archibald Colin Lomas DCM,+; Alfred Frederick Long; Arthur Long
C F W Long; Henry A Long; James Charles Long; John Long; T Long,+
Walter Long; O W Longstaff; Samuel Looker,+; George Looms; George Henry
Lord; Robert Charles Lord,+; Herbert L G Lott; A E Love; Frederick Love
S Love; T J Love; W R Love,+; Harold Edward Lovell; Arthur William Lovedav
DCM + Bar,+; Albert Jeremy Loveday; Frederick Loveday,+; Frederick W
Loveday; George Albert Loveday; Hedley Uriah Loveday,+; James B Loveday
John Loveday; Johnathan W Loveday; R G Loveday,+; Thomas G Loveday
Frederick W Loveday; B Lovegrove,+; William Lovegrove,+; Charles Lovelock,+
Ernest William Lovelock; F A J Lovelock; Frederick Graham Lovelock,+; Herbert
Sidney Lovelock; Victor Rowland Lovelock,+; E Loveridge; Edward Loveridge,+
S Loveridge; Thomas Loveridge,+; Ernest Edward George Lovesey; F I Lovibond
W J Low; Arthur Lowe; Ernest Lowe; Herbert Lowe; Wilfred J Loff; Ernest
Lucas; J Lucas; T H Lucas,+; W J Lugg,+; Joseph J Luse; Frederick Luckman
Reginald Lumkin; Arthur George Lusty; Charles Lusty; Edward Johnathan Lusty
George Thomas Lusty; Herbert Lydiard; Alfred Lye; Charles E Lye; Henry Ernest
Lyne; George Lyne; Norman Lynes,+; Henry Thomas Lynn,+;

Thomas William Mabley; Alfred Charles Mabberley; Arthur Reginald Mabberley
Frank Mabberley; Henry Mabberley,+; James Edward Mackman; Charles Stuart
Macpherson (Became Mayor of Swindon 1944); George T Macpherson
John Macpherson; Thomas Henry Madden; Ronald Kirkpatrick Macqillvray,+
D Mahoney; Walter Maisey,+; Alfred Edward Major; E J Major; Harold Major
William George Major; C Malin; Charles Malin,+; Frank Malken; William John
Manfield; Frederick Manly; Bertrand Manners,+; Edward C Manners; Frederick
James Manners,+; Herbert F Manners; William Frederick George Manners,+
Arthur Thomas Manning; Edward William Manning (Dvr 21st Dorset Bty RFA
Moredon); John Thomas Manning,+; Alfred Mannings,+; Frank Mant,+; Henry
George Mant; Charles Henry Mantell; J Mantell; Ernest Edward Manton
Charles Mansbridge; Thomas William Mansfield; Edgar Mapstone; James Albert
March; Alfred Marchant,+; Arthur Ernest Marchant,+; Frederick G Margetts
C Marks,+; Frederick C Marks; Robert George Marks; Thomas J Marks; William
Thomas Marks; Frederick T Marley; Arthur J Marsh; Charles J Marsh; Eric
Marsh; Frederick Marsh; Harry Marsh; Henry William Marsh; Jesse Lewellyn
Marsh,+; John Marsh; Lemuel Enos Marsh,+; William John Marsh; William
Thomas Marsh; Arthur Marshall,+; Frederick E Marshall; Wilfred H Marshall
T W Marshall,+; Thomas O Marshman; Edgar Marston,+; Albert R Martin
Arthur Martin; Arthur A Martin; E Martin; Frank Martin; Frederick Martin,+
Frank Clewley Martin,+; Herbert A Martin; Lesley Frenk Martin,+; Ralph F
Martin; Reginald J Martin; Tom Martin,+; W H Martin; William Martin
William D Martin; W F Martin,+; William Henry Martin; W J Martin +; Gaetano

Masetto; Ernest Nelson Maskell,+; Francis H Maskell; James A Maskelyne; William Maskelyne; H Maslen; A Maslin; Thomas Henry Maslin,+; Albert Edward Mason; Arthur Mason,+; Bert A Mason; Bert E Mason; Harold F Mason; Henry J Mason; John William Mason; Dr P Mason; A E Massey; Wilfred Raymond Massey; A T Matthews; Albert Victor Matthews; Arthur R Matthews; Charles James Matthews; Edmond J Matthews; Ernest R Matthews; Frank Matthews; G W Matthews; George L E Matthews; George O Matthews; George Sidney Matthews; Harold James Matthews,+; Harold Reginald Matthews; Henry O Matthews; Harold W Matthews; John Matthews; James Matthews; John Edgar Matthews,+; James Edward Matthews; John F Matthews; Jacob Ernest Matthews,+; Leslie Henry Matthews; P Matthews; Stanley Welcome Matthews,+; Trevor C J Matthews; Victor Rowland Matthews; Walter Matthews ,+; Walter Henry Matthews; William E Matthews; William J Matthews; William Matthews; George Mattingly; George E J Mattingly; Frederick Ernest Mattock,+; Arthur Henry Maunder; George C Maunders; W L Mawer; Arthur E May; Arthur G May; Douglas G May; Ernest May; Harold May; Johnathan S May; Percy H May; William R May; Vernon J Maybury; Sidney Ernest Mayell; William John Mayell; George Henry Maynard; Thomas Alec Maynard; Thomas C Mayo; Walter C Mayo; William Albert Mayo (Wilts Regt); Cecil F Mazzoleni; James H Mazey; Joseph McCarthy; John McCarthy; Johnathan F McCarthy; Matthew McCue; A Mc Dougal,+; Daniel McGovern; Richard T McGrath; William Arthur Mc Grath,+; George Mc Ilvride,+; Alexander McKay,+; Matthew McLean; Johnathan Henry McLellan; W L McLoughlin; George Mc Nally,+; Sidney B McNally; William Thomas McNally; C Mead; Leonard F Mead; William George Mead; A E Meader; William Henry Meader; Albert Edward Mears; George N Mears,+; Harold Medhurst; G E Mees; John Melhuish; Percival Mellon ,+; Reginald William Menham,+; Sidney Merchant,+; H J Merrett,+; Alfred J Messenger; George Frederick Messenger; Joseph William Messenger; Charles Henry Metcalfe; Albert Middleton; Hubert Midwinter; Arthur M Mildenhall; Cecil John Mildenhall,+; Walter Mildenhall; Alfred Miles; Albert Johnathan Miles; Arthur Bertie Miles,+; Christopher Miles; Charles Albert Miles,+; Charles D Miles; Ernest Miles; Edward Albert Miles; Frederick Edmond Miles (Coldstream Guards); Frederick Henry Miles,+; F V Miles; Harold Miles; Humphrey J Miles; Joseph Miles; R E H Miles,+; William Miles; Ernest W Millard; Reginald H Millard; Albert Miller; E Miller; Herbert Edward Bowen Miller,+; Henry John Gardner Miller,+; R Miller; Sidney James Millet; Thomas Geoffrey Millin,+; William Richard Millin,+; Arthur William Mills,+; Arthur S Mills; Albert Mills; Edward George Mills,+; Frederick Mills (RE); Henry Mills,+; Harry George Mills,+; Sidney John Mills,+; Victor Mills; Albert Milsom; Ernest Milsom; Frederick G Milsom; Samual J Milton; Charles Minchin; Thomas H Minchin; J Minett,+; Alexander B Minto; Archie J Minto; William H L Minto; Frederick Edward Minty; George Mitchell; H C Mitchell; James Frederick Mitchell; S W Mitchell; Thomas Edgar Mitchell; Edwin L Mittens; Ernest Charles Mobey; F R Mobey; Francis Richard Mobey,+; Lewis Richard Mockridge; William Henry Modley; Ernest Johnathan Money; H Monks; K Monks; William Joseph Moody,+; William George Moody; Alfred Moore; Francis George Moore,+; George Ernest Moore,+; Henry Moore; Henry George Moore; H Moore; Joseph Moore; L F Moore,+; Thomas Moore; T H Moore; William Henry Walker Moore,+; Samual Frederick John Moon; Frederick Charles Moorman; Patrick Moran; Thomas Moran,+; L R Moreman; Reginald Percy Edgar Moreman,+; Wilfred B Moreman; W H Moreman,+; Alfred Charles Morgan,+; Alfred John Morgan; Clarence W Morgan; Francis James William Morgan,+; Frederick John Morgan,+; Henry Edward Morgan,+; Victor Johnathan F Morgan; Ralph Morkett; Charles V Morris,+; Frederick Morris; Harry Morris; Johnathan Charles Morris; James Edward Morris; L Morris; Sidney Morris,+; S R Morris,+; Septimus Summers Morris,+; Walter Gilbert Morris,+; W T Morris,+; Andrew W J Morrison; Albert Arthur Morse; Albert James Morse,+; Cecil Morse; Charles William Morse;

Ewart Morse;   Edwin Morse;   Ernest William George Morse;   Frank Morse,+;
Frederick Mark Morse;   G Morse,+;   Henry Jacob Morse MM;   John Morse,+;
Jesse Morse;   Percy Lapper Morse,+;   Ralph Raymond Morse;   Richard Hun
Dennis Morse,+;   Sidney Morse;   Sidney Frederick Morse;   Thomas Morse,+
W Morse;   William Charles Morse (11085 Wilts Regt);   A H Mosely;   A E W Moses
Bert T Moses;   Alfred Sidney Moss;   James Moss,+;   Thomas Alfred Moss;   William
Moss;   R H Mortimer;   William Mortimer;   Edward Johnathan Morton;   Samua
Moulding;   Percy Moulder;   F Mountjoy;   G Mountjoy;   James Mountjoy;   Percy
Moxey;   Edward Johnathan Mudge;   H N Mugford,+;   Ernest Mullarney,+
Albert Edward Mulcock;   George James Mulcock;   Thomas Mullins;   Alfred James
Mullis;   William Johnathan Mullis;   Christopher Mulraney;   G G Mulraney
Johnathan Mulraney;   Henry F C Munday;   A M Mundy;   Albert H Mundy;   Alfred
James Mundy;   George B Mundy;   Lloyd Alexander Munro;   James W T Murrel
Wilfred Henry Murphy;   Donald William Musetano;   S H J Musty;   Charles A L
Mutton;   Ernest Granville Mutton,+;   Edwin George Myall Order of St George 4th
Class (Russia),+;   C Myers;

A Nash;   Charles E Nash,+;   Edgar T Nash;   Francis Henry Nash;   George William
Frederick Nash,+;   Harold G Nash;   Percy G Nash;   Percy William Nash;   S G Nash
Walter William Nash;   William Nash;   Dennis John Neabard;   Arthur T Neal
Joseph C Neal;   William F Neale;   William George Neale,+;   F Neate;   G C Nei
Herbert Harold Nethercot,+;   Reginald Nethercot;   Richard Nethercot;   William
Neeves;   Charles E Neville,+;   Reginald Neville;   William C Neville;   A J New
Bertram Henry Charles New,+;   Frederick G New;   Frederick W New;   H T New
Raymond New;   Thomas New;   Thomas Henry New;   William Charles New,+
Albert Newman;   Bennett Newman,+;   E Newman;   Ernest E Newman
F W Newman,+;   Frank Newman,+;   Harold V Newman;   Ivor G Newman
H Newman;   James Newman;   James W Newman;   John Newman,+;   L
Newman;   Norman T Newman;   Robert Newman;   Sidney A Newman;   Victo
Reuben Newman,+;   Walter J Newman;   Wilfred Newman;   Percy J Newport
Albert Edward Newton,+;   A H Niblett;   C W Niblett;   Edgar John Nicholas,+
John Nicholas,+;   Alfred Nicholls;   Ben Nicholls;   David Nicholls;   Frank Nicholls
Jesse Nicholls;   Rowland Nicholls;   Ernest Nichols;   William E Nichols,+;   Ernes
Nippress;   Frank Nippress,+;   George Nippress;   Michael J Nixon;   Philip H Noad
C J Noble;   E L D Noble,+;   I H Noble;   S Nock;   Edgar John Norgrove,+;   Henr
A Norman;   C Norris;   Henry V Norris;   Henry Norris;   J Norris,+;   Lawrence
Norris;   Lewis Norris;   R S Norris;   Walter J Norris;   William A Norris;   Albert E
North;   Arthur Sydney North,+;   Percy George North (139 Cricklade Road);   Rober
W Northover;   Samual J Northway;   Edgar George Norton,+;   W O Norton;   James
H Notley;   Vernon George Nott,+;   Bernard W Nunn;   William Charles Nunney
Frederick J Nurden;   W J Nurden,+;   Claude Nutbeam;   Frederick C Nutbeam
E Nutman;

John Park Oak,+;   C Oakford;   Leonard Oaks,+;   Aeneas O'Brien;   D O'Brien,+
Felix O'Brien;   Harold Frederick O'Brien,+;   Dennis G O'Callaghan;   Charles M
Ockwell;   Ernest J Ockwell;   E Ockwell;   Johnathan Ockwell;   L F F Ockwell
R T Okwell,+;   Sidney Ockwell;   William George Ockwell;   Daniel James
O'Connell,+;   Charles O'Connor;   E C Odey;   John Henry Odey,+;   W R Odey
William Ody;   Reginald O'Keefe;   Timothy O'Keefe,+;   E T Oldrewe;   J R T O'Neil
L H O'Neil;   T J O'Neil;   Enoch Onions;   Charles Oram;   F Oram,+;   P T Oram
E F R Orpwood;   A E Orum;   Charles Orum;   Christopher Orum;   George Henry
Osborn,+;   H L Osborn;   H V Osborn;   J W Osborn;   W J Osborn;   T O'Shea
R H Osman   H G Ostler;   E Ovens;   F S Ovens;   H J Ovens;   S H Ovens;   H
Owens;   F Oxborrow;   Arthur Oxley (AOC);   H P Oxley;

Clemence J Packer;   Edward George Packer,+;   Frederick W Packer;   Herber
Joseph Packer;   Joseph Packer,+;   John Packer,+;   Joseph George Packe
27 Summers Street);   M I Packer;   Thomas Packer;   William M Packer +

Frederick Charles Packford (9 Omdurman Street);   Norman Percy Packford (9 Omdurman Street);   William George Padget ,+;   Alfred Padgett;   John Joseph Padgett (29 Ferndale Road);   Albert Edward Page;   Frank Page;   Frederick James Page,+;   Harry Page;   Henry Stephen Page;   Sidney Charles Page;   Sidney Arthur Page;   Thomas William Page;   V L Page;   William John Page,+;   Ernest John Paget ,+;   M R Paget,+;   Joseph Pagett;   George Arthur Paginton,+;   W J Paginton (42 Cricklade Street);   Albert Painter;   Albert Johnathan Painter (Chapel Street);   Albert William Painter,+;   Arthur William Painter;   C H Painter;   Edward George Painter;   Ernest William Painter;   Edwin C Painter;   Frederick C Painter;   G Painter , +;   Henry Edward Painter;   H Painter;   John Painter;   Mervyn Painter;   R Painter;   Thomas Painter;   William Edward Painter,+;   J E Paintin,+;   Albert Edward Paisley;   Arthur William Paisey;   Oscar Henry Pakeman MM;   Percy Palfrey;   lbert Edward Palmer;   Arthur Gilbert Palmer,+;   A W Palmer;   Frederick Hazel Palmer;   James Edward Palmer;   Richard Thomas Palmer;   Richard Thomas Palmer ,+;   Robert J A Palmer;   William Palmer;   Walter William Palmer,+;   Arthur Pane; Alfred John Pannell,+;   Alfred James Pantoll,+;   Frederick Panting;   James Parbutt; Frederick George Parfitt;   H M Parfitt;   Frederick Arthur Parker;   Rev G W Parker; John Parker;   George Clemence Parkinson;   Harold Thomas Parratt;   George William Parrish (99 Albion Street);   Simon George Parrott,+;   A E Parry;   J Parry; George Thomas Parsonage;   Ernest Charles Parsons,+;   Frank Parsons,+;   Robert E V Parsons;   Stephen Charles Parsons;   William Parsons;   F E Part,+;   Thomas Parton,+;   Ernest Partridge;   Percy Partridge;   Ralph Allen Partridge,+;   Joseph Douglas Partington;   Cyril J Paterson;   Francis Paterson;   Gordon Paterson; Henry James Patterson;   George L Patton;   Ralph N Patton;   Frederick J Paulding (51 Winifred Street);   Charles T Paul;   Frederick George Paul MM;   Arthur Payne; Arthur Robert Payne;   Edwin P Payne;   Frank Payne;   Frederick George Payne,+; G F Payne;   John Henry Payne;   William Payne;   Albert Edward Payntor,+;   Alfred Peake;   Andrew H Peaple;   H Peaple;   Joseph E Pearson;   Thomas Pearson; Albert Pearce;   A C Pearce,+;   Albert Edward Pearce;   Alfred James Pearce,+; Alexander S Pearce;   B Pearce;   Cyril A Pearce;   Edward Pearce;   Edward Frederick Pearce;   Frederick Henry Pearce;   Frederick James Pearce;   F S Pearce,+;   George Ewart Pearce,+;   John Andrew Pearce;   Joseph Edward Pearce;   Lionel H Pearce; Percy Johnathan Pearce;   Reginald Pearce;   Thomas I Pearce;   Victor Pearce; William James Pearce;   William S Pearce;   William Pearse,+;   Charles G Peart; Horace George Peart,+;   Henry John Peart;   Joseph John Peart,+;   William G Peart; George Peck (102 Linsdale Street);   Alfred Leslie King Pedder,+;   Leonard Thomas Pegler;   Percy John Pegler,+;   A J Pelling;   William J Pelly;   Thomas Frederick Pengilly;   A V Pennycook;   Owen Cyril People,+;   Albert W Pepler;   John K Perham MM (RFA);   H Perham (RFC);   Albert H Perkins;   Joseph Johnathan Perrett; William Perrett;   Francis H R Perry;   Frederick Charles Perry;   Frederick G Perry DCM;   Frederick S Perry;   John Lewis Perry;   Thomas Henry Perry,+;   Alfred Peter; Wallace William Petters;   Edward Henry William Pettiford,+;   Harry Pewsey; George James Peyton;   Johnathan W Phelps (Cpt 4th Wilts);   Thomas C Phelps; Charles Phillimore,+;   Alfred C Phillips;   Arthur Henry Phillips,+;   Elton J Phillips; Ernest Cecil Phillips;   Ernest Johnathan Phillips;   George Nigel Victor Phillips,+; George P Phillips;   Henry James Phillips;   John Phillips;   Johnathan Gordon Phillips;   Richard Phillips;   Sidney Richard Phillips,+;   William Edward Phillips; Johnathan H Philp;   William S Philpott;   Arthur Charles Pickering;   Frederick F W Pickering;   N S J Pickering;   V G A Pickering,+;   Robert William Pickernell,+; Arthur Ernest Pickett;   Alfred Reginald Pickett;   E H Pickett;   Hubert William Pickett;   John Pickett;   William Edward Pickett,+;   L Pickford;   Edward J Picton; Tom Pictor,+;   W E Pictor;   Herbert F Pidgeon;   George Harold Pidgeon,+;   Orbrey W Pierce;   William Harold Piff MM;   Edward Piggott;   George Piggott;   Charles Pike,+;   Cecil Hurbert Pike;   E A Pike;   Edgar Frank Pike,+;   E J Pike;   John Pike ,+;   William J C Pike (RE Wilts Fortress Engineers);   Richard Johnathan Pile;   Percy Herbert Pill,+;   Ernest H Pillinger;   A G Pilot;   Ernest E Pilot;   W E Pilot;   Arthur James Pincott;   Ralph Pincott;   Frederick Bertram Pinfield,+;   Arthur Henry

Pinnegar; Arthur Pinnegar; P Pinnigar; William E Pithouse; Harold J Pitt;
Lancelot Pitt; William James Pitt,+; Ernest Henry Pitman,+; Horace Raymond
Plaister; A Plaister MM; Arthur Leslie Platt; Gordon R Platt; Percy Harold Platt;
Stanley C Platt; Stanley H Platt; William Johnathan Platt; George W Plenty;
E Plimley; Arthur Reginald Plomer; Albert T Plowman; James J Plumb (RE);
E Plumley; F Plyer; George E Poake; A E Poletti (56 Kingshill); Gerald Maurice
Ponsonby,+; AT Pontin; Arthur A Ponting; A H Ponting; Albert James Ponting
,+; Alfred Joseph Ponting; Charles R Ponting,+; Edwin C Ponting (RE); Edwin
Stanley Ponting,+; Henry Johnathan Ponting; Henry William Ponting MID (Sgt
Wilts Fortress Engineers); James Ponting; Leonard George Ponting; Reginald
Arthur Ponting,+; Robert Ponting; Sidney Henry Ponting; Walter Ponting;
William Johnathan Ponting; Frank Pooke; Albert Edward Poole; Albert Theobald
Poole; Harold T Poole; Harry James Poole; James Frederick Poole; Thomas
Poole,+; William Poole,+; Charles Pope; Alick Porter; Albert Edward Porter;
Arthur John Porter,+; Ernest Henry Porter; Ernest George Porter; Frank Porter
,+; George Henry Porter; Hubert G Porter; Oliver W Porter; Reginald H Porter;

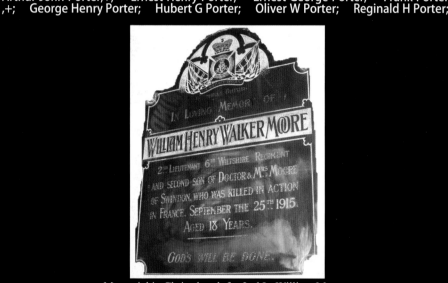

Memorial in Christchurch for 2nd Lt William Moore

Stanley E Porter; Thomas Edgar Porter,+; Richard Portlock; Morton Ewart
Postlethwaite,+; Maurice A Potbury; John Potter,+; Steven Potter; Robert
Johnathan Poulton; Edgar W Pounds; Arthur Henry Powell,+; Ernest W Powell;
Reginald Powell; W J Powell; Charles William Powers; Charles William Poynter;
Robert Poynter; Wallace Frederick Poynter; William George Poynter; Norman
Conway Prangley,+; Ernest Pratt,+; Frederick Thomas Pratt; Johnathan Stephen
Pratt; Arthur Benjamin Preater,+; Charles Lewis Preater,+; Herbert Frederick
Preater,+; William Henry Press,+; Albert Edgar Preston,+; J Preston; William
Alfred Preston; Albert William C Price; Albert Edward Price; Frederick William
Price; Harry Price; James Price,+; John Price,+; Richard Johnathan Price;
Richard George Price; Reynallt Price; William Price,+; William Johnathan Price;
William S Price; Christopher J Prictor; Henry James Priddle,+; Christopher
George Prince; G Prince; Issac Johnathan Prince; George Harry Prior,+; Alfred
F Probets; F Probets; Herbert Probets; J Probets; T Probets; W Probets,+;
Thomas Proberts,+; F Proffitt; W B Prosser; Hedly A K Proudler; H G Provis;
Nelson J Provis,+; William Prowton; Henry Pryce; Henry E V Pryor; Arthur
Puffet; Harry Macock Puffet,+; Sidney Puffet; Walter G Puffet; William Puffet;

Percy G Pugh; Percy William Pullen,+; Thomas Pullen; Ernest John Purbrick (ERA Royal Navy. 114 Beatrice St); Thomas Purbrick (Royal Navy. 114 Beatrice St); E Purdue; Arthur William Purnell; Frederick G Purnell (Wilts Fortress Engineers); William C Purnell; Johnathan Henry Puzey; Edward C Pymm (141 Broad Street);

A Quarrell; H Quest; Edwin R Quick; Charles Henry Racey; Edward James Radbourne; P Radmore; Albert Henry Radway; William Lawrence Raison,+; Sidney Ralph; Alfred J H Rand; Alfred Randall; Charles Henry Portlock Randall,+; Edward J Randall; Frederick Randell; Reginald Randell; Walter E Randell; W Rashley; James William Ratcliffe; Francis Henry Rawlings,+; James Rawlings,+; Arthur Edward Read,+; W C Rawlings; Frederick Rawlinson; Harold Rayer; Alfred S Razey; G E Razey; William Charles Razey; Arthur Ernest Read; George William Read; Harry Read; Henry Read; Thomas Read; Walter George Read; William Edward Read; William John Read; George Charles Reason; William F Reason; J A Rebbeck; W T Rebbeck; George William Redman; Henry John Redman; David C Reed; E Reed; Sydney George Herbert Reed,+; Albert Charles Rees,+; Harold M Rees; William James Rees; H Reeson; V Reeson; C E Reeves; Ernest Walter Reeves; Ernest Thomas Reeves; Frederick James Reeves,+; George Reeves; Henry Reeves; James Reeves; Johnathan Reeves; Reginald G Reeves; R H Reeves,+; William Reeves; William Charles Reeves; W H Reeves; Raymond G Rendel; Stanley E Rendell; Albert Retter; Robert R Retter; Vernon Melville Reveley,+; Albert Reynolds; Ernest Harold Reynolds; G W Reynolds; Hubert Harry Reynolds,+; William Arthur Reynolds,+; W A Reynolds; Henry Rennison; Sidney Rhymes,+; Albert Harold Rice; Eric T Rice; Henry Rice; Stanley Rice; W J Rice; John Benjamin Rich; Benjamin J Richards; Clifford John Richards; George V Richards (26 Newhall Street); Henry James Richards; Percy Stanley Richards; Thomas E Richards; William Henry Richards; Edward Richardson; Henry Richardson; George Richens,+; Henry Richens; Jack W Richens; Frederick Albert Richens; Sidney Joseph Richens; Thomas Richens; William E Richens; William Thomas Richens; Archibald David Richman,+; Alfred George Richman,+; Harold George Richmond; Richard R Ricketts; Percy Thomas Ricketts,+; F J Ricks; Jack Ricks; John William Ricks; Percy Riddall; Edward Henry Rigden; Charles Herbert Righton,+; Edward J Riley; Albert Edward Rivers; Arthur Reginald Rivers; Charles Rivers; Ernest Abraham Rivers; William Rivers,+; Walter John Rixon,+; Charles Ernest Roach; A H Robbins; David Robbins,+; Henry Robbins,+; William J Robbins; Samual Ernest Robbins; A Roberts; Albert Ernest Roberts; Alfred L Roberts; Arthur James Roberts; A J Roberts; C L Roberts; Charles William Henry Roberts,+; Clifford J S Roberts; Even L Roberts; F F Roberts,+; George Reece Roberts; George Roberts; Harold David Roberts; Henry Charles Roberts (Sgt Major); J A Roberts; John F C Roberts; L Roberts; W N Roberts; Walter R Roberts; Albert Robertson; Frank Aston Robertson,+; E W Robie; Edward R Robins; Frank Robins; Harold Richard Robins,+; John Robins; Walter Henry Robins; William E Robins; William Henry Robins; Albert Joseph Robinson; A M C Robinson; F Robinson MSM,+; F Robinson MM; Frederick Isaac Robinson,+; Frederick Stephen Robinson,+; Henry George Robinson; J Robinson; Norman F Robinson; Stephen Robinson; T Robinson; T H J Robinson; William Charles Robinson; William Henry Robinson; William Robinson; W J Robinson,+; R Robson; William Tom Rodbourne ,+; H Rochester; H C Rodda MC Medaille Militaire (Lt Wilts Fortress Engineers); L Roe,+; T F Roe,+; Charles Harold Rogers; Edward Rogers; Herbert Rogers; J Rogers; Laurence E Rogers; Lewis Rogers; Thomas S Rogers; W J Rogers; Sidney Rolfe; Thomas Rolfe; Albert Ernest Rolls; A G Romans; F R Rootes; Leonard Victor Roots,+; Leonard W H Roper; Ralph W Rosby; Albert Charles Rose; Edward Victor Rose,+; Francis George Rose; Frederick William Rose; George T Rose; Henry John Rose; Nathan Rose; P A Rose; Edward G Rouse; G S Rouse; John Thomas Rouse; Thomas D Row; (25 Goddard Avenue); Arthur Herbert Rowles MM,+; John Rowse; Arthur

Rowland; L H Thomas Rowland,+; John D Rowland; S H Rowland; Thomas J Rowland; Herbert George Ruddle,+; J Ruddle; Henry C Rudman; William F Rudman; Walter J Rudman; Frederick Edward Rumble; Leonard Rumble; William Edward Rumble; Albert Rummery; Henry Rumming; Phillip S Rushan; George Edward Russ,+; Frederick Russell; F E Russell (Canadian Forces – Born Haydon Wick); Frank Edward Russell MID,+; Howard Russell; James Russell; James Thomas Russell; William Edward Russell; W G Russell,+; William James Russell; William Russell; William Albert Rymills;

George Sadler; W Sadler,+; W G N Sadler; William George Sadler; Thomas Saddler; T W Sage (6 Westcott Place); James Sainsbury; Thomas Sainsbury; William Thomas Sainsbury; H F Salter; Cyril M Salvage; L H Sanderman; Clifford W Sanders; David Sanders,+; George Sanders; A O Sandle; Wallace Sansom; Albert John Sansum,+; Frederick Charles Sansum,+; Frederick C Sarahs; George H Sarahs; John Edward Sarahs; George Samworth; Percy Samworth; A W Saunders; Anthony Saunders; Charles William Saunders; E F Saunders; Ernest Saunders,+; E A Saunders,+; J G Saunders; J O Saunders; Richard Saunders; Sanuel Saunders,+; Sidney George Saunders; William James Saunders; Percy Sidney Saville DSM; Ben Saw; George Sawford; Hugh Sawtell (13 Hunt Street); A J Sawyer; A E Sawyer; Charlie Sawyer; George Francis Sawyer,+; William Thomas Sawyer; Sidney James Scadding; Maurice Frederick Scammell,+; Sidney Harold Scammell,+; S Scarlett; B F Schmitz; Henry Schoerthal; Stanley William Schofield,+; S J Schorn; George W Schulze; A G Scott DCM; Fred James Scott; George William Scott; John Andrew Scott; Walter Scott,+; William Scott; William J L Scott; Edward J Scrivens; William Scrivens; William Samuel Scruby,+; Albert Scull,+; James Thomas Scull,+; Percy Francis Scull,+; Reginald Wakefield Scull,+; Bert Scutts; Charles Scutts; E W Scutts; Henry Scutts; Henry George Scutts; Richard Scutts; William Scutts; Edwin Robert Seager,+; Henry James Seager,+; James Seager; John Seager,+; Percy Seager,+; Thomas R Seager; John Sealey,+; Stephen Sealey; Harold D Seaman; John Seddon; Charles Frederick Sedgwick,+; Joseph Thomas Sedgwick; Arthur Henry Selby,+; Frederick B Selby; George A Selby; William J Selby; Ashley William Sellars,+; Charles Frederick Selman,+; Arthur Sellwood; Arthur James Sellwood; William Joseph Henry Sellwood,+; Charles Selman; George Selman; Albert William Selwood; Edward T Selwood; Frederick C Selwood; Frederick R G Selwood; Herbert William Selwood; Henry Selwood; John Robert Selwood,+; William Henry Selwood; William Serridge; D W H Sexton; George Henry Sexton,+; John Seymour; Reginald George Shachel; Percy S Shackell; A Shadwell; Edgar William Shail; Robert G Shail; Albert E Shakespeare; Walter Frank Shakespeare,+; Henry Harold Shallcroft; William George Shaldon,+; N Shalwell; A E Sharland; Frederick George Sharland; Henry Sharland (L/cpl Wilts Fortress Engineers); Joseph Henry Sharland,+; William J Sharland; Albert William Sharman; F R Sharman; Sydney Sharman; William Sharman; Alfred Sharp; Charles Henry Sharp; George A Sharpe; William G Sharpe; William Henry Sharpe; Charles Sharpes,+; W J Sharpes (L/cpl D Coy 2nd Wilts); James Sharps MM,+; George Edward Shaylor,+; Alfred Charles Shaw; Jack E Shaw; Ernest John Sheldon; Frederick George Sheldon; Frederick Granville Sheldon; Henry J Sheldon; Stanley H Sheffield; Archibald Walter Sheppard,+; Ashley Francis Sheppard; Bert Sheppard; E Sheppard; Frederick Sheppard; Henry Sheppard; Harold Sheppard; L A F Sheppard; Percy John Sheppard,+; Robert H Sheppard; Samual Charles Sheppard; S E Sheppard; Thomas Albert Sheppard; William Charles Sheppard; Walter W N Sheppard; Ernest William Shergold; Frederick D W Shergold (RE); Herbert James Shergold; Herbert Stanley Shergold (ASC); Reginald Donald Shergold,+; Thomas A Shergold (ASC); Henry Bert Sherman,+; William E Sherman; William H Sherman; Alfred Sherwood,+; Arthur James Sherwood; T Sherwood; Walter Sherwood; D H Sheward; Henry Shewry; William Shewry; Ernest Shipner; Edward Shipton

Frances William Shipton;   John Charles Shipway;   Walter Thomas Shipway;
Arthur Shirney;   Charles Shittrall;   E W Shorrock;   William Shorten;   Ernest W
Shurgold;   Herbert J Shurgold;   Arthur Shurmer;   Henry Shurmer,+;   Henry
Albert Shurmer;   Thomas Shute,+;   William Shuttlewood;   R E Silk;   Herbert
Sillett;   William Silto;   C Simmonds;   William Abner Simmonds,+;   William
Simmons;   F H Simons;   Philip Simons;   Thomas H Simons;   Charles Henry

Simkins,+;   Enos William Simpkins;   Frederick Albert Simkins,+;   George Henry
Simpkins;   Ernest H Simpkins;   George Henry Simpkins;   George Simpkins;
G J Simpkins;   G W Simpkins;   Harry C Simpkins;   M Simpkins;
Sidney T Simpkins;   W A Simpkins;   Arthur Sims MM,+;   Charles Sims;
D W Sims;   David E Sims;   E J V Sims;   James William Sims,+;   L Sims;   W G Sims;
A Sinclair;   L C Singer;   William Harold Singer,+;   James E Single;   Sidney A
Sinnett,+;   Edwin J Sinnister;   Arthur James Skane;   Edward George Skeates;
Samual A Skeates;   Thomas Skeates;   Arthur Skinner;   E H Skinner;   G E Skinner;
Stuart Edward Skinner;   William Robert Skinner,+;   Arthur George Skull;   Henry
Edward Skull;   Stanley Skull;   Hubert James Skyrme,+;   C E Slade;   F Slade,+;
James William Slade;   John Henry Bowman Slade,+;   Martin J Slade (RE);   William
A Slade;   A J Slater;   Frederick Conway Slater,+;   George Slater;   Percy A Slatter;
Charles Sleeman;   E S Slempson;   Lemuel Sly,+;   Herbert Henry Small,+;
A J A Smart;   Albert Edwin Smart;   Charles Smart;   Ernest George Smart;   Herbert
Charles Smart;   Henry James Smart;   Hubert Sidney Smart;   William Elijah Smart
,+;   William James Smart;   Archibald Smith,+;   Arthur William Smith;   Albert
E Smith;   Arthur Laurence Smith;   Alex William Smith;   Albert Smith;   Alfred
Edward Smith;   Arthur Smith;   Austin George Smith;   Alfred Smith;   Albert Henry
Smith;   Albert Edward W Smith;   Arthur Sidney Alfred Smith,+;   Arthur William
Smith;   Albert Charles Smith;   Bertie Smith;   Charles C Smith;   Charles Henry
Smith;   Cyril Charles Bosworth Smith,+;   David Smith,+;   E A Smith;   E H Smith;
Edward J Smith;   Edward Frederick Smith;   Ernest A M L Smith;   F Smith;   Francis
William Smith,+;   Frank Smith,+;   Frederick Charles Smith,+;   Frederick William
Smith,+;   George Alfred Smith,+;   G T D Smith;   G V Smith (RFC);   George
Frances Smith;   George Charles Smith;   George Cornelius Smith;   Gilbert Charles
Smith;   George James Smith,+;   George John Smith,+;   George Smith;   Harold
Smith,+;   Henry James Smith;   Henri Smith;   Horace Smith (York Road);   Herbert
Frederick Smith;   Herbert Walter Smith;   Herbert A T Smith;   Herbert Issac Smith;
Henry John Smith;   H Smith;   John Smith;   Jesse Smith;   John Smith,+;   John
Smith,+;   John Smith,+;   Joseph Smith,+;   P E K Smith,+;   Percy Sidney Smith;
Raymond Reginald Smith,+;   Robert John Smith;   Ralph Smith;   Reginald Albert
Smith;   S C Smith,+;   Sydney H Smith;   Sidney Walter Smith,+;   Sidney Rowland
Smith,+;   Stanley G Smith;   Samual N Smith;   T F Smith;   Thomas M Smith;

W Smith; W A Smith (RFA); Walter G Smith; Walter Thomas Smith; Walter S Smith; William Henry Smith; William P Smith; William Robert Edward Smith; William John Smith; William Charles Smith; W H Smith; William James Smith; William George J Smith; A G H Smithson; John William Smithson; Henry James Smoker,+; Robert Smythe; William Richard Snelgrove; H Snell; Ben Charles Snook; Charles Albert Snook; George Frederick Snook; James Henry Snook; Sidney Snook; Charles William Snowden,+; P W Sobey; William Edward Sollis; B J Soloman; Stanley B Solven; Austin Somers; Frank Souerbutts; Arthur Soul; William Frederick Soul; James Southall; Arthur Southam; Albert James Southby; F G Southern; Harry A Southwell,+; C W Spackman; Ernest C Spackman; George Spackman; H Spackman; John Walter Spackman; Sidney Frederick Spackman; T Spackman; Walter John Spackman; William Spackman; William Edward Spackman,+; William Peter Spackman; Charles R Sparkes; Frederick Charles Sparkes; Frederick William Sparrow; Edwin George Speake; Harold Victor Speake,+; Albert Victor Speck; George Fred Speck,+; Herbert Speck; H Speed; A T Speller; A Spicer; Herbert Thomas Spicer; Charles H Spong; W Spong; Bertram Byron; Spreadbury,+; F F Spreadbury; R R Spreadbury; Thomas William Springford; Cecil H Spruce; Ernest P Spurlock MM (RE); Herbert J Spurlock; W Spry; Frederick Robert Squire,+; Ernest Frederick Stacey; Edward Tom Stacey,+; Frank Stacey; Mark Stacey; Stephen Charles Stacey,+; A Stafford; Edward Ernest Stafford; Edwin E Stafford; George Stafford,+; Frederick J Stagg; V H Stagg; W F Stagg; Walter Staite,+; Francis Stallard,+; Robert George Stallard; William Edward Stallard,+; William George Stanaway; V Stanier; Alexander Standish; Irvin Standish; F E Stanley; H G Stanley; H W Stanley; Oscar James Stanley,+; W C Stanley; Sidney Stapleford; Herbert Staples,+; Frederick R Steer; Frank Stephens,+; Frederick Stephens; Thomas Alfred Stephens; Thomas Stratton Stephens,+; W H F Stephens; George Stephenson (S/Mjr Princes Street); Alfred Stevens; Charles Stevens,+; Edward James Stevens,+; Frank Stevens; Francis E Stevens; George A Stevens; George W Stevens,+; Herbert Arthur Stevens,+; Henry Stevens (32 Jennings Street); Henry F Stevens; John Stevens; Norman Stevens; V Stevens; William A Stevens; William Frederick Stevens,+; Frederick Stevenson; Robert Stevenson; Eric Stinchcombe,+; Percy Charles Stokes; A H Stone; Charles Stone,+; E Stone; Frank Stone,+; George Stone; Herbert Stone; Herbert Henry Stone; Joseph Stone,+; J R Stone; Mark Stone; Rupert J Stone; W Stone; William Stone,+; William Ephrame Stone,+; S L Stow; Alfred George Strange; Augustus Strange,+; A W E Strange; Ernest Wilfred Strange; H P Strange; John A Strange,+; Reginald Charles J Strange; Rupert E Strange; Stanley Victor Strange; Thomas Strange,+; Walter George Strange; A G Statford; Alfred V Stratford; Charles Stratford; Frederick G Stratford; George William Stratford,+; William John Stratford; William Stratford William Frederick Stratford,+; William Henry Stratford,+; Ernest Stratton; Edward John Stratton,+; F G Stratton; E J Stratlow; W Street; Charles W J Streetly; H W T Streetly; Herbert George Strong; Charles Edward Stroud,+; Edward C Stroud; George H Stroud; William Bert Stroud,+; E F Stuart; Ernest John Sturgess,+; Edward A Sturgess; A Sturmy; H R Sturmy; John Edward Sturmy; Albert Ernest Styles; Albert Edward Henry Styles,+; C Styles; Patrick Styles; Ernest William Suddrick; Joseph Sullivan,+; R J Sully; Edgar Charles Summers,+; V Summers; Cyril Arthur Sutcliff; Gordon Eric Sutcliff; Richard N Sutcliff; Victor Sutcliff; Arthur Thomas Sutton; George Fred Sutton,+; James Sutton; J E Sutton; Jesse Frederick Sutton; Lewis M Sutton; Owen Sutton; Raymond James Sutton; S W Sutton; William Edward George Sutton,+; William Henry Sutton; Frederick Swallow; W Swan; Ernest George Swatton; Harry Swatton; P F Swatton; Dr R M Swinhoe (Chief GWR Doctor); W Sylvester; Harry Syrett MM,+;

E Talbot; Edward James Talbot; Leslie George Tamkin; Gilbert Tandy; Albert Tanner; Edward William Tanner; Fred Tanner,+; Henry Richard Tanner; Jesse

Tanner; William J Tanner.+; Percy Robert Neville Taphouse (RAF); Alfred Tanner ,+; Austin Tarrant; Harry Tarrant (4 Beckhampton Street); Herbert Edwin Tarrant; Herbert Cecil Tatnell; F Tatnell; Percy Taverner,+; Albert Ernest Taylor; Albert George Taylor; Albert V R Taylor; Alfred Taylor; Arthur Richard Taylor; Charles Henry Taylor; Clarence Taylor; Charles Stewart Taylor,+; Clifford Taylor; Coleridge David Beale Taylor,+; Edward John Taylor; Edwin Taylor; Ernest George Taylor; George Taylor,+; George Henry Green Taylor,+; Gilbert Taylor; Henry Taylor; Herbert William Taylor; Jack Taylor DCM MM; James Taylor; John Taylor; Reginald R Taylor; R E Taylor; Samual Taylor; Stanley D Taylor; Thomas Alfred Taylor; Victor R S Taylor; Walter Henry Taylor; William Henry Taylor William George John Taylor; W T B Taylor; Walter Lewis Taylor; Henry Tee; A W Telling; Bert Charles Telling,+; Edward Walton Telling,+; Ernest John Telling; Francis Edward Telling; Henry Frederick Telling; Victor Arthur Telling; S Temblett; T Temblett; David Charles Temple; Frederick Charles Temple; William Royston Temple; Frederick James Terry; Frederick W Terry; Wilfred Sidney Terry; Alfred Thatcher; H E H Thatcher; Reginald William Thatcher; S Thatcher; Thomas Rice Thatcher; William James Thatcher; Walter John Thatcher,+; William Thatcher; George William Theobald; Algernon Thomas; Atcherley Thomas; Charles Thomas; Dudley H Giles Thomas; Frederick Alfred Thomas,+; Frederick George Thomas; Gilbert William Thomas; Henry Thomas,+; Joseph Thomas; J E Thomas,+; J H Thomas; Robert Ernest Thomas; William E Thomas; William Frances Thomas; William Henry Thomas,+; Albert Edgar Thompson (RAF – Hawkins Street); Albert Edward Thompson; Charles Edward Thompson; Ernest Albert Thompson; Henry Thompson; William James Thompson; Albert R Thorley; Henry John Thornbury,+; William A Thornbury; Charles Aldridge Thorne DCM; Frederick Charles Thorne DCM + BAR. MID,+; James J Thorne; Arthur Thorpe; Charles Thorpe; Ernest Thorpe; Frederick George Thorpe; Harold Thorpe; William Thorpe; Ben Thrush,+; George Thrush ,+; Edward Thumurod; J Tillbury; William Mark Timbrell; Arthur Percy Tilley,+; Charles Tiltman,+; H Timms; Percy Leonard Timms,+; Stuart Pike Tindle (2nd Lt RHA); T Tindle; Percy L Tinker; Charles Reginald Tipper; Frank Titchener,+; Herbert Beezley Titchener.+; Percy John Titchener; Ernest F Titcomb; H Titcomb; John Titcomb; Albert George Titcombe; Albert Henry Titcombe; Arthur John Titcombe; E Titcombe; Frederick Titcombe; Frederick J Titcombe; George Thomas Titcombe; Henry Titcombe; Henry R J Titcombe; John Thomas Titcombe ,+; Joseph Cornelius Titcombe,+; Rupert Ernest Titcombe,+; Sydney F Titcombe; William Titcombe; Walter Charles Tombleson; A J L Tombs; Edward Richard Mark Tombs,+; H D S Tombs; R E Tombs; Ruford H C Tombs; Bernett Tomes; Christopher B Tomes; Frederick Charles Tomes; George B Tomes; Joseph B Tomes; Arthur Leonard Austin Tomlyn,+; Bram Tomkins; Edgar Tomkins; George Charles Tomkins; Montgomery F Tomkins; Stanley W Tomkins; Walter G Tomkinson; Frederick John Tompkins,+; George James Tompkins,+; Hugh Toner; Arthur Harold Toop,+; Samual E Topp; Victor R Topp; William J Topple; Leonard Henry Toombs; Charles Toomer (RE Apsley House, Bath Road); James P Toomer; Sidney Toomer (RFC Apsley House, Bath Road); William George Toose; Albert William Tovey; Archibald Arthur Tovey,+; Frederick Norman Tovey; Francis William Towell; A J Townsend; Charles Townsend,+; Charlie Townsend,+; Charles L Townsend; Cecil George Townsend; David Frederick Townsend; Ernest Arthur Townsend,+; E J Townsend; Frederick G Townsend; George Townsend MM; George Edward Townsend; George William Townsend; Henry Townsend; Henry John Townsend; Joseph Townsend; N Townsend; Reginald George Townsend,+; Sidney Herbert Townsend; Thomas William Townsend; William Townsend,+; Wilfred Townsend; Henry Trapnell; A E W Treherne (ASC); Thomas Trigg; Thomas A Trimmer; F A Trimmex; Henry Trollope; Walter A E Trollope; George Henry Trotman,+; P T E Trott (Colonel); A R Trueman; Arthur William Trueman; H Trueman; Henry G J Trueman; Montgomery G Trueman; William Trueman; William Charles Truman,+; William John Trueman; W G

Trueman; Arthur N Tuck; B Tuck; Frederick George Tuck,+; H W Tuck; Sidney W K Tuck; William Albert Tuck; William James Tuck; William John Tuck,+; Albert James Tucker; Alfred Henry Tucker; Charles William Tucker; Mervyn A E Tucker; Stanley William Tucker; Victor William Tucker; J Tuckey; Alfred Charles Tuckwell; Thomas Henry Tuckwell; Charles Edward Tudor – Jones,+; F T Tuffley; T Tugby,+; Joseph Mark Washington Tugwell,+; Percy T Tuley; Arthur E Tunley; Cyril C Tunley; Albert Edward Turner,+; Arthur George Turner; Charles Turner; Edward Turner; Frederick Turner; Frederick R Turner; George F Turner (23 Jennings Street); George J Turner; Henry James Turner; Stephen H Turner; Thomas H Turner MC; William Benjamin Turk; Herbert Thomas Turton,+; Walter Twining,+; Thomas Twitchell; John Robert Twyford,+; F C Turton; Thomas William Turyford; Albert E Tylee; Charles Henry Tylee; F J S Tylee; George J I Tylee; Herbert S Tylee; Sidney W Tylee; Thomas F H Tylee; Arthur George Tyler ,+; Richard Tyler; W Tyler; W G Tyler (Sgt – 17 William Street);

George Edward Underhill; H J I Underhill; J Underhill; W E Underhill; James W Underwood; W Underwood; Arthur Unit; A G Upton; Herbert Lyle Urch; William Edward Usher; Charles Uzzell (6 Cambria Houses); William George Uzzell,+;

F A Vaughan; S Vaughan; Arthur Venn; Frederick Albert Venn; Wilfred Venning; Percy Verrinder; John FrancisVickery,+; William Victor Vickery; Hugh Cecil Vickes; A W Vines; Charles William Vines; Edgar Vines,+; Edwin Vines; Sydney Vines,+; Walter John Vines; William Vines,+; A Viner; C Viner; Frederick Reginald Viner,+; Cecil William H Vincent; Jacob Bunce Vivash,+; Cecil Charles Viveash; Frederick John Viveash; Leonard Viveash; Thomas James Viveash; William Percy Viveash; Bernard Vokins,+; Frederick Allan Vowles; R VVowles;

F Wade,+; A Wait; A E Wait; Charles Wait MM; H A Wait; Samual Wait; Albert George Waite,+; Cyril Henry Waite; William Waite; Joseph Thomas Wakefield; Walter Wakefield; William Vincent Wakefield; G Wakeling; James Victor Wakeling,+; Leslie James Wakeling; Wilfred Wakeling; Arthur E Wakely (RFA); Alfred Harry Waldron,+; E J Waldron; Francis John Waldron; William Charles Waldron; E J Walker; F Walker; Frederick James Walker; George Edward Walker,+; Henry John Walker,+; Herbert S Walker; James H Walker; Nathaniel William Walker; William Henry G Walker; Walter James Walker; William F Walker; E Walklate; Robert Walklate; Frederick Harry Walklett; Arthur H Wall; G W Wall; Llewellyn Wall; W Wall; Bernard Wallace; William E Wallace; William Wallbridge; Edgar Walling; R Wallington; Ernest Wallis; F C Wallis (RFC); Frank Wallis; Frederick Wallis; S Wallis; William Henry Walman; R A Walsh; Rev W H Walsham; William Henry Walstow,+; Edward Joseph Walter; Robert John Walter; Frederick Walter; W H Walter; A W Walters; Ernest Charles Walters,+; Francis Frederick Walters; Harold Walters; E Walton; Harry Walton,+; Henry A Warburton; Herbert James Warburton,+; Albert Ward; John William Ward; Alfred George Warham,+; C Wareham; J Wareham; H V Warman MM,+; William Warman; Stephen James Warner,+; Albert Warren; Arthur Warren; Edward Warren; F E Warren; Frank Warren; James R F Warren; John Warren; John E Warren; R Warren; A F Warrick; Henry Warwick; Samual Warwick; Walter Warwick; William George Wasley,+; A E Waterhouse; Charles John Watkins; Henry Watkins; H W Watling,+; Albert E Watson; James Watson; Jesse W Watson; E G Watt; Alfred C Watts; Albert Edward Watts; Benjamin Thomas Watts; Charles Watts; Isaac Charles Watts,+; Thomas Watts; William Watts,+; William Walter Victor Watts; Albert Edward Weaver; James Christopher Weaver; William Reuben Weaver,+; A Webb MM; Albert H Webb; Albert George Webb; Arthur Charles Webb; Arthur Webb,+; C E Webb; Charles Henry Webb; Cyril Gordon Webb,+; Charles S Webb; Frederick Webb; F G D Webb; George Henry Webb; George Webb; Harry Webb; H W Webb; Mewyn

Thomas Webb,+;   Norman P Webb;   Percy William Webb;   R M Webb;   S F Webb;   Thomas George Webb,+;   William John Webb;   William Thomas Webb; A F Webber;   Albert Henry Webber,+;   F A Webber;   F J Webber;   H J Webber; Alfred Percy Webster;   A R Weeden;   Albert Weeks;   Adgar Weeks;   Frederick Weeks,+;   Arthur Weight;   Bertie W Weight;   Reginald Weight;   Charles C Wells; Charles Wells;   Francis James Wells;   H E L Wells;   Herbert George Long Wells ,+;   T Wells;   G A Welson;   F H Welsh;   F G Westall;   Sidney H Westall; T C Westall,+;   W Westall;   Alfred George Westbrook,+;   E Westbury;   A S Westcott;   Alfred Longhurst Westlake,+;   E D Westlake;   G H Westlake; H R Westlake;   A G Weston;   A N Weston;   Arthur Weston,+;   B W Weston; Frederick Weston;   J R Weston;   Frederick Westwood;   Arthur Whale,+;   H J Whale;   M Whale;   W W C Whale;   F C Whatley,+;   W E Whatly;   W L Whatley; Frederick George Wheatcroft,+;   J H Wheatly;   C J Wheeler;   F E Wheeler DCM; Frederick James Wheeler,+;   Harry Wheeler;   R S E Wheeler;   Walter Wheeler,+; W H Wheeler;   W J Wheeler;   W R Wheeler;   Charles Edward Whetham,+;   George Joseph Whetham,+;   F G Whetham;   Charles Edward White;   Clement White; Edwin Gordon White MC,+;   Dennis White;   Frederick Charles White;   G F White; Henry Charles White;   H J White;   H T White;   Jack White;   L H White;   Lionel A White;   Sidney White;   T E White;   T H White;   W M A White;   William George White;   W H White,+;   W W White;   W G Whitefoot;   W D Whitehouse;   Hubert Whiting;   Edwin Riley Whiteman,+;   J E F Whiteman;   Lancelot Charles Whiteman; R R Whiteman;   W F J Whiteman;   C Whittaker;   Edward G Whittaker;   William Whittington;   Harold A Whitworth (Hampshire Regt);   Leslie Whipp;   T L Whipp; Charles Wiblin;   W E B Wickenden;   Frank Wicks;   Joseph William Wicks; F Wiggin;   F T Wiggins;   Wilfred Wiggins,+;   Edgar Frank Wilcox;   Frederick Wilcox; A E Wild;   S E Wild;   Percy Wilder;   Alfred James Wildman,+;   Francis George Wildman,+;   A E Wilkins;   Frederick Wilkins;   Nelson W Wilkins;   Rev B Wilkins;Sidney Wilkins;   William Henry Wilkins;   Walter Issac Wilkins;   George H Wilkinson;A O G Wilks;   Charles Peter Wilks,+;   E E Wilks;   O Wilks;   Edward Willawoys;Francis Willcock;   H E Willcock;   A J T Willcocks;   A Williams;   Albert HenryWilliams;   Arthur Edmund Williams,+;   David Williams;   E M F Williams; Edward Albert Williams,+;   Edward James Williams,+;   Frederick Albert Williams; Frederick Henry Williams;   Francis Sydney Williams,+;   Frank Williams;   Frederick Charles Williams;   Frederick James Williams;   Frederick Thomas Williams;   George Williams;   Herbert Henry Williams MID,+;   Hubert Williams,+;   John Williams; Leonard Henry Williams;   Reuben J Williams;   Raymond A Williams;   R I Williams; R W Williams;   W E Williams;   William George Williams;   William Henry Williams; William James Williams,+;   William James Williams,+;   W John Harris Williams,+; Albert Edward Willis,+;   Albert Harry Willis,+;   Cecil Willis;   Francis James Willis,+; Frederick Willis;   George Valentine Willis;   Sydney George Willis;   Thomas Willis (Glos Regt – Princes Street);   Albert V Willoughby;   Frederick Willoughby;   Stanley Willoughby;   Thomas W Willoughby;   Elijah John Willows;   William Henry Wills ,+;   Bert S Wilson;   Cyril Spencer Wilson MC MID,+;   Edwin John Wilson,+;   Frank Wilson;   Frederick W Wilson;   George Charles Wilson;   Henry Day Wilson,+; James Wilson,+;   Jesse Wilson;   Percy T Wilson;   Thomas J Wilson;   Thomas William Wilson;   William Henry Richard Wilson,+;   Arthur Ernest Wiltshire;   Charles Henry Wiltshire,+;   E G Wiltshire;   Frederick E Wiltshire;   H Wiltshire;   Percy R Wiltshire;   P T Wiltshire;   William Wilshire;   W G E Wiltshire;   Bert Winchurst; Samual J Winchurst;   William E Winchurst;   A E Winchcombe;   Frederick Winchcombe;   Sydney Wilfred Winchcombe,+;   Wallace Henry Winchcombe; William G Winchcombe;   Bert Winchurst,+;   Frederick G Windman;   Albert E Windslow;   James Frederick Winslow,+;   Joseph Winslow;   Oliver F Winslow; S M Winslow;   Charles Winter,+;   H Winter;   Wallace George Winter;   Ernest George Wise;   Frank Wise;   Albert Edward Withers;   A G Withers;   Henry Withers; Alfred James Witt;   Dennis Witt;   A J Witts;   Ernest E Witts;   Frederick Witts; F P Witts;   F T Witts;   Henry Witts;   Edwin Wombey;   Edward Clarence G Wood; G C Wood;   Leslie S P Wood;   Harold E Woodall;   Leslie J Woodcock;

Sidney H Woodcock (RFC);   A W G Woodfield;   James Herbert Woodham,+; Vincent Woodham;   Jesse V Woodhouse;   H T Woodley (RFC);   F Woodley;   S Woodley; Thomas H Woodley;   William Henry Woodley,+;   Albert Frederick James Woodman ,+;   E Woodman;   H Woodman;   William Woodroffe;   Albert Woodward (Wilts Regt);   Albert Victor Woodward,+;   Augustus George Woodward;   Ernest Maurice Woodward;   Francis J Woodward;   GeorgeWilliam John Woodward,+;   Harry Hall Woodward,+;   P R H Woodward;   Walter Woodward;   W H J Woodward;   William Henry Woodward;   William E Woodward;   William John Woodward;   Frank Woof; Arthur Charles Woolford;   Albert Edward Woolford,+;   Ernest Woolford;   Ernest Edward Woolford;   Frederick Jesse Woolford;   Henry Woolford;   James Edward Woolford;   Sidney Frank Woolford,+;   F W Woolford,+;   Joseph John Woolford,+; William James Woolford;   William Thomas Woolford;   Charles Wooster;   Percy James Wootten;   George Wordley,+;   Sidney Workman;   G Worthy;   Alfred Thomas Wright DCM,+;   Ernest Chivers Wright,+;   F G Wright;   Frederick Johnson Wright,+;   Frederick John Wright;   Harry Francis Wright,+;   Henry Wright; Robert Wright;   Thomas James Wright;   Walter Wright (L/Cpl D coy 2nd Wilts); William Wright;   Alfred Wyatt;   Arthur Wyatt;   David Wyatt;   Edward Wyatt; Frank Wyatt;   Harry Wyatt,+;   James Wyatt;   Stephen Wyatt;   William Wyatt; John Joseph Wyley,+;

W Yarnton;   Charles William Yates;   H Yates;   Henry Charles Yates;   H R Yates; F C Yeo;   Harold Henry Yeo (79 Bright Street);   John Herbert Yeo;   Thomas David Yeo,+;   Percy Henry York;   A E Young;   C E Young;   Charles James Young; Daniel Young (AOC);   G H Young;   Dr Gordon Young;   John Henry Young;   Robert Jason Young;   William Alfred Young (RE);   Edward T Zebedee (180 Cricklade Road);

Memorial Window in Christchurch. The inscription at the bottom of the window reads, -
To the Glory of God and the memory of the men of the Wiltshire Regiment and Lt Sidney G H
Reed, 104th Batt MGC who died in the service of the country in the Great War 1914 - 1918

*Nation shall not lift up sword against Nation,
neither shall they learn War any more*

Isaiah 2:4

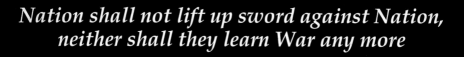

APPENDIX

Private. 203069 Frederick Isaacs.
2nd Btn Wiltshire Regt.
Died of wounds 3rd August 1917

2nd Lieutenant
Ernest Millard

Major Dr. Surgeon General
R Swinhoe. RAMC

William Harold Piff. MM.
Royal Engineers

Lieutenant William Jobson
MC. RFA

John, Charles and George

Macpherson Brothers of 184 Victoria Road in 1918. John and George both served with the Royal Flying Corps. Charles enlisted with the Wiltshire Yeomanry in January 1917. After training as a signaler he was transferred to the 5th Battalion South Lancashire Regiment, serving on the western front from April 1918. After the war he became an optician working for Hyslop and Co, of which he became Managing Director. He served as a Swindon councior and gave 42 years service to Swindon. In 1944 he became Mayor of the Town with Phyllis his wife as Mayoress. He was later made an honourary freeman of Swindon.

ACKNOWLEDGEMENTS
Additions to contributors

Bob Barrett, Peter Goldsworthy. Old Town and Thamesdown Rotary Clubs. BBC Radio Swindon & Wiltshire. Stuart Macpherson.

A very special thank you also to go to the publisher of this book, Melvyn Mckeown Thank you for your design ideas, your patience and care in this work.

and - Very finally!

A lot of reference material used for this book was from handwritten sources, I offer my sincerest appologies if any mistakes arise.